Rick Steves'

FLORENCE & TUSCANY
2005

Rick Steves & Gene Openshaw

TUSCANY

A24 Freeway	
S68 Major Road	
—— Major Rail Line	✈ Airport
Siena Recommended location*	
Livorno Just passing through**	
■ Ruin, Museum, other Point of Interest	

* Cities with names in black are of touristic interest.
Many shown in Tuscany are covered in this book.

** Cities with names in gray are of no touristic interest.

FLORENCE

1. Accademia
2. Baptistery
3. Bargello
4. Boboli Gardens Entry
5. to Brancacci Chapel
6. Duomo (Cathedral)
7. Duomo Museum
8. Giotto's Tower
9. Medici Chapels
10. Medici-Riccardi Palace
11. Mercato Nuovo
12. Michelangelo's House
13. Museum of Precious Stones
14. Orsanmichele Church
15. Palazzo Vecchio
16. Piazza della Repubblica
17. Piazza Signoria
18. to Piazzale Michelangelo
19. Pitti Palace
20. Ponte Vecchio
21. San Lorenzo Church
22. to San Marco Museum
23. Santo Spirito Church
24. Santa Croce Church
25. to Santa Maria del Carmine Church
26. Santa Maria Novella Church
27. Santa Maria Novella Perfumery
28. Science Museum
29. Uffizi Gallery
30. Main Tourist Info
31. Train Station
32. Bus Station
33. San Lorenzo Market

KEY

Pedestrian-friendly Area

Popular Shopping Area

■ Landmark or Point of Interest (sight number marks entrance)

�832 Tourist Information

0 200 meters
200 yards

Rick Steves'

FLORENCE & TUSCANY

2005

AVALON
TRAVEL

CONTENTS

INTRODUCTION

Florence is Europe's cultural capital. As the home of the Renaissance and the birthplace of the modern world, Florence practiced the art of civilized living back when the rest of Europe was rural and crude. Democracy, science, and literature, as well as painting, sculpture, and architecture were all championed by the proud and energetic Florentines of the 1400s.

When the Florentine poet Dante saw teenaged Beatrice, her beauty so inspired him that he spent the rest of his life writing poems to her. The Renaissance opened people's eyes to the physical beauty of the world around them, inspiring them to write, paint, sculpt, and build.

Today, Florence is geographically small but culturally rich, with more artistic masterpieces per square mile than anyplace else. In a single day, you could look Michelangelo's *David* in the eyes, fall under the seductive sway of Botticelli's *Birth of Venus*, and climb the modern world's first dome, which still dominates the skyline.

Stroll the same pedestrian streets walked by Michelangelo, Leonardo, and Botticelli; window-shop the high-fashion boutiques; drag your tongue slowly over the world's best gelato; and end the day bumping elbows with fellow diners in a crowded *osteria*.

Then escape to the Tuscan countryside. With its manicured hills, rustic farms, and towns clinging to nearly every hill, Tuscany is our image of village Italy. Venture beyond the fringes of Florence and you'll find a series of sun- and wine-soaked villages, each with its own appeal. Stretching from the Umbrian border to the Ligurian Sea, the landscape changes from idyllic (Crete Senese) to mountainous (the Montagnola) to flat and brushed with sea breezes (Pisa).

During your visit, you'll discover that the peaceful Tuscan villages and bustling Florence—with its rough-stone beauty, art-packed museums, children chasing pigeons, students riding Vespas, artisans sipping Chianti, and supermodels wearing Gucci fashions—offer many of the very things you came to Italy to see.

This Information is Accurate and Up-to-Date

This book is updated every year. Most publishers of guidebooks can afford an update only every two or three years (and even then, it's often by fax or e-mail). Since this book is selective, we can personally update it annually. Even so, things change. But if you're traveling with the current edition of this book, we guarantee you're using the most up-to-date information available in print. For the very latest, visit www.ricksteves.com/update. Also at our Web site, check our Graffiti Wall (select "Rick Steves' Guidebooks," then "Florence & Tuscany") for a huge, valuable list of reports and experiences—good and bad—from fellow travelers. This book will help you have an inexpensive, hassle-free trip. Your trip costs about $10 per waking hour. Your time is valuable. This guidebook saves lots of time.

About This Book

This book is organized this way:

Each **Orientation** includes tourist information and public transportation. The "Planning Your Time" section offers a suggested schedule with thoughts on how to best use your limited time.

Sights provide a succinct overview of the most important sights, arranged by neighborhood, with ratings: ▲▲▲—Don't miss; ▲▲—Try hard to see; ▲—Worthwhile if you can make it; no rating—Worth knowing about.

The **Renaissance Walk** takes you through the core of Renaissance Florence, starting with Michelangelo's *David* and cutting through the heart of the city to the Ponte Vecchio on the Arno River.

The **Self-Guided Tours** lead you through Tuscany's most important sights, with tours of Florence's Uffizi Gallery, Bargello, Museum of San Marco, Duomo Museum, Medici Chapels, Medici-Riccardi Palace, Church of Santa Maria Novella, Brancacci Chapel, and the Science Museum, as well as Siena's Duomo and Civic Museum and Pisa's Duomo and Baptistery.

Sleeping is a guide to our favorite budget hotels, conveniently located near the sights.

Eating offers restaurants ranging from inexpensive eateries to splurges, with an emphasis on good value.

Florence with Children, Nightlife, and **Shopping** contain our best suggestions on these topics.

Transportation Connections covers connections by train, bus, and plane, laying the groundwork for your smooth arrival and departure.

Siena covers the highlights in this captivating Gothic city, from the stay-awhile central piazza to the 13th-century cathedral. **Pisa** takes you beyond the Leaning Tower. **Lucca** introduces you to the charms of this little-touristed, well-preserved city. And **Tuscan Hill Towns** brings you the best of village Italy, featuring Montalcino, Pienza, San Gimignano, Montepulciano, Cortona, and Volterra.

History takes you on a whirlwind tour through the ages, covering eight centuries from ancient Tuscany to the present.

The **appendix** includes a climate chart for Florence, a list of festivals, and Italian survival phrases.

Throughout this book, when you see a ✪ in a listing, it means that the sight is covered in more detail in one of our self-guided tours. A page number will tell you where to look to find more information.

Browse through this book and choose your favorite sights. Then have a great trip! You'll become your own guide with our tours. You won't waste time on mediocre sights because, unlike other guidebooks, this one covers only the best. Since your major financial pitfall is lousy, expensive hotels, we've worked hard to assemble the best accommodations values. Traveling like a temporary local, you'll get the absolute most out of every mile, minute, and euro.

PLANNING

Trip Costs

Six components make up your trip costs: airfare, surface transportation, room and board, sightseeing/entertainment, shopping/miscellany, and gelato.

Airfare: Don't try to sort through the mess. Find and use a good travel agent. A basic, round-trip United States-to-Florence (or even cheaper, Milan or Rome) flight should cost $700 to $1,000, depending on where you fly from and when. Always consider saving time and money in Europe by flying "open jaw" (into one city and out of another).

Surface Transportation: Most of Florence's sights, clustered in the downtown core, are within easy walking distance of each other. If you'd rather use taxis than walk, allow about $60–80 over the course of a one-week visit (taxis can be shared by up to four people). The cost of round-trip transportation to the recommended nearby destinations is affordable ($25 by train, second class, to Pisa; about $20 by bus to San Gimignano; and $30 by train, second class, to Siena). For a one-way trip between Florence's airport and the city center, allow $7 by bus or $25 by taxi (can be shared). The other cities and villages covered in this book are made for walking.

Room and Board: You can thrive in Tuscany in 2005 on $100 a day per person for room and board. This allows $10 for lunch, $5 for snacks, $20 for dinner, and $65 for lodging (based on two people splitting the cost of a $130 double room that includes breakfast). If you have more money, we've listed great ways to spend it. Students and tightwads can enjoy Tuscany for as little as $40 a day ($20 for a bed, $20 for meals and snacks), but budget sleeping and eating require the skills covered later in this chapter (and in greater detail in *Rick Steves' Europe Through the Back Door*).

Sightseeing and Entertainment: Figure about $8–13 per major sight (Michelangelo's *David,* Uffizi Gallery), $4–6 for smaller ones (museums, climbing church towers), and $25 for splurge experiences (e.g., walking tours and concerts). An overall average of $20 a day works for most. Don't skimp here. After all, this category directly powers most of the experiences that all the other expenses are designed to make possible.

Shopping and Miscellany: Figure $1 per postcard, coffee, and soft drink and $2 per gelato. Shopping can vary in cost from nearly nothing to a small fortune. Good budget travelers find that this category has little to do with assembling a trip full of lifelong, wonderful memories.

When to Go

Tuscany's best travel months (and busiest, most expensive months) are May, June, September, and October. Between November and April you can usually expect pleasant weather and none of the sweat and stress of the tourist season.

The most grueling thing about travel in Tuscany is the summer heat in July and August, when temperatures hit the high 80s and 90s. Florence is fine in the winter, when temperatures drop to the 40s and 50s. Spring and fall can be chilly, and many hotels do not turn on their heat. Air-conditioning, when available, usually only operates from June through September. Most mid-range hotels come with air-conditioning—a worthwhile splurge in the summer. (See climate chart in the appendix.)

Resources
Tourist Offices in the United States
Virtually every place you'll visit has a tourist information office (abbreviated **TI** in this book); Florence has several—see page 23.

Before your trip, contact the nearest Italian TI in the United States and briefly describe your trip and request information. You'll get the general packet and, if you ask for specifics (city map, calendar of festivals, etc.), an impressive amount of help. If you have a specific problem, they're a good source of sympathy.

Contact the office nearest you:

In New York: 630 Fifth Ave. #1565, New York, NY 10111, tel. 212/245-5618, brochure hotline 212/245-4822, fax 212/586-9249, enitny@italiantourism.com.

In California: 12400 Wilshire Blvd. #550, Los Angeles, CA 90025, tel. 310/820-1898, brochure hotline 310/820-0098, fax 310/820-6357, enitla@italiantourism.com.

Web sites: www.firenzeturismo.it (Florence tourist information), www.italiantourism.com (Italian Tourist Board in the United States), www.museionline.it (museums in Italy, in English), and www.fs-on-line.com (train info and schedules).

Rick Steves' Books and Public Television Shows

Rick Steves' Europe Through the Back Door 2005 gives you budget-travel skills, such as minimizing jet lag, packing light, planning your itinerary, traveling by car or train, finding rooms, changing money, avoiding rip-offs, buying a mobile phone, hurdling the language barrier, staying healthy, taking great photographs, using a bidet, and much more. The book also includes chapters on 38 of Rick's favorite "Back Door" destinations.

Rick Steves' Country Guides, an annually updated series that covers Europe, offer you the latest on the top sights and destinations, with tips on how to make your trip efficient and fun.

Rick Steves' Florence & Tuscany 2005 is one of our **City and Regional Guides.** Updated every year, these focus on Europe's most compelling destinations. Along with specifics on sights, restaurants, hotels, and nightlife, you'll get self-guided, illustrated tours of the outstanding museums and most characteristic neighborhoods.

Rick Steves' Easy Access Europe, written for travelers with limited mobility, covers London, Paris, Bruges, Amsterdam, and the Rhine River.

Rick Steves' Europe 101: History and Art for the Traveler (with Gene Openshaw) gives you the story of Europe's people, history, and art. Written for smart people who were sleeping in their history and art classes before they knew they were going to Europe, *101* brings Europe's sights to life.

Rick Steves' Best European City Walks & Museums (with Gene Openshaw) gives you self-guided tours of the major museums and historic neighborhoods in Amsterdam, London, Paris, Madrid, Rome, Florence, and Venice.

In Italy, a phrase book is as fun as it is necessary. *Rick Steves' Italian Phrase Book* helps you meet the people and stretch your budget. It's written by a monoglot who, for 25 years, has fumbled through Italy struggling with all the other phrase books. Use this practical book to make hotel reservations over the telephone, have the man in the deli make you a sandwich, and ask for a free taste of cantaloupe-flavored gelato at the *gelateria.*

My public television series, *Rick Steves' Europe,* keeps churning out shows. Several of the 95 episodes (from the new series and from *Travels in Europe with Rick Steves*) feature destinations covered in this book.

Rick Steves' Guidebooks

Rick Steves' Europe Through the Back Door
Rick Steves' Best European City Walks & Museums
Rick Steves' Easy Access Europe

Country Guides
Rick Steves' Best of Europe
Rick Steves' Best of Eastern Europe
Rick Steves' France
Rick Steves' Germany & Austria
Rick Steves' Great Britain
Rick Steves' Ireland
Rick Steves' Italy
Rick Steves' Portugal
Rick Steves' Scandinavia
Rick Steves' Spain
Rick Steves' Switzerland

City and Regional Guides
Rick Steves' Amsterdam, Bruges & Brussels
Rick Steves' Florence & Tuscany
Rick Steves' London
Rick Steves' Paris
Rick Steves' Prague & the Czech Republic*
Rick Steves' Provence & the French Riviera
Rick Steves' Rome
Rick Steves' Venice

*Coming in 2005

(Avalon Travel Publishing)

Rick Steves' Postcards from Europe, Rick's autobiographical book, packs 25 years of travel anecdotes and insights into the ultimate 2,000-mile European adventure.

Other Guidebooks

For most travelers, this book is all you need. The well-researched Access guide (which combines Florence and Venice) and the colorful Eyewitness guide (on Florence and Tuscany) are popular with travelers. Eyewitness is fun for its great, easy-to-grasp graphics and photos, and it's just right for people who want only factoids. But the Eyewitness books are relatively skimpy on content and they weigh a ton. You can buy them in Florence (no more expensive than in the United States) or simply borrow them for a minute from other travelers at certain sights to make sure you're aware of that place's high-

Begin Your Trip at
www.ricksteves.com

At ricksteves.com you'll find a wealth of **free information** on destinations covered in this book, including fresh European travel and tour news and helpful "Graffiti Wall" tips from thousands of fellow travelers.

While you're there, Rick Steves' **online Travel Store** is a great place to save money on travel bags and accessories specially designed by Rick Steves to help you travel smarter and lighter. These include Rick's popular carry-on bags (wheeled and rucksack versions), money belts, day bags, totes, toiletries kits, packing cubes, clotheslines, locks, clocks, sleep sacks, adapters, and a wide selection of guidebooks, planning maps, and *Rick Steves' Europe* DVDs.

Traveling through Europe by rail is a breeze, but choosing the right railpass for your trip (amidst hundreds of options) can drive you nutty. At ricksteves.com you'll find **Rick Steves' Annual Guide to European Railpasses**—your best way to convert chaos into pure travel energy. Buy your railpass from Rick, and you'll get a bunch of free extras to boot.

Travel agents will tell you about mainstream tours of Europe, but they won't tell you about **Rick Steves' tours.** Rick Steves' Europe Through the Back Door travel company offers more than two dozen itineraries and 250+ departures reaching the best destinations in this book...and beyond. You'll enjoy the services of a great guide, a fun bunch of travel partners (with group sizes in the mid-20s), and plenty of room to spread out in a big, comfy bus. You'll find tours to fit every vacation size, from week-long city getaways (Paris, London, Venice, Florence, Rome), to 12–18 day country tours, to three-week "Best of Europe" adventures. For details, visit www.ricksteves.com or call 425/771-8303 ext 217.

lights. If you'll be traveling elsewhere in Italy, consider the 2005 editions of *Rick Steves' Italy, Venice,* and *Rome.*

In Florence, local guidebooks (sold at kiosks) are cheap and give you a map and a decent commentary on the sights. For brand-name guidebooks, try **Feltrinelli International** (Mon–Sat 9:00–19:30, closed Sun, Via Cavour 20 red, a few blocks north of the Duomo and across the street from the TI on Via Cavour, tel. 055-219-524), **Edison Bookstore** (daily 9:00–24:00, sells CDs and novels on Renaissance, facing Piazza della Repubblica, tel. 055-213-110), or **Paperback Exchange** (cheaper but smaller selection, Mon–Fri 9:00–19:30, Sat 10:00–13:00 & 15:30–19:30, closed Sun, shorter hours in Aug, Via Fiesolana 31 red, at corner of Via Fiesolana and Via dei Pilastri, 6 blocks east of Duomo, tel. 055-247-8154).

Recommended Reading and Movies

To get the feel of Tuscany past and present, consider reading some of these books or seeing these films:

Non-Fiction: *The City of Florence* (R. W. B. Lewis), *The Stones of Florence* (Mary McCarthy), *Brunelleschi's Dome* (Ross King), *Lives of the Artists* (Giorgio Vasari), *The Architecture of the Italian Renaissance* (Peter Murray), *Florence: A Portrait* (Michael Levey), *The House of Medici* (Christopher Hibbert), *The Prince* and *Florentine Histories* (Niccolò Machiavelli), *Italian Days* (Barbara Grizzuti Harrison), *Desiring Italy* (Susan N. Cahill), *The Italians* (Luigi Barzini), *That Fine Italian Hand* (Paul Hofmann), *Italian Neighbors* and *An Italian Education* (Tim Parks), *Travelers' Tales: Italy* (Anne Calcagno), and *Under the Tuscan Sun* (Frances Mayes).

Fiction: *The Agony & the Ecstasy* (Irving Stone), *A Room With a View* (E. M. Forster), *The Sixteen Pleasures* (Robert Hellenga), *The Light in the Piazza* (Elizabeth Spencer), *A Rich Full Death* (Michael Dibdin), *Death of an Englishman* (Magdalen Nabb), *Bella Donna* (Barbara Cherne), and *Romola* (George Eliot).

Flicks: *A Room With a View* (1986), *Tea with Mussolini* (1999), and *The Light in the Piazza* (1962).

Maps

The black-and-white maps in this book are drawn by Dave Hoerlein, one of our veteran tour guides who is well-traveled in Tuscany and Italy. His concise and simple maps are designed to help you get oriented and find places listed in the text quickly and painlessly. Any TI and some hotels will have free maps. Better maps that list all the roads are sold at newsstands for €3–4; take a look before you buy to be sure the map has the level of detail you want.

PRACTICALITIES

Red Tape: You need a passport but no visa or shots to travel in Italy.

Time: In Tuscany—and in this book—you'll use the 24-hour clock. It's the same through 12:00 noon, then keep going: 13:00, 14:00, and so on. For anything over 12, subtract 12 and add p.m. (14:00 is 2:00 p.m.).

Business Hours: Traditionally, Italy uses the siesta plan. People generally work from about 8:00 to 13:00 and from 15:30 to 19:00, Monday through Saturday. Nowadays, though, many businesses have adopted the government's recommended 8:00 to 14:00 workday. In tourist areas, shops are open longer.

Shopping: Shoppers interested in customs regulations and VAT refunds (the tax refunded on large purchases made by non-EU residents) can refer to page 194.

Discounts: Discounts for sights are not listed in this book because they are generally limited to European residents and countries that offer reciprocal deals (the U.S. doesn't).

Watt's up? If you're bringing electrical gear, you'll need a two-prong adapter plug (sold cheap at travel stores in the United States) and a converter. Travel appliances often have convenient, built-in converters; look for a voltage switch marked 120V (U.S.) and 240V (Europe).

MONEY

Banking

You'll want to spend local hard cash. The best and fastest way to get it is by using plastic: your ATM, credit, or debit card at a cash machine *(Bancomat)*.

To get a cash advance from a bank machine, you'll need a PIN (numbers only, no letters) with your bank card. Before you go, verify with your bank that your card will work and alert them that you'll be making withdrawals in Europe (otherwise, the bank may not approve transactions if it perceives unusual spending patterns).

Visa and MasterCard are more commonly accepted than American Express. Bring two cards in case one is demagnetized, rejected, or eaten by a temperamental cash machine. If your card is rejected, try again, and request a smaller amount; some cash machines won't let you take out more than about €150—don't take it personally. Be aware that some ATMs will tell you to take your cash within 30 seconds, and if you aren't fast enough, your cash will be sucked back into the machine and you'll have a hassle trying to get it from the bank.

Just as at home, credit or debit cards work easily at larger hotels, restaurants, and shops, but smaller businesses prefer payment in hard cash.

For a backup, we bring several hundred dollars in U.S. cash

Exchange Rate

We've priced things throughout this book in the euro currency.

1 euro (€) = about $1.20

To convert prices in euros to dollars, add 20 percent: €20 = about $24, €45 = about $55.

Just like the dollar, one euro is broken down into 100 cents. You'll find coins ranging from 1 cent to 2 euros, and bills ranging from 5 euros to 500 euros.

Damage Control for Lost or Stolen Cards

You can stop thieves from using your ATM, debit, or credit card by reporting the loss immediately to the proper company. Call these 24-hour U.S. numbers collect: VISA (tel. 410/581-9994), MasterCard (tel. 636/722-7111), and American Express (tel. 336/393-1111).

Providing the following information will help expedite the process: the name of the financial institution that issued you the card, full card number, the cardholder's name as printed on the card, billing address, home phone number, circumstances of the loss or theft, and identification verification including a Social Security number or birthdate and your mother's maiden name. (Packing along a photocopy of the front and back of your cards helps you answer the harder questions.) If you are the secondary cardholder, you'll also need to provide the primary cardholder's identification-verification details. You can generally receive a temporary card within two or three business days in Europe.

If you promptly report your card lost or stolen, you typically won't be responsible for any unauthorized transactions on your account, although many banks charge a liability fee of $50.

rather than traveler's checks (which we feel are a waste of time and fees). But if you prefer traveler's checks, note that banks—not exchange offices—have the best rates for cashing them. For a large exchange, it pays to compare rates and fees. Banking hours are generally from 8:30 to 13:30 and from 15:30 to 16:30 Monday through Friday, but can vary wildly. Banks are slow; simple transactions can take 15–30 minutes. Post offices and train stations usually change money if you can't get to a bank.

Use a money belt. Thieves target tourists. A money belt provides peace of mind and allows you to carry lots of cash safely. Don't be petty about changing money. The greatest avoidable money-changing expense is wasting time every few days to return to a bank. Change a week's worth of money, get big bills, stuff them in your money belt, and travel!

Tipping

Tipping in Italy isn't as automatic and generous as it is in the United States, but for special service, tips are appreciated, if not expected. As in the United States, the proper amount depends on your resources, tipping philosophy, and the circumstance, but some general guidelines apply.

Restaurants: Check the menu to see if the service is included (*servizio incluso*—generally 15 percent); if not, a tip of 5–10 percent is fine (for details, see page 178), though Italians rarely tip.

Taxis: To tip the cabbie, round up. For a typical ride, round up to the next euro on the fare (to pay a €13 fare, give €14); for a long ride, to the nearest €10 (for a €75 fare, give €80). If the cabbie hauls your bags and zips you to the airport to help you catch your flight, you might want to toss in a little more. But if you feel like you're being driven in circles or otherwise ripped off, skip the tip.

Special Services: It's thoughtful to tip a couple of euros to someone who shows you a special sight and who is paid in no other way (such as the man who shows you an Etruscan tomb in his backyard). Tour guides at public sites often hold out their hands for tips after they give their spiel; if I've already paid for the tour, I don't tip extra, though some tourists do give a euro or two, particularly for a job well done. I don't tip at hotels, but if you do, give the porter a euro for carrying bags and leave a couple of euros in your room at the end of your stay for the maid if the room was kept clean. In general, if someone in the service industry does a super job for you, a tip of a couple of euros is appropriate...but not required.

When in doubt, ask. If you're not sure whether (or how much) to tip for a service, ask your hotelier or the tourist information office; they'll fill you in on how it's done on their turf.

TRAVEL SMART

Many people travel through Italy thinking it's a chaotic mess. They feel any attempt at efficient travel is futile. This is dead wrong—and expensive. Italy, which seems as orderly as spilled spaghetti, actually functions well. Only those who understand this and travel smart can enjoy Italy on a budget.

Buy a phone card and use it for reservations and double-checking hours of sights. (We've included phone numbers for this purpose.) Enjoy the friendliness of the local people. Ask questions. Most locals are eager to point you in their idea of the right direction. Pack along a pocket-size notebook to organize your thoughts. Those who expect to travel smart, do.

Sundays have the same pros and cons as they do for travelers in the United States: Sightseeing attractions are generally open; banks and many shops are closed. City traffic is light. Rowdy evenings are rare on Sundays. Saturdays are virtually weekdays with earlier closing hours.

Museums and sights, especially the biggies, usually stop admitting people 30–60 minutes before closing time.

Hotels are often booked up on Easter (March 27 in 2005), April 25, May 1, June 24 (in Florence), in August, November 1, and on Fridays and Saturdays. Religious holidays and train strikes can catch you by surprise anywhere in Italy.

Really, this book can save you lots of time and money. But to have an A trip, you need to be an A student. Read it all before your trip; note the days when museums are closed and whether reservations are mandatory. For instance, you can wait two hours in line to get into the Uffizi, or make a quick phone call to get a reservation in advance and walk right in. Saving Michelangelo's *David* for your Florentine finale is risky, and on Monday, impossible. If you cut your Siena day trip short, you'll miss the city's medieval magic at twilight. A smart trip is a puzzle—a fun, doable, and worthwhile challenge.

Transportation

The downtown core of Florence is walkable, though it involves dodging swarms of noisy Vespa motorscooters. For information on taking buses and taxis, see "Getting Around Florence" in the Orientation chapter. If you have a car, park it. Drivers who don't follow the strict rules get fined (see page 202).

Getting around the Tuscan countryside is easiest by rental car and doable by bus and train; you'll find specifics on public transportation in each chapter. For information on transportation throughout Italy, see *Rick Steves' Italy 2005*.

In Florence, get train tickets, reservations, and supplements at travel agencies rather than at the congested train station. The cost is either the same or there's a minimal charge. Ask your hotel for the nearest travel agency, or try American Express.

American Express offers all the normal services, but is most helpful as an easy place to get your train tickets, reservations, supplements (all the same price as at the station), or even just information on train schedules (Mon–Fri 9:00–17:30, Sat money exchange only 9:00–12:30, 3 short blocks north of Palazzo Vecchio on Via Dante Alighieri 22 red, tel. 055-50981).

COMMUNICATING

Telephones

Savvy travelers use the telephone every day to confirm hotel reservations, check opening hours, and phone home.

Phone Cards: Instead of putting coins in pay phones, you can buy cards with pre-paid time. There are two kinds of phone cards available.

1. Insertable phone cards that you stick into the slot of a public pay phone. These work like coins in a pay phone. Buy them (in denominations of €5, €10, etc.) at tobacco shops, post offices, and machines near phone booths (many phone booths indicate where the nearest phone-card sales outlet is located). Rip off the perforated corner to "activate" the card, then physically insert it into a slot in the pay phone. It displays how much money you have remaining on the card. Then just dial away to anywhere in the world. These cards give you your best deal for calls within Italy, and are reasonable for international calls.

2. International phone cards that can be used from virtually any phone. These are not inserted into the phone. You dial the toll-free number listed on the card to reach an automated operator. When prompted (English is always available), you dial in a code number, also written on the card. A voice tells you how much is left in your account. Then dial your number. Since you don't insert the card in the phone, you can use these to make inexpensive calls from most phones, including the one in your hotel room, avoiding pricey hotel rates (if your phone is set on pulse, switch it to tone). Calls to the United States cost about €1 for 10 minutes. You can use the cards to make local and long-distance calls as well. Buy cards at small newsstand kiosks and hole-in-the-wall long-distance phone shops (in denominations of €5, €10, etc.; buy a cheapie in case the card is a dud.) Because there are so many brand names, ask for an international telephone card (*carta telefonica prepagata internazionale*, KAR-tah teh-leh-FOHN-ee-kah pray-pah-GAH-tah in-ter-naht-zee-oh-NAH-lay). Tell the vendor where you'll be making most calls ("to America"), and he'll select the brand with the best deal.

Phones: The Telecom public telephones are everywhere and take cards only (no coins). About a quarter of the phones are broken. The rest work reluctantly. Dial slowly and deliberately, as if the phone doesn't understand numbers very well. Often a recorded message in Italian will break in, brusquely informing you that the phone number does not exist *(non-esistente)*, even if you're dialing your own home phone number. Dial again with an increasing show of confidence, in an attempt to convince the phone of your number's existence. If you fail, try a different phone. Repeat as needed.

When spelling out your name on the phone, you'll find *a* (pronounced "ah" in Italian), *i* (pronounced "ee"), and *e* (pronounced "ay") are confusing to Americans. Say "*a*, Ancona," "*e*, Empoli," and "*i*, Imola" to clear up that problem. If you plan to access your voice mail from Italy, be advised that you can't always dial extensions or secret codes once you connect (you're on vacation—relax).

Dialing within Italy: Italy has a direct-dial phone system (no area codes). To call anywhere within Italy, just dial the number. For example, the number of one of our recommended Florence hotels is 055-293-451. To call it from the Florence train station, dial 055-293-451. If you call it from Venice, it's the same: 055-293-451. Mobile phone numbers no longer start with zero (these are dialed direct like fixed phone numbers).

Florence's phone numbers vary in length; a hotel can have, say, an eight-digit phone number and a nine-digit fax number.

Italy's toll-free numbers start with 800 (like U.S. 800 numbers, though in Italy you don't need to dial a "1" first). In Italy, you can dial these 800 numbers—called *freephone* or *numero verde* (green number)—free from any phone without using a phone card or coins. Note that you can't call Italy's toll-free numbers from America, nor can you count on reaching America's toll-free numbers from Italy.

Dialing International Calls: When calling internationally, dial the international access code (00 if you're calling from Europe, 011 from the United States or Canada), the country code of the country you're calling (39 for Italy; see appendix for list of other countries), and the local number. To call the Florence hotel from the United States, dial 011 (the U.S. international access code), 39 (Italy's country code), then 055-293-451. To call our office in Edmonds, Washington, from Italy, we dial 00 (Europe's international access code), 1 (the U.S. country code), 425 (Edmonds' area code), and 771-8303. European time is six/nine hours ahead of the East/West Coasts of the United States.

Hotel-room phones are reasonable for calls within Italy (the faint beeps stand for €0.10 phone units) but a terrible rip-off for calls to the United States (unless you use an international telephone card or your hotel allows toll-free access to your calling-card service—see below).

Calling-Card Services: While still convenient, these services, such as AT&T, MCI, and Sprint, are no longer a good value. It's much cheaper to call the United States using an international or insertable phone card, but some people prefer to use their easier, pricier calling cards. Each card company has a toll-free number in each European country that puts you in touch with an English-speaking operator. For Italy, AT&T's toll-free number is 172-444, Sprint's is 172-1877, and MCI has three numbers: dial 172-403 from a pay phone, 800-172-402 from a mobile phone, or 800-905-825 from all other phones. The operator takes your card number and the number you want to call, puts you through, and bills your home phone number for the call. Oddly, you need to use a small-value coin or Italian phone card to dial the toll-free number.

Plans vary wildly within the big-three companies, and many have extra fees that can add up in a hurry. Given the service charge, connection fee, and first-minute cost, it can cost you $7–8 to say "Hi, sorry I missed you" if you reach an answering machine at the number you're trying to call. It's even more expensive to use a calling card to make calls between European countries; it's far cheaper to simply call direct using a phone card purchased in Italy.

Mobile Phones: Many travelers now buy cheap mobile phones in Europe to make both local and international calls. (Typical American mobile phones don't work in Europe, and those that do have horrendous per-minute costs.) For about $75 you can get a phone with $20 worth of calls that will work in the country where you purchased it. (You can buy more time at newsstands or mobile phone shops.) For about $100 you can get a phone that will work in most countries once you pick up the necessary chip per country. If you're interested, stop by any European shop that sells mobile phones (you'll see prominent store-window displays). Depending on your trip and budget, ask for a phone that works only in that country or one that can be used throughout Europe. If you're on a budget, skip mobile phones and use cheap international phone cards instead.

E-mail and Mail

E-mail: E-mail use among Italian hoteliers is common. Drab little Internet cafés are popular in big cities like Florence. Your hotelier can steer you to the one nearest your hotel.

Mail: Mail service is miserable throughout Italy. Postcards get last priority. If you must receive mail while traveling, consider a few pre-reserved hotels along your route. (American Express offices will hold mail for a month for people who have an AmEx card.) Allow 14 days for U.S.-to-Italy mail delivery, but don't count on it. Federal Express makes pricey two-day deliveries. E-mailing and phoning is so easy that we've completely dispensed with mail stops. If possible, mail nothing precious from Italy.

TRAVELING AS A TEMPORARY LOCAL

We travel all the way to Italy to enjoy differences—to become temporary locals. You'll experience frustrations. Certain truths that we find "God-given" or "self-evident," such as cold beer, ice in drinks, bottomless cups of coffee, hot showers, and bigger being better, are suddenly not so true. One of the benefits of travel is the eye-opening realization that there are logical, civil, and even better alternatives. A willingness to go local ensures that you'll enjoy a full dose of Italian hospitality.

If there is a negative aspect to the image Italians have of Americans, it is that we are big, loud, aggressive, impolite, rich, and a bit naive. While Italians, flabbergasted by our Yankee excesses, say in disbelief, *"Mi sono cadute le braccia!"* ("I throw my arms down!"), they nearly always afford us individual travelers all the warmth we deserve.

Send Us a Postcard, Drop Us a Line

If you enjoy a successful trip with the help of this book and would like to share your discoveries, please fill out the survey at www .ricksteves.com/feedback, or e-mail us at rick@ricksteves.com. We personally read and value all feedback.

Judging from all the happy postcards we receive from travelers who have used this book, it's safe to assume you'll enjoy a great, affordable vacation—with the finesse of an independent, experienced traveler.

From this point, "we" (your coauthors) will drop our respective egos and become "I."

Thanks, and *buon viaggio!*

BACK DOOR TRAVEL PHILOSOPHY
From *Rick Steves' Europe Through the Back Door*

Travel is intensified living—maximum thrills per minute and one of the last great sources of legal adventure. Travel is freedom. It's recess, and we need it.

Experiencing the real Europe requires catching it by surprise, going casual..."through the Back Door."

Affording travel is a matter of priorities. (Make do with the old car.) You can travel—simply, safely, and comfortably—anywhere in Europe for $100 a day plus transportation costs. In many ways, spending more money only builds a thicker wall between you and what you came to see. Europe is a cultural carnival, and, time after time, you'll find that its best acts are free and the best seats are the cheap ones.

A tight budget forces you to travel close to the ground, meeting and communicating with the people, not relying on service with a purchased smile. Never sacrifice sleep, nutrition, safety, or cleanliness in the name of budget. Simply enjoy the local-style alternatives to expensive hotels and restaurants.

Extroverts have more fun. If your trip is low on magic moments, kick yourself and make things happen. If you don't enjoy a place, maybe you don't know enough about it. Seek the truth. Recognize tourist traps. Give a culture the benefit of your open mind. See things as different but not better or worse. Any culture has much to share.

Of course, travel, like the world, is a series of hills and valleys. Be fanatically positive and militantly optimistic. If something's not to your liking, change your liking. Travel is addictive. It can make you a happier American as well as a citizen of the world. Our Earth is home to six billion equally important people. It's humbling to travel and find that people don't envy Americans. They like us, but, with all due respect, they wouldn't trade passports.

Globe-trotting destroys ethnocentricity. It helps you understand and appreciate different cultures. Travel changes people. It broadens perspectives and teaches new ways to measure quality of life. Many travelers toss aside their hometown blinders. Their prized souvenirs are the strands of different cultures they decide to knit into their own character. The world is a cultural yarn shop. And Back Door travelers are weaving the ultimate tapestry. Come on, join in!

FLORENCE

ORIENTATION

The best of Florence lies mostly on the north bank of the Arno River. The main historical sights cluster around the red-brick dome of the cathedral *(Duomo)*. Everything is within a 20-minute walk of the train station, cathedral, or Ponte Vecchio (Old Bridge). The less impressive but more characteristic Oltrarno area (south bank) is just over the bridge. Though small, Florence is intense. Prepare for scorching summer heat, kamikaze motor scooters, slick pickpockets, few WCs, and erratic museum hours.

Planning Your Time

Plan your sightseeing carefully. The major sights—the Uffizi Gallery and the Accademia (starring Michelangelo's *David*)—close on Monday. While many travelers spend several hours a day in lines at the Uffizi and Accademia, you can avoid this by making reservations (see page 35). Do our recommended Renaissance Walk in the morning or late afternoon to avoid heat and crowds. Stop often for gelato.

Florence in One Day

  8:30 Accademia *(David)*; reserve in advance.

10:00 Renaissance Walk through town center, climb Giotto's Tower.

12:00 Bargello Museum (best statues), lunch at Cantinetta dei Verrazzano.

14:00 Shop around San Lorenzo.

17:00 Uffizi Gallery (finest paintings); reserve in advance.

19:00 Dinner on/near Piazza della Signoria, or hikers can take the Oltrarno Walk (best local color) and have dinner at 20:00 at Trattoria Sabatino.

Florence Overview

Florence in Two Days
Day 1
8:30	Accademia *(David)*; reserve in advance.
10:00	Museum of San Marco (art by Fra Angelico).
12:00	Medici Chapels (Michelangelo).
14:00	Lunch, market, wander, shop.
16:30	Baptistery.
17:00	Climb Giotto's Tower.
18:00	Renaissance Walk through heart of old town.
20:00	Dinner on or near Piazza della Signoria.

Day 2
9:00	Bargello (greatest statues).
11:00	Duomo Museum (intriguing statues by Donatello and Michelangelo) or Science Museum.
13:00	Lunch, free to wander and shop.
15:00	Church of Santa Maria Novella (Masaccio painting), old perfumery.
17:00	Uffizi Gallery (best paintings); reserve in advance.
19:00	Oltrarno Walk.
20:00	Dinner in Oltrarno.

Florence in Three (or More) Days
Day 1
8:30	Accademia *(David)*; reserve in advance.
10:00	Museum of San Marco (Fra Angelico).
12:00	Markets, shop, wander.

13:00   Lunch.
14:00   Medici Chapels (Michelangelo).
15:00   Church of Santa Maria Novella and old perfumery.
16:30   Baptistery.
17:00   Giotto's Tower.
18:00   Renaissance Walk through heart of old town.
20:00   Dinner on or near Piazza della Signoria.

Day 2
 9:00   Bargello (top statues).
11:00   Science Museum.
13:00   Lunch, free to wander and shop.
16:30   Uffizi Gallery (unforgettable paintings); reserve in advance.
19:00   Sunset at Piazzale Michelangelo (consider a dinner picnic).

Day 3
10:00   Duomo Museum.
12:00   Santa Croce Church.
14:00   Lunch.
15:00   Pitti Palace, Boboli Gardens.
18:00   Oltrarno Walk.
20:00   Dinner in Oltrarno.

Day 4
Side-trip to Siena (sights open daily; 1–2 hrs by bus), or consider an
overnight stay to enjoy the town at twilight.

Day 5, 6, and so on
Visit your pick of Pisa, Lucca, and Tuscan hill towns.

Arrival in Florence

For a rundown on Florence's train station, the bus station next door, and airport, see "Transportation Connections," page 198. The taxi stand in front of the train station often has a line. To catch a cab without the line, wander deeper into the city. Most recommended hotels are within a 10- or 15-minute walk. Many of the hotels listed are in the direction of the Church of Santa Maria Novella. From the station (with your back to the tracks), cross the wide square to reach the church and continue to the piazza in front of the church. The underground Galleria S. M. Novella tunnel that leads from the station under the square to the church keeps you out of the traffic but is popular with thieves. Skip it or use with caution.

Tourist Information

There are three **TI**s in Florence: across from the train station, near Santa Croce Church, and on Via Cavour.

The TI across the square from the train station is most crowded—expect long lines (Mon–Sat 8:30–19:00, Sun 8:30–13:30; with your back to tracks, exit the station—it's across the square in wall near corner of church, Piazza Stazione, tel. 055-212-245). In the train station, avoid the Hotel Reservations "Tourist Information" window (marked *Informazioni Turistiche Alberghiere*) near the McDonald's; it's not a real TI, but a hotel reservation business instead.

The TI near Santa Croce Church is pleasant, helpful, and uncrowded (Mon–Sat 9:00–19:00, Sun 9:00–14:00, shorter hours off-season, Borgo Santa Croce 29 red, tel. 055-234-0444).

Another winner is the TI three blocks north of the Duomo (Mon–Sat 8:30–18:30, Sun 8:30–13:30, closed Sun in winter, Via Cavour 1 red, tel. 055-290-832 or 055-276-0383, international bookstore across street).

At any TI, pick up a map, a current museum-hours listing (extremely important, since no guidebook—including this one—has ever been able to accurately predict the hours of Florence's sights), and any information on entertainment. The free monthly *Florence Concierge Information* magazine lists museums, plus lots that I don't: concerts, markets, sporting events, church services, shopping ideas, bus and train connections, and an entire similar section on Siena. Get yours at the TI or from any expensive hotel (pick one up, as if you're staying there).

Helpful Hints

Theft Alert: Florence has particularly hardworking thief gangs. They specialize in tourists and hang out where you do: near the train station, the station's underpass (especially where the tunnel surfaces), and major sights. Also be on guard at two squares frequented by drug pushers (Santa Maria Novella and Santo

Daily Reminder

Sunday: Today the Duomo's dome, Science Museum, and Museum of Precious Stones are closed. These sights close early: Duomo Museum (at 13:40) and the Baptistery's interior (at 14:00). A few sights are open only in the afternoon: Duomo (13:30–16:45), Santa Croce Church (13:00–17:30), and Brancacci Chapel and the Church of Santa Maria Novella (both 13:00–17:00).

The Museum of San Marco, which is open on the second and fourth Sunday of the month until 19:00, closes entirely—as does the Bargello—on the first, third, and fifth Sunday. The Medici Chapels and the Modern Art Gallery (in the Pitti Palace) close on the second and fourth Sunday. (Need a calendar? Look in the appendix.)

It's not possible to reserve tickets today by phone for the major sights (Accademia, Uffizi Gallery) because the booking office is closed; see page 35 for alternatives.

Monday: The biggies are closed, including Accademia *(David)* and Uffizi Gallery, as well as the Palatine Gallery/Royal Apartments in the Pitti Palace.

The Medici Chapels and the Modern Art Gallery (in the Pitti Palace) close on the first, third, and fifth Monday of the month. The Museum of San Marco and the Bargello close on the second and fourth Monday. Boboli Gardens close on the first and last Monday. The Palazzo Vecchio may stay open until 23:00 in summer.

Target these sights on Mondays: Duomo Museum, Giotto's Tower, Brancacci Chapel, Michelangelo's House, Science Museum, Palazzo Vecchio, and churches. Or take a walking tour.

Tuesday: All sights are open except for Michelangelo's House and the Brancacci Chapel. The Science Museum closes early (13:00).

Wednesday: All sights are open except for Medici-Riccardi Palace and Santo Spirito Church (closed in afternoon).

Thursday: All sights are open. The Museum of Precious Stones stays open late (19:00) while these sights close early: Duomo (15:30) and Palazzo Vecchio (14:00).

Friday: All sights are open. The Church of Santa Maria Novella opens late (13:00–17:00) and Palazzo Vecchio closes late (may be open until 23:00 in summer).

Saturday: All sights are open, but the Science Museum closes at 13:00. These sights close early on the first Saturday of the month: Duomo (15:30) and the Duomo's dome (16:00). The Museum of San Marco stays open until 19:00. The Accademia, Uffizi, and Palatine Gallery/Royal Apartments may stay open until 22:00 in summer.

Spirito). American tourists—especially older ones—are considered easy targets.

Churches: Many churches now operate like museums, charging an admission fee to see their art treasures. Modest dress is required in some churches, and recommended for all of them—no short shorts (or short skirts) and no bare shoulders. Be respectful of worshipers; don't use a flash. Churches usually close from 12:30 to 15:00 or 16:00.

Chill Out: Schedule into your sightseeing several cool breaks where you can sit, pause, and refresh yourself with a sandwich, gelato, or coffee.

Medical Help: To track down a doctor who speaks English, call 055-475-411 (reasonable hotel calls, cheaper if you go to the clinic at Via L. Magnifico 59, near Piazza Libertà) or get a list of English-speaking doctors from the TI. There are 24-hour pharmacies at the train station and near the Duomo on Borgo San Lorenzo.

Addresses: Street addresses list businesses in red and residences in black (color-coded on the actual street number and indicated by a letter following the number in printed addresses: r = red, no indication = black). *Pensioni* are usually black but can be either. The red and black numbers each appear in roughly consecutive order on streets but bear no apparent connection with each other. I'm lazy and don't concern myself with the distinction (if one number's wrong, I look for the other) and can easily find my way around.

Launderettes: The Wash & Dry Lavarapido chain offers long hours and efficient, self-service launderettes at several locations (about €6.20 for wash and dry, daily 8:00–22:00, tel. 055-580-480). These are close to recommended hotels: Via dei Servi 105 (and a rival launderette at Via Guelfa 22 red, off Via Cavour; both near *David*); Via del Sole 29 red and Via della Scala 52 red (between train station and river); and Via dei Serragli 87 red (across the river in Oltrarno neighborhood).

Getting Around Florence

I organize my sightseeing geographically and do it all on foot.

If you take **buses,** a €1 ticket gets you one hour (€1.80/3 hrs, €4/24 hrs, tickets not sold on bus before 21:00—buy in *tabacchi* shops or newsstands, validate on bus, after 21:00 buy tickets on bus, route map available at TI). Multiday passes are also available.

The minimum cost for a **taxi** ride is €4 or, after 22:00, €5 (rides in the center of town should be charged as tariff #1). A taxi ride from the train station to Ponte Vecchio costs about €8. Taxi fares and supplements (e.g., €2 extra if you telephone a cab) are clearly explained on signs in each taxi.

Tips for Tackling Our Self-Guided Tours

Sightseeing can be hard work. Our self-guided tours are designed to help make your visits to Italy's finest museums meaningful, fun, fast, and painless. Make reservations for the more crowded sights (see page 35). To make the most of our tours, read the tour the night before your visit.

Because of labor demands, hours of sights change without warning. Pick up the latest listing of museum hours at a TI. Don't put off visiting a must-see sight such as *David;* you never know when a place will close unexpectedly for a holiday, strike, or restoration.

When you arrive at the sight, use the overview map to get the lay of the land and the basic tour route. Expect a few changes—paintings can be on tour, on loan, out sick, or shifted at the whim of the curator. To adapt, pick up any available free floor plans as you enter, ask an information person to glance at this book's maps to confirm they're current, or if you can't find a particular painting, just ask any museum worker. Point to the photograph in this book and ask, *"Dov'è?"* (DOH-vay; it means "Where?").

We cover the highlights at sights. You might want to supplement with an audioguide (dry-but-useful recorded descriptions in English, about $5, usually available on site), or a guided tour (usually $6 or more). Tours in English are most likely to occur during peak season. The quality of a tour depends on the guide's knowledge, fluency, and enthusiasm.

Museums have their rules; if you're aware of them in advance, they're no big deal. Keep in mind that many sights have "last entry" times 30–60 minutes before closing. Guards usher people out before the official closing time.

Cameras are normally allowed, but no flashes or tripods (without special permission). Flashes damage oil paintings and distract others in the room. Even without a flash, a handheld camera will take a decent picture (or buy postcards or posters at the museum bookstore). Video cameras are usually allowed.

For security reasons, you're often required to check even small bags. Many museums have a free checkroom at the entrance. They're safe. If you have something you can't bear to part with, be prepared to stash it in a pocket or purse.

At the museum bookshop, thumb through the biggest guidebook (or scan its index) to be sure you haven't overlooked something that is of particular interest to you. If there's an on-site cafeteria, it's usually a good place to rest and have a snack or light meal. Museum WCs are free and generally clean.

And finally, every sight or museum offers infinitely more than the few stops we cover. Use these tours as an introduction—not the final word.

Tours of Florence

Note that big bus companies offer tours of Florence but for most, the city is really best on foot.

Walking Tours of Florence—This company offers a variety of tours (up to 12/day Mon–Sat year-round plus summer Sundays) featuring downtown Florence, Uffizi highlights, or Tuscany (countryside, Siena, San Gimignano, Pisa, or the Cinque Terre), presented by informative, entertaining, native English–speaking guides. The "Original Florence" walk hits the main sights but gets offbeat to weave a picture of Florentine life in medieval and Renaissance times. You can expect lots of talking, which is great if you like history. Tours, offered throughout the year regardless of the weather, start at their office and are limited to 22 people, but will go with as few as two participants. Extra guides are available if more people show up (€25 for 3-hr Original Florence walk, office open Mon–Sat 8:30–18:00, Sun 8:30–13:30 but off-season closed on Sun and for lunch, Piazza Santo Stefano 2 black, a short block north of Ponte Vecchio; go east on tiny Vicolo San Stefano, in Piazza Santo Stefano at #2—see map on page 29, booking necessary for Uffizi tour, private tours available, tel. 055-264-5033, mobile 329-613-2730, www.artviva.com, staff@artviva.com). For all the schedule details, pick up their extensive brochure in your hotel lobby.

Florentia—Top-notch, private walking tours—geared for thoughtful, well-heeled travelers with good attention spans—are led by local scholars. The tours range from introductory city walks and museum visits to in-depth thematic walks such as the Golden Age of Florence, Medici Dynasty, and more. Excursions to Siena, Lucca, and the Tuscan countryside are available (tours start at €175 for a half-day tour, reserve in advance, tel. 338-890-8625, U.S. tel. 510-549-1707, www.florentia.org, info@florentia.org).

Local Guide—Paola Migliorini offers museum tours, city walking tours, and Tuscan excursions by van. You (and your group) can tailor tours as you like. The van allows slow walkers to enjoy the city nearly sweat-free (€50/hr or €65/hr with 8-seat van, Via S. Gallo 120, tel. 055-472-448, mobile 347-657-2611, www.florencetour.com, info @florencetour.com).

SIGHTS

In this chapter, Florence's most important museums have the shortest listings and are marked with a ○ (and page number). These sights are covered in greater detail in one of the self-guided tours included in this book.

The Renaissance Walk (see page 48) connects a number of these sights, from Michelangelo's *David* to the Ponte Vecchio over the Arno River. You can book ahead to visit the major museums on this walk (Accademia and Uffizi Gallery); see page 35 for details.

Price Hike Alert: Museums jack up their prices if they host special exhibitions.

North of the Duomo (Cathedral)

▲▲▲Accademia (Galleria dell' Accademia)— This museum houses Michelangelo's *David,* the consummate Renaissance statue of the buff, Biblical shepherd boy ready to take on the giant. Nearby are some of the master's other works, including his powerful (unfinished) *Prisoners, St. Matthew,* and a *Pietà* (possibly by one of his disciples). Florentine Michelangelo Buonarotti, who would work tirelessly through the night, believed that the sculptor was a tool of God, responsible only for chipping away at the stone until the intended sculpture emerged. Beyond the magic marble are two floors of mildly interesting pre-Renaissance and Renaissance paintings, including a couple of lighter-than-air Botticellis.

Cost, Hours, Location: €6.50 (plus €3 reservation fee), Tue–Sun 8:15–18:50, 8:15–22:00 on holidays and maybe on summer Sat, closed Mon (last entry 45 min before closing, Via Ricasoli 60, tel.

Florence Sights

400 METERS

400 YARDS

TO FORTEZZA DA BASSO

TRAIN STN.

PIAZZA ADUA

MUSEUM OF SAN MARCO

TO PIAZZA LIBERTA

ACCADEMIA (DAVID)

PIAZZA S.S. ANNUNZIATA

MERCATO CENTRALE

SAN LORENZO CHURCH & STREET MKT.

BUS STN.

MEDICI CHAPELS

MEDICI RICCARDI PALACE

PRECIOUS STONES MUSEUM

S. MARIA NOVELLA

LAUR. LIB.

CERRETANI

DUOMO

DUOMO MUSEUM

PERFUMERY

BAPT.

AGLI

PIAZZA REPUBBLICA

CORSO

Dante's House

BARGELLO

MICHELANGELO'S HOUSE

S. TRINITA

VIGNA NUOVA

ORSAN-MICHELE

PORTA ROSSI

MERC. NUOVO

RIVER

TO BRANCACCI CHAPEL

OLTRARNO

B. D. GRECI

P. S. CROCE

SANTA CROCE

S. SPIRITO

B. S. JACOPO

PALAZZO VECCHIO

SCIENCE MUSEUM

TINTORI

ARNO

PONTE VECCHIO

UFFIZI

VIA SAN NICCOLO

PITTI PALACE

BOBOLI GARDENS

DCH

FORTE BELVEDERE

PIAZZALE MICHELANGELO

★ PIAZZA SIGNORIA

VIEW

G = GELATERIA

055-238-8609). ❂ See page 51 of the Renaissance Walk.

Nearby: Piazza Santissima Annunziata, behind the Accademia, displays lovely Renaissance harmony. Facing the square are two fine buildings: the 15th-century Santissima Annunziata church (worth a peek) and Brunelleschi's Hospital of the Innocents (*Spedale degli Innocenti,* not worth going inside), with terra-cotta medallions by Luca della Robbia. Built in the 1420s, the hospital is considered the first Renaissance building.

▲▲**Museum of San Marco (Museo di San Marco)**—One block north of the Accademia, this 15th-century monastery houses the

 greatest collection anywhere of frescoes and paintings by the early Renaissance master Fra Angelico. The ground floor features the monk's paintings, along with some works by Fra Bartolomeo. Upstairs are 43 cells decorated by Fra Angelico and his assistants. While the monk/painter was trained in the medieval religious style, he also learned and adopted Renaissance

techniques and sensibilities, producing works that blended Christian symbols and Renaissance realism. Don't miss the cell of Savonarola, the charismatic monk who rode in from the Christian right, threw out the Medicis, turned Florence into a theocracy, sponsored "bon-fires of the vanities" (burning books, paintings, and so on), and was finally burned himself when Florence decided to change channels (€4, Mon–Fri 8:15–13:50, Sat–Sun 8:15–19:00, but closed first, third, and fifth Sun and second and fourth Mon of each month, on Piazza San Marco, tel. 055-238-8608).

The ticket office can issue reserved tickets and even sell tickets (often with immediate reservation) to the Uffizi and Accademia. ❂ See Museum of San Marco Tour on page 93.

Museum of Precious Stones (Museo dell' Opificio delle Pietre Dure)—This unusual gem of a museum features mosaics of inlaid marble and stones. You'll see remnants of the Medici workshop from 1588, including 500 different precious stones, the tools used to cut and inlay them, and room after room of the sumptuous finished product. The fine loaner booklet describes it all in English (€2, Mon–Sat 8:15–14:00, Thu until 19:00, closed Sun; Via degli Alfani 78, around corner from Accademia). This ticket booth can also sell tickets with reservations (often for the same day) to the Uffizi and Accademia.

▲▲**Medici Chapels (Cappelle Medicee)**—The burial site of the ruling Medici family in the church of San Lorenzo comprises the dusky Crypt; the big, domed Chapel of Princes; and the magnificent, all-Michelangelo New Sacristy featuring the master's architecture, tombs, and statues. The Medicis made their money in textiles and banking and patronized a dream team of Renaissance artists who put Florence on the cultural map. Michelangelo, who spent his teen years living with the Medicis, was commissioned for the family's final tribute (€6, daily 8:15–16:50 but closed the second and fourth Sun and the first, third, and fifth Mon of each month, tel. 055-238-8602). ✪ See Medici Chapels Tour on page 123.

Nearby: Behind the chapels on Piazza Madonna di degli Aldobrandini is a lively market scene that I find just as interesting. Take a stroll through the huge double-decker Mercato Centrale (central food market) one block north.

▲**Medici-Riccardi Palace (Palazzo Medici-Riccardi)**—Lorenzo the Magnificent's home is worth a look for its art. The tiny Chapel of the Magi contains colorful Renaissance gems like the *Procession of the Magi* frescoes by Benozzo Gozzoli. The former library has a Baroque ceiling fresco by Luca Giordano, a prolific artist from Naples known as Fast Luke *(Luca fa presto)* for his ambidextrous painting abilities. While the Medicis originally occupied this 1444 house, in the 1700s it became home to the Riccardi family, who added the Baroque flourishes (€4, Thu–Tue 9:00–19:00, closed Wed, Via Cavour 3, kitty-corner from San Lorenzo Church, 1 long block north of Baptistery, tel. 055-276-0340). ✪ See Medici-Riccardi Palace Tour on page 132.

Duomo and Nearby

▲▲**Duomo (Santa Maria del Fiore)**—Florence's Gothic cathedral has the third-longest nave in Christendom (free, Mon–Wed and Fri–Sat 10:00–17:00 except first Sat of month 10:00–15:30, Thu 10:00–15:30, Sun 13:30–16:45, modest dress code enforced, tel. 055-230-2885). The church's noisy neo-Gothic facade from the 1870s is covered with pink, green, and white Tuscan marble. Since

nearly all of its great art is stored in the Duomo Museum (behind the church), the best thing about the interior is the shade. The inside of the dome is decorated by one of the largest paintings of the Renaissance, a huge *Last Judgment* by Giorgio Vasari and Federico Zuccari. Note: The massive crowds that overwhelm the entrance in the morning clear out by afternoon.

The cathedral's claim to artistic fame is Brunelleschi's magnificent dome—the first Renaissance dome and the model for domes to follow. ✪ See page 54 of the Renaissance Walk.

Florence at a Glance

▲▲▲**Uffizi Gallery** Greatest collection of Italian paintings any-where—reserve ahead. **Hours:** Tue–Sun 8:15–18:50, 8:15–22:00 on holidays and maybe on summer Sat, closed Mon.

▲▲▲**Accademia** Michelangelo's *David* and powerful (unfinished) *Prisoners*—reserve ahead. **Hours:** Tue–Sun 8:15–18:50, 8:15–22:00 on holidays and maybe on summer Sat, closed Mon.

▲▲▲**Bargello** Underappreciated sculpture museum (Michelangelo, Donatello, Medici treasures). **Hours:** Daily 8:15–13:50; closed first, third, and fifth Sun and second and fourth Mon of each month.

▲▲**Museum of San Marco** Best collection anywhere of frescoes and paintings by the early Renaissance master Fra Angelico. **Hours:** Mon–Fri 8:15–13:50, Sat–Sun 8:15–19:00; closed first, third, and fifth Sun and second and fourth Mon of each month.

▲▲**Medici Chapels** Tombs of Florence's great ruling family, designed and carved by Michelangelo. **Hours:** Daily 8:15–16:50; closed the second and fourth Sun and the first, third, and fifth Mon of each month.

▲▲**Church of Santa Maria Novella** 13th-century Dominican church with Masaccio's famous 3-D painting. **Hours:** Mon–Thu and Sat 9:30–17:00, Fri and Sun 13:00–17:00.

▲▲**Santa Croce Church** 14th-century Franciscan church with pre-cious art, tombs of famous Florentines, and Brunelleschi's Pazzi Chapel. **Hours:** Mon–Sat 9:30–17:30, Sun 15:00–17:30; winter Mon–Sat 9:30–12:30 & 15:00–17:30, Sun 13:00–17:30.

▲▲**Science Museum** Fascinating collection of old clocks, tele-scopes, maps, and Galileo's finger. **Hours:** Mon and Wed–Fri 9:30–17:00, Tue and Sat 9:30–13:00, closed Sun.

▲▲**Pitti Palace** Three museums in lavish palace: Palatine Gallery (Raphael art), Modern Art Gallery, Grand Ducal Treasures (Medici treasure chest), plus sprawling Boboli Gardens. **Hours:** Palatine: Tue–Sun 8:15–18:50, closed Mon; Modern Art and Treasures: daily 8:15–13:50, closed second and fourth Sun and first, third, and fifth Mon; Boboli: daily 9:00–19:30 June–Aug, 9:00–18:30 fall and spring, 9:00–16:30 in winter, closed first and last Mon of month.

▲▲**Brancacci Chapel** Works of Masaccio, early Renaissance master who reinvented perspective. **Hours:** Mon and Wed–Sat 10:00–17:00, Sun 13:00–17:00, closed Tue.

▲▲**Duomo (Santa Maria del Fiore)** Gothic Cathedral with colorful facade, long nave, and the first dome built since ancient Roman times. **Hours:** Mon–Wed and Fri–Sat 10:00–17:00 except first Sat of month 10:00–15:30, Thu 10:00–15:30, Sun 13:30–16:45.

▲▲**Duomo Museum** Underrated cathedral museum with great sculpture. **Hours:** Mon–Sat 9:00–19:30, Sun 9:00–13:40.

▲**Climbing Duomo's Dome** Grand view into the cathedral, close-up of dome architecture, and, after 463 steps, a glorious Florence vista. **Hours:** Mon–Fri 8:30–19:00, Sat 8:30–17:40 except first Sat of month 8:30–16:00, closed Sun.

▲**Giotto's Tower** Bell tower with views equaling Duomo's, 50 fewer steps, and fewer lines. **Hours:** Daily 8:30–19:30.

▲**Baptistery** Bronze doors fit to be the gates of Paradise. **Hours:** Doors always viewable; Baptistery open Mon–Sat 12:00–19:00, Sun 8:30–14:00.

▲**Medici-Riccardi Palace** Lorenzo the Magnificent's home, with fine art, frescoed ceilings, and a lovely Chapel of the Magi. **Hours:** Tue–Thu 9:00–19:00, closed Wed.

▲**Palazzo Vecchio** Fortified palace once the home of the Medici family, wallpapered with mediocre art. **Hours:** Fri–Wed 9:00–19:00, Thu 9:00–14:00, in summer maybe 9:00–23:00 on Mon and Fri.

▲**Ponte Vecchio** Famous bridge lined with gold and silver shops. **Hours:** Bridge always open.

▲**Mercato Nuovo** Bustling market in loggia. **Hours:** Open daily.

▲**Michelangelo's House** Museum featuring early, lesser-known works of the master. **Hours:** Wed–Mon 9:30–14:00, closed Tue.

▲**Piazzale Michelangelo** Hilltop square in south Florence offering stunning view of city and Duomo. **Hours:** Always open.

▲**Climbing the Duomo's Dome**—For a grand view into the cathedral from the base of the dome, a peek at some of the tools used in the dome's construction, a chance to see Brunelleschi's "dome-within-a-dome" construction, a glorious Florence view from the top, and the equivalent of 463 plunges on a Stairmaster, climb the dome. To avoid the *long*, dreadfully slow-moving line, arrive by 8:30 (€6, Mon–Fri 8:30–19:00, Sat 8:30–17:40 except first Sat of month 8:30–16:00, closed Sun, enter from outside church on north side, tel. 055-230-2885).

▲**Giotto's Tower (Campanile)**—If you're not interested in experiencing dome-within-a-dome architecture, you'll likely feel that climbing Giotto's 270-foot bell tower beats scaling the neighboring Duomo's dome. With 50 fewer steps, it's a faster climb with a similar view—plus the dome (€6, daily 8:30–19:30, last entry 40 min before closing). ✪ See page 56 of the Renaissance Walk.

▲**Baptistery**—Michelangelo said its bronze doors were fit to be the gates of Paradise. Check out the gleaming copies of Lorenzo Ghiberti's bronze doors facing the Duomo. Making a breakthrough in perspective, Ghiberti used mathematical laws to create the illusion of receding distance on a basically flat surface.

The doors on the north side of the building were designed by Ghiberti when he was young; he'd won the honor and opportunity by beating Brunelleschi in a competition (the rivals' original entries are in the Duomo Museum, see below).

Inside, sit and savor the medieval mosaic ceiling where it's always Judgment Day. Jesus is giving the ultimate thumbs up and thumbs down (€3, interior open Mon–Sat 12:00–19:00, Sun 8:30–14:00; bronze doors are on the outside, so always "open"; original panels are in the Bargello Museum). ✪ See page 88 of the Bargello Tour.

▲▲**Duomo Museum (Museo dell' Opera del Duomo)**—The underrated cathedral museum, behind the church at #9, is great if you like sculpture. On the ground floor, look for a late Michelangelo *Pietà*, the eight restored panels of Ghiberti's north doors for the Baptistery, and statues from the original Baptistery facade. Upstairs, you'll find Brunelleschi's models for his dome, as well as Donatello's anorexic *Mary Magdalene* and playful choir loft. The museum features most of Ghiberti's original "Gates of Paradise" panels; the panels on the Baptistery's doors today are copies (€6, Mon–Sat 9:00–19:30, Sun 9:00–13:40, last entry 40 min before closing, closed on holidays, one of the few museums in Florence open on Mon, tel. 055-230-2885). ✪ See Duomo Museum Tour on page 108.

Make Reservations to Avoid Lines

Florence has a reservation system for its top five sights—Uffizi, Accademia, Bargello, Medici Chapels, and the Pitti Palace. Two of these sights always have long lines: the Accademia (Michelangelo's *David*) and the Uffizi (Renaissance paintings). To avoid long waits—up to two hours at the Uffizi—reserve by phone. Frankly, it's stupid not to.

While you can generally make a reservation a day in advance (upon arrival in Florence), you'll have a wider selection of entry times by calling a few days ahead. You dial 055-294-883 (Mon–Fri 8:30–18:30, Sat 8:30–12:30, closed Sun), an English-speaking operator walks you through the process, and two minutes later you say *grazie,* with appointments (15-min entry window) and six-digit confirmation numbers for each of the top museums and galleries. The ticket phone number is often busy; be persistent. If you call months in advance (during off-season) or request your hotel to make the appointment for you (when you confirm your hotel booking), you may save some frustration. Some booking agencies offer reservations online for a fee (such as www.weekendafirenze.it).

If you haven't booked ahead, you can make reservations for the top sights at the minor, less-crowded sights (such as the Museum of San Marco or Museum of Precious Stones). Clerks at the ticket booths at these sleepy sights can reserve and sell tickets to the major sights, often for admission the same day, allowing you to skip right past the dreary mob scene.

Lines occasionally form at the Uffizi even for those with reservations who are waiting to pick up tickets. If you have reservations, consider picking up your Uffizi ticket at a less-crowded sight (any ticket office can issue reserved tickets).

Between the Duomo and Piazza della Signoria

▲▲▲Bargello (Museo Nazionale)—This under-appreciated sculpture museum is in a former police-station-turned-prison that looks like a mini–Palazzo Vecchio. It has Donatello's painfully beautiful *David* (the very influential first male nude to be sculpted in a thousand years), works by Michelangelo, and rooms of Medici treasures cruelly explained in Italian only (politely suggest to the staff that English descriptions would be wonderful). Moody Donatello, who embraced realism with his lifelike statues, set the personal and artistic style for many Renaissance artists to follow. The best works are in the ground-floor room at the foot of the outdoor staircase and in the room directly above (€4, daily 8:15–13:50 but closed first, third, and fifth Sun and second and fourth Mon of each month, last entry 40 min before closing, Via del Proconsolo 4, tel. 055-238-8606). ✪ See Bargello Tour on page 84.

▲**Dante's House (Casa di Dante)**—Dante's house is closed indefinitely for restoration. It's actually a copy built near his house just a hundred years ago, consisting of five rooms in an old building with lots of documents and photos relating to his life and work. Well-described in English, it's interesting to literary buffs (across the street and around the corner from Bargello, at Via S. Margherita 1, tel. 055-219-416).

Orsanmichele Church—In the 9th century, this *loggia* (a covered courtyard) was a market used for selling grain (stored upstairs). Later, it was closed in to make a church. Outside, check out the dynamic statue-filled niches, some with accompanying symbols from the guilds that sponsored the art. Donatello's *St. Mark* and *St. George* (on the northeast and northwest corners) step out boldly in the new Renaissance style. The interior, viewable only during evening concerts (see page 58), has a glorious Gothic tabernacle (1359) by Orcagna. The iron bars spanning the vaults were the Italian Gothic answer to the French Gothic external buttresses. ✪ See page 58 of the Renaissance Walk.

The museum upstairs holds many of the church's precious originals. Someday tourists may be able to enjoy its fine statues by Ghiberti, Donatello, and company. (But don't hold your breath.)

A block away, you'll find the...

▲**Mercato Nuovo (a.k.a. the Straw Market)**—This market loggia is how Orsanmichele looked before it became a church. Originally a silk and straw market, Mercato Nuovo still functions as a rustic market today (at the intersection of Via Calimala and Via Porta Rossa). Prices are soft. Notice the circled X in the center, marking the spot where people hit after being hoisted up to the top and dropped as punishment for bankruptcy. You'll also find *Porcellino* (a statue of a wild boar nicknamed "little pig"), which people rub and give coins to in order to ensure their return to Florence. Nearby, a wagon sells tripe (cow innards) sandwiches.

▲**Piazza della Repubblica**—This large square sits on the site of Florence's original Roman Forum. The lone column—nicknamed the belly button of Florence—is the only remaining bit of Roman Florence except for its grid street plan. Look at the map (by the benches—where the old boys hang out to talk sports and politics) to see the ghost of Rome. Roman Florence was a garrison town—a rectangular fort with this square marking the intersection of the two main roads (Via Corso and Via Roma).

Today's piazza, framed by a triumphal arch, is really a nationalistic statement celebrating the unification of Italy. Florence, the capital of the country (1865–1870) until Rome was liberated, lacked a square worthy of this grand new country. So the neighborhood here was razed to open up an imposing modern forum surrounded by stately circa-1890 buildings.

Between here and the river you'll find characteristic parts of the medieval city that give a sense of what this neighborhood felt like before it was bulldozed. Back in the Middle Ages, writers described Florence as so densely built up that when it rained, pedestrians didn't get wet. Torches were used to light the lanes in midday. The city was prickly with noble family towers (like San Gimignano) and had Romeo-and-Juliet-type family feuds. But with the rise of the Medicis (c. 1300), no noble family was allowed to have an architectural ego trip taller then theirs, and nearly all other towers were taken down.

The fancy La Rinascente department store, facing the Piazza della Repubblica, is one of the city's finest (WC on fourth floor, view terrace in small pricey bar above that).

On and near Piazza della Signoria

▲▲▲Uffizi Gallery—This greatest collection of Italian paintings anywhere features works by Giotto, Leonardo, Raphael, Caravaggio, Rubens, Titian, and Michelangelo, and a roomful of Botticellis, including his *Birth of Venus*. Start with Giotto's early stabs at Renaissance-style realism, then move on through the 3-D experimentation of the early 1400s to the real thing rendered by the likes of Botticelli and Leonardo. Finish off with the High Renaissance— Michelangelo, Rubens, and Titian. Because only 780 visitors are allowed inside the building at any one time, during the day there's generally a very long wait. The good news: no Louvre-style mob scenes. The museum is nowhere near as big as it is great. Few tourists spend more than two hours inside. The paintings are displayed on one comfortable U-shaped floor in chronological order from the 13th through 17th centuries (left wing—the best: Florentine Middle Ages to Renaissance; connecting corridor: sculpture; right wing: High Renaissance to Baroque).

Cost, Hours, Reservations: €9.50, plus €3 for recommended reservation, Tue–Sun 8:15–18:50, 8:15–22:00 on holidays and maybe on summer Sat, closed Mon (last entry 45 min before closing; after entering take elevator or climb 4 long flights of stairs). To avoid the long lines, it's smart to call ahead to reserve an entry time. ✪ For details on making reservations and for a self-guided tour, see Uffizi Gallery Tour on page 64.

In Courtyard of Uffizi: Enjoy the Uffizi's courtyard (free), full of artists and souvenir stalls. The surrounding statues honor earthshaking Florentines: artists (Michelangelo), philosophers (Machiavelli), scientists (Galileo), writers (Dante), and explorers (Amerigo

Vespucci), and the great patron of so much Renaissance thinking, Lorenzo "the Magnificent" de Medici. ✪ For more, see page 62 of the Renaissance Walk.

▲Palazzo Vecchio—With its distinctive castle turret, this fortified palace—once the town hall, then the home of the Medici family—is a Florentine landmark. But if you're visiting only one palace interior in town, the Pitti Palace is better. The Palazzo Vecchio interior is worthwhile only if you're a real fan of Florentine history or of the artist Giorgio Vasari, who wallpapered the place with mediocre magnificence.

Highlights include the 13,000-square-foot Grand Hall *(Sala Grande)*, lined with huge Vasari paintings of Florence at war. The central ceiling painting shows Cosimo I de' Medici (The Younger), the patron who financed "Vasari's Sistine Chapel." In the hall stands Michelangelo's statue of *Victory* (*La Vittoria*, 1533–34), showing a young man triumphing over an older man (who may be a self-portrait). This was the prototype of the many spiral-shaped statues by other artists that also line the Grand Hall.

Pass through a dozen richly-decorated rooms to the Room of the Lilies *(Sala dei Gigli)* with Duomo views out the window and Donatello's bronze statue of *Judith and Holofernes*. The statue was commissioned by the Medici, who saw themselves as the noble Judith slaying their (drunken, sleepy) enemies. When the Medici were driven out, the Florentines took it from the Medici-Riccardi Palace and placed it at the Palazzo Vecchio doorway (where the fake *David* stands) as a symbol of their triumph over the corrupt Medici. A decade later, it was replaced by Michelangelo's *David* as the symbol of Florence victorious.

The adjoining Chancery Room *(Cancelleria)* was once Machiavelli's office. In the nearby Map Chamber *(Sala delle Carte Geografiche)*, Southern Californians can find their hometown on maps (far right corner, upper level) charting the known world in the 16th century.

Cost, Hours: €5.70, €8 combo-ticket with Brancacci Chapel, Fri–Wed 9:00–19:00, Thu 9:00–14:00, in summer maybe open 9:00–23:00 on Mon and Fri, ticket office closes one hour earlier (tel. 055-276-8465). ✪ See page 59 of the Renaissance Walk.

Even if you don't go to the museum, do step into the **free court-yard** (behind the fake *David*) just to feel the essence of the Medicis. Until 1873, Michelangelo's *David* stood at the entrance, where the copy is today. While the huge statues in the square are important only as the whipping boys of art critics and as rest stops for pigeons, the nearby **Loggia dei Lanzi** has several important statues. Look for Cellini's bronze statue of Perseus holding the head of Medusa. The plaque on the pavement in front of the fountain marks the spot where the monk Savonarola was burned in MCDXCVIII, or 1498 (for more on the monk, see Museum of San Marco Tour on page 93).

▲▲**Science Museum (Istituto e Museo di Storia della Scienza)**—This is a fascinating collection of Renaissance and later clocks, telescopes, maps, and ingenious gadgets. Trace the technical innovations as modern science emerges from 1000 to 1900. One of the most talked-about bottles in Florence is the one here containing Galileo's finger. The first floor features various tools for gauging the world, from a compass and thermometer to Galileo's telescopes. The second floor delves into clocks, pumps, medicine, and chemistry. Loaner English guide-booklets are available. It's friendly, comfortably cool, never crowded, and just a block east of the Uffizi on the Arno River (€6.50, Mon and Wed–Fri 9:30–17:00, Tue and Sat 9:30–13:00, closed Sun, Piazza dei Giudici 1, tel. 055-265-311). ✪ See Science Museum Tour on page 152.

▲**Ponte Vecchio**—Florence's most famous bridge is lined with shops that have traditionally sold gold and silver. A statue of Cellini, the master goldsmith of the Renaissance, stands in the center, ignored by the flood of tacky tourism. ✪ See page 63 of Renaissance Walk.

Notice the "prince's passageway" above the bridge. In less secure times, the city leaders had a fortified passageway connecting the Vecchio Palace and Uffizi with the mighty Pitti Palace, to which they could flee in times of attack. This passageway, called the **Vasari Corridor,** is technically open to the public, but good luck getting an appointment (open "seasonally," try the museum reservation line, tel. 055-294-883).

Santa Croce Church and Nearby

▲▲**Santa Croce Church**—This 14th-century Franciscan church, decorated with centuries of precious art, holds the tombs of great Florentines (€4, Mon–Sat 9:30–17:30, Sun 13:00–17:30; winter Mon–Sat 9:30–12:30 & 15:00–17:30, Sun 13:00–17:30, modest dress code enforced, tel. 055-246-6105). The loud 19th-century Victorian Gothic facade faces a huge square ringed with tempting shops and littered with tired tourists. Escape into the church and admire its sheer height and spaciousness.

On your left as you enter is the **tomb of Galileo Galilei** (1564–1642), the Pisan who lived his last years under house arrest near Florence. Having defied the Church by saying the earth revolved around the sun, his heretical remains were only allowed in the church long after his death.

Directly opposite (on the right side of the nave) is the **tomb of Michelangelo Buonarroti** (1475–1564). Santa Croce was Michelangelo's childhood church, as he grew up a block east of here at Via dei Bentaccordi 15 (where nothing but a plaque marks the spot). The tomb, with the allegorical figures of painting, architecture, and

Floods in Florence

Summer visitors to Florence gaze at the lazy green creek called the Arno River and have a tough time imagining it being a destructive giant. But rare, powerful flooding is a part of life in Florence. The Arno River washed away the Ponte Vecchio in 1177 and 1333. And on November 4, 1966, a huge rain turned the Arno into a wall of water inundating the city with mud stacked as high as 20 feet. Nearly 14,000 families were left homeless, and a huge amount of art was destroyed or damaged.

Almost as impressive as the flood was the huge outpouring of support, as the art-loving world came to the city's rescue. While money poured in from far and wide, volunteers nicknamed "mud angels" mopped things up. After the flood, scientists made great gains in restoration techniques as they cleaned and repaired masterpieces from medieval and Renaissance times.

Today you'll see plaques around town showing the high-water marks (about six feet high at the Duomo). But now that a new dam has tamed the Arno, kayakers glide peacefully on the river, sightseers enjoy the great art with no thought of a flood, and locals...still get nervous after every heavy rain.

sculpture, was designed by Michelangelo's great admirer, the artist/biographer Vasari. Vasari also did the series of paintings that line the left side of the nave, using the twisting poses and bulky muscles that Michelangelo pioneered.

You'll find several sights along the right side of the nave, including a memorial to the poet **Dante Alighieri** (1265–1321). There's no body inside—he was banished by his hometown because of political differences. Exiled Dante looks weary, the Muse of Poetry mourns, and Lady Florence gestures to say, "Look what we missed out on."

At the **tomb of Niccolo Machiavelli** (1469–1527), Lady Justice presents a medallion with his portrait on it. Macchiavelli, a champion of democratic Florence, opposed the Medici as tyrants. When they returned to power, he was arrested and tortured. He retired to his farm to write *The Prince,* a how-to manual on hardball politics.

A carved and gilded relief by Donatello of the Annunciation shows a kneeling angel gently breaking the news to an astonished Mary.

Gioachino Rossini (1792–1868), composer of many operas and the *William Tell Overture* (a.k.a. the *Lone Ranger* theme), died in Paris, but was later moved here to his homeland during a wave of Italian nationalism in the late 19th century.

The first chapel to the right of the main altar features the famous fresco by Giotto of the *Death of Saint Francis.* Santa Croce was one of the first (and still is the biggest) churches built in honor of the humanist monk of Assisi. With simple but eloquent gestures, Francis' brothers bid him a sad farewell, one of the first expressions of human emotion in modern painting.

In the next chapel to the right, Giotto paints one of the first 3-D "scenes," showing Francis preaching to monks and nuns in a crude arcade.

At the end of the right transept, a door leads into the sacristy where you'll find a rumpled bit of St. Francis' tunic *(Parte di Tunica)* and old sheets of music. In the bookshop, notice the photos of the devastating flood of 1966 high on the wall. Beyond that is the "leather school" that's really more of a touristy leather store, but is mildly interesting. Exit between the Rossini and Machiavelli tombs into the cloisters. On the left enter Brunelleschi's **Pazzi Chapel,** considered one of the finest pieces of Florentine Renaissance architecture.

▲**Michelangelo's House (Casa Buonarroti)**—Fans enjoy a house standing on property once owned by Michelangelo, built by his grand-nephew, who turned it into a little museum honoring his famous relative. You'll see some of Michelangelo's early, much-less-monumental statues and sketches (€6.50, Wed–Mon 9:30–14:00, closed Tue, English descriptions, Via Ghibellina 70, tel. 055-241-752).

The highlights are on the first floor, in rooms that adjoin the first-floor landing. Climb the stairs to the landing, where you come face-to-face with portraits of 60-year-old Michelangelo (by his contemporaries), the Buonarroti family sword, and some leather shoes thought to be Michelangelo's. The room to the right displays small clay and wax models—some by Michelangelo, some by pupils—that the artist used to sketch out ideas for his statues.

The room to the left of the landing displays two relief panels, his earliest known sculptures. Teenage Michelangelo carved every inch of the *Battle of the Centaurs* (1490–92), a squirming tangle of battling nudes. Michelangelo kept this in his personal collection all his life. *The Madonna of the Stairs* (c. 1490) is as contemplative as the *Centaurs* is dramatic. Throughout his long career, bipolar Michelangelo veered between these two styles—moving or still, emotional or thoughtful, pagan or Christian.

The small, darkened room adjoining the landing is for the museum's vast collection of Michelangelo's sketches. Unfortunately, only a handful of works can be displayed at any one time. Vasari claims that Michelangelo wanted to burn his preliminary sketches, lest anyone think him less than perfect.

And finally, true Michelangemaniacs will complete their visit by exiting outside to gaze at Via Ghibellina 67 (next door to a Farmacia). This humble doorway lined with grey-green stone was once the entrance to Michelangelo's residence, circa 1520.

Near the Train Station

▲▲**Church of Santa Maria Novella**—This 13th-century Dominican church is rich in art. Along with crucifixes by Giotto and Brunelleschi, there's every textbook's example of the early Renaissance mastery of perspective: *The Holy Trinity* by Masaccio; it's opposite the side entrance. The exquisite chapels trace art in Florence from medieval times to early Baroque. The outside of the church features a dash of Romanesque (horizontal stripes), Gothic (pointed arches), Renaissance (geometric shapes), and Baroque (scrolls). Step in and look down the 330-foot nave for a 14th-century optical illusion (€2.50, Mon–Thu and Sat 9:30–17:00, Fri and Sun 13:00–17:00). ✪ See Santa Maria Novella Tour on page 135.

Nearby: A palatial **perfumery** is around the corner 100 yards down Via della Scala at #16 (free but shopping encouraged, Mon–Sat 9:30–19:30, closed Sun, tel. 055-216-276). Thick with the lingering aroma of centuries of spritzes, it started as the herb garden of the Santa Maria Novella monks. Well-known even today for its top-quality products, it is extremely Florentine. Pick up the history sheet at the desk and wander deep into the shop. From the back room, you can peek at Santa Maria Novella's cloister with its dreamy frescoes and imagine a time before Vespas and tourists.

South of the Arno River

▲▲**Pitti Palace**—From the Uffizi, follow the course of the elevated passageway (closed to non-Medicis) across the Ponte Vecchio to the gargantuan Pitti Palace, which has several separate museums.

The **Palatine Gallery/Royal Apartments (Galleria Palatina)** is the biggie, featuring palatial room after chandeliered room, its walls sagging with masterpieces by minor artists and minor pieces by masters. Its Raphael collection is the biggest anywhere (first floor, €8.50, Tue–Sun 8:15–18:50, closed Mon, buy tickets on right-hand side of courtyard, tel. 055-238-8614).

The **Modern Art Gallery** features Romanticism, neoclassicism, and Impressionism by 19th- and 20th-century Tuscan painters (second floor, €5, admission includes mildly interesting Costume Museum, daily 8:15–13:50 but closed second and fourth Sun and first, third, and fifth Mon).

The **Grand Ducal Treasures (Museo degli Argenti)** is the Medici treasure chest, with jeweled crucifixes, exotic porcelain, gilded ostrich eggs, and so on, made to entertain fans of applied arts (ground floor, €6, includes Porcelain Museum and Boboli Gardens, same hours as Boboli Gardens, listed below).

Behind the palace, the huge landscaped **Boboli Gardens** offer a shady refuge from the city heat (€6, daily 9:00–18:30 fall and spring, 9:00–19:30 June–Aug, 9:00–16:30 winter, but closed first and last Mon of month).

▲▲**Brancacci Chapel**—For the best
look at Masaccio's works (he's the early
Renaissance master who re-invented perspective), see his restored frescoes here.
Instead of medieval religious symbols,
Masaccio's paintings feature simple,
strong human figures with facial expressions that reflect their emotions. The
accompanying works of Masolino and
Filippino Lippi provide illuminating contrasts (€4, free reservations required, €8

combo-ticket with Palazzo Vecchio, limit of 30 visitors every 15
minutes, Mon and Wed–Sat 10:00–17:00, Sun 13:00–17:00, closed
Tue, ticket office closes at 16:30, cross Ponte Vecchio and turn right
and hike to Piazza del Carmine, tel. 055-276-8224). ❍ See
Brancacci Chapel Tour on page 144.

The neighborhoods around the church are considered the last
surviving bits of old Florence.

Santo Spirito Church—This has a classic Brunelleschi interior and
a very early Michelangelo crucifix, painted on carved wood, given by
the sculptor to the monastery in appreciation for the opportunity
that they gave him to dissect and learn about bodies. Pop in here for
a delightful Renaissance space and a chance to marvel at a Michelangelo all alone (free, most days 10:00–12:00 & 16:00–17:30,
Sat–Sun only 16:00–17:30, closed Wed afternoon, Piazza Santo
Spirito, tel. 055-210-030).

▲**Piazzale Michelangelo**—Overlooking the city from across the
river (look for the huge statue of David), this square is worth the 30-
minute hike, drive, or bus ride (either #12 or #13 from the train
station) for the view of Florence and the stunning dome of the
Duomo. After dark, it's packed with local schoolkids feeding their
dates slices of watermelon and then licking them clean. Just beyond it
is the stark, beautiful, crowd-free, Romanesque San Miniato Church.

Oltrarno Walk—If you never leave the touristy center, you won't really
see Florence. There's more to the city than tourism. Ninety percent of
its people live and work in the Oltrarno neighborhood, south of the
Arno River, where tourists rarely venture. This self-guided tour follows
a perfectly straight line (you can't get lost). Cross the Ponte Vecchio,
turn right, and walk west on the busy, noisy road toward Pisa—it
changes names, from Borgo San Jacopo and Via di Santo Spirito to
Borgo San Frediano—until you reach the city wall at Porta San
Frediano. Along this route, you can check out several recommended
restaurants (see Eating, page 177). As you walk, consider these points:

After one block, at the fancy **Hotel Lungarno,** step up to the
Arno River viewpoint for a great look at the Ponte Vecchio. Recall
the story of Kesserling, the Nazi commander-in-chief of Italy who

happened to be an art-lover. As the Nazis retreated in 1944, he was commanded to blow up all the bridges. Rather than destroy the venerable Ponte Vecchio, he disabled it by blowing up the surrounding neighborhood. Turn around and cross the street to see the ivy-covered nub of a medieval tower—ruined August 6, 1944.

Along this walk, you'll see plenty of artisans at work and lots of inviting little **shops.** You're welcome to drop in, but remember, it's polite to say *"Buon giorno"* and *"Ciao."* "Can I take a look?" is *"Posso guardare?"* (POH-soh gwahr-DAH-ray).

The streets are busy with *motorini* (Vespas and other motor bikes). While these are allowed in the city, nonresident cars are not (unless they are electric). Notice that parked cars have a *residente* permit on their dash. You'll see a police officer (likely a woman) later on the walk, keeping out traffic.

Look for little architectural details. Tiny shrines protect the corners of many blocks. Once upon a time, the iron spikes on the walls impaled huge candles, which provided a little light. Electricity changed all that, but notice there are no electric wires visible. They're under the streets.

This street is lined with apartment buildings punctuated by the occasional *palazzo.* The skyline and architecture are typical of the 13th to 16th centuries. Huge *palazzi* (recognized by their immense doors, lush courtyards, and grand stonework) were for big-shot merchants. Many have small wooden doors designed to look like stones (like those at 3b on Borgo San Frediano). While originally for one family, these buildings are now subdivided, as evidenced by the huge banks of doorbells at the door.

The **Church of Santa Maria del Carmine,** with its famous Brancacci Chapel and Masaccio frescoes, is a short detour off Borgo San Frediano (see Brancacci Chapel Tour on page 144).

A couple of blocks before Porta San Frediano (and its tower), look left up Piazza dei Nerli. The bold yellow schoolhouse was built during Mussolini's rule—grandly proclaiming the resurrection of the Italian empire.

Porta San Frediano, built about 1300, is part of Florence's medieval wall, which stretches impressively from here to the river. In medieval times, a three-quarter-mile-wide strip outside the wall was cleared to deny attackers any cover. The tower was originally twice as high, built when gravity ruled warfare. During the Renaissance, when gunpowder dominated warfare, the tower—now just an easy target—was lopped. Notice the original doors—immense and studded with fat iron nails to withstand battering rams. Got a horse? Lash it to a ring.

Tour over. You passed several fun eateries, and the colorful Trattoria Sabatino is just outside the wall (all described in Eating, page 177). *Ciao.*

Near Florence: Fiesole

Perched on a hill overlooking the Arno valley, Fiesole gives weary travelers a break in the action and, during the heat of summer, a breezy location from which to admire the city below. The ancient Etruscans knew a good spot when they saw one, and chose to settle here, establishing Fiesole about 400 years before the Romans founded Florence. Wealthy Renaissance families in pre-air-conditioning days also chose Fiesole as a preferred vacation spot and built villas in the surrounding hillsides. Later, 19th-century Romantics spent part of the Grand Tour admiring the vistas, much like the hordes of tourists do today. Most come here for the view—the actual sights pale in comparison to those in Florence.

Getting to Fiesole: From the Florence train station, take bus #7—enjoying a peek at gardens, vineyards, orchards, and villas—to the last stop, Piazza Mino (€1, 3/hr, fewer after 20:00, 30 min, departs Florence from Piazza Adua at northeast side of train station and also from south side of Piazza San Marco). Taxis from Florence cost about €15 (take taxi to highest point you want to visit—La Reggia Ristorante for view terrace, or Church of San Francesco—then explore downhill).

Tourist Information: To reach the TI from the bus stop, walk toward the bell tower and take the first right. Pick up a free map (Mon–Sat 9:00–18:00, Sun 10:00–13:00 & 14:00–18:00, closes 1 hour earlier in winter, Via Portigiani 3, tel. 055-598-720). Market day is Saturday, when a modest selection of food and household items fills Piazza Mino (early–13:00).

SIGHTS

▲▲**Terrace with a View**—Catch the sunset (and your breath) from the view terrace just below La Reggia Ristorante. It's a steep hike from the Fiesole bus stop (face bell tower, take Via San Francesco on left).

Church of San Francesco—For even more hill-climbing, continue up from the view terrace to this charming little church. Several colorful altar paintings and an intimate scale make this church more enjoyable than Fiesole's Duomo (free, Mon–Sat 10:00–12:00 & 15:00–19:00, Sun 15:00–19:00, Via San Francesco 13).

Duomo—While this church has a drab 19th-century exterior, the interior is worth a look, if only for the blue- and white-glazed Giovanni della Robbia statue of St. Romulus over the entry door (free, daily 7:30–12:00 & 15:00–18:00, across Piazza Mino from the bus stop).

Roman Theater and Archaeological Park—Occasionally used today for plays, this well-preserved theater held up to 2,000 people. The site's other ruins are...well...ruined, and lacking in explanation. But the valley view and peaceful setting are lovely (€6.50 combo-ticket includes the Civic and Bandini Museums, daily 9:30–19:00, until 17:00 in winter, from the bus stop, cross Piazza Mino toward the back of the Duomo, entrance is on the right).

Civic Museum (Museo Civico)—As the mandatory exit to the Archaeological Park, the museum might seem like a funnel into the gift shop, but its decent collection of Roman artifacts is fairly interesting. Look for English explanations (€6.50 combo-ticket, daily 10:00–19:00).

Bandini Museum (Museo Bandini)—This teensy museum displays a modest morsel of quality Gothic and Renaissance art (€6.50 combo-ticket, daily 10:00–19:00, behind Duomo, Via Dupre 1).

Private Villas—Although most villas in the area are privately owned, many open their gardens to the public on a seriously limited, reservation-only basis. For the tenacious tourist, the TI can sort out schedules and entries (€4, not practical without a car, reservations and information in Italian, tel. 800-414-240).

SLEEPING

(€1 = about $1.20, country code: 39)
For the Sleep Code, see page 167.

$$$ **Hotel Villa Bonelli** is a three-star place with 20 rooms and a view from the breakfast room (Sb-€75, Db-€124, Tb-€160, Qb-€190, 10 percent less in winter, air-con, walk 8 min from bus stop up Via Gramsci, right on Via Poeti to #1, tel. 055-59513 or 055-598-941, fax 055-598-942, www.hotelvillabonelli.com, info@hotelvillabonelli.com).

EATING

The first two restaurants are on Piazza Mino, where the bus stops from Florence.

Ristorante Perseus serves authentic Tuscan dishes at a fair price. A local favorite with its rambling interior, the specials are scrawled on a scrap of paper (daily 12:30–14:30 & 19:30–23:30, Piazza Mino 9, tel. 055-59143, friendly Ago SE).

Ristorante Aurora is an upscale alternative with a territorial view terrace (daily 12:30–14:30 & 19:30–22:30, next to bus stop on Piazza Mino).

Imagine eating in a Michelangelo-designed Tuscan villa with a fabulous view—that's **Villa San Michele.** While the hotel may be unaffordable, the entrées at the restaurant, and a visit to the splendid gardens and public spaces, can be yours for €20–40. If the terrace is open, sit there (daily 12:00–14:45 & 19:30–22:00, closed Nov–March, reservations smart, Via Doccia 4, tel. 055-567-8200). From Piazza Mino, it's a five-minute taxi ride.

Fiesole is made to order for a scenic and breezy **picnic.** Pick up your goodies at the Co-Op supermarket on Via Gramsci and walk to the panoramic terrace (see "Sights," page 45). Or, for more convenience and less view, picnic at the shaded park on the way to the view terrace (walk up Via San Francesco about halfway to the terrace and climb the stairs to the right).

RENAISSANCE WALK

From David *to the Arno River*

After centuries of labor, Florence gave birth to the Renaissance. We'll start with the Renaissance poster boy, Michelangelo's *David*. A short walk away are the Baptistery doors that opened the Renaissance and the dome that captured its soaring spirit. Finally, we'll reach Florence's political center, dotted with monuments of that proud time. Great and rich as this city is, it's easily covered on foot. Our walk through the top sights is less than a mile long, running from the Accademia (home of *David*), past the Duomo to the Arno River.

ORIENTATION

Accademia (Michelangelo's *David*): €6.50 (plus €3 reservation fee), Tue–Sun 8:15–18:50, 8:15–22:00 on holidays and maybe on summer Sat, closed Mon (last entry 45 min before closing, Via Ricasoli 60, tel. 055-238-8609). No photos or videos are allowed. The museum is most crowded on Sun, Tue, and right when it opens. It's smart to reserve ahead; see page 35 for details.

Duomo (cathedral): Free, Mon–Wed and Fri–Sat 10:00–17:00 (except first Sat of month 10:00–15:30), Thu 10:00–15:30, Sun 13:30–16:45. Tel. 055-230-2885.

Climbing the **dome** costs €6 (Mon–Fri 8:30–19:00, Sat 8:30–17:40 except first Sat of month 8:30–16:00, closed Sun and holidays; enter from outside church on new north-side entrance, though entry could be switched back to south side, arrive by 8:30 to avoid a long wait in line).

Giotto's Tower (Campanile): €6, daily 8:30–19:30, last entry 40 min before closing.

Baptistery: €3, interior open Mon–Sat 12:00–19:00, Sun 8:30–14:00.

The famous bronze doors are on the outside so they're always "open" (viewable) and free. The original panels are in the Duomo Museum.

Getting There: The Accademia is a 15-minute walk from the train station or a 10-minute walk from the cathedral (head northeast on Via Ricasoli). Taxis are reasonable.

Information and Services: The nearest TI is on Via Cavour, two blocks from the Accademia (pick up update of current museum hours). WCs are in the Accademia basement and in cafés along the walk.

Length of This Tour: Three hours.

Photography: Photos are prohibited in the Accademia. In churches and other museums, photos without a flash are generally OK.

Cuisine Art: You'll find cafés, self-service cafeterias, bars, and gelato shops along the route. Many good eateries along this route are described in the Eating chapter.

Starring: Michelangelo, Brunelleschi, and Ghiberti.

THE TOUR BEGINS

The Duomo, the cathedral with the distinctive red dome, is the center of Florence and the orientation point for this walk. If you ever get lost, home's the dome.

We'll start at the Accademia (2.5 long blocks north of the Duomo), though you could easily start at the Duomo and visit the Accademia later.

• *Head to the Accademia. If there's a line, as you shuffle your way along, notice the perspective tricks on the walls of the ticket room.*

The Florentine Renaissance (1400–1550)

In the 13th and 14th centuries, Florence was a powerful center of banking, trading, and textile manufacturing. The resulting wealth fertilized the cultural soil. Then came the Black Plague in 1348. Nearly half of the population died, but the infrastructure remained strong, and the city rebuilt stronger than ever. Led by Florence's chief family, the art-crazy Medicis, and with the naturally aggressive and creative spirit of the Florentines, it's no wonder the long-awaited Renaissance finally took root here.

The Renaissance—the "rebirth" of Greek and Roman culture that swept across Europe—started around 1400 and lasted about 150 years. In politics, the Renaissance meant democracy; in science, a renewed interest in exploring nature. The general mood was optimistic and "humanistic," with a confidence in the power of the individual.

In medieval times, poverty and ignorance had made life "nasty, brutish, and short" (for lack of a better cliché). The church was the people's opiate, and their lives were only a preparation for a happier

Renaissance Walk

time in heaven after leaving this miserable vale of tears.

Medieval art was the church's servant. The noblest art form was architecture—churches themselves—and other arts were considered most worthwhile if they embellished the house of God. Painting and sculpture were narrative and symbolic, to tell Bible stories to the devout and illiterate masses.

As prosperity rose in Florence, so did people's confidence in life and themselves. Middle-class craftsmen, merchants, and bankers felt they could control their own destinies, rather than being at the whim of nature. They found much in common with the ancient Greeks and Romans, who valued logic and reason above superstition and blind faith.

Renaissance art was a return to the realism and balance of Greek and Roman sculpture and architecture. Domes and round arches replaced Gothic spires and pointed arches. In painting and sculpture, Renaissance artists strove for realism. Merging art and science, they used mathematics, the laws of perspective, and direct observation of nature to paint the world on a flat surface.

This was not an anti-Christian movement, though it was a logical and scientific age. Artists saw themselves as an extension of God's creative powers. At times, the church even supported the Renaissance and commissioned many of its greatest works. Raphael frescoed Plato and Aristotle on the walls of the Vatican. But for the first time in Europe since Roman times, we also find rich laymen who wanted art simply for art's sake.

After 1,000 years of waiting, the smoldering fires of Europe's classical heritage burst into flame in Florence.

The Accademia—Michelangelo's *David*

Start with the ultimate. When you look into the eyes of Michelangelo's *David,* you're looking into the eyes of Renaissance Man. This 14-foot-tall symbol of divine victory over evil represents a new century and a whole new Renaissance outlook. This is the age of Columbus and classicism, Galileo and Gutenberg, Luther and Leonardo—of Florence and the Renaissance.

In 1501, Michelangelo Buonarotti, age 26, a Florentine, was

commissioned to carve a large-scale work for the Duomo. He was given a block of marble that other sculptors had rejected as too tall, shallow, and flawed to be of any value. But Michelangelo picked up his hammer and chisel, knocked a knot off what became *David*'s heart, and started to work.

The figure comes from a Bible story. The Israelites, God's chosen people, are surrounded by barbarian warriors led by a brutish giant named Goliath. The giant challenges the Israelites to send out someone to fight him. Everyone is afraid except one young shepherd boy—David. Armed only with a sling, which he throws over his shoulder, David cradles some stones in his other hand and heads out to face Goliath.

The statue captures David as he's sizing up his enemy. He stands relaxed but alert, leaning on one leg in a classical pose. In his powerful

More Michelangelo

If you're a fan of Earth's greatest sculptor, you won't leave Florence until there's a check next to each of these:

- Bargello Museum: several Michelangelo sculptures (see Bargello Tour on page 84).
- Duomo Museum: another moving Pietà (see Duomo Museum Tour on page 108).
- Medici Chapels: The Night and Day statues, plus others done for the Medici tomb, located at Church of San Lorenzo (see Medici Chapels Tour on page 123).
- Palazzo Vecchio: his "Victory" statue.
- Laurentian Library: Michelangelo designed the entrance staircase, located at Church of San Lorenzo.
- Uffizi: A rare Michelangelo painting (see Uffizi Gallery Tour on page 64).
- Michelangelo's House (Casa Buonarroti): Built on property Michelangelo once owned, at Via Ghibellina 70, containing some early works.
- Church of Santa Croce: Michelangelo's tomb.

right hand, he fondles the stones he'll fling at the giant. His gaze is steady—searching with intense concentration, but also with extreme confidence. Michelangelo has caught the precise moment when David is saying to himself, "I can take this guy."

David is a symbol of Renaissance optimism. He's no brute but a civilized, thinking individual who can grapple with and overcome problems. He needs no armor, only his God-given body and wits. Look at his right hand, with the raised veins and strong, relaxed fingers. Many complained that it was too big and overdeveloped. But this is the hand of a man with the strength of God. No mere boy could slay the giant. But David, powered by God, could...and did.

Originally, the statue was commissioned to go on top of the Duomo, but the people loved it so much they put it next to the Palazzo Vecchio on the main square, where a copy stands today. (If the relationship between the head and body seems a bit out of proportion, it's because Michelangelo designed it to be seen "correctly" from far below the rooftop of the church.) Note the crack in *David*'s left arm where it was broken off during a riot near the Palazzo Vecchio. The recently-cleaned statue is slightly whiter than a year ago.

Florentines could identify with David. Like him, they considered themselves God-blessed underdogs fighting their city-state rivals. In a deeper sense, they were civilized Renaissance people slaying the ugly giant of medieval superstition, pessimism, and oppression.

• *Hang around awhile. Eavesdrop on tour guides.* David *stands under a wonderful Renaissance-style dome. Lining the hall leading up to* David *are other statues by Michelangelo—his* Prisoners (Prigioni), St. Matthew, *and a* Pietà.

Prisoners

These unfinished figures seem to be fighting to free themselves from the stone. Michelangelo believed the sculptor was a tool of God, not creating but simply revealing the powerful and beautiful figures He put in the marble. Michelangelo's job was to chip away the excess, to reveal. He needed to be in tune with God's will, and whenever the spirit came upon him, Michelangelo worked in a frenzy, often for days on end without sleep.

The *Prisoners* gives us a glimpse of this fitful process, showing the restless energy of someone possessed, struggling against the rock that binds him. Michelangelo was known to shout at his figures in frustration: "Speak!" You can still see the grooves from the chisel, and you can picture Michelangelo hacking away in a cloud of dust. Unlike most sculptors, who built a model and then marked up their block of marble to know where to chip, Michelangelo always worked freehand, starting from the front and working back. These figures emerge from the stone (as his colleague Vasari put it) "as though surfacing from a pool of water."

The *Prisoners* was designed for the never-completed tomb of Pope Julius II (who also commissioned the Sistine Chapel ceiling). Michelangelo may have abandoned them simply because the project itself petered out, but he may have deliberately left them unfinished. Having satisfied himself that he'd accomplished what he set out to do, and seeing no point in polishing them into their shiny, finished state, he went on to a new project.

As you study the *Prisoners,* notice Michelangelo's love and understanding of the human body. His greatest days were spent sketching the muscular, tanned, and sweating bodies of the workers in the Carrara marble quarries. Here, the prisoners' heads and faces are the least-developed part—they "speak" with their poses. Comparing these restless, claustrophobic *Prisoners* with the serene and confident *David* gives an idea of the sheer emotional range in Michelangelo's work.

Pietà (by Michelangelo or, more likely, by his followers)

In the unfinished *Pietà* (the threesome closest to *David*), they struggle to hold up the sagging body of Christ. Michelangelo emphasizes the heaviness of Jesus' dead body, driving home the point that this divine being suffered a very human death. Christ's massive arm is almost the size of his bent and broken legs. By stretching his body—

if he stood up he'd be over seven feet tall—its weight is exaggerated.
• *Leaving the Accademia (possibly after a look at its paintings, including two Botticellis), turn left and walk toward the Duomo down Via Ricasoli. About halfway to the big church, turn right on Via dei Pucci. Directly ahead is the bustling San Lorenzo street market. Just before that (on the first corner) is the imposing Medici-Riccardi Palace.*

Medici-Riccardi Palace

Renaissance Florence was ruled by the rich banking family, the Medici, who lived here. Studying this grand Florentine palace you'll notice fortified lower walls and elegance limited to the upper fancy stories. The Medici family may have been the local Rockefellers but, having self-made wealth rather than actual noble blood, they were always a bit defensive. The Greek motifs along the eaves highlight the palace's Renaissance roots. Back then, rather than having parking spots, grand buildings came with iron rings to tether your horse.

The interior shows off a quintessential Florentine palazzo with a courtyard and a couple of impressive rooms, most notably the sumptuous little Chapel of the Magi (€4 palace entry, Thu–Tue 9:00–19:00, closed Wed). ◉ See Medici-Riccardi Palace Tour on page 132.
• *From the palace, head for the Duomo—down Via Martelli, with a possible detour to explore the San Lorenzo street market and, perhaps, the neighboring Medici Chapels (◉ See Medici Chapels Tour, page 123). The dome of the Duomo is best viewed just to the right of the facade on the corner of the pedestrian-only street.*

The Duomo—Florence's Cathedral

The dome of Florence's cathedral—visible from all over the city—inspired Florentines to do great things. The big but unremarkable church itself (nicknamed the Duomo) is Gothic, built in the Middle Ages by architects who left it unfinished.

Think of the confidence of the age: The Duomo was built with a big hole in its roof awaiting a dome. This was before the technology to span it with a dome was available. *No problema.* They knew that someone soon could handle the challenge. In the 1400s, the architect Brunelleschi was called on to finish the job. Brunelleschi capped the church Roman-style—with a tall, self-supporting dome as grand as the ancient Pantheon, which he had studied.

He used a dome within a dome. First, he built the grand white skeletal ribs, which you can see, then filled them in with interlocking bricks in a herringbone pattern. The dome grew upward igloo-style, supporting itself as it proceeded from the base. When they reached

The Duomo

TO S. LORENZO
& MARKET
(3 MIN. WALK)

VIA RICASOLI

TO
ACCADEMIA (DAVID)
(10 MIN. WALK)

TO
TRAIN
STATION
& INFO
(10 MIN.
WALK)

❹

❺

DUOMO

❶

❸

BAPTISTERY

GIOTTO'S
TOWER

❷

CALZAIUOLI

ORSAN-
MICHELE

N

TO
PIAZZA SIGNORIA,
UFFIZI, & ARNO RIVER

DCH

❶ BRUNELLESCHI – Dome
❷ Best place to view the Dome
❸ Duomo Museum (statues)

❹ GHIBERTI – His contest-winning doors
❺ GHIBERTI – The "Gates of Paradise" 25 years later

the top, Brunelleschi arched the ribs in and fixed them in place with the lantern. His dome, built in only 14 years, was the largest since Rome's Pantheon.

Brunelleschi's dome was the wonder of the age, the model for many domes to follow, from St. Peter's to the U.S. Capitol. People gave it the ultimate compliment, saying "not even the ancients could have done it." Michelangelo, setting out to construct the dome of St. Peter's, drew inspiration from the dome of Florence. He said, "I'll make its sister…bigger, but not more beautiful."

The church's facade looks old, but is actually neo-Gothic—only from 1870. Its "retro" look captures the feel of the original medieval facade—green, white, and pink marble sheets that cover the brick construction; Gothic (pointed) arches; and three horizontal stories decorated with mosaics and statues. Still, the facade is generally ridiculed. (While one of this book's authors thinks it's the most beautiful church facade this side of heaven, the other one naively agrees with those who call it "the cathedral in pajamas.") The inside of the church is worth a walk only for its coolness and a look at how bare the terrible flood of 1966 left it.

Bell Tower ("Giotto's Tower")

You can climb the dome, but the bell tower (to the right of the facade) is easier, less crowded, and faster, and it rewards you with a view of the dome. Giotto, like any good Renaissance genius, wore several artistic hats. Considered the father of modern painting, he designed this 270-foot-tall bell tower for the Duomo two centuries before the age of Michelangelo. In his day, Giotto was called the ugliest man to ever walk the streets of Florence, but he left the city what, in our day, many call the most beautiful bell tower in all of Europe.

The bell tower served as a sculpture gallery for Renaissance artists—notice Donatello's four prophets on the side that faces out (west side). These are copies, but the originals are at the wonderful Duomo Museum, just behind the church (❂ see Duomo Museum Tour on page 108). In the museum you'll also get a close-up look at Brunelleschi's wooden model of his dome, Ghiberti's doors (described below), and a late *Pietà* by Michelangelo.

• *The Baptistery is the small octagonal building in front of the church.*

Baptistery and Ghiberti's Bronze Doors

Florence's Baptistery is dear to the soul of the city. The locals, eager to link themselves to the classical past, believed (wrongly) that this was a Roman building. It *is* Florence's oldest building (11th century). Most festivals and parades either started or ended here. Go inside (for a modest €3 fee) for a fine example of pre-Renaissance mosaic art (1200s–1300s) in the Byzantine style.

The Last Judgment on the ceiling gives us a glimpse of the medieval worldview. Life was a preparation for the afterlife, when you would be judged good or bad, black or white, with no in-between. Christ, peaceful and reassuring, would bless you with heaven (on His right hand) or send you to hell (below Christ's double-jointed left hand, at the base of the ceiling) to be tortured by demons and gnashed between the teeth of monsters.

This hellish scene looks like something right out of the *Inferno* by Dante...who was dipped into the baptismal waters right here.

The Baptistery's bronze doors bring us out of the Middle Ages and into the Renaissance. Florence had great civic spirit, with different guilds and merchant groups embellishing their city with great art. The city staged a competition in 1401 for the commission of the Baptistery's north doors (on the right side as you face the Baptistery with the Duomo at your back). All the greats entered, and 25-year-old Lorenzo Ghiberti won easily, beating out heavyweights such as Brunelleschi (who, having lost the Baptistery gig, was free to go to Rome, study the Pantheon, and later design the Duomo's dome). The original entries of Brunelleschi and Ghiberti are in the Bargello, where you can judge them for yourself.

Later, in 1425, Ghiberti was given another commission, for the east doors (facing the church), and this time there was literally no contest. The bronze panels of these doors (the ones with the crowd of tourists looking on) added a whole new dimension to art—depth. Michelangelo said these doors were fit to be the gates of Paradise. (These panels are copies. The originals are in the nearby Duomo Museum.) Here we see how the Renaissance was a merging of art and science. Realism was in, and Renaissance artists used math, illusion, and dissection to get it.

In the "Jacob and Esau" panel (just above eye level on the left), receding arches, floor tiles, and banisters create a background for a realistic scene. The figures in the foreground stand and move like real people, telling the Bible story

with human details. Amazingly, this spacious, three-dimensional scene is made from bronze only a few inches deep.

Ghiberti spent 27 years (1425–1452) working on these panels. That's him in the center of the door frame, atop the second row of panels—the head on the left with the shiny male pattern baldness.

• *Facing the Duomo, turn right onto the pedestrian-only street that runs south from here toward the Arno River.*

Via dei Calzaiuoli

The pedestrian-only Via dei Calzaiuoli (kahlts-ay-WOH-lee) was part of the ancient Roman grid plan that became Florence. Throughout the city's history, this street has connected the religious center (where we are now) with the political center (where we're heading), a five-minute walk away. In the last decade, traffic jams have been replaced by potted plants, and this is a pleasant place to stroll, people-watch, window-shop, catch the drips on your gelato cone, and wonder why American cities can't become pedestrian-friendly.

Two blocks down, look right on Via degli Speziali to see a triumphal arch celebrating the unification of Italy. In ancient Roman times, the Piazza della Repubblica where the arch stands was the city center.

If you're in the mood for some of the world's best edible art, you're in the right place. Drop by one of several nearby ice-cream parlors for a cup of gelato. *Perchè no?* (Why not?)

Gelati tips: *Artiginale, Nostra Produzione,* and *Produzione Propia* mean gelato is made on the premises. Also, gelato displayed in metal tins, rather than the normal white plastic, indicates it's likely to be homemade. A simple cone or cup will do; avoid fancy, rip-off €10 "tourist specials." Look at the price list, which usually shows pictures of scoops (1, 2, or 3) followed by the pertinent price.

Orsanmichele Church—Florence's Medieval Roots

The Orsanmichele Church (at the inter-section with Via dei Tavolini) provides an interesting look at Florentine values. It's a combo church/granary. Originally this was an open loggia (covered porch) with a huge warehouse upstairs to store grain to feed the city during sieges. The arches of the loggia were artfully filled in (14th century) and the building gained a new purpose—as a church.

Circle the church. Each niche was filled with an important statue. In earlier Gothic times, statues were set deeply in the niches, simply embellishing the house of God. Here we see statues (as restless as man on the verge of the Renaissance) stepping out from the protection of the church.

Donatello's *St. George* (at northwest corner of church) is alert, perched on the edge of his niche, scanning the horizon for dragons, and announcing the new age with its new outlook. (The original statue is in the Bargello.) Compare this Renaissance-style *St. George* with Nanni's smaller-scale, deeply set, and less sophisticated *Four Saints* statue to its left.

Below some of the niches, you'll find the symbols of the various guilds and groups that paid for the art. The relief below the *Four Saints* is a good example. Art historians differ here. It was commissioned either by the guys who do the discount circumcisions or by the carpenters' and masons' guild.

You can visit the interior only during evening concerts (tickets sold on day of concert from door facing Via dei Calzaiuoli). If you make it inside for a performance, look for the pillars with spouts in them (three feet off the

Orsanmichele Church

1 DONATELLO – St. George

2 NANNI – Four Saints

3 Tabernacle (viewable during evening concerts)

FROM DUOMO

VIA ORSANMICHELE

VIA CALZAIUOLI

VIA LAMBERTI

TO PALAZZO VECCHIO & UFFIZI

DCH

ground), used for delivering grain from the storage rooms upstairs. Notice the Gothic tabernacle's medieval elegance, color, and lack of depth and realism. This is a wonderful scene—Florence in 1350. Remember the candlelit medieval atmosphere that surrounds this altarpiece as you view similar altarpieces out of context in the Uffizi Gallery.

• *Florence's best collection of sculpture, the Bargello (see page 84), is a few blocks east down Via dei Tavolini. But let's continue down the mall 50 more yards, to the huge and historic square.*

Palazzo Vecchio—Florence's Political Center

The main civic center of Florence is dominated by the Palazzo Vecchio, the Uffizi Gallery, and the marble greatness of old Florence littering the cobbles. This square still vibrates with the echoes of Florence's past—executions, riots, and great celebrations. There's even Roman history—look for the chart showing the ancient city (on a waist-high, freestanding display to your right as you enter the square). Today, it's a tourist's world with pigeons, postcards, horse buggies, and tired hubbies. And, if it would make your tired hubby happy, the ritzy Café Rivoire—with the best view seats in town—is famous for its fancy desserts and hot chocolate (closed Mon).

Before you towers the Palazzo Vecchio, the Medicis' palatial city hall—a fortress designed to contain riches and survive the many riots that went with local politics. The windows are just beyond the reach of angry stones, the tower was a handy lookout post, and

Sights on Piazza della Signoria

VIA DEI
← CALZAIUOLI

ORSAN-
MICHELE

TO
BARGELLO

TO
SANTA
CROCE

❶ PIAZZA SIGNORIA

❺ ❹

❷ PALAZZO VECCHIO

LOGGIA ↘

❸

❻

UFFIZI

🔭❼

❽ A R N O   R I V E R

PONTE VECCHIO   DCH

❶ Roman city plan
❷ MICHELANGELO –
   David (copy)
❸ Loggia: Perseus
   & other statues
❹ AMMANATI - Fountain
   of Neptune
❺ Savonarola plaque
❻ Entry to Uffizi Gallery
❼ View spot
❽ Bust of Cellini
   (& padlocks of love)

justice was doled out sternly on this square. Michelangelo's *David* once stood (until 1873) where the replica stands today. The original *David*, damaged in a riot (when a bench thrown out of a palace window knocked its left arm off), was moved indoors for its own protection.

While the palace interior is not worth touring on a short visit, be sure to step past the replica *David* through the front door into the Palazzo Vecchio's courtyard (free). This palace was Florence's civic center. You're surrounded by art for art's sake—a statue frivolously marking the courtyard's center, and ornate walls and columns. Such luxury was a big change 500 years ago. The squiggly, ornate wall painting is called *grotteschi*, inspired by the art that decorated the walls of ancient Roman villas being excavated at the time (c. 1500, named for "grotto" because the ancient villas were actually well below 15th-century Roman street level).

• *Back outside, check out the statue-filled Loggia.*

The Loggia, once a forum for public debate, was perfect for a city that prided itself on its democratic traditions. But later, when the Medicis figured good art was more desirable than free speech, it was turned into an outdoor sculpture gallery. Notice the squirming

Florentine themes—conquest, dominance, rapes, and severed heads. The statues lining the back are Roman originals brought back to Florence by a Medici when he moved home after living in Rome. Two statues in the front deserve a closer look.

Benvenuto Cellini's *Perseus,* the Loggia's most noteworthy piece, shows the Greek hero who decapitated the snake-headed Medusa. They say Medusa was so ugly she turned humans who looked at her to stone—though one of this book's authors thinks she's kinda cute.

The Rape of the Sabines, with its pulse-quickening rhythm of muscles, is Mannerist, from the restless period following the stately and confident Renaissance (c. 1560). The sculptor, Giambologna, proved his mastery of the medium by sculpting three entangled bodies from one piece of marble. The composition is best viewed from below in front. The relief panel below shows a wider view of the terrible scene. Note what looks like an IV tube on the arm of the horrified husband. It's an electrified wire that effectively keeps the pigeons away.

• *Cross the square to the big fountain of Neptune by Ammanati that Florentines (including Michelangelo) consider a huge waste of marble—though one of this book's authors.... Find the round bronze plaque in the cobbles 10 steps in front of the fountain.*

Savonarola

The Medici family was briefly thrown from power by an austere monk named Savonarola, who made Florence a constitutional republic. He organized huge rallies lit by roaring bonfires here on the square where he preached. While children sang hymns, the devout brought their rich "vanities" (such as paintings, musical instruments, and playing cards) and threw them into the flames.

But not everyone wanted a return to the medieval past. Encouraged by the pope, the Florentines fought back, and arrested Savonarola. For two days, they tortured him, trying unsuccessfully to persuade him to see their side of things. Finally, on the very spot where Savonarola's followers had built bonfires of vanities, the monk was burned. The bronze plaque, engraved in Italian *("Qui dove…"),* reads: "Here, Girolamo Savonarola and his Dominican brothers were hanged and burned" in the year "MCCCCXCVIII" (1498).

• *Stay cool, we have 100 yards to go. Follow the gaze of the fake David into the courtyard of the two-toned horseshoe-shaped building…*

Uffizi Courtyard—The Renaissance Hall of Fame

The top floor of this building, known as the *uffizi* ("offices") during Medici days, is filled with the greatest collection of Florentine painting anywhere. It's one of Europe's top four or five galleries (see next chapter).

The Uffizi courtyard, filled with merchants and hustling young artists, is watched over by statues of the great figures of the Renaissance. Tourists zero in on the visual accomplishments of the era—not realizing that it was many-faceted. Let's pay tribute to the nonvisual Renaissance as well as we wander through Florence's Hall of Fame.

• *Stroll down the left side of the courtyard from Palazzo Vecchio to the river, noticing…*

1. **Lorenzo the Magnificent** was a great art patron and cunning power broker. Excelling in everything except modesty, he set the tone for the Renaissance.
2. **Giotto,** an architect (he holds the plan to the city's great bell tower—named for him), was the first great modern painter.
3. **Donatello,** the sculptor who served as a role model for Michelangelo, holds a hammer and chisel.
4. **Leonardo da Vinci** was a scientist, sculptor, musician, engineer…and not a bad painter either.
5. **Michelangelo** ponders the universe and/or stifles a belch.
6. **Dante,** with the laurel-leaf crown and lyre of a poet, says, "I am the father of the Italian language." He was the first Italian to write a popular work *(The Divine Comedy)* in non-Latin, using the Florentine dialect, which soon became "Italian" throughout the country.
7. The poet **Petrarch** wears laurel leaves from Greece, a robe from Rome, and a belt from Wal-Mart.
8. **Boccaccio** wrote *The Decameron,* stories told to pass the time during the 1348 Black Plague.
9. The devious-looking **Machiavelli** is hatching a plot—his book *The Prince* taught that the end justifies the means, paving the way for the slick and cunning "Machiavellian" politics of today.
10. **Amerigo Vespucci** (in the corner) was an explorer who gave his name to a fledgling New World.
11. **Galileo Galilei** (in the other corner) holds the humble telescope he used to spot the moons of Jupiter.

• *Finish our walk at the Arno River, overlooking the Ponte Vecchio.*

Ponte Vecchio

Before you is the Ponte Vecchio (Old Bridge). A bridge has spanned this narrowest part of the Arno since Roman times. While Rome "fell," Florence really didn't, remaining a bustling trade center along the river. To get into the exclusive little park below, you'll need to join the Florence rowing club.

• *Finish by hiking to the center of the bridge.*

A fine bust of the great gold-smith, Cellini, graces the central point of the bridge. This statue is a reminder that, in the 1500s, the Medicis booted out the bridge's butchers and tanners and installed the gold- and silversmiths who still tempt visitors to this day. This is a very romantic spot late at night. In fact, hanging over the edge of the bridge (on either side of the Cellini bust) are piles of padlocks. Guys demonstrate the enduring quality of their love by ceremonially taking their girls here, locking a lock, and throwing the key into the Arno. (But what's with the combination lock?)

Notice the Medicis' protected and elevated passageway that led from the Palazzo Vecchio through the Uffizi, across the Ponte Vecchio, and up to the immense Pitti Palace, four blocks beyond the bridge.

During World War II, the local German commander was instructed to blow the bridge up. But even some Nazis appreciate history—he blew up the buildings at either end, leaving the bridge impassable but intact. *Grazie.*

UFFIZI GALLERY TOUR
(Galleria degli Uffizi)

In the Renaissance, Florentine artists rediscovered the beauty of the natural world. Medieval art had been symbolic, telling Bible stories. Realism didn't matter. But Renaissance people saw the beauty of God in nature and the human body. They used math and science to capture the natural world on canvas as realistically as possible.

The Uffizi Gallery (oo-FEET-zee) has the greatest overall collection anywhere of Italian painting. We'll trace the rise of realism and savor the optimistic spirit that marked the Renaissance.

> *My eyes love things that are fair,*
> *and my soul for salvation cries.*
> *But neither will to Heaven rise*
> *unless the sight of Beauty lifts them there.*
> —Michelangelo Buonarroti, sculptor, painter, poet

ORIENTATION

Cost: €9.50, plus €3 for optional but recommended reservation fee.

Hours: Tue–Sun 8:15–18:50, 8:15–22:00 on holidays and maybe summer Sat (last entry 45 min before closing), closed Mon.

Reservations: Avoid the two-hour peak-season midday wait by making a telephone reservation. It's easy, slick, and costs only €3. Dial 055-294-883 during office hours (Mon–Fri 8:30–18:30, Sat 8:30–12:30, closed Sun) at least a day before your visit and ideally at least a few days in advance for a better selection. With the help of an English-speaking operator, you'll get an entry slot (15-min window) and a six-digit confirmation number. Off-season, it can be possible to get a same-day reservation. Using the same phone number, you can reserve in advance for the Accademia, Bargello, Medici Chapels, and Pitti

Uffizi Gallery Overview

Palace; of these, the Accademia has the worst lines.

After you've booked your reservation, go to the Uffizi at your appointed time. Walk briskly past the 200-yard-long line—pondering the IQ of this gang—to the special ticket office (across the courtyard from the entry) for those with reservations (labeled in English "Entrance for Reservations Only"), give your number, pay (cash only), and scoot right in.

If you haven't called ahead, there are other ways to make an Uffizi reservation—sometimes for the same day, depending on luck and availability: 1) buy Uffizi tickets with reservations at the Museum of San Marco, the Museum of Precious Stones, or another Florence sight; 2) try booking directly at the Uffizi (ask the clerk at the reserved-ticket office if you can reserve in person); 3) take a tour of the museum with Walking Tours of Florence (booking required, see "Walking Tours," page 27); or 4) for a fee, you can reserve online through various agencies such as www.weekendafirenze.it or www.florenceart.it.

Getting There: It's on the Arno River between Palazzo Vecchio and Ponte Vecchio, a 15-minute walk from the train station.

Information: You can buy cheap Uffizi guidebooks from street vendors. The Uffizi (www.arca.net/uffizi/) has a gift shop (at exit on ground floor, has entrance for public). The only WC is on the top floor, near the snack bar and the stairs leading down to the exit.

Length of This Tour: Two hours.

Cloakroom: At the start, far from the finish.

Cuisine Art: The simple café at the end of the gallery has salads, desserts, fruit cups, and a terrace with a Duomo/Palazzo Vecchio view. A cappuccino here is one of Europe's great $2 treats.

Photography: Cameras not allowed.

Starring: Botticelli, Venus, Raphael, Giotto, Titian, Leonardo, and Michelangelo.

THE TOUR BEGINS

The Ascent

• *Buy your ticket, then walk up the four long flights of the monumental staircase to the top floor. Your brain should be fully aerated from the hike up. Past the ticket-taker, look out the window.*

The U-ffizi is U-shaped, running around the courtyard. The entire collection is on this one floor, displayed chronologically. This left wing contains Florentine painting from medieval to Renaissance times. The right wing (which you can see across the courtyard) has art from the Roman and Venetian High Renaissance, works from the Baroque that followed, and a café terrace facing the Duomo. Connecting the two wings is a short corridor with sculpture. We'll concentrate on the Uffizi's forte, the Florentine section, then get a taste of the art it inspired.

• *Down the hall, enter the first door on the left and face Giotto's giant* Madonna and Child.

Medieval—When Art Was As Flat As The World (1200–1400)

Giotto (c. 1266–1337)—*Madonna and Child* (*Madonna col Bambino Gesu, Santi e Angeli*)

Mary and baby Jesus sit on a throne in a golden never-never land symbolizing heaven. It's as if medieval Christians couldn't imagine holy people inhabiting our dreary material world. It took Renaissance

Giotto and Medieval Art

1. GIOTTO – Madonna and Child
2. Medieval Crucifixion
3. DUCCIO – Madonna and Child with Angels
4. CIMABUE – Madonna and Child with Angels
5. SIMONE MARTINI – Annunciation
6. GENTILE DA FABRIANO – Adoration of the Magi

painters to bring Mary down to earth and give her human realism. For the Florentines, "realism" meant "three-dimensional." In this room, pre-Renaissance paintings show the slow process of learning to paint a 3-D world on a 2-D surface.

Before concentrating on the Giotto, look at some others in the room. The **crucifixion** (on your right as you face the Giotto) was medieval 3-D—paint a crude two-dimensional work...then physically tilt the head forward. Nice try.

The three similar-looking Madonna-and-Bambinos in this room—all painted within a few decades of each other around the year 1300—show small baby steps in the march to realism. **Duccio**'s (on the left as you face Giotto) is the most medieval and two-dimensional. There's no background. The angels are just stacked one on top of the other, floating in the golden atmosphere. Mary's throne is crudely drawn—the left side is at a three-quarters angle while the right is practically straight on. Mary herself is a wispy cardboard-

cutout figure seemingly floating just above the throne.

On the opposite wall, **Cimabue**'s is an improvement. The large throne creates an illusion of depth. Mary's foot actually sticks out over the lip of the throne. Still, the angels are stacked like sardines, serving as a pair of heavenly bookends.

Giotto (JOT-oh) creates a space and fills it. Like a set designer, he builds a three-dimensional "stage"—the canopied throne—then peoples it with real beings. The throne has angels in front, prophets behind, and a canopy over the top, clearly defining the throne's three dimensions. The steps leading up to it lead from our space to Mary's, making the scene an extension of our world. But the real triumph here is Mary herself—big and monumental, like a Roman statue. Beneath her robe, she has a real live body—her knees and breasts stick out at us. This three-dimensionality was revolutionary in its day, a taste of the Renaissance a century before it began.

Giotto was one of the first "famous" artists. In the Middle Ages, artists were mostly unglamorous craftsmen, like carpenters or cable-TV repairmen. They cranked out generic art and could have signed their work with a bar code. But Giotto was recognized as a genius, a unique individual. He died in a plague that devastated Florence. If there had been no plague, would the Renaissance have started 100 years earlier?

• *Enter Room 3, to the left of Giotto.*

Simone Martini (c. 1285–1344)—*Annunciation* (*Annunciazione con i Santi Ansano e Giulitta*)

Simone Martini boils things down to the basic figures needed to get the message across: (1) The angel appears to sternly tell (2) Mary that she'll be the mother of Jesus. In the center is (3) a vase of lilies, a symbol of purity. Above is the (4) Holy Spirit as a dove about to descend on her. If the symbols aren't enough to get the message across, Simone Martini has spelled it right out for us in Latin: "*Ave Gratia Plena*...Hail, favored one, the Lord is with you." Mary doesn't look exactly pleased as punch.

This is not a three-dimensional work. The point was not to recreate reality but to teach religion, especially to the illiterate masses. This isn't a beautiful Mary or even a real Mary. She's a generic woman without distinctive features. We know she's pure—not from her face but only because of the halo and symbolic flowers. Before the Renaissance, artists didn't care about the beauty of individual people.

Simone Martini's *Annunciation* has medieval features you'll see in many of the paintings in the next few rooms: (1) religious subject, (2) gold background, (3) two-dimensionality, and (4) meticulous detail.

• *Pass through Room 4, full of golden altarpieces, stopping at the far end of Room 5.*

Gentile da Fabriano (c. 1370–1427)— *Adoration of the Magi (Adorazione dei Magi)*

Look at the incredible detail of the Three Kings' costumes, the fine horses, and the cow in the cave. The canvas is filled from top to bottom with realistic details—but it's far from realistic. While the Magi worship Jesus in the foreground, their return trip home dangles over their heads in the "background."

This is a textbook example of the International Gothic style popular with Europe's aristocrats in the early 1400s: well-dressed, elegant people in a colorful, design-oriented setting. The religious subject is just an excuse to paint secular luxuries like brocade-pattern clothes and jewelry. And the scene's background and foreground are compressed together to create an overall design that's pleasing to the eye.

Such exquisite detail work raises the question: Was Renaissance three-dimensionality truly an improvement over Gothic, or simply a different style?

• *Exit to your right and hang a U-turn left into Room 6.*

Early Renaissance (Mid-1400s)

Paolo Uccello (1397–1475)—*The Battle of San Romano* (*La Battaglia di S. Romano*)

In the 1400s, painters worked out the problems of painting realistically, using mathematics to create the illusion of three-dimensionality. This colorful battle scene is not so much a piece of art as an exercise in perspective. Paolo Uccello (oo-CHEL-loh) has challenged himself with every possible problem.

The broken lances at left set up a 3-D "grid" in which to place this crowded scene. The fallen horses and soldiers are experiments in "foreshortening"—shortening the things that are farther away from us (which appear smaller) to create the illusion of distance. Some of the figures are definitely A-plus material, like the fallen gray horse in the center and the white horse at the far right walking away. But some are more like B-minus work—the kicking red horse's legs look like ham hocks at this angle, and the fallen soldier at far right would only be child-sized if he stood up.

And then there's the D-minus "Are-you-on-drugs?" work. The converging hedges in the background create a nice illusion of a distant hillside maybe 250 feet away. So what are those soldiers the size of the foreground figures doing there? And jumping the hedge, is that rabbit 40 feet tall?

Paolo Uccello almost literally went crazy trying to master the three dimensions (thank God he was born before Einstein discovered one

Early Renaissance

1 UCCELLO – Battle of San Romano
2 FILIPPO LIPPI – Madonna and Child with Two Angels
3 POLLAIUOLO – Labors of Hercules

more). Uccello got so wrapped up in it he kind of lost...perspective.
• *Enter Room 8.*

Fra Filippo Lippi (1406–1469)—*Madonna and Child with Two Angels (Madonna col Bambino e Due Angeli)*

Compare this Mary with the generic female in Simone Martini's *Annunciation*. We don't need the wispy halo over her head to tell us she's holy—she radiates sweetness and light from her divine face. Heavenly beauty is expressed by a physically beautiful woman.

Fra (Brother) Lippi, an orphan raised as a monk, lived a less-than-monkish life. He lived with a nun who bore him two children. He spent his entire life searching for the perfect Virgin. Through his studio passed Florence's prettiest girls, many of whom decorate the walls here in this room.

Lippi painted idealized beauty, but his models were real flesh-and-blood human beings. You could look through all the thousands of paintings from the Middle Ages and not find anything so human as the mischievous face of one of Lippi's little angel boys.

• *Enter Room 9, with two small works by Pollaiuolo in the glass case between the windows.*

Antonio Pollaiuolo (c. 1431–1498)—*Labors of Hercules (Fatiche di Ercole)*

Hercules gets a workout in these two small panels showing the human form at odd angles. The poses are the wildest imaginable, to show how each muscle twists and tightens. While Uccello worked on perspective, Pollaiuolo studied anatomy. In medieval times, dissection of corpses was a sin and a crime (the two were one then)—a desecration of the human body, which was the temple of God. But Pollaiuolo was willing to sell his soul to the devil for artistic knowledge. He dissected.

There's something funny about this room that I can't put my finger on...I've got it—no Madonnas. Not one.

We've seen how Early Renaissance artists worked to conquer reality. Now let's see the fruits of their work, the flowering of Florence's Renaissance.

• *Enter the large Botticelli room and take a seat.*

Florence—The Renaissance Blossoms (1450–1500)

Florence in 1450 was in a Firenz-y of activity. There was a can-do spirit of optimism in the air, led by prosperous merchants and bankers and a strong middle class. The government was reasonably democratic, and Florentines saw themselves as citizens of a strong Republic like ancient Rome. Their civic pride showed in the public monuments and artworks they built. Man was leaving the protection of the church to stand on his own two feet.

Lorenzo de' Medici, head of the powerful Medici family, epitomized this new humanistic spirit. Strong, decisive, handsome, poetic, athletic, sensitive, charismatic, intelligent, brave, clean, and reverent, Lorenzo was a true Renaissance Man, deserving of the nickname he went by—"the Magnificent." He gathered Florence's best and brightest around him for evening wine and discussions of great ideas. One of this circle was the painter Botticelli (bot-i-CHEL-ee).

Sandro Botticelli (1444–1510)—*Allegory of Spring (Allegoria della Primavera)*

It's springtime in a citrus grove. The winds of spring blow in (Mr. Blue, at right), causing the woman on the right to sprout flowers from her lips as she morphs into Flora, or Spring—who walks by, spreading flowers from her dress. At the left are Mercury and the Three Graces, dancing a delicate maypole dance. The Graces may be symbolic of the three forms of love—love of beauty, love of people, and sexual love, suggested

The Renaissance Blossoms

TO
VENUS DE' MEDICI

LEONARDO

MAIN CORRIDOR

BOTTICELLI

FROM
EARLY REN.

DCH

❶ BOTTICELLI – Allegory of Spring
❷ BOTTICELLI – Adoration of the Magi
❸ BOTTICELLI – Birth of Venus
❹ BOTTICELLI – Slander
❺ LEONARDO DA VINCI – Annunciation
❻ LEONARDO DA VINCI – Adoration of the Magi
❼ VERROCHIO – Baptism of Christ

by the raised intertwined fingers. (They forgot love of peanut butter on toast.) In the center stands Venus, the Greek goddess of love. Above her flies a blindfolded Cupid, happily shooting his arrows of love without worrying whom they'll hit.

Here is the Renaissance in its first bloom, its "springtime" of innocence. Madonna is out, Venus is in. Adam and Eve hiding their nakedness are out, glorious flesh is in. This is a return to the pre-Christian pagan world of classical Greece, where things of the flesh are not sinful. But this is certainly no orgy—just fresh-faced innocence and playfulness.

Botticelli emphasizes pristine beauty over gritty realism. The lines of the bodies, especially of the Graces in their see-through nighties, have pleasing, S-like curves. The faces are idealized but have real human features. There's a look of thoughtfulness and even melancholy in the faces—as though everyone knows that the innocence of spring will not last forever.

• *Look at the next painting to the right.*

Botticelli—*Adoration of the Magi (Adorazione dei Magi)*

Here's the rat pack of confident young Florentines who reveled in the optimistic pagan spirit—even in a religious scene. Botticelli included himself among the adorers, looking vain in the yellow robe at far right. Lorenzo's the Magnificent-looking guy at the far left.

Botticelli—*Birth of Venus (Nascita di Venere)*

According to myth, Venus was born from the foam of a wave. Still only half awake, this fragile newborn beauty floats ashore on a clam shell, blown by the winds, where her maid waits to dress her. The pose is the same S-curve of classical statues (as we'll soon see). Botticelli's pastel colors make the world itself seem fresh and newly born.

This is the purest expression of Renaissance beauty. Venus' naked body is not sensual but innocent. Botticelli thought that physical beauty was a way of appreciating God. Remember Michelangelo's poem: souls will never ascend to Heaven "...until the sight of Beauty lifts them there."

Botticelli finds God in the details—Venus' windblown hair, the translucent skin, the maid's braided hair, the slight ripple of the wind's abs, and the flowers tumbling in the slowest of slow motions, suspended like musical notes, caught at the peak of their brief life.

Mr. and Mrs. Wind intertwine—notice her hands clasped around his body. Their hair, wings, and robes mingle like the wind. But what happened to those splayed toes?

• *"Venus on the Half-Shell" (as many tourists call this) is one of the masterpieces of Western art. Take some time with it. Then find the small canvas on the wall to the right, near La Primavera.*

Botticelli—*Slander (La Calumnia)*

The spring of Florence's Renaissance had to end. Lorenzo died young. The economy faltered. Into town rode the monk Savonarola, preaching medieval hellfire and damnation for those who embraced the "pagan" Renaissance spirit. "Down, down with all gold and decoration," he roared. "Down where the body is food for the worms." He presided over huge bonfires, where the people threw in their fine clothes, jewelry, pagan books...and paintings.

Slander spells the end of the Florentine Renaissance. The setting is classic Brunelleschian architecture, but look what's taking place beneath those stately arches. These aren't proud Renaissance Men and Women but a ragtag, medieval-looking bunch, a Court of Thieves in an abandoned hall

of justice. The accusations fly and everyone is condemned. The naked man pleads for mercy but the hooded black figure, a symbol of his execution, turns away. The figure of Truth (naked Truth)— straight out of *The Birth of Venus*—looks up to heaven as if to ask "What has happened to us?" The classical statues in their niches look on in disbelief.

Botticelli listened to Savonarola. He burned some of his own paintings and changed his tune. The last works of his life were darker, more somber, and pessimistic of humanity.

The German poet Heine said, "When they start by burning books, they'll end by burning people." Savonarola, after four short years of power, was burned on his own bonfire in the Piazza della Signoria, but by then the city was in shambles. The first flowering of the Renaissance was over.

• *Enter the next room.*

Leonardo da Vinci (1452–1519)—*Annunciation*

A scientist, architect, engineer, musician, and painter, Leonardo was a true Renaissance Man. He worked at his own pace rather than to please an employer, so he often left works unfinished. The two in this room aren't his best, but even a lesser Leonardo is enough to put a museum on the map, and they're definitely worth a look.

Gabriel has walked up to Mary and now kneels on one knee

like an ambassador, saluting her. See how relaxed his other hand is, draped over his knee. Mary, who's been reading, looks up with a gesture of surprise and curiosity.

Leonardo constructs a beautifully landscaped "stage" and puts his characters in it. Look at the bricks on the right wall. If you extended lines from them, the lines would all converge at the center of the painting, the distant blue mountain. Same with the edge of the sarcophagus and the railing. Subconsciously, this subtle touch creates a feeling of balance, order, and spaciousness.

Think back to Simone Martini's *Annunciation* to realize how much more natural, relaxed, and realistic Leonardo's version is. He's taken a miraculous event—an angel appearing out of the blue—and presented it in a very human way.

Leonardo—*Adoration of the Magi*

Leonardo's human insight is even more apparent here, in this unfinished work. The poor kings are amazed at the Christ child—even afraid of him. They scurry around like chimps around fire. This work is as agitated as the *Annunciation* is calm, giving us an idea of Leonardo's range. Leonardo was pioneering a new era of painting, showing not just the outer features but the inner personality.

The next painting to the right, *Baptism of Christ*, is by Verrochio, Leonardo's teacher. Legend has it that Leonardo painted the angel on the far left when he was only 14 years old. When Verrocchio saw that some kid had painted an angel better than he ever would...he hung up his brush for good.

Florence saw the first blossoming of the Renaissance. But when the cultural climate turned chilly, artists flew south to warmer climes. The Renaissance shifted to Rome.

• *Exit into the main corridor. Breathe. Sit. Admire the ceiling. Look out the window. See you in five.*

Back already? Now continue down the corridor and turn left into the octagonal Venus de' Medici room (they only allow 25 people in at a time). If you skip this because there's a line, you'll also be missing the next five rooms, which include works by Cranach, Dürer, Memling, Holbein, Giorgione, and others.

Classical Sculpture

If the Renaissance was the foundation of the modern world, the foundation of the Renaissance was classical sculpture. Sculptors, painters, and poets alike turned for inspiration to these ancient Greek and Roman works as the epitome of balance, 3-D, human anatomy, and beauty.

The *Venus de' Medici*, or *Medici Venus* (*Venere de' Medici*, Ancient Greece)

Is this pose familiar? Botticelli's *Birth of Venus* has the same position of the arms, the same S-curved body, and the same lifting of the right leg. A copy of this statue stood in Lorenzo the Magnificent's garden, where Botticelli used to hang out. This one is a Roman copy of the lost original by the great Greek sculptor Praxiteles. The *Medici Venus* is a balanced, harmonious, serene statue from Greece's "Golden Age," when balance was admired in every aspect of life.

Perhaps more than any other work of art, this statue has been

Classical Sculpture and Northern Renaissance

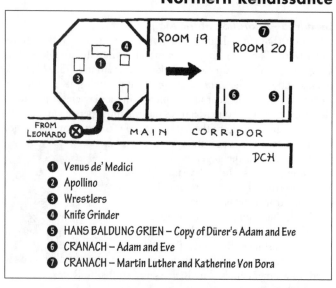

① Venus de' Medici
② Apollino
③ Wrestlers
④ Knife Grinder
⑤ HANS BALDUNG GRIEN – Copy of Dürer's Adam and Eve
⑥ CRANACH – Adam and Eve
⑦ CRANACH – Martin Luther and Katherine Von Bora

the epitome of both ideal beauty and sexuality. In the 18th and 19th centuries, sex was "dirty," so the sex drive of cultured aristocrats was channeled into a love of pure beauty. Wealthy sons and daughters of Europe's aristocrats made the pilgrimage to the Uffizi to complete their classical education...where they swooned in ecstasy before the cold beauty of this goddess of love.

Louis XIV had a bronze copy made. Napoleon stole her away to Paris for himself. And in Philadelphia in the 1800s, a copy had to be kept under lock and key to prevent the innocent from catching the Venere-al disease. At first, it may be difficult for us to appreciate such passionate love of art, but if any generation knows the power of sex to sell something—be it art or underarm deodorant—it's ours.

The Other Statues

Venus de' Medici's male counterpart is on the right, facing Venus. *Apollino* (a.k.a. "Venus with a Penis") is also by the master of smooth, cool lines: Praxiteles.

The other works are later Greek (Hellenistic), when quiet balance was replaced by violent motion and emotion. *The Wrestlers,* to the left of Venus, is a study in anatomy and twisted limbs—like Pollaiuolo's paintings a thousand years later.

The drama of *The Knife Grinder* to the right of Venus stems from the off-stage action—he's sharpening the knife to flay a man alive.

• *Exit the octagonal room and pass through Room 19 into Room 20.*

Northern Renaissance

Hans Baldung Grien (c.1484–1545)— Copy of Dürer's *Adam and Eve*

The warm spirit of the Renaissance blew north into Germany. Albrecht Dürer (1471–1528), the famous German painter and engraver, traveled to Venice, where he fell in love with all things Italian. Returning home, he painted the First Couple in the Italian style—full-bodied, muscular (check out Adam's abs and Eve's knees), "carved" with strong shading, fresh-faced, and innocent in their earthly Paradise.

This copy by Hans Baldung Grien of Dürer's original (now in the Prado) was a training exercise. Like many of Europe's artists—including Michelangelo and Raphael—Baldung Grien learned technique by studying Dürer's meticulous engravings, spread by the newly invented printing press.

Lucas Cranach (1472–1553)—*Adam and Eve*

Eve sashays forward, with heavy-lidded eyes, to offer the forbidden fruit. Adam stretches to display himself and his foliage to Eve. The two panels are linked by smoldering eye contact, as Man and Woman awaken to their own nakedness. The Garden of Eden is about to be rocked by new ideas that are both liberating and troubling.

Though the German Lucas Cranach occasionally dabbled in the "Italian style," he chose to portray his Adam and Eve in the now-retro look of International Gothic.

They are slimmer than Dürer's, smoother, more S-shaped, elegant, graceful, shapely, and erotic, with the dainty pinkies of the refined aristocrats signing Cranach's paycheck.

Though life-sized, Adam and Eve are not lifelike, not monumental, not full-bodied or muscular, and are not placed in a real-world landscape with distant perspectives. Even so, Cranach was very much a man of the Renaissance, a friend of Martin Luther, and a champion of humanism.

Cranach—*Martin Luther*

Martin Luther—German monk, fiery orator, and religious whistle-blower—sparked a century of European wars by speaking out against the Catholic Church.

Luther (1483–1546) lived a turbulent life. In early adulthood, the newly ordained priest suffered a severe personal crisis of faith, before

finally emerging "born again." In 1517 he openly protested against church corruption and was excommunicated. Defying both the pope and the emperor, he lived on the run as an outlaw, watching as his ideas sparked peasant riots. He still found time to translate the New Testament from Latin to modern German, write hymns such as "A Mighty Fortress," and spar with the humanist Erasmus and fellow-Reformer Zwingli.

Now 46 years old, Martin Luther is easing out of the fast lane. Recently married to an ex-nun, he has traded his monk's habit for street clothes, bought a house, had several kids...and has clearly been enjoying his wife's home cooking and home-brewed beer.

Cranach—*Katherine von Bora* (Luther's wife)

When "Katie" decided to leave her convent, the famous Martin Luther agreed to help find her a husband. She rejected his nominees, saying she'd marry no one...except Luther himself. In 1525 the 42-year-old ex-priest married the 26-year-old ex-nun "to please my father and annoy the pope." Martin turned his checkbook over to "my lord Katie," who also ran the family farm, raised their six children and 11 adopted orphans, and hosted Martin's circle of friends (including Cranach) at loud, chatty dinner parties.

• *Pass through the next couple of rooms, exiting to a great view of the Arno. Stroll through the sculpture wing.*

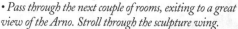

The Sculpture Wing

A hundred years ago, no one even looked at Botticelli—they came to the Uffizi to see the sculpture collection. And today, these 2,000-year-old Roman copies of 2,500-year-old Greek originals are hardly noticed.

• *There are benches at the other end of the wing with a superb view.*

View of the Arno

Enjoy Florence's best view of the Arno and Ponte Vecchio. You can also see the red-tiled roof of the Vasari Corridor, the "secret" passage

connecting the Palazzo Vecchio, Uffizi, Ponte Vecchio, and Pitti Palace on the other side of the river—a half-mile in all. This was a private walkway, wallpapered in great art, for the Medici family's commute from home to work.

As you appreciate the view (best at sunset), remember that it's this sort of pleasure that Renaissance painters wanted you to get from their paintings. For them, a canvas was a window you looked through to see the wide world.

We're headed down the home stretch now. If your little U-feetsies are killing you and it feels like torture, remind yourself it's a pleasant torture and smile...like the statue next to you.

• *In the far corridor, turn left into the first room (#25) and grab a blast of cold from the air-conditioner vent on the floor to the left.*

High Renaissance (1500–1550)— Michelangelo, Raphael, Titian

Michelangelo Buonarroti (1475–1564)—*Holy Family (Sacra Famiglia)*

This is the only completed easel painting by the greatest sculptor in history. Florentine painters were sculptors with brushes. This shows it. Instead of a painting, it's more like three clusters of statues with some clothes painted on.

The main subject is the holy family—Mary, Joseph, and baby Jesus—and in the background are two groups of nudes looking like classical statues. The background represents the old pagan world, while Jesus in the foreground is the new age of Christianity. The figure of young John the Baptist at right is the link between the two.

This is a "peasant" Mary, with a plain face and sunburned arms. Michelangelo shows her from a very unflattering angle—we're looking up her nostrils. But Michelangelo himself was an ugly man, and he was among the first artists to recognize the beauty in everyday people.

High Renaissance

① MICHELANGELO – Holy Family
② RAPHAEL – Madonna of the Goldfinch
③ RAPHAEL – Pope Leo X
④ TITIAN – Venus of Urbino
⑤ PARMIGIANINO – Madonna of the Long Neck

Michelangelo was a Florentine—in fact he was like an adopted son of the Medicis, who recognized his talent—but much of his greatest work was done in Rome as part of the Pope's face-lift of the city. We can see here some of the techniques he used on the Sistine Chapel ceiling that revolutionized painting—monumental figures; dramatic angles (we're looking up Mary's nose); accentuated, rippling muscles; and bright, clashing colors (all the more apparent since both this work and the Sistine have been recently cleaned). These added an element of dramatic tension lacking in the graceful work of Leonardo and Botticelli.

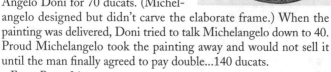

Michelangelo painted this for Angelo Doni for 70 ducats. (Michelangelo designed but didn't carve the elaborate frame.) When the painting was delivered, Doni tried to talk Michelangelo down to 40. Proud Michelangelo took the painting away and would not sell it until the man finally agreed to pay double...140 ducats.
• Enter Room 26.

Raphael (Raffaello Sanzio, 1483–1520)—
Madonna of the Goldfinch (La Madonna del Cardellino)
Raphael (roff-eye-ELL) brings Mary and Bambino down from heaven and into the real world of trees, water, and sky. He gives baby Jesus (right) and John the Baptist a realistic, human playfulness. It's a

tender scene painted with warm colors and a hazy background that matches the golden skin of the children.

Raphael perfected his craft in Florence, following the graceful style of Leonardo. In typical Leonardo fashion, this group of Mary, John the Baptist, and Jesus is arranged in the shape of a pyramid, with Mary's head at the peak.

The two halves of the painting balance perfectly. Draw a line down the middle, through Mary's nose and down through her knee. John the Baptist on the left is balanced by Jesus on the right. Even the trees in the background balance each other, left and right. These things aren't immediately noticeable, but they help create the subconscious feelings of balance and order that reinforce the atmosphere of maternal security in this domestic scene—pure Renaissance.

Raphael—*Leo X and Cardinals (Leone X con i Cardinali)*

Raphael was called to Rome at the same time as Michelangelo, working next door while Michelangelo did the Sistine ceiling. Raphael peeked in from time to time, learning from Michelangelo's monumental, dramatic figures. His later work is grittier and more realistic than the idealized, graceful, and "Leonardoesque" Madonna.

Pope Leo is big, like a Michelangelo statue. And Raphael captures some of the seamier side of Vatican life in the cardinals' eyes—shrewd, suspicious, and somewhat cynical. With Raphael, the photographic realism pursued by painters ever since Giotto was finally achieved.

The Florentine Renaissance ended in 1520 with the death of Raphael. Raphael (see his self-portrait to the left of the Madonna) is considered both the culmination and conclusion of the Renaissance. The realism, balance, and humanism we associate with the Renaissance are all found in Raphael's work. He combined the grace of Leonardo with the power of Michelangelo. With his death, the Renaissance shifted again—to Venice.

• *Pass through the next room and enter Room 28.*

Titian (Tiziano Vecelli, c. 1490–1576)—*Venus of Urbino (La Venere di Urbino)*

Compare this *Venus* with Botticelli's newly hatched *Venus* and you get a good idea of the difference between the Florentine and

Six Degrees of Leo X

This sophisticated, luxury-loving pope was at the center of an inter-national, Renaissance world that spread across Europe. He crossed paths with many of the Renaissance Men of his generation. Based on the theory that any two people are linked by only "six degrees of separation," let's link Leo X with the actor Kevin Bacon:

- Leo X's father was Lorenzo the Magnificent, patron of Botticelli and Leonardo.
- When Leo X was age 13, his family took in 13-year-old Michelangelo.
- Michelangelo inspired Raphael, who was later hired by Leo X.
- Raphael exchanged masterpieces with fellow genius Albrecht Dürer, who was personally converted by Martin Luther (who was friends with Lucas Cranach), who was excommunicated by...Leo X.
- Leo X was portrayed in the movie *The Agony and the Ecstasy*, which starred Charlton Heston, who was in *Planet of the Apes* with Burgess Meredith, who was in *Rocky* with Sylvester Stallone...who ultimately connects with...Kevin Bacon.

Venetian Renaissance. Botticelli's was pure, innocent, and other-worldly. Titian's should have a staple in her belly button. This isn't a Venus, it's a centerfold—with no purpose but to please the eye and other organs. While Botticelli's allegorical Venus is a message, this is a massage.

Titian and his fellow Venetians took the pagan spirit pioneered in Florence and carried it to its logical hedonistic conclusion. Using bright, rich colors, they captured the luxurious life of happy-go-lucky Venice.

While Raphael's *Madonna of the Goldfinch* was balanced with a figure on the left and one on the right, Titian balances his painting in a different way—with color. The canvas is split down the middle by the curtain. The left half is dark, the right half warmer. The two halves are connected by a diagonal slash of luminous gold—the nude woman. The girl in the background is trying to find her some clothes.

By the way, visitors from centuries past also panted in front of this Venus. The poet Byron called it "*the* Venus." With her sensual skin, hey-sailor look, and suggestively placed hand, she must have left them blithering idiots.

• *Find the n–n–n–next painting.*

Parmigianino (1503–1540)—*Madonna of the Long Neck (Madonna dal Collo Lungo)*

Raphael, Michelangelo, Leonardo, and Titian mastered reality. They could place any scene onto a canvas with photographic accuracy. How could future artists top that?

Mannerists such as Parmigianino tried by going beyond realism, exaggerating it for effect. Using brighter colors and twisting

poses (two techniques explored by Michelangelo), they created scenes more elegant and more exciting than real life.

By stretching the neck of his Madonna, Parmigianino (like the cheese) gives her an unnatural swanlike beauty. She has the same pose and position of hands as Botticelli's *Venus* and the *Venus de' Medici.* Her body forms an arcing S-curve—down her neck as far as her elbow, then back the other way along Jesus' body to her knee, then down to her foot. The baby Jesus seems to be blissfully gliding down this slippery slide of sheer beauty.

In the Uffizi, we've seen many images of female beauty: from ancient goddesses to medieval Madonnas to wicked Eves, from Botticelli's pristine nymphs to Michelangelo's peasant Mary, from Raphael's Madonna-and-baby to Titian's babe. Their physical beauty expresses different aspects of the human spirit.

• *Pass through several rooms, returning to the main corridor.*

The Rest of the Uffizi

As art moved into the Baroque period, artists took Renaissance realism and exaggerated it still more—more beauty, more emotion, or more drama. There's lots of great stuff in the following rooms, and I'd especially recommend the enormous canvases of Rubens, Rembrandt's *Self-Portrait,* and the shocking ultra-realism of Caravaggio's *Bacchus* and *Abraham Sacrificing Isaac.*

• *But first, head to the end of the corridor (WCs en route) for a true aesthetic experience.*

The Little Cappuccin Monk (Cappuccino)

This drinkable art form, born in Italy, is now enjoyed all over the world.

It's called *The Little Cappuccin Monk* because the coffee's frothy light-and-dark-brown foam looks like the two-toned cowls of the Cappuccin order. Drink it on the terrace in the shadow of the towering Palazzo Vecchio and argue the philosophy of Marx and Hegel—was the Renaissance an economic phenomenon or a spiritual one? *Salute.*

BARGELLO TOUR

The Renaissance began with sculpture. The great Florentine painters were "sculptors with brushes." You can see the birth of this revolution of 3-D in the Bargello (bar-JEL-oh), which boasts the best collection of Florentine sculpture. It's a small, uncrowded museum and a pleasant break from the intensity of the rest of Florence.

ORIENTATION

Cost: €4 (higher if a special exhibition is offered).

Hours: Daily 8:15–13:50 but closed first, third, and fifth Sun and second and fourth Mon of each month. Last entry 40 minutes before closing.

Getting There: It's located at Via del Proconsolo 4, a three-minute walk northeast of the Uffizi. Facing the Palazzo Vecchio, go behind the Palazzo and turn left. Look for a rustic brick building with a spire that looks like a baby Palazzo Vecchio. If lost ask, "DOH-vay bar-JEL-oh?"

Information: Nothing in English. Tel. 055-238-8606.

Length of This Tour: One hour.

Cuisine Art: Inexpensive bars and cafés await in the surrounding streets. See recommended eateries "Near Palazzo Vecchio" on page 187.

Photography: No.

Starring: Michelangelo, Donatello, Brunelleschi, Ghiberti, and four different *David*s.

THE TOUR BEGINS

Sculpture In Florence

• *Buy your ticket and take a seat in the courtyard.*

The Bargello, built in 1255, was an early Florence police station *(bargello)* and then a prison. The heavy fortifications tell us that politics in medieval Florence had its occupational hazards.

The Bargello, a three-story rectangular building, surrounds this cool and peaceful courtyard. The best statues are found in two rooms—one on the ground floor at the foot of the outdoor staircase, and another one flight up, directly above. We'll proceed logically, in a chrono kind of way, from Donatello to Verrocchio to Michelangelo.

But first, meander around this courtyard and get a feel for sculpture in general and rocks in particular. Sculpture is a much more robust art form than painting. Think of the engineering problems alone of the sculpting process: quarrying and cutting the stone, transporting the block to the artist's studio, all the hours of chiseling chips away, then the painstaking process of sanding the final product by hand. A sculptor must be strong enough to gouge into the stone but delicate enough to groove out the smallest details. Think of Michelangelo's approach to sculpting—he wasn't creating a figure, he was liberating it from the rock that surrounded it.

If the Renaissance is humanism, then sculpture is the perfect medium to express it in. It shows the human form, standing alone, independent of church, state, or society, ready to create himself.

Finally, a viewing note. Every sculpture has an invisible "frame" around it—the stone block it was cut from. Visualizing this frame helps you find the center of the composition.

• *Climb the courtyard staircase to the next floor up and turn right into the large Donatello room. Pause at Donatello's painted bust of* Niccolo da Uzzanò.

Donatello—*Niccolo da Uzzanò* (c. 1420)

Not an emperor, not a king, not a pope or prince, this is one of Florence's leading businessmen in a toga, portrayed in the style of an ancient Roman bust. In the 1400s, when Florence was inventing the Renaissance that all Europe would soon follow, there was an optimistic spirit of democracy that gloried in everyday people. With wrinkles, quizzical look, and bags under the eyes, Donatello has portrayed this man literally wart (left cheek) and all.

Donatello Room

① DONATELLO – Bust of Niccolo da Uzzano

② DONATELLO – Early David

③ DONATELLO – St. George

④ DONATELLO – David

⑤ DESIDERIO (or DONATELLO) – St. John the Baptist

⑥ GHIBERTI and BRUNELLESCHI – Bronze panels for Baptistery door competition

⑦ DELLA ROBBIA – Terra-cotta panels

Donatello—An early *David* (marble, 1408)

This is the first of several *David*s we'll see in the Bargello. His dainty pose makes him a little unsteady on his feet. He's dressed like a medieval knight (fully clothed but showing some leg through the slit skirt). The generic face and blank, vacant eyes give him the look not of a real man but of an anonymous decoration on a church facade. At age 22, Donatello still had one foot in the old Gothic style. To tell the story of David, Donatello plants a huge rock right in the middle of Goliath's forehead.

• *At the far end of the room, St. George stands in a niche in the wall.*

Donatello—*St. George* (*S. Giorgio*, 1416)

The proud warrior has both feet planted firmly on the ground. He stands on the edge of his niche looking out alertly. He tenses his powerful right hand as he prepares to attack. George, the Christian slayer of dragons, was just the sort of righteous warrior that proud Renaissance Florentines could rally around in their struggles with nearby cities. Nearly a century later, Michelangelo's *David* replaced *George* as the unofficial symbol of Florence, but *David* was clearly inspired by *George*'s relaxed intensity and determination. (This is the original marble statue. A bronze version stands in its original niche at Orsanmichele Church.)

The relief panel below shows George doing what he's been pondering. To *George*'s right, the sketchy arches and trees create the illusion of a distant landscape. Donatello, who apprenticed in

Donatello
(1386–1466)

Donatello was the first great Renaissance genius, a model for Michelangelo and others. He mastered realism, creating the first truly lifelike statues of people since ancient times. Donatello's work is highly personal. Unlike the ancient Greeks—but like the ancient Romans—he often sculpted real people, not idealized versions of pretty gods and goddesses. Some of these people are downright ugly. In the true spirit of Renaissance humanism, Donatello appreciated the beauty of flesh-and-blood human beings.

Donatello's personality was also a model for later artists. He was moody and irascible, purposely setting himself apart from others in order to concentrate on his sculpting. He developed the role of the "mad genius" that Michelangelo would later perfect.

Ghiberti's studio, is credited with teaching his master how to create 3-D illusions like this.

• *On the floor to your left, you'll find...*

Donatello—*David* (bronze, c. 1430)

He's naked. Donatello, who never married, sees David as a teenage boy wearing only a helmet, boots, and sword. The smooth-skinned warrior sways gracefully, poking his sword playfully at the severed head of the giant Goliath. His *contrapposto* stance is similar to Michelangelo's *David*, resting his weight on one leg in the classical style, but it gives him a feminine rather than masculine look. Gazing into his coy eyes and at his bulging belly is a very different experience from confronting Michelangelo's older and sturdier Renaissance Man.

This *David* paved the way for Michelangelo's. Europe hadn't seen a free-standing male nude like this in a thousand years. In the Middle Ages, the human body was considered a dirty thing, a symbol of man's weakness, something to be covered up in shame. The church prohibited exhibitions of nudity like this one and certainly would never decorate a church with it. But in the Renaissance, a new class of rich and powerful merchants appeared that bought art for personal enjoyment. Reading Plato's *Symposium*, they saw the ideal of Beauty in the form of a young man. This particular statue stood in the Medicis' palace...where Michelangelo, practically an adopted son, grew up admiring it.

As we see the different *David*s in the Bargello, compare and contrast the artists' styles. How many ways can you slay a giant?

• St. John the Baptist, *done by Donatello or his student, is to the right of the boyish, naked* David.

Desiderio da Settignano (or Donatello)— St. John the Baptist (S. Giovanni Battista)

John the Baptist was the wild-eyed, wildcat prophet who lived in the desert preaching, living on bugs 'n' honey, and baptizing Saviors of the World. Donatello, the mad prophet of the coming Renaissance, might have identified with this original eccentric.

• *On the wall next to* George, *you'll find some bronze relief panels. Don't look at the labels just yet.*

Ghiberti and Brunelleschi— Baptistery Door Competition Entries (two different relief panels, titled *Il Sacrificio di Abramo*)

Some would say these two panels are the first works of the Renaissance. These two versions of *Abraham Sacrificing Isaac* were finalists in the contest held in 1401 to decide who would do the bronze doors of the Baptistery. The contest sparked citywide excitement that evolved into the Renaissance spirit. Lorenzo Ghiberti won, and later did the doors known as the Gates of Paradise. Filippo Brunelleschi lost—fortunately for us—freeing him to design the Duomo's dome.

Both artists catch the crucial moment when Abraham, obeying God's orders, prepares to slaughter and burn his only son as a sacrifice. At the last moment—after Abraham passed this test of faith—an angel of God appears to stop the bloodshed.

Is one panel clearly better than the other? Composition: One is integrated and cohesive, the other a balanced knickknack shelf of segments. Human drama: One has bodies and faces that speak.

You be the judge. Here are the two finalists for the Baptisery door competition—Ghiberti's and Brunelleschi's. Which do you like best?

Ghiberti's, on the left.

The boy's body is a fine classical nude in itself, so real and vulnerable. Abraham's face is intense and ready to follow God's will. Perspective: An angel zooms in from out of nowhere to save the boy in the nick of time. Detail: One lamb's ram's wool is curlier than the other, one altar is more intricate.

It was obviously a tough call, but Ghiberti's was chosen, perhaps because his goldsmith training made him better suited for the technical end.

• *Along the walls, you'll find several colorful terra-cotta reliefs.*

Luca della Robbia—Terra-cotta Relief Panels

Mary and baby Jesus with accompanying angels look their most serene in these panels by the master of painted, glazed porcelain. Polished blue, white, green, and yellow, they have a gentle and feminine look that softens the rough masculine stone of this room. Luca was just one of a family of della Robbias that pioneered art in terra-cotta.

• *Exit the Donatello room through the same door you entered. Cross to the rooms on the other side of the courtyard. Take your first left, then turn right and climb the red-carpeted stairs to the next floor. At the top of the stairs, turn left, then left again. Verrocchio's David stands (when not out for restoration) in the center of the room.*

Verrocchio—*David* (c. 1470)

Andrea del Verrocchio (1435–1488) is best known as the teacher of Leonardo da Vinci, but he was also the premier sculptor of the generation between Donatello and Michelangelo. This saucy, impertinent *David* is younger and more masculine than Donatello's, but a far cry from Michelangelo's monumental version. He's definitely the shepherd "boy" described in the Bible. He leans on one leg, not with a firm, commanding stance but a nimble one (especially noticeable from behind).

Compare the smug smile of the victor with Goliath's "Oh, have I got a headache" expression.

• *The doorway to your right leads to a room of glass cases filled with small statues. In the center of the room, you'll find...*

Pollaiuolo—*Hercules and Antaeus* (*Ercole e Anteo,* 1498)

Antaeus was invincible as long as he was in contact with the earth, his mother. So Hercules just picked him up like "The Rock" of the Renaissance and crushed him to death.

More than any early artist from this period, Antonio Pollaiuolo studied the human body in motion. These figures are not dignified Renaissance Men. Yet, in this tangled pose of flailing arms and legs, there still is a Renaissance sense of balance—all the motion spins around the center of gravity where their bodies grind together.

• *In the nearby glass cases are small-scale, alternate versions of the* Mercury *that we'll soon see.*

The Rest of the Bargello

Before we lose elevation to visit the final room downstairs, browse around the upper floors. On this floor, you'll find ivories, jewelry, and terra-cotta Mary-baby-and-angel panels by other members of the della Robbia clan. The top floor has armor and medallions.

• *Now descend back to the courtyard on the ground floor. The final room we'll visit is through the door to your left at the bottom of the stairs. We'll begin with three lesser Michelangelos.*

Michelangelo—*Bacchus (Baccho,* c. 1497)

Bacchus, the god of wine and revelry, raises another cup to his lips, while his little companion goes straight for the grapes.

Maybe Michelangelo had a sense of humor after all. Compare this tipsy Greek god of wine with his sturdy, sober *David,* begun a few years later. *Bacchus* isn't nearly so muscular, so monumental...or so sure on his feet. Hope he's not driving. The pose, the smooth muscles, the beer belly, and swaying hips look more like Donatello's boyish *David.*

This was Michelangelo's first major commission. He often vacillated between showing man as strong and noble, and as weak and perverse. This isn't the nobility of the classical world, but the decadent side of orgies and indulgence.

• *Just to the left, you'll find...*

Michelangelo—*Brutus (Bruto,* 1540)

Another example of the influence of Donatello is this so-ugly-he's-beautiful bust by Michelangelo. His rough intensity gives him the look of a man who has succeeded against all odds, a dignity and heroic quality that would be missing if he were too pretty.

The subject is Brutus, the Roman

Bargello—Ground Floor

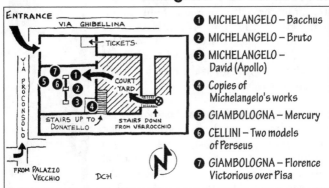

ENTRANCE
VIA GHIBELLINA
TICKETS
COURTYARD
STAIRS UP TO DONATELLO
STAIRS DOWN FROM VERROCCHIO
VIA PROCONSOLO
FROM PALAZZO VECCHIO
DCH

❶ MICHELANGELO – Bacchus

❷ MICHELANGELO – Bruto

❸ MICHELANGELO – David (Apollo)

❹ Copies of Michelangelo's works

❺ GIAMBOLOGNA – Mercury

❻ CELLINI – Two models of Perseus

❼ GIAMBOLOGNA – Florence Victorious over Pisa

who, for the love of liberty, murdered his friend and dictator, Julius Caesar (*Et tu...?*). Michelangelo could understand this man's dilemma. He himself was torn between his love of the democratic tradition of Florence and loyalty to his friends the Medicis, who had become dictators.

So he gives us two sides of a political assassin. The right profile (the front view) is heroic. But the hidden side, with the drooping mouth and squinting eye, makes him more cunning, sneering, and ominous.

Michelangelo—*David* (also known as *Apollo,* 1530–32)

This restless, twisting man is either David or Apollo (is he reaching for a sling or a quiver?). As the last of the *David*s in the Bargello, it's a good time to think back on those we've seen: Donatello's generic warrior and girlish, gloating *David*; Verrocchio's boyish, impish version; and now this unfinished one by Michelangelo. Michelangelo certainly learned from these earlier versions, even copying certain elements, but what's truly amazing is that his famous *David* in the Accademia is so completely different from the others, so much larger than life in every way.

In the glass cases in the corner are small-scale copies of some of Michelangelo's most famous works. Back near the entrance there's a bust of Michelangelo by his fellow sculptor da Volterra, capturing Michelangelo's broken nose and brooding nature.

• *On the other side of the room...*

Giambologna—*Mercury*

Catch this statue while you can—he's got flowers waiting to be delivered. Despite all the bustle and motion, *Mercury* has a solid

Renaissance core: the line of balance that runs straight up the center, from toes to hip to fingertip. He's caught in mid-stride. His top half leans forward, counterbalanced by his right leg in back, while the center of gravity rests firmly at the hip-bone. Down at the toes, notice the cupid practicing up for the circus.

Cellini—*Models of Perseus (Perseo)*

The life-size statue of Perseus slaying Medusa, located in the open-air loggia next to Palazzo Vecchio, is cast bronze. Benvenuto Cellini started with these smaller models in wax and bronze to get the difficult process down. When it came time to cast the full-size work, everything was going fine...until he realized he didn't have enough metal! He ran around the studio, gathering up pewterware and throwing it in, narrowly avoiding a messterpiece.

Giambologna—*Florence Victorious over Pisa (Firenze Vittoriosa su Pisa)*

This shows the fierce Florentine chauvinism born in an era when Italy's cities struggled for economic and political dominance...and Florence won.

MUSEUM OF SAN MARCO TOUR

(Museo di San Marco)

Two of Florence's brightest lights lived in the San Marco Monastery, a reminder that the Renaissance was not just a secular phenomenon. At the Museum of San Marco, you'll find these two different expressions of 15th-century Christianity—Fra Angelico's radiant paintings, fusing medieval faith with Renaissance realism, and Savonarola's moral reforms, fusing medieval faith with modern politics.

ORIENTATION

Cost: €4.

Hours: Mon–Fri 8:15–13:50, Sat–Sun 8:15–19:00, but closed the first, third, and fifth Sun and the second and fourth Mon of each month.

Getting There: It's on Piazza San Marco, around the corner from the Accademia, and several long blocks northeast of the Duomo (head up Via Ricasoli or Via Cavour).

Information: Tel. 055-238-8608. You can buy Uffizi and Accademia tickets with reservations here.

Length of This Tour: One hour.

Cuisine Art: Gran Caffè San Marco Self-Service, on Piazza San Marco, offers a fast, basic, and cheap buffet (opposite the square from the museum entrance; the cafeteria door is around the corner on Via Cavour, near #50). For a fresh-baked focaccia and pizza to go, try Pugi (on Piazza San Marco, next to main entrance of Gran Caffè San Marco).

Starring: Fra Angelico's paintings and Savonarola's living quarters.

San Marco—Ground Floor

THE TOUR BEGINS

Overview

Ground floor: The world's best collection of Fra Angelico paintings.
Upstairs: The monks' cells (living quarters), decorated by Fra Angelico, and the cell of the most famous resident, Savonarola.

• *Buy ticket and enter the courtyard/cloister.*

GROUND FLOOR

The Courtyard/Cloister

Renaissance arches frame Gothic cross-vaulting—an apt introduction to a monastery built during the optimistic time (1439) when Renaissance humanism dovetailed with medieval spirituality.

Fra Angelico—*Fresco of St. Dominic and Crucifixion*

The fresco by Fra Angelico (in the corner of the cloister, straight ahead from the entrance) shows Dominic, the founder of the order, hugging the bloody cross like a groupie adoring a rock star. Monks who lived here—including Fra Angelico, Savonarola, and Fra Bartolomeo—renounced money, sex, ego, and rock music to follow a simple, regimented life, meditating on Christ's ultimate sacrifice.

• *We'll tour the rooms around the courtyard moving counterclockwise. The first one, by the entrance, is the Hospice (Ospizio).*

The Hospice (Ospizio), with paintings by Fra Angelico (Beato Angelico)

Fra Angelico (c. 1400–1455)—equal parts monk and painter—fused early-Renaissance technique with medieval spirituality. His works can be admired for their beauty or contemplated as spiritual visions. Browse the room and you'll find serene-faced Marys, Christs, and saints wearing gold halos (often painted on altarpieces), bright primary colors (red-blue-yellow/gold), evenly lit scenes, and meticulous detail—all creating a mystical world of their own, glowing from within like stained-glass windows.

• *Start with the large altarpiece* (The Deposition) *at the near end of the room.*

Fra Angelico—*Deposition of Christ from the Cross (Pala di Santa Trinità)*

Christ's body is lowered from the cross, mourned by haloed women (on the left) and contemporary Florentines (right). There's a clearly defined foreground (the kneeling, curly-headed man and the woman with her back to us), background (the distant city and hills), and middle distance (the trees).

Fra Angelico, trained in medieval religious painting, never closed his eyes to the innovations of the budding Renaissance, using both styles all his life. There are Gothic elements, such as the altarpiece frame, inherited from his former teacher (who painted the pinnacles on top). The holy wear halos, and the stretched-out "body of Christ" is symbolically "displayed" like the communion bread.

But it's truly a Renaissance work. The man in green lowering Christ bends forward at a strongly foreshortened (difficult to draw) angle. Christ's toes, kissed by Mary Magdalene, cross the triptych wall, ignoring the frame's traditional three-arch divisions. Fra Angelico was boldly "coloring outside the lines" to create a single, realistic scene.

And the holy scene has been removed from its golden heaven and placed in the first great Renaissance landscape—on a lawn, among flowers, trees, cloud masses, real people, and the hillsides of Fiesole overlooking Florence. Fra Angelico, the ascetic monk, refused to renounce one pleasure—his joy in the natural beauty of God's creation.

• *Working counterclockwise around the room, you'll find the following works (among others).*

Fra Angelico—*Triptych of St. Peter the Martyr* (*Trittico di San Pietro Martire*)

In this early, more "medieval" work, Fra Angelico sets (big) Mary and Child in a gold background flanked by (small) saints standing obediently in their niches. Having recently joined the Dominican community in Fiesole, young Brother Giovanni (as he was known in his lifetime) now dressed like these famous Dominicans—white robe, blue cape, and tonsured haircut.

Peter the Martyr (next to Mary, with bloody head) exemplified the unbending Dominican spirit. Attacked by heretics (see the scene above Peter), he was hacked in the head with a dagger, but died still preaching, writing with his own blood: *"Credo in Deum"* (I believe in God).

• *Continuing counterclockwise...*

Fra Angelico—Two Panels: *Wedding and Funeral of the Virgin* (*Sposalizio e Funerali della Vergine*)

Fra Angelico's teenage training was as a miniaturist, so even these small *predella* panels (part of a larger altarpiece) are surprisingly realistic—the folds in the clothes, the gold-brocade hemlines, and the precisely outlined people, as though etched in glass. Notice the

Renaissance perspective tricks he was exploring, setting the wedding in front of receding buildings and the funeral among candles that get shorter at the back of the scene.

Fra Angelico—*Last Judgment (Giudizio Universale)*

Despite the Renaissance, Florence in the 1420s was still a city in the Christian universe described by Dante. Hell (to the right) is a hierarchical barbecue where sinners are burned, boiled, and tortured

by a minotaur-like Satan, who rules the bottom of the pit. The blessed in Heaven (left) play ring-around-the-rosy with angels. In the center, a row of open tombs creates a 3-D Highway to Hell, stretching ominously to that Final Judgment Day.

Fra Angelico (and assistants)—*Thirty-five Scenes Painted on Doors of a Silverware Storeroom (Panelli dell' Armadio degli Argenti)*

The first nine scenes in this Life of Christ are by Fra Angelico himself (the rest by assistants). Like storyboards for a movie, these natural, realistic, and straightforward panels "show" through action, they don't just "tell" through symbols. (The Latin inscription beneath each panel is redundant.) The miraculous is presented as matter-of-factly as an everyday occurrence.

1. The Wheel of Ezekiel (OK, that's medieval symbolism) prophesies Christ's coming.
2. In the Annunciation, the angel gestures to tell Mary she'll give birth.
3. Newborn Jesus glows, amazing his parents, while timid shepherds sneak a peek.
4. Precocious Jesus splays himself and says, "Cut me."
5. One of the Magi kneels to kiss the babe's foot.
6. In the temple, the tiny baby is dwarfed by elongated priests and columns.
7. Mary and the baby ride, while Joseph carries the luggage.

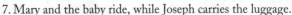

8. Meanwhile, babies are slaughtered in a jumble of gore, dramatic poses, and agonized faces.

9. The commotion contrasts with the serenity of child Jesus in the temple.

This work by 50-year-old Fra Angelico—master of many styles, famous in Italy, recently returned from a gig in the Vatican—has the fresh, simple, spontaneous storytelling of a children's book.

Fra Angelico—Lamentation (Compianto sul Cristo Morto)

This painting of the executed Christ being mourned silently by loved ones was the last thing many con-demned prisoners saw during their final hours. It once hung in a church where the soon-to-be executed were incarcerated.

The melancholy mood is under-stated, suggested by a series of horizontal layers—Christ's body, the line of mourners, the city walls, landscape horizon, layered clouds, and the crossbar. It's as though Christ is being welcomed into peace-ful rest, a comforting message from Fra Angelico to the condemned.

"Fra Angelico" (Angelic Brother) is a nickname that describes his reputation for sweetness, humility, and compassion. It's said he couldn't paint a crucifixion without crying. In 1984, he was beati-fied by Pope John Paul II and made patron of artists.

• *At the far end of the room hangs the...*

Fra Angelico—Altarpiece of the Linen-Drapers (Tabernacolo dei Linaioli)

The impressive size and marble frame (by Ghiberti) attest to Fra Angelico's worldly success and collaboration with Renaissance greats. The monumental Mary and Child and the saints on the doors are gold-backed and elegant to please conservative patrons. In the three *predella* panels below, Fra Angelico gets to display his Renaissance chops, showing haloed saints mingling with well-dressed Florentines amid local city- and landscapes. (Find Ghi-berti in the left panel, kneeling, in blue.)

• *On the long wall are three similar-looking altarpieces. These are examples of a scene known as a* sacra conversazione.

Evolution of the *Sacra Conversazione*

Fra Angelico (largely) invented what became a common Renaissance theme: Mary and Child surrounded by saints "conversing" informally about holy matters. Four examples in this room show how Fra Angelico, exploring Renaissance techniques, developed the idea over his lifetime.

The *Triptych of St. Peter the Martyr,* shown on page 96, is not a true *sacra conversazione,* even though it shows Mary and saints. But Mary is unnaturally big, flanked by smaller saints in a line. The gold background gives no hint they inhabit the same space, and there is no eye contact between them and no "conversation."

• *Left-to-right along the long wall, you'll find the following three altar-pieces in the* sacra conversazione *style.*

Fra Angelico—*Annalena Altarpiece (Pala d'Annalena)*

In the *Annalena Altarpiece*—considered Florence's first true *sacra conversazione*—the saints emerge from their niches, gather cautiously in a semicircle, and tentatively acknowledge each other with eyes and gestures. The background is traditional gold, but now in the form of a curtain hanging behind the throne.

Still, everyone's either facing out or in profile—not the natural poses of a true crowd. Mary and Jesus direct our eye to Mary's brooch, the first in a series of circles radiating out from the center: brooch, halo, canopy arch, circle of saints. Set in a square frame, this painting has the circle-in-a-square composition that marks many *sacra*s.

Fra Angelico—*San Marco Altarpiece (Pala di San Marco)*

In 1439, Cosimo de' Medici built this monastery, inviting Fra Angelico's Dominican community to move here from Fiesole. Fra Angelico soon became prior (head monk), turning down an offer to be archbishop of Florence.

Cosimo commissioned this painting as the centerpiece of the new church (next door). For the dedication Mass, Fra Angelico theatrically "opens the curtain," revealing a stage set with a distant backdrop of trees, kneeling saints in the foreground, and a crowd gathered around Mary and Child at center stage on a raised, canopied throne. The altarpiece was like a window onto a marvelous world where holies mill about on Earth as naturally as mortals.

The *San Marco Altarpiece* places the holy saints clearly in the 3-D world we inhabit. The carpet makes a "chessboard" pattern to establish 3-D space. To show just how far we've come from Gothic,

Fra Angelico gives us a painting-in-a-painting—a crude, gold-backed crucifixion.

Fra Angelico—*Bosco ai Frati Altarpiece* (*Pala di Bosco ai Frati*)

This altarpiece is Fra Angelico's last great work, and he uses every stylistic arrow in his quiver: detailed friezes of the miniaturist;

medieval halos and gold backdrop; monumental, naturally posed figures in the style of Masaccio (especially St. Francis, on the left, with his relaxed *contrapposto*); 3-D perspective established by the floor tiles; and Renaissance love of natural beauty (the trees and sky).

Fra Angelico's bright colors are eye-catching. The gold backdrop sets off the red-pink handmaidens, which set off Jesus' pale skin. The deep blue of Mary's dress, frosted with a precious gold hem, turns out at her feet to show a swath of the green inner lining, suggesting the 3-D body within.

Despite Renaissance realism, Fra Angelico creates a world of his own—perfectly lit, with no moody shadows, no dirt, frayed clothing, or imperfection. The faces are certainly realistic, but they express no human emotion. These mortals, through sacrifice and meditation, have risen above the petty passions celebrated by humanist painters to achieve a serenity that lights them from within.

• *Exit the Hospice into the courtyard. Continue counterclockwise and enter the next set of rooms (marked* Lavabo e Refettorio). *The small room on the left has paintings and fresco fragments by Fra Bartolomeo. Working clockwise around the room, you'll find these works by...*

Fra Bartolomeo (1473–1517)

Fra Bartolomeo lived and worked in this monastery a generation after the "Angelic" brother. *Ecce Homo* shows the kind of Christ that young, idealistic Dominican monks (like Fra Bartolomeo) adored in their meditations—curly-haired, creamy-faced, dreamy-eyed, bearing the torments of the secular world with humble serenity.

Fra Bartolomeo—*St. Dominic (San Domenico)*

St. Dominic holds a finger to his lips—"Shh! We have strict rules in my order." Dominic (c. 1170–1221), a friend of St. Francis of Assisi, formed his rules after seeing the austere *perfetti* (perfect ones) of the heretical Cathar sect of southern France. He figured they could only be converted by someone just as extreme, following Christ's simple, possession-free lifestyle. Nearing 50, Dominic made a 3,400-mile preaching tour—on foot, carrying his luggage—from Rome to Spain to Paris and back. Dominic is often portrayed with the star of revelation over his head.

Fra Bartolomeo—*St. Thomas Aquinas* (*San Tommaso d'Aquino*)

St. Thomas Aquinas (c. 1225–1274), the intellectual giant of the U. of Paris, used logic and Aristotelian models to defend and explain Christianity (building the hierarchical belief system known as Scholasticism). He's often shown with a heavy build and the sun of knowledge burning in his chest.

Fra Bartolomeo—*Portrait of Savonarola* (*Ritratto di Fra Girolamo Savonarola*)

This is the famous portrait—in profile, hooded, with big nose and clear eyes, gazing intently into the darkness—of the man reviled as the evil opponent of Renaissance goodness. Would it surprise you to learn that it was Savonarola who inspired Fra Bartolomeo's art? Bartolomeo was so moved by Savonarola's sermons that he burned his early nude paintings (and back issues of *Penthouse*), became a monk, gave up painting for a few years...then resurfaced to paint the simple, sweet frescoes we see here.

• *Leaving the world of Fra Bartolomeo, return to the courtyard and continue to the next room (Capitolo), which contains the large wall fresco...*

Fra Angelico—*Crucifixion with Saints* (*Crocifissione dell' Angelico*)

Shortly after the Fiesole monks moved into their new digs here (c. 1440), Fra Angelico began decorating the walls with frescoes. This crucifixion, against a bleak background, is one of more than 20 versions in the monastery of Christ's torture/execution. It was in this room that naughty monks were examined and judged.

Among the group of hermits, martyrs, and religious extremists that surround the cross, locate Dominic (kneeling at the foot of the cross, in Dominican white robe, blue cape, and tonsured hair, with star on head), Peter the Martyr (kneeling in right corner, with bloody head), and Thomas Aquinas (standing behind Peter, with jowls and sun on chest).

The bell in the room is the original church bell, the one that rang a warning to Savonarola the night he was arrested. (The mob was so enraged that they exiled the bell for 10 years.)

• *Head upstairs to the first floor.*

FIRST FLOOR

• *At the top of the stairs, you come face to face with Fra Angelico's* Annunciation *fresco (pictured on page 30). Get oriented from here. A few steps to the left is a corridor lined with "cells" (monks' bedrooms) decorated with frescoes by Fra Angelico.*

Stretching to the right are more cells (by Fra Angelico and assistants) and the library, displaying old manuscripts. In the far corner (not visible from here, reached by circling clockwise) is Savonarola's cell.

Fra Angelico—*The Annunciation*
Monks gathered in this corner for common prayers, contemplating Christ's life from beginning *(The Annunciation)* to end (the *Crucifixion with St. Dominic,* over your shoulder).

The angel with rainbow wings (sway back and forth and watch them sparkle) greets Mary under an arcade remarkably similar to the one in the monastery courtyard, literally bringing this scene home to unimaginative monks. It was paintings such as this that made Fra Angelico so famous that the pope would call him to paint the Vatican. Yet this, like the other frescoes here, was meant only for the private eyes of humble monks.

• *From* The Annunciation, *take a few steps to the left and look down the (east) corridor lined with cells.*

Fra Angelico's frescoes (in monks' cells of the east corridor)
After a long day of prayer, meditation, reading, frugal meals, chopping wood, hauling water, translating Greek, attending Mass, and more prayer—a monk retired to one of these small, bare, lamplit rooms. His "late-night TV" was programmed by the prior—Fra Angelico—in the form of a fresco to meditate on before sleep.

All in all, 43 cells were decorated in the early 1440s under Fra Angelico's direction, but many were executed by assistants. Some of Fra Angelico's best work is found in the 10 cells along the left-hand side.

San Marco—First Floor

STAIRS UP FROM GROUND FLOOR

LIBRARY

ANNUNCIATION →

FRA ANGELICO FRESCOES

CLOISTER (BELOW)

SAVONAROLA'S CELLS & POSSESSIONS

DCH

❶ ❷ ❸ ❹ ❺ ❻ ❼ ❽ ❾ ❿

⓮ ⓭ ⓫
⓬

❶ Noli me Tangere
❷ Lamentation
❸ Annunciation
❹ Crucifixion
❺ Birth of Jesus
❻ Transfiguration
❼ The Mocking of Christ
❽ The Empty Tomb
❾ Mary Crowned
❿ Presentation in the Temple
⓫-⓮ Savonarola's Cells

Cell ❶—*Noli me Tangere* (the first of 10 rooms on the left-hand side of the corridor): The resurrected Jesus, appearing as a hoe-carrying

gardener, says "Don't touch me," and gingerly sidesteps Mary Magdalene's grasp. The flowers and trees represent the blossoming of new life, and they're about the last we'll see. Most scenes have stark, bare backgrounds, to concentrate the monk's focus on just the essential subject.

Cell ❷—Lamentation: Christ and mourners are a reverse image of the *Lamentation* downstairs. Christ levitates, not really supported by the ladies' laps. The colors are muted grays, browns, and pinks. Dominic (star on head) stands contemplating, just as the monk should do by mentally transporting himself to the scene.

Cell ❸—Annunciation: The painting's arches echo the room's real arch. (And they, in turn, harmoniously "frame" the "arch" of Mary and the angel bending toward each other to talk.) Peter the Martyr (bloody head) looks on.

You can't call these cells a wrap until you've found at least six crosses, three Dominics, three Peters, and a Thomas Aquinas. Ready, go.

Cell ❹—Crucifixion: That's one. And another Dominic.

Cell ❺—Birth of Jesus: And there's your second Peter.

Cell ❻—Transfiguration: Forsaking Renaissance realism, Fra Angelico emphasizes the miraculous. In an aura of blinding light, Christ spreads his arms cross-like, dazzling the three witnesses at the bottom of the "mountain." He's joined by disembodied heads of prophets, all spinning in a circle echoed by the room's arch.

Cell ❼—The Mocking of Christ: From Renaissance realism to Dalí surrealism. Dominic, while reading the Passion, conjures an image of Christ—the true king, on a throne with globe and scepter—now blindfolded, spit upon, slapped, and clubbed by...a painting of medieval symbols of torment. This must have been a puzzling riddle from the Master to a novice monk.

Cell ❽—The Empty Tomb: The worried women are reassured by an angel that "He is risen." Jesus, far away in the clouds, seems annoyed that they didn't listen to him.

Cell ❾—*Mary Crowned:*...triumphantly in Heaven, while Dominic, Peter, Aquinas, Francis, and others prepare to celebrate with high-fives.

Cell ❿—*Presentation in the Temple:* Baby Jesus is swaddled like a mummy. And there's your final Peter.
• *Continue around the bend—Savonarola's three rooms are at the far end of the corridor. Stop at the last room on the right in the corridor.*

Girolamo Savonarola (1452–1498)— His Rooms and Possessions *(Celle del Savonarola)*

⓫–⓮—Savonarola's Cells
You'll find a number of Savonarola's possessions scattered about this room and the adjacent cluster of three rooms, his living quarters. Browse around while reading about his life.

Last Room in the Corridor
The room displays Savonarola's **blue cloak** and personal **crucifix.** Home-schooled by his Scholastic grandfather, the 22-year-old had his life changed by hearing a sermon on repentance. He traded his scholar's robes for the blue cloak of a simple Dominican monk. He quickly became known for his asceticism, devotion, and knowledge of the Bible.
• *Now enter the* Celle del Savonarola.

First Room of Savonarola's Living Quarters
The **portrait bust** shows the hooded monk whose personal charisma and prophetic fervor led him from humble scholar to celebrity preacher to prior of San Marco to leader of Florence to controversial martyrdom. The **relief** under the portrait bust shows Savonarola at his greatest moment. He stands before the Florence city council and pledges allegiance to Florence's constitution, assuming control of the city after the exile of the Medici (1494). Reviled as a fanatical, regressive tyrant and praised as a saint, reformer, and champion of democracy, Savonarola was a complex man in turbulent times.

Various **paintings** show Savonarola in action, including one by Federico Andreotti with Savonarola reproaching two troublemakers in his study.
• *The next room is...*

Savonarola's Study *(Studiolo)*
Seated at this **desk,** in his ecclesiastical folding **chair** *(La sedia del Savonarola),* Savonarola scoured his **Bible** for clues to solve Florence's civic strife.

In 1482 at age 30, the monk had come to San Marco as a lecturer. He was bright, humble...and boring. Then, after experiencing divine revelations, he spiced his sermons with prophecies of future events...which started coming true. His sermons on Ezekiel, Amos, Exodus, and the Apocalypse predicted doom for the Medici family. He made brazen references to the pope's embezzling and stable of mistresses, and preached hope for a glorious future after city and church were cleansed.

Packed houses heard him rail against the "prostitute church...the monster of abomination." Witnesses wrote that "the church echoed with weeping and wailing," and afterward "everyone wandered the city streets dazed and speechless." From this humble desk, he corresponded with the worldly pope, the humanist Pico della Mirandola, and fans, such as Lorenzo the Magnificent, who begrudgingly admired his courage.

Lorenzo died, the bankrupt Medicis were exiled, and Florence was invaded by France...as Savonarola had prophesied. In the power vacuum, Savonarola was seen as a moderate voice who championed a return to Florence's traditional constitution. He was made head of a Christian commonwealth.

Room with Savonarola's Possessions
(Le Reliquie di Savonarola)

Savonarola's personal moral authority was unquestioned, as his simple **wool clothes** and **rosary** attest.

At first, his rule was just. He cut taxes, reduced street crime, shifted power from rich Medicis to citizens, and even boldly proposed banning Vespas from tourist zones.

However, Savonarola had an uncompromising and fanatical side, as his **hair-shirt girdle** attests. His government passed strict morality laws against swearing, blasphemy, gambling, and ostentatious clothes, which were enforced by gangs of thuggish teenagers. At the height of the Christian Republic, during Lent of 1497, followers built a huge "bonfire of vanities" on the Piazza della Signoria where they threw wigs, carnival masks, dice, playing cards, musical instruments, and discredited books and paintings.

In 1498 several forces undermined Savonarola's Republic: scheming Medici, crop failure, rival cities, a pissed-off pope threatening excommunication for Savonarola and political isolation for Florence, and a public tiring of puritanism. Gangs of opponents (called *Arrabbiati*, Rabid Dogs) battled Savonarola's supporters (the "Weepers"). Meanwhile, Savonarola was slowly easing out of public life, refusing to embroil the church in a lengthy trial, retiring to his routine of study, prayer, and personal austerity.

During Lent, a Franciscan monk challenged a Dominican to a public ordeal by fire to prove Savonarola right or wrong. (The righteous one would supposedly survive.) The Franciscan chickened out, but a bloodthirsty mob—with the blessing of city leaders and the pope—marched on San Marco to arrest Savonarola. *Arrabbiati* fought monks with clubs (imagine it in the **courtyard** out the window), while the church bells clanged and the monks shouted, *"Salvum fac populum tuum, Domine!"* ("Save thy people, Lord!"). The Arrabbiati stormed up the stairs to this floor, and Savonarola was

handed over to the authorities in the library doorway (back near Fra Angelico's *Annunciation,* where you can also see the appropriate *Kiss of Judas* fresco in the cell nearby). He was taken to Palazzo Vecchio, tortured, tried, and sentenced.

On May 23, 1498 (see the **painting** *Suplizio del Savonarola in Piazza della Signoria*), before a huge crowd in the square in front of the Palazzo Vecchio (where today there's a memorial plaque embedded in the pavement in front of the Neptune fountain), Savonarola was publicly defrocked, then publicly forgiven by a papal emissary. Then he was hanged—not American execution–style, where the neck snaps—but slowly strangled, dangling from a rope, while teenage boys hooted and threw rocks.

The crowd looked on the lifeless body of this man who had once captivated their minds, as they lit a pyre under the scaffold— see the **stick** *(palo)* from the fire. The flames rose up, engulfing the body, when suddenly...his arm shot upward!—like a final blessing or curse—and the terrified crowd stampeded, killing several. His ashes were thrown in the Arno.

The Rest of the Museum

The corridor near Fra Angelico's *Annuniciation* has the Library, with music and other manuscripts. In a cell across the hall is Fra Angelico's *Kiss of Judas* fresco. At the end of the corridor (right side) are the Cells of Cosimo de' Medici, the founder of the Medici ruling dynasty and builder of this monastery. Inside, the painting of the Magi includes a kneeling Magus kissing the baby's feet—a portrait of Cosimo.

• *To exit, return to the stairway and descend. Take a right at the bottom into a bookshop decorated with a fine Ghirlandaio* Last Supper *fresco (are you as tired as John is?), then exit. On the street, turn right, then right again, and you'll see the Duomo.*

DUOMO MUSEUM TOUR

(Museo dell' Opera del Duomo)

Brunelleschi's dome, Ghiberti's bronze doors, and Donatello's statues—these three define the 1400s in Florence (the "Quattrocento"), when the city blossomed and classical arts were reborn. All three are featured at the Duomo Museum, plus a Michelangelo *Pietà* intended as his sculptural epitaph. While copies now decorate the exteriors of the cathedral, Baptistery, and bell tower, the original sculptured masterpieces of the complex are now restored and displayed safely indoors, filling the Duomo Museum. This newly refurbished museum is a delight that most visitors to Florence overlook.

ORIENTATION

Cost: €6.

Hours: Mon–Sat 9:00–19:30, Sun 9:00–13:40, closed on holidays. Last entry 40 minutes before closing. (This is one of the few museums in Florence open on Monday.)

Getting There: The museum is across the street from the Duomo on the east side, at Via del Proconsolo 9.

Information: Tel. 055-230-2885. If you find all this church art intriguing, look through the open doorway of the Duomo art studio, which has been making and restoring church art since the days of Brunelleschi (a block toward the river from the Duomo at 23a Via dello Studio).

Length of This Tour: 90 minutes.

Starring: Brunelleschi, Ghiberti, Donatello, and Michelangelo.

THE TOUR BEGINS

Ghiberti's doors are on the ground floor, while Donatello's statues are on the first floor. The *Pietà* is on a landing halfway between floors.

Duomo Museum—Ground Floor

❶ Roman, Etruscan,
   Baptistery Fragments

❷ Madonna
   with the Glass Eyes

❸ Pope Boniface VIII

❹ DONATELLO –
   St. John the Evangelist

❺ Room of Altarpieces
   & Reliquaries

❻ GHIBERTI – Bronze
   Baptistery Panels

❼ MICHELANGELO –
   Pietà (on mezzanine)

GROUND FLOOR

The Medieval Cathedral

• *Browse the first few small rooms.*

Roman sarcophagi, Etruscan fragments, a chronological chart, and broken **Baptistery statues** attest to the 2,000-year history of Florence's cathedral, Baptistery, and campanile (bell tower, called Giotto's Tower). The Baptistery was likely built on the site of a

pagan Roman temple. It was flanked by a humble church that, by the 1200s, was not big enough to contain the exuberant spirit of a city growing rich from the wool trade and banking. In 1296, the cornerstone was laid for a huge church—today's cathedral, or Duomo—intended to be the biggest in Christendom.

• *The first large room (with a pope sitting at one end) is lined with statues from the original facade. On the long wall you'll find...*

Madonna with the Glass Eyes (Madonna col Bambino)

The church was dedicated to Mary—starry-eyed over the birth of baby Jesus—who sat, crowned like a chess-set queen, above the main

door, framed with a dazzling mosaic halo. She's accompanied (to our right) by St. Zenobius, Florence's first bishop during Roman times, whose raised hand consecrates the former pagan ground as Christian.

This room displays the statues that sat in niches on the original facade (1296–1587), designed by the church's architect, Arnolfo di Cambio. The facade looked much like today's colorful neo-Gothic facade, with white, pink, and green marble, pointed arches, three horizontal stories, gleaming with gold mosaics, and studded with the statues in this room.

But only the ground story was ever finished, the work stalled by the plague, stylistic debates, and the construction of the cathedral itself. The upper two-thirds remained bare brown brick all through medieval and Renaissance times, until 1587, when the still-incomplete facade was torn down.

Large, Seated Statue of Pope Boniface VIII

Despised by Dante for meddling in politics, this pope paid 3,000 florins to get his image in a box seat on the facade. His XL shirt size made him look correct when viewed from below. Though the statue is stylized, Arnolfo di Cambio realistically shows the pope's custom-made, extra-tall hat and bony face. (Most of the room's statues are straight-backed to hang on the facade.)

• *On the long wall opposite the Madonna, find...*

Donatello—St. John the Evangelist (San Giovanni Evangelista)

A hundred years later, di Cambio's medieval facade became a showcase for Renaissance sculptors.

John sits gazing at a distant horizon, his tall head rising high above the massive body. This visionary foresees a new age...and the coming Renaissance. The right hand is massive—as relaxed as though it were dangling over the back of a chair, but full of powerful tension. With the powerful right hand of Michelangelo's *David*, and the beard of Michelangelo's *Moses*, this work is a hundred years ahead of its time.

At 22 years old, Donatello (c. 1386–1466) sculpted this just before becoming a celebrity for his Rebirth-inducing statue of *St. George* (original in Bargello, copy on exterior of the Orsanmichele Church). Donatello, like most early Renaissance artists, was a blue-collar worker, raised as a workshop apprentice among knuckle-dragging muscle-men. He proudly combined physical skill with technical know-how to create beauty (Art + Science = Renaissance Beauty). His statues are thinkers with big hands who can put theory into practice.

• *Up a few steps at the end of the room is a...*

Room of Altarpieces and Reliquaries

These medieval altarpieces, which once adorned chapels and altars inside the Duomo, show saints and angels suspended in a gold never-never land. In the adjoining room, the ornate reliquaries hold bones and objects of the saints (Peter's chains, Jerome's jawbone, and so on), many bought from a single, slick 14th-century con artist preying on medieval superstition.

In the 1400s, tastes changed, and these symbols of crude, superstitious medievalism were purged from the Duomo and stacked in storage. Soon artists replaced the golden heavenly scenes with flesh-and-blood humans inhabiting the physical world of rocks, trees, and sky...the Renaissance.

• *In the ground-floor courtyard, you'll find...*

Ghiberti—Eight Bronze Panels from the Baptistery Doors Called the "Gates of Paradise" (1425–1452)

The Renaissance began in 1401 with a citywide competition to build new doors for the Baptistery. Lorenzo Ghiberti (c. 1378–1455) won the job and built the doors (now on the Baptistery's north side), which everyone loved. He then was hired to make another set of doors—these panels—for the main entrance facing the Duomo. These "Gates of Paradise" revolutionized the way Renaissance people saw the world around them.

Of the 10 panels from the Gates of Paradise, the museum displays eight, as the rest are still being cleaned. (Copies now adorn the Baptistery itself.) Restoration is difficult, because the corrosive oxides gather inside, between the bronze panel and gilding. (Even these cleaned panels are pitted and blotched.) The panels are under glass to protect against natural light, and gassed with nitrogen against oxygen and humidity.

Joseph
(Storie di Giuseppe e Beniamino)

With just the depth of a thumbnail, Ghiberti creates a temple in the round inhabited by workers. This round temple wowed Florence. Armed with the rules of perspective, Ghiberti rendered reality with a mathematical precision we don't normally notice in everyday life, when our eyes and mind settle for ballpark estimates. For Florentines, suddenly the world acquired a whole new dimension—depth.

Adam and Eve (La Creazione e Storie di Adamo ed Eva)

Ghiberti tells several stories in one panel—a common medieval technique—using different thickness in the relief. In the sketchy back-

ground (very low relief), God in a bubble conducts the Creation. In the center (a little thicker), Eve springs from Adam's side. Finally, in the lower left (in high relief), an elegantly robed God pulls Adam, as naked as the day he was born, from the mud.

Ghiberti welcomed the innovations of other artists. See the angel flying through an arch (right side). This arch is in very low relief but still looks fully 3-D because it's rendered sideways, using painters'-perspective tricks—a relief technique Ghiberti learned from one of his employees, the young Donatello.

Jacob and Esau
(Storie di Giacobbe ed Esau)

The "background" arches and the space they create are as interesting as the scenes themselves. At the center is the "vanishing point" on the distant horizon, where all the arches and floor tiles converge. This calm center gives us an eye-level reference point for all the figures. Those closest to us are big, clearly defined, and at the bottom of the panel. Distant figures are smaller, fuzzier, and higher up.

Ghiberti has placed us about 20 feet away from the scene, part of this casual crowd of holy people—some with their backs to us—milling around an arcade.

Labors of Adam, and Cain and Abel
(Il lavoro dei progenitori e Storie di Caino e Abele)
On one mountain, we see Cain and Abel offering a sacrifice at the top, Adam waving at the bottom, and the first murder in between. In

early panels such as this one, Ghiberti used only a sketchy landscape as a backdrop for human activities.

Ghiberti, the illegitimate son of a goldsmith, labored all his working life (over 50 years) on the two Baptistery doors. These were major manufacturing jobs, employing a large workshop of artists and artisans for each stage of the process: making the door frames that hold the panels, designing and making models of the panels, casting the design in bronze, gilding the panels (by bathing them in powdered gold dissolved in mercury, then heating until the gold and bronze blended), polishing the panels, mounting them, installing the doors...and signing paychecks for everyone along the way. Ghiberti was as much businessman as artist.

Solomon and the Queen of Sheba
The receding arches stretch into infinity, giving the airy feeling we could see forever. All the arches and stair steps converge at the center of the panel, where the two monarchs meet, uniting their respective peoples. Ghiberti's subject was likely influenced by the warm ecumenical breeze blowing through Florence in 1439, as religious leaders convened here in an attempt to reunite the eastern

(Constantinople) and western (Rome) realms of Christendom.

If the Renaissance began in 1401 with Ghiberti's doors, it ended in 1555 with Michelangelo's *Pietà*.

• *In the courtyard are two staircases almost side by side. Ascend the old (not new) staircase to the first landing.*

Michelangelo—*Pietà* (1547–1555)

Eighty-year-old Michelangelo (1475–1564) was designing his own tomb, with this as the centerpiece. He was depressed by old age, the recent death of his soul mate, and the grim reality that sculpting this statue was writing his own obituary.

The broken body of the crucified Christ is tended by three mourners—Mary, his mother (the shadowy figure on our right); Mary Magdalene (on the left, polished up by a pupil); and Nicodemus, the converted Pharisee, whose face is clearly that of Michelangelo himself. The polished body of Christ stands out from the unfinished background. Michelangelo (as Nicodemus), who spent a lifetime bringing statues to life by "freeing" them from the stone, looks down at what could be his final creation, the once-perfect body of Renaissance Man that is now twisted, disfigured, and dead.

Seen face-on, the four figures form a powerful geometric shape of a circle inside a triangle, split down the middle by Christ's massive but very dead arm. Seen from the right side, they seem to interact with each other, their sketchy faces changing emotions from grief to melancholy to peaceful acceptance.

Fifty years earlier, a confident Michelangelo had worked here on these very premises, skillfully carving *David* from an imperfect block. But he hated this marble for the *Pietà*; it was hard and grainy and gave off sparks when hit wrong. (The chisel grooves in the base remind us of the sheer physical effort of a senior citizen sculpting.) Worst of all, his housekeeper kept bugging him with the same question that Pope Julius II used to ask about the Sistine Chapel—"When will you finish?" Pushed to the edge, Michelangelo grabbed a hammer and attacked the statue, hacking away and breaking off limbs, then turned to the servant and said, "There! It's finished!" (An assistant later repaired some of the damage, but cracks are still visible in Christ's left arm and only leg.)

• *Continue upstairs to the first floor, entering a large room lined with statues and two balconies. Donatello's four prophets are at the far end.*

FIRST FLOOR

Room of the Cantorie *(Le Cantorie)*— Donatello's Prophets

The room displays the original 16 statues (by several sculptors) that ring the bell tower's third story (where copies stand today).

Duomo Museum—First Floor

❽ DONATELLO –
   Habakkuk and Jeremiah

❾ PISANO'S 4 Prophets

❿ DELLA ROBBIA – Cantoria

⓫ "Lamb of God" Panel

⓬ DONATELLO – Cantoria

⓭ DONATELLO –
   Mary Magdalene

⓮ Medieval Crucifix

⓯ John the Baptist's Finger

⓰ PISANO (& Others) –
   Campanile Panels

⓱ BRUNELLESCHI –
   Dome Model, Death Mask,
   Scaffolding, Tools

⓲ MICHELANGELO –
   Balcony Models

⓳ Facade Models

⓴ Laying of 1860 Facade

㉑ Emilio de Fabris & Designs

Donatello did five of them, plus some others in collaboration.

Donatello ("Little Donato") invented the Renaissance style that Michelangelo would later perfect—powerful statues that are ultra-realistic, even ugly, sculpted in an "unfinished" style by an artist known for experimentation and a prickly, brooding personality, who was famous but lived like a peasant, married only to his work.

Donatello—*Habakkuk (Abacuc)*

Donatello's signature piece shows us the wiry man beneath the heavy mantle of a prophet. His rumpled cloak falls down the front, dividing the body lengthwise. From the deep furrows emerges a bare arm with well-defined tendons and that powerful right hand. His long, muscled neck leads to a bald, squash-like head (the Italians call the statue *Lo Zuccone*).

The ugly face, with several days' growth of beard, crossed eyes, and tongue-tied mouth, looks crazed. This is no confident Charlton Heston prophet, but a man who's spent too much time alone, fasting in the wilderness, searching for his calling, and who now returns to babble his vision on a street corner.

Donatello, the eccentric prophet of a new style, identified with this statue, talking to it, swearing at it, yelling at it: "Speak!"

• *Nearby, look for...*

Donatello—*Jeremiah (Geremia)*

Watching Jerusalem burn in the distance, the ignored prophet reflects on why the Israelites wouldn't listen to his warning. He purses his lips bitterly, and his downturned mouth is accentuated by his plunging neck muscle and sagging shoulders. The folds in the clothes are very deep, suggesting the anger, sorrow, and disgust that Jeremiah feels but cannot share, as it is too late.

Movement, realism, and human drama were Donatello's great contributions to sculpture.

• *Along the long, left-hand wall are four dark-stained statues.*

Andrea and Nino Pisano's Four Prophets

Pisano's prophets are elegant but smaller and two-dimensional, with flat backs to stand obediently in their niches. The faces are generic and calm. Little wonder that these stuffy prophets were replaced on the bell tower by Donatello's younger and more energetic *Habakkuk* and *Jeremiah*.

• *The two balconies in Room 12 are the Cantorie—Donatello's on the right (from the entrance), della Robbia's on the left. Della Robbia's is a reconstruction from casts, with the original 10 panels below.*

Luca della Robbia—*Cantoria* (1431–1438)

After almost 150 years of construction, the cathedral was nearly done, and they began preparing the interior for the celebration. Brunelleschi hired a little-known sculptor, 30-year-old Luca della Robbia, to make this choir box—a balcony for singers next to the organ in the cathedral—and it summed up the exuberance of the Quattrocento. The panels are a celebration of music, song, and dance performed by toddlers, children, and teenagers.

The *cantoria* brings Psalm 150 to life like an MTV video. Latin speakers can read the text, while the rest can follow along with the pictures. Start in the upper left:

"Praise the Lord" *(Laudate D.N.M)*, reads the banner along the top. "Praise him in his holy place, in the firmament *(Firmamento)* for his mighty deeds *(Virtu)* and greatness *(Magnitudinus)*." Then come the panels:

1. (Upper left panel): Teenagers laugh and dance to the sound of trumpets, as the text reads "Praise with the sound of trumpets" *(sono Tubae)*.

2. and 3. Babysitters put down infants and pick up guitars and autoharps ("Praise him with psalter and zither," *Psaltero et Cythera)*.

4. "... Praise him with tambourines..." *(Timpano)*

5. "...and dancing" *(Choro)*. Seven kids dance ring-around-the-rosy as della Robbia sculpts a scene in the round on an almost-flat surface, showing front, back, and in-between poses.

6. "...with pipes and strings" *(Organo)*. A child Apollo pumps a hand organ.

7. "...and with jubilant cymbals" *(Cimbales)*. The kids make a joyful racket. "Everybody praise the Lord!"

Della Robbia's choir box was a triumph, a celebration of Florence's youthful boom time. Perhaps sensing he could never top it, the young sculptor hung up his hammer and chisel and concentrated on the colorful glazed terra-cotta for which he's best known. (Find the **round "Lamb of God" panel** over your left shoulder, above a doorway nearby, by Luca's nephew, who took over the workshop.)

Donatello—*Cantoria*

If della Robbia's balcony looks like afternoon recess, Donatello's is an all-night rave. Donatello's figures are sketchier, murky, and filled with frenetic activity, as the dancing kids hurl themselves around the balcony.

Recently returned from a trip to Rome, Donatello carved in the style of classical friezes of dancing *putti* (chubby, playful toddlers).

This choir box stood in a dark area of the Duomo, so Donatello chose colorful mosaics and marbles to catch the eye, while purposely leaving the dancers unfinished, shadowy, tangled figures flitting inside the columns. In the dim light, worshipers swore they saw them move.

• *Enter an adjoining room full of bishops' robes, a half-ton silver altarpiece, and...*

Donatello—*Mary Magdalene (Maddalena)*

Carved out of white poplar, originally painted with realistic colors (like the **medieval crucifix** displayed nearby), this statue is less a Renaissance work of beauty than a medieval object of intense devotion.

Mary Magdalene—the legendary prostitute rescued from the streets by Jesus—folds her hands in humble prayer. Her once-beautiful face and body have been scarred by the fires of her own remorse, fasting, and repentance. The matted hair sticks to her face; veins and tendons line the anorexic arms and neck. The rippling animal-skin dress and hair suggest emotional turmoil within. But from her hollow, tired eyes, a new beauty shines, an enlightened soul that doesn't rely on the external beauty of human flesh.

The man who helped re-birth the classical style now shocked Florence by turning his back on it. Picking up a knife, he experimented in the difficult medium of wood carving, where subtlety can get lost when the wood splits off in larger-than-wanted slivers.

Sixty-five-year-old Donatello had just returned to Florence, after years away. His city had changed. Friends were dying (Brunelleschi died before they could reconcile after a bitter fight), favorite pubs were overrun with frat boys, and Florence was gaga over Greek gods in pretty, gleaming marble. Donatello fell into a five-year funk, completing only two statues, including this one.

• *In the display case to the left of* Mary, *you'll find...*

John the Baptist's Finger in a Reliquary (*Artista fiorentino: Reliquario di un osso di dito di S. Giovanni Battista*)

The severed index finger of the beheaded prophet is the most revered relic of all the holy body parts in this museum.

Pop. 100,000... but Still a Small Town

Ghiberti won the bronze-door competition. Brunelleschi lost and took teenage Donatello with him to Rome. Donatello returned to join Ghiberti's workshop. Ghiberti helped Brunelleschi with dome plans. Brunelleschi, Donatello, and Luca della Robbia collaborated on the Pazzi Chapel. And so on, and so on.

• *Pass back through the large room of the Cantorie and into the next room. Work clockwise from the entrance.*

Andrea Pisano (and others)—*The Campanile Panels* (c. 1334–1359)

These 28 hexagonal and 28 diamond-shaped, blue-glazed panels decorated Giotto's Tower, seven per side (where copies stand today).

The original design scheme was perhaps Giotto's, but most were executed by his successor, Andrea Pisano, and assistants.

The panels celebrate technology, showing workers, inventors, and thinkers. Allegorically, they depict man's long march to "civilization"—a blend of art and science, brain and brawn. But realistically, they're snapshots of that industrious generation that helped Florence bounce back ferociously from the Black Death of 1347–1348.

The lower, **hexagonal panels** (reading clockwise from the entrance) show God starting the chain of creation by inventing (1) man and (2) woman, then (3) Adam and Eve continuing the work, (4) Jabal learning to domesticate sheep, (5) Jubal blowing a horn, inventing music...

• *Continuing along the next wall...*

(6) Tubalcain the blacksmith, and (7) Noah inventing wine and Miller Time. (8) An astronomer sights along a quadrant to chart the heavens and the (round, tilted-on-axis, pre-Columbus) Earth, (9) a master builder supervises his little apprentices building a brick wall, (10) a doctor holds a flask of urine to the light for analysis, etc.

• *On the fourth wall, check out...*

(20) The invention of sculpture, as a man chisels a figure to life.

The upper **diamond-shaped panels,** of marble on blue majolica (tin-glazed pottery tinged blue with copper sulfate), add religion (Sacraments and Virtues) to the civilization equation.

• *Enter the next, narrow room to find tools, scaffolding, and, at the end of the corridor, a wooden model of the cathedral dome's lantern.*

Brunelleschi's Dome—*Model of the Lantern* (*Cupola di S. Maria del Fiore*)

Brunelleschi's dome (look at this model of the dome, or out the window at the real thing) put mathematics in stone, a feat of engineering that was functional and beautiful. It rises 330 feet from the ground, with eight white, pointed-arch ribs, filled in with red brick and capped with a "lantern" to hold it all in place.

The dome had to cover a gaping 140-foot hole in the roof of the church (a drag on rainy Sundays), a hole too wide to be spanned by the wooden scaffolding traditionally used to support a dome while it was being built. (An earlier architect suggested supporting the dome with a great mound of dirt inside the church...filled with coins, so peasants would later cart it away for free.) In addition, the eight-sided "drum" the dome was to rest on was too weak to support a heavy

dome, and there were no side buildings on the church on which to attach Gothic-style buttresses.

The solution was a dome within a dome, leaving a hollow space between to make it lighter. And the dome had to be self-supporting, both while being built and when finished, so as not to require buttresses.

Brunelleschi used wooden models such as these to demonstrate his ideas to skeptical approval committees.

• *In the display cases are scaffolding and tools.*

Scaffolding

Although no scaffolding supported the dome, they needed exterior scaffolding for the stone and brick masons. The support timbers were stuck into postholes in the drum (some are visible on the church today).

The dome rose in rings. First, they'd stack a few blocks of white marble to create part of the ribs, then connect the ribs with horizontal crosspieces, then fill in the space with red brick in a herringbone pattern. When the ring was complete and self-supporting, they'd move the scaffolding up and do another section.

Tools

The dome weighs 80 million pounds—as much as the entire population of Florence—so Brunelleschi had to design special tools and machines to lift and work all that stone. (The lantern alone—which caps the dome—is a marble building nearly as tall as the Baptistery.) You'll see sun-dried bricks, brick molds, rope, a tool belt, compasses, stone pincers, and various pulleys for lifting. Brunelleschi also designed a machine (not on display) where horses turned a shaft that reeled in rope, lifting heavy loads.

The dome was completed in 16 short years, capping 150 years of construction on the church. Brunelleschi enjoyed the dedication ceremonies, but died before the lantern was completed. His legacy is a dome that stands as a proud symbol of man's ingenuity, proving that art and science can unite to make beauty.

• *Next to the lantern model, find...*

Brunelleschi's Death Mask *(Anonimo: Maschera funebre)*

Filippo Brunelleschi (1377–1446) was uniquely qualified to create the dome. Trained in sculpture, he gave it up in disgust after losing

the Baptistery gig. In Rome, he visualized placing the Pantheon on top of the Duomo, and dissected its mathematics and engineering.

Back home, he astounded Florence with a super-realistic painting of the Baptistery, as seen from the Duomo's front steps. Florentines lined up to see the painting (now lost) displayed side by side with the real thing, marveling at the 3-D realism. (Brunelleschi's mathematics of linear perspective were later expanded and popularized by Alberti.)

In 1420 Brunelleschi was declared *capomaestro* of the dome project. He was a jack-of-all-trades and now master of all as well, overseeing every aspect of the dome, the lantern, and the machinery to build them. Despite all his planning, it's clear from documentary evidence that he was making it up as he went along, exuding confidence to workers and city officials while privately improvising.

• *In the next room, behind glass, you'll see...*

Two Wooden Models for the Duomo's Balcony

But the church wasn't done. Even today, there's bare brick on much of the drum at the base of the dome. In 1507 a competition was held to cover that brick with a marble balustrade. Baccio d'Agnolo won, and covered part of the southeast section before others with better taste stopped him.

• *The next room deals with...*

Facade from the 16th to the 19th Centuries

In 1587 the medieval facade by di Cambio was considered hopelessly outdated and was torn down like so much old linoleum. But work on a replacement never got off the ground, and the church front sat bare for nearly 300 years while they debated proposal after proposal (like the models in this room) by many famous architects. Most versions champion the Renaissance style to match Brunelleschi's dome rather than Gothic to fit the church.

• *Enter the next room.*

Laying of the First Stone of the Facade in 1860

In the 1800s, with the Romantic movement, there was a renaissance of the Gothic style (so to speak). In 1860 a ceremonial first stone was laid—using the hammer and trowel displayed here—by King Vittorio Emmanuel II, the future leader of a newly unified modern Italy.

• *In the last room...*

The 19th-Century Facade

Emilio de Fabris (portrait) won the competition with a neo-Gothic facade echoing the original work of di Cambio, and the new-old facade was dedicated in 1887. Notice that even de Fabris changed designs as he went—the spikes along the roofline in some of the designs are not there today.

Critics may charge that this facade is too retro, but it was the style of the church beloved by Ghiberti, Donatello, Brunelleschi, and the industrious citizens of Florence's Quattrocento, who saw it as Florence's finest art gallery.

MEDICI CHAPELS TOUR

(Cappelle Medicee)

The Medici (MED-ee-chee) Chapels contain tombs of Florence's great ruling family, from Lorenzo the Magnificent to those less so. The highlight is a chapel designed by Michelangelo at the height of his creative powers. This is the Renaissance Man's greatest "installation," a room completely under his artistic control, featuring innovative architecture, tombs, and sculpture. His statues are a middle-aged man's brooding meditation on mortality, the fall of the Medici Golden Age, and the relentless passage of time—from *Dawn* to *Day* to *Dusk* to *Night*.

ORIENTATION

Cost: €6.

Hours: Daily 8:15–16:50 but closed the second and fourth Sun and the first, third, and fifth Mon of each month.

Getting There: It's in the church of San Lorenzo—the one with the smaller dome on Florence's skyline (5-min walk northwest of Duomo). The bustling outdoor market almost obscures the chapel entrance at the back (west end) of the church.

Information: Tel. 055-238-8602.

Length of This Tour: One hour.

Photography: Not allowed.

Starring: Michelangelo's statues *Day, Night, Dawn,* and *Dusk.*

THE TOUR BEGINS

Overview

The Medici Chapels consist of three burial places: the unimpressive Crypt, the large and gaudy Chapel of Princes, and—the highlight—Michelangelo's New Sacristy, a room completely designed by him,

with architecture, tombs, and statues to honor four Medicis.
• *Buy tickets and enter at the back (west) end of the church of San Lorenzo. Immediately past the turnstile, you're in...*

The Crypt

This gloomy, low-ceilinged room with gravestones underfoot reminds us that these "chapels" are really tombs. You'll see lots of "Lorenzos" here (the family's patron saint)...but none that are "Magnificent" (he's later). Historians will search for the slab of **Cosimo the First** (look for "Cosmus Magnus Dux Etr" in the first chapel to right of entry), a shrewd banker and politician, grandfather of Lorenzo the Magnificent, and founder of the first Medici dynasty.
• *Head upstairs via either staircase into the large, domed, multicolored...*

Chapel of Princes
(La Cappella dei Principi, 1602–1743)

The impressive **dome** overhead (seen from outside, it's the big, red-brick "mini-Duomo") tops an octagonal room that echoes the Baptistery and Duomo drum. It's lined with six tombs of Medici rulers. It's decorated every-where with the **Medici coat of arms**—a shield with six balls representing the pills of doctors *(medici)*, their original occupation. Along with many different colored marbles, geologists will recognize jasper, porphyry, quartz, alabaster, coral, mother-of-pearl, and lapis lazuli.

Sixteen shields ring the room at eye level, the Tuscan cities ("Civitas") ruled by Florence's dukes. Find Florence, with its fleur-de-lis ("Florentiae"), and Pisa ("Pisarum"), both just left of the altar.

The bronze **statues** honor two of the "later" Medicis (1531–1743), the cultured but oppressive dukes who ruled Florence after

the city's glorious Renaissance. Ferdinando I (ruled 1587–1609), in ermine cape and jewels, started the work on this Chapel of Princes and tore down the Duomo's medieval facade. His son, Cosimo II (ruled 1609–1621, to the right), appointed Galileo "first professor" of science at Pisa U., inspiring him to label the moons of Jupiter "the Medici Stars."

Apart from the **altar,** finished in 1939 for a visit from Hitler and Mussolini, there is no Christian

New Sacristy

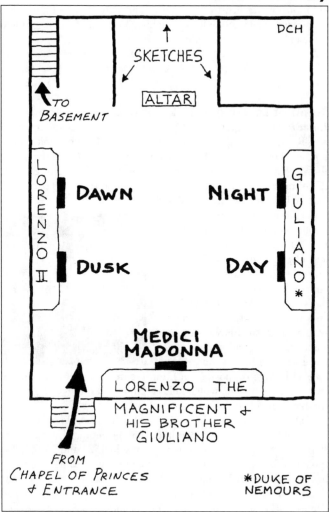

symbolism in this spacious but stifling temple to power, wealth, and mediocre Medicis.

• *Continue down the hall, passing statues of Roman armor with worms sprouting out, to Michelangelo's New Sacristy.*

New Sacristy (Sagrestia Nuova)—Michelangelo

The entire room—architecture, tombs, and statues—was designed by Michelangelo (1520–34) to house the bodies of four of the Medici family. Michelangelo, who spent his teen years in the Medici household and personally knew three of the four buried here, was emotionally attached to the project. This is the work of a middle-aged man (age 45–59) reflecting on his contemporaries dying around him, and on his own mortality.

• *There are tombs decorated with statues against three of the walls, and an altar on the fourth. Start with the tomb on the left wall (as you enter and face the altar).*

Tomb of Lorenzo II, Duke of Urbino

Lorenzo II—the grandson of Lorenzo the Magnificent—is shown as a Roman general, seated, arm resting on a Medici-bank money box, and bowing his head in contemplation. He had been the model for Machiavelli's *The Prince*, and when he died without a male heir at 27 (of tuberculosis and syphilis), the line of great princes stretching back to Cosimo the Elder died with him.

His sarcophagus, with a curved, scrolled lid, bears the reclining statues that Michelangelo named *Dusk* and *Dawn*. **Dusk** (the man), worn out after a long day, slumps his chin on his chest and reflects on the day's events. **Dawn** (the woman) stirs restlessly after a long night, with an anguished face, as though waking from a bad dream. *Dusk* and *Dawn*, with their counterparts
Day and *Night* (opposite wall), represented to Michelangelo the swift passage of time, which kills everyone and causes our glorious deeds on earth to quickly fade.

During the 14 years he worked here, Michelangelo suffered the deaths of his father, favorite brother, and his unofficial stepbrother, Pope Leo X Medici. In addition, plagues in 1522 and 1527 killed thousands in Florence. In 1527 his adoptive city of Rome was looted by mercenaries. Michelangelo's letters reveal that, turning 50, he was feeling old, tired ("If I work one day, I need four to recuperate"), and depressed (he called it *mio pazzo*, "my madness"), facing the sad fact that the masterpiece of his youth—the grand tomb of Pope Julius II—was never going to be completed.

Overachievers in severe midlife crises may wish to avoid the Medici Chapels.

• *On the opposite wall...*

Tomb of Giuliano, Duke of Nemours

Overshadowed by his famous father (Lorenzo the Magnificent) and big brother (Pope Leo X), **Giuliano** led a wine-women-and-song life, dying young without a male heir. His statue as a Roman general, with scepter, powerful Moses-esque pose, and alert, intelligent face, looks in the direction of the Madonna statue, as though asking forgiveness for a wasted life. The likeness is not at all accurate. Michelangelo said, "In a thousand years, no one will know how they looked."

Giuliano's "active" pose complements the "contemplative" one of Lorenzo, showing the two elements (thought + action) that Plato and Michelangelo believed made up the soul of man.

Night (the woman) does a crossover sit-up in her sleep, toning the fleshy abs that look marvelously supple and waxlike, not like hard stone. She's highly polished, shimmering, and finished with minute details. Michelangelo's females—musclemen with coconut-shell breasts—are generally more complete and (some think) less interesting than his men.

Theories abound that Michelangelo was homosexual. While his private sex life (or lack thereof) ultimately remains a mystery, his public expressions of affection were clearly weighted toward men. Some say he was less interested in female bodies and felt he could easily sum them up in a statue.

Day (the man) works out a crick in his back, each limb twisting a different direction, turning away from us. He looks over his shoulder with an expression (suspicious? angry? arrogant?) forever veiled behind chisel marks suggestive of Impressionist brush strokes. In fact, none of the four reclining statues' faces expresses a clear emotion, as all are turned inward, letting body language speak.

If, as some say, Michelangelo purposely left these statues "unfinished" while liberating them from their stone prison, it certainly adds mystery and a contrast in color and texture. *Night*'s moonlit clarity and *Day*'s rough-hewn grogginess may also reflect Michelangelo's own work schedule—a notorious day-sleeper and guilt-ridden layabout ("Dear to me is sleep") who, when inspired (as a friend wrote), "works much, eats little, and sleeps less."

Among *Night*'s symbols (the crescent moon on her forehead, owl under knee, and poppies underfoot) is a grotesque **mask** with, perhaps, a self-portrait. Michelangelo, a serious poet (so much so he almost considered sculpting his "day job"), has *Night* say in one of his poems: "As long as shame and sorrow exist/I'd rather not see or hear/So speak softly and let me sleep."

Day, Night, Dawn, and *Dusk*—brought to life in this room where Michelangelo had his workshop, and where they've been ever

The Medicis in a Minute and a Half

The Medici family—part *Sopranos*, part Kennedys, part John-D-and-Catherine-T art patrons—dominated Florentine politics for 300 years (c. 1434–1737). Originally a hardworking, middle-class family in the cloth, silk, and banking business, they used their wealth, blue-collar popularity, and philanthropy to rise into Europe's nobility, producing popes and queens.

1400s: The Princes

Cosimo the Elder (ruled 1434–1464), a shrewd moneylender, had free-spending popes and nobles in his pocket, becoming the richest man in Europe and virtual dictator of Florence. He was the patron of Brunelleschi, Donatello, Ghiberti, and Fra Angelico.

Lorenzo the Magnificent (ruled 1469–1492), Cosimo's grandson, epitomized the Medici ruling style: publicly praising Florence's constitution while privately holding the purse strings. A true Renaissance Man, Lorenzo's personal charisma, public festivals, and support of da Vinci, Botticelli, and teenage Michelangelo made Florence Europe's most enlightened city.

1494–1532: Exile in Rome

After Lorenzo's early death, the family was exiled by the Florentines, a victim of bank failure, Savonarola's reforms, and the Florentine tradition of democracy. They built a power base in Rome under Lorenzo's son (Pope Leo X, who made forays into Florence) and nephew (Pope Clement VII, who finally invaded Florence and crushed the republic).

1537–1737: The Grand Duchy—Mediocre Medicis

Backed by Europe's popes and kings, the "later" Medicis—descendants of Cosimo the Elder's brother—ruled Florence and Tuscany as just another duchy. Politically repressive but generous patrons of the arts (the Uffizi, Pitti Palace, Cellini, Galileo), they married into Europe's royal families (Catherine and Marie de Medici were queens of France) while Florence declined as a political and economic power.

since—meditate eternally on Death, squirming restlessly, unable to come to terms with it.

Tomb of Lorenzo the Magnificent and his Brother Giuliano

As the tomb was never completed, all that really marks where The Magnificent One's body lies is the marble base that the Madonna and saints stand on. Perhaps Michelangelo was working up to the grand finale to honor the man who not only was the greatest Medici but who also plucked a poor 13-year-old Michelangelo from an

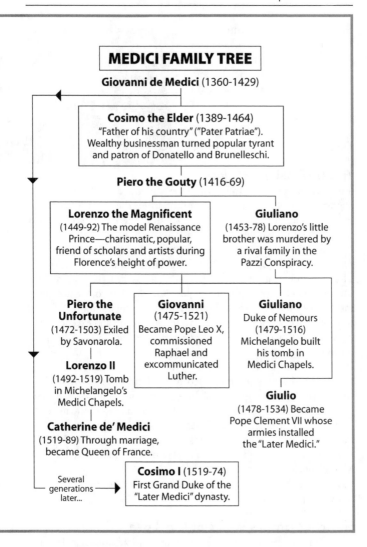

MEDICI FAMILY TREE

Giovanni de Medici (1360-1429)

Cosimo the Elder (1389-1464)
"Father of his country" ("Pater Patriae").
Wealthy businessman turned popular tyrant
and patron of Donatello and Brunelleschi.

Piero the Gouty (1416-69)

Lorenzo the Magnificent
(1449-92) The model Renaissance
Prince—charismatic, popular,
friend of scholars and artists during
Florence's height of power.

Giuliano
(1453-78) Lorenzo's little
brother was murdered by
a rival family in the
Pazzi Conspiracy.

Piero the Unfortunate
(1472-1503) Exiled
by Savonarola.

Lorenzo II
(1492-1519) Tomb
in Michelangelo's
Medici Chapels.

Catherine de' Medici
(1519-89) Through marriage,
became Queen of France.

Giovanni
(1475-1521)
Became Pope Leo X,
commissioned
Raphael and
excommunicated
Luther.

Giuliano
Duke of Nemours
(1479-1516)
Michelangelo built
his tomb in
Medici Chapels.

Giulio
(1478-1534) Became
Pope Clement VII whose
armies installed
the "Later Medici."

Several
generations
later...

Cosimo I (1519-74)
First Grand Duke of the
"Later Medici" dynasty.

obscure apprenticeship to dine at the Medici table with cardinals
and kings.

Lorenzo's beloved younger brother, Giuliano, died in 1478 in a
"hit" by a rival family, stabbed to death before the altar of the
Duomo during Easter Mass. (Lorenzo, wounded, drew his sword
and backpedaled to safety. Enraged supporters grabbed the assas-
sins—including two priests planted there by the pope—and literally
tore them apart.)

The **Medici Madonna,** unlike many Michelangelo women, is
thin, vertical, and elegant, her sad face veiled under chisel marks.

She tolerates the squirming, two-year-old Jesus, who still seems to want to breast-feed, aware of the hard life her son has ahead of him. Mary's right foot is still buried in stone, so this unfinished statue was certainly meant to be worked on more. The saints **Cosmas** and **Damian** were done by assistants.

The Unfinished Project

The Chapel project (1520–1534) was plagued by delays: design changes, late shipments of Carrara marble, the death of patrons, Michelangelo's other obligations (including the Laurentian Library next door), his own depression, and...revolution.

In 1527 Florence rose up against the Medici pope and declared an independent republic. Michelangelo, torn between his love of Florence and loyalty to the Medicis of his youth, walked a fine line. He continued to work for the pope while simultaneously designing fortified city walls to defend Florence from the pope's troops. In 1530 the besieged city fell, Republicans were rounded up and executed, and Michelangelo went into hiding (perhaps in the chapel basement, down the steps to the left of the altar). Fortunately, his status both as artist and staunch Florentine spared him from reprisals.

In 1534 a new pope enticed Michelangelo to come back to Rome with a challenging new project: painting the *Last Judgment* over the altar in the Sistine Chapel. Michelangelo left, never to return to the Medici Chapels. Assistants gathered up statues and fragments from the chapel floor (and the Madonna from Michelangelo's house) and did their best to assemble the pieces according to Michelangelo's designs.

• *The apse is the area behind the altar. This has the best view of the chapel as a whole.*

Sketches on the Walls of the Apse

Michelangelo's many design changes and improvisational style come to life in these (dimly lit and hard to see behind Plexiglas) black chalk and charcoal doodles, presumably by Michelangelo and assistants.

• *Starting on the left wall and working clockwise at about eye level...*

I think I saw hash marks counting off days worked, a window frame for the Laurentian Library, scribbles, a face, an arch, a bearded face, and (on the right wall) squares, a nude figure crouching in a doorway, a twisting female nude with her dog, and a tiny, wacky cartoon Roman soldier with shield and spurs. You really do get a sense of Michelangelo and staff working, sweating, arguing, and just goofing off as the hammers pound and dust flies.

The Whole Ensemble—Michelangelo's Vision

The New Sacristy was the first chance for Michelangelo, the quintessential well-rounded Renaissance Man, to use his arsenal of talents—as sculptor, architect, and Thinker of Big Ideas—on a single, multimedia project. The resulting "installation" (a 20th-century term) produces a powerful overall effect that's different for everyone—"somber," "meditative," "redemptive," "ugly."

The room is a cube topped with a Pantheon-style dome, with three distinct stories—the heavy tombs at ground level, upper-level windows with simpler wall decoration, and the dome, better lit and simpler still. The whole effect draws the eye upward, from dark and "busy" to light and airy. (It's intensified by an optical illusion—Michelangelo made the dome's coffers, the upper windows, and round lunettes all taper imperceptibly at the top to make them look taller and higher.)

The white walls are lined in gray-brown-green stone. The half columns, arches, and triangular pediments are traditional Renaissance forms, but with no regard for the traditional "orders" of the time (matching the right capital with the right base, the correct width-to-height ratio of columns, upper story taller than lower, etc.). Michelangelo had Baroque-en the rules, baffling his contemporaries and pointing the way to a new, more ornate style that used old forms as mere decoration.

Finally, Michelangelo, a serious neo-Platonist, wanted this room to symbolize the big philosophical questions that death presents to the survivors. Summing up these capital-letter concepts (far, far more crudely than was ever intended), the room might say:

Time (the four reclining statues) kills Mortal Men (statues of Lorenzo and Giuliano) and mocks their Glory (Roman power symbols). But if we Focus (Lorenzo and Giuliano's gaze) on God's Grace (Madonna and Child), our Souls (both Active and Contemplative parts) can be Resurrected (the Chapel was consecrated to this) and rise from this drab Earth (the dark, heavy ground floor) up into the Light (the windows and lantern) of Heaven (the geometrically perfect dome) where God and Plato's Ideas are forever Immortal.

And that, folks, is a Mouthful.

MEDICI-RICCARDI PALACE TOUR

Cosimo (The Elder) de' Medici, the founder of the ruling family dynasty, lived here with his upwardly-mobile clan, including Lorenzo the Magnificent. Besides the immediate family, the palace also hosted many famous Florentines: teenage Michelangelo, who lived almost as an adopted son; Leonardo da Vinci, who played lute for Medici parties; and Botticelli, who studied the classical sculpture that dotted the gardens. The historical ambience is captured in a few well-preserved rooms and in a 15th-century fresco that brings the colorful Medici world to life.

ORIENTATION

Cost: €4.
Hours: Thu–Tue 9:00–19:00, closed Wed.
Getting There: Via Cavour 3, kitty-corner from San Lorenzo Church, one long block north of Baptistery, tel. 055-276-0340.

THE TOUR BEGINS

Exterior
Cosimo de' Medici hired the architect Michelozzo to build the palace (1444), whose three-story facade set the tone throughout Florence—rough stones at bottom, rising to smooth and elegant on top. Two generations later, Michelangelo added the distinctive "kneeling windows" (with scrolls), an innovation that cropped up on palaces the world over. In the 1700s the palace was extended northward (keeping the same style) by the next owners, the Riccardi family.

Courtyard

As with many Italian homes, the courtyard served as an open-air meeting point and "living room" for the extended family. The statue of Orpheus (who calmed wild animals with his harp) reminded visitors that the Medici family calmed wild Florence with smart and soothing politics. Find the family shield above the arches, with the six pills of these doctors *(medici)* turned cloth merchants turned international bankers. The Riccardi family later gilded this Renaissance lily with Baroque decor and adorned this courtyard with their collection of classical sculpture.

The room that opens onto the courtyard (now the Multimedia Reference Area) was Lorenzo the Magnificent's public office. Today the palace is a functioning county government building. As you wander around, notice staff at work.

Garden

Pop out into the fragrant garden with its greenhouse for lemon

trees. The tiny garden is a mere fraction of the once-spacious gardens that stretched for a city block to the north. The grounds were studded with fountains and statues, including the *Venus de' Medici* (Uffizi) and Donatello's *David* (Bargello). Teenage Michelangelo studied sculpture and the liberal arts in the family school located in the gardens.

• *From the courtyard, separate stairways lead to the Chapel of the Magi and the Luca Giordano-decorated library, both on the first floor.*

Chapel of the Magi (Cappella di Gozzoli)

This sumptuous little room was the nuclear family's private chapel, where they could kneel at the altar and pray to a *Madonna and Child* by Filippo Lippi (where a copy stands now). The other three walls display *The Journey of the Magi*—one Magus per wall—by Benozzo Gozzoli (1459).

On the biggest wall, a curly-haired young Magus on a white horse leads a parade of men through a rocky landscape. But the scene takes you not to Bethlehem but to 15th-century, Medici-populated Tuscany. Riding behind the Magus are Cosimo (in red hat, riding modest brown donkey) and his son Piero (red hat, grey-white horse), who succeeded Cosimo as ruler of Florence. In the line of red-hatted young men behind them, find Piero's 10-year-old son and future ruler—Lorenzo the Magnificent (far left, in red cap, with scoop nose, brown bowl-cut hair, and intense gaze). In fact, every year on Epiphany, the Medici men would dress up like this and parade down Via Larga to celebrate the holiday of the Three Kings.

The next wall (working clockwise) sets the Magus and his entourage in a green, spacious, and obviously Tuscan landscape. The men wear colorful clothes that set trends throughout Europe.

On the last wall, notice that the white-bearded Magus on his white donkey (far left) got cut off when the room was later remodeled. But the fresco was preserved—find the horse's ass on the other side of the doorway.

Gozzoli's crystal-clear, shadowless scenes reflect the style of his teacher, Fra Angelico. Pristine red, white, and green predominate—the Medici family colors.

• *Return to the courtyard and find the other staircase to the Luca Giordano-decorated library.*

Luca Giordano Library ("Gallery")

This Baroque, Versailles-like former library is part of a later extension added by the Riccardi family. The ceiling (*Allegory of Divine Wisdom*, frescoed in 1685 by the Naples artist Luca Giordano) honors Medici big shots through the ages. They're the guys with stars on their heads frolicking with Greek gods. The blue-robed woman over the entrance is Florence, immersed in the nobility of the classical world.

Also on display is Filippo Lippi's cheek-to-cheek *Madonna and Child,* the original that once stood on the altar of the Chapel of the Magi.

SANTA MARIA NOVELLA TOUR

Santa Maria Novella, chock-full of groundbreaking paintings and statues, is a reminder that the Renaissance was not simply a secular phenomenon. Many wealthy families paid for chapels inside the church that today are appreciated for their fine art.

Masaccio's fresco *The Trinity,* the first painting of modern times to portray three-dimensional space (1427), blew a "hole in the wall" of this church. From then on, a painting wasn't just a decorated panel, but a window into the spacious 3-D world of light and color. With Masaccio's *Trinity* as the centerpiece, the church traces Florentine art from the medieval to the Quattrocento (1400s) to the onset of Baroque.

ORIENTATION

Cost: €2.50.

Hours: Mon–Thu and Sat 9:30–17:00, Fri and Sun 13:00–17:00.

Dress Code: Shorts are allowed, but please no short shorts or bare arms.

Getting There: It's on Piazza Santa Maria Novella, a block south of the train station.

Note: Art lovers can seek out the adjacent **cloisters** (separate fee and entry to the left of the church's facade); the Chapel of the Spaniards—currently under restoration—is notable for Bonaiuto's fresco *Allegory of the Dominican Order.*

Around the corner from the church is a fancy **perfumery** that's fun to visit (free, Mon–Sat 9:30–19:30, closed Sun, Via della Scala 16, tel. 055-216-276); see page 42 for details.

Length of This Tour: One hour.

Photography: Not allowed.

Starring: Masaccio, Giotto, Brunelleschi, Ghirlandaio, and Filippino Lippi.

THE TOUR BEGINS

❶ Exterior—The Facade

The green-and-white marble facade by Leon Battista Alberti (1456–70) contains elements of Florence's whole history: Romanesque (horizontal stripes, like the Baptistery), Gothic (pointed arches on the bottom level), Renaissance (geometric squares and circles on the upper level), and even proto-Baroque (the scrolls).

The church itself is cross-shaped, with a high central nave and low-ceilinged side aisles—the scrolls on the facade help bridge the two levels.

• *Enter the courtyard to the right of the main door, passing through the cemetery, where you'll pay to enter. Masaccio's* Trinity *is on the opposite wall from the entrance. But we'll start our tour at the central doorway in the facade, looking down the long nave to the altar.*

❷ Interior—View down the Nave from the Main Entrance

The long, 330-foot nave looks even longer thanks to a 14th-century perspective illusion. The columns converge as you approach the altar, their number increases, the arches get lower and the floor gets higher, creating a tunnel effect. Gothic architects were aware of the rules of perspective, just not how to render it on a two-dimensional canvas.

• *Hanging from the ceiling in the middle of the nave is...*

❸ Giotto (c. 1266–1337)—*Crucifixion*

Giotto's altarpiece originally stood on the main altar. Stately and under-stated, it avoids the gruesome excesses of many medieval crucifixes. The tragic tilt of Christ's head, the parted lips, and the stretched rib cage tell more about human suffering than the excessive spurting of blood.

On either side of the crossbar, Mary and John sit in a golden iconic heaven, but they are fully human, turned at a three-quarter angle, with

Santa Maria Novella

1. Facade by Alberti
2. View of the Nave
3. GIOTTO – *Crucifixion*
4. MASACCIO – *The Trinity*
5. ORCAGNA BROTHERS – Last Judgment Frescos
6. BRUNELLESCHI – *Crucifixion*
7. GHIRLANDAIO – *Fresco Cycles of Mary and John the Baptist*
8. FILIPPINO LIPPI – *St. Philip* (right wall) *St. John* (left wall)
9. VASARI – *Madonna of the Rosary*

knowing, sympathetic expressions. Giotto, the proto-Renaissance experimenter in perspective, creates the illusion that Christ's hands are actually turned out, palms down, not hammered flat against the cross.

• *Masaccio's* Trinity *is on the left wall, about midway along the nave (opposite the entrance). For the best perspective, stand about 20 feet from it, then take four steps to your left. Masaccio positioned it to be seen by the faithful as they dipped fingers into a (missing) font and crossed themselves—"Father, Son, and Holy Ghost."*

❹ Masaccio (1401–1428)—The Trinity (1425–1427)

In his short but influential five-year career, Masaccio was the first painter since ancient times to portray Man in Nature—real humans with real emotions, in a spacious three-dimensional world. (Unfortunately for tourists, he did the best 3-D space here, and the best humans in the Brancacci Chapel across the river.)

With simple pinks and blues (now pretty faded), Masaccio creates the illusion that we're looking into a raised, cube-shaped chapel

(about three yards by three yards by three yards) topped with an arched ceiling and framed at the entrance with classical columns. Inside the chapel, God the Father stands on an altar, holding up the cross of Christ. (Where's the dove of the Holy Spirit? Why is God's "white collar" crooked?) John looks up at Christ while Mary looks down at us. Two donors (husband and wife, most likely) kneel on the front step outside the chapel, their cloaks spilling out of the niche. Below this fake chapel sits a fake tomb with the skeleton of Adam; compare it with the real tomb and niche to the right.

The checkerboard ceiling creates a 3-D tunnel effect, with rows of panels that appear to converge at the back, the panels getting smaller, lower, and closer together. Earlier painters had played with tricks like this, but Masaccio went further. He gave such thought to the proper perspective that we, as viewers, know right where we stand in relation to this virtual chapel.

He knew that, in real life, the rows of checks would, if extended, stretch to the distant horizon. Lay a mental ruler along them, and you'll find the "vanishing point"—where all the lines intersect—all the way down below the foot of the cross. Masaccio places us there, with that at eye level, looking "up" into the chapel.

Having fixed where the distant horizon is and where the viewer is, Masaccio draws a checkerboard grid in between, then places the figures on it (actually underneath it) like chess pieces. What's truly amazing is that young Masaccio seemed to grasp this stuff intuitively—a "natural," eyeballing it and sketching freehand what later artists would have to work out with a pencil and paper.

What Masaccio learned intuitively, Brunelleschi analyzed mathematically and Alberti (who did the facade) codified in his famous 1435 treatise, *On Painting*. Soon, artists everywhere were drawing Alberti checkerboards on the ground, creating spacious, perfectly lit, 3-D scenes filled with chess-piece humans.

• *The Orcagna Chapel is at the far end of the left transept. As you approach, view the chapel from a distance. This is the illusion that Masaccio tried to create—of a raised chapel set in a wall—using only paint on a flat surface. Climb the steps to enter.*

❺ Orcagna Brothers (a.k.a. the di Cione brothers)

Frescoes of the Last Judgment: *Inferno, Purgatorio,* and *Paradiso* (1340–1357)

In 1347–1348, Florence was hit with the terrible Black Death (bubonic plague) that killed half the population. Here, in the Orcagna Chapel, the fading frescoes from that grim time show hundreds of figures, and not a single smile.

It's the Day of Judgment (center wall), and God (above the stained-glass window) spreads his hands to divide the good and evil. God has selected Dante as the interior decorator for heaven and hell. (Find Dante all in white, with his ear-flap cap, among the crowd to the left of the window, about a third of the way up.) Notice that God is bigger than the angels, who dwarf the hallowed saints, who are bigger than ordinary souls such as Dante, mirroring the feudal

hierarchy of king, nobles, knights, and serfs.

In *Heaven* (left wall), Hotel Paradiso is *completo*, stacked with gold-haloed saints. *Hell* (faded right wall) is a series of layers, the descending rings of Dante's Inferno. A river of fire runs through it, dividing *Purgatory* (above) and *Hell* (below). At the bottom of the pit, where dogs and winged demons run wild, naked souls in caves beg for mercy and get none.

• *In a chapel to the left of the church's main altar, you'll find...*

❻ Filippo Brunelleschi—*Crucifixion*

Filippo Brunelleschi (1377–1446)—architect, painter, sculptor—used his skills as an analyst of nature to carve (in wood) a perfectly

realistic *Crucifixion*, neither prettified nor with the grotesque exaggeration of medieval religious objects. His Christ is buck naked, not particularly muscular or handsome, with bulging veins, armpit hair, tensed leg muscles, and bent feet. The tilt of Christ's head frees a tendril of hair that directs our eye down to the wound and the dripping blood, dropping straight from his side to his thigh to his calf—a strong vertical line that sets off the curve of Christ's body. Brunelleschi carved this to outdo his friend Donatello's crucifix in Santa Croce. Donatello's is an agonized peasant; Brunelleschi's a dignified noble.

• *In the choir area behind the main altar are Ghirlandaio's 21 frescoes, stacked seven to a wall. We'll concentrate on just the six panels on the bottom.*

❼ Domenico Ghirlandaio—Fresco Cycles of Mary and John the Baptist (1485–1490)

At the peak of Florence's power, wealth, and confidence, Domenico Ghirlandaio (1449–1494) painted portraits of his fellow Florentines in their Sunday best, inhabiting video-game landscapes of classical buildings, rubbing shoulders with saints and angels. The religious subjects get lost in the colorful scenes of everyday life—perhaps a metaphor for how Renaissance humanism was marginalizing religion.

• *Start with the left wall and work clockwise along the bottom. The first scene is...*

Expulsion of Joachim from the Temple

Proud, young Florentine men (the group at left) seem oblivious to bearded, robed saints rushing from the arcade. There's Ghirlandaio himself (in the group on the right) looking out at us, with one hand proudly on his hip and the other gesturing, "I did this." The scene is perfectly lit, almost shadow-free, allowing us to look deep into the receding arches.

• *Continue clockwise to the next scene.*

Birth of the Virgin

Five beautiful young women, led by the pregnant daughter of Ghirlandaio's patron, parade up to newborn Mary. The pregnant girl's brocade dress is a microcosm of the room's decorations. Dancing babies in the room's classical frieze celebrate Mary's birth, obviously echoing della Robbia's beloved Cantoria in Florence's Duomo Museum.

True, Ghirlandaio's works are "busy"—each scene crammed with portraits, designs, fantasy architecture, and great costumes—but if you mentally frame off small sections, you discover a collection of mini-masterpieces.
• *On the center wall, flanking the stained-glass window, are two matching panels.*

Giovanni Tornabuoni Kneeling and
Francesca Tornabuoni (his wife) Kneeling

Giovanni Tornabuoni, who paid for these frescoes, was a successful executive in the Medici Company (and Lorenzo the Magnificent's uncle). However, by the time these frescoes were being finished, the Medici bank was slipping seriously into the red, and soon the family had to flee Florence, creditors on their heels.
• *On the right wall...*

Mary Meets Elizabeth

In a spacious, airy landscape (with the pointed steeple of S. M. Novella in the distance), Mary and Elizabeth embrace, uniting their respective

entourages. The parade of ladies in contemporary dress echoes the one on the opposite wall. This panel celebrates youth, beauty, the city, trees, rocks, and life.

A generation after Brunelleschi and Alberti, all artists—including the near-genius Ghirlandaio—had mastered perspective tricks. Here, Alberti's famed checkerboard is laid on its side, making a sharply receding wall to create the illusion of great distance.

Ghirlandaio employed many assistants in his productive workshop: "Johnson, you do the ladies' dresses. Anderson, you're great at birds and trees. And Michelangelo...you do young men's butts." The three small figures leaning over the wall (above Mary and Elizabeth) were likely done by 13-year-old Michelangelo, an apprentice here before being "discovered" by Lorenzo the Magnificent. Relaxed and natural, they cast real shadows, as true to life as anyone in Ghirlandaio's perfect-posture, face-the-camera world.

Ghirlandaio was reportedly jealous (and talented Michelangelo contemptuous), but, before they parted ways, Michelangelo learned how to lay fresco from the man who did it as well as anyone in Florence.

The Birth of John the Baptist

Set in a typical (rich) Florentine bedroom, John's birth is attended by none other than Lorenzo de Medici's mom (second figure from right), with the broad face, thin lips, and scooped nose Lorenzo would inherit.

• *In the chapel to the right of the altar, Filippino Lippi did the frescoes on the left and right walls. Look first at the right wall, lower level (there's a decent view from the altar steps)...*

❽ Filippino Lippi

St. Philip at the Temple of Mars

In an elaborate shrine, a statue of the angry god Mars waves his broken lance menacingly. The Christian Philip points back up and says, "I'm not afraid of him—that's a false god." To prove it, he opens a hole in the base of the altar, letting out a little dragon, who promptly farts (believe it when you see it), causing the pagan king's son to swoon and die. The overcome spectators clutch their foreheads and noses.

If Ghirlandaio was "busy," Lippi is downright hyperactive, filling every square inch with something frilly—rumpled hair, folds in clothes, dramatic gestures, twisting friezes, wind-blown flags, and gassy dragons.

• *On the left wall, lower level...*

St. John the Evangelist Raising Drusiana from the Dead

The miracle takes place in a spacious 3-D architectural setting, but Lippi has all his actors in a chorus line across the front of the stage. Filippino Lippi (1457–1504, the son of the more famous Fra Filippo

Lippi) was apprenticed to Botticelli and exaggerated his bright colors, shadowless lighting, and elegant curves.

The sober, dignified realism of Florence's Quattrocento was ending. Michelangelo would extend it, building on Masaccio's spacious, solemn, dimly lit scenes. But Lippi championed a style (later called Mannerism, leading to Baroque) that loved color and dramatic excitement.

• *In the next chapel to the right of the altar, on the central wall, find...*

❾ Giorgio Vasari—*Madonna of the Rosary*

The picture-plane is saturated with images from top to bottom. Saints and angels twist and squirm around Mary (the red patch in the center), but their body language is gibberish, just an excuse for Vasari to exhibit his technique.

Giorgio Vasari (1511–1574), best known as the writer of *The Lives of the Artists,* was a prolific artist himself. As a Mannerist, he copied the "manner" of, say, a twisting Michelangelo statue, but violated the sober spirit, multiplying by 100 and cramming the canvas. I've tried to defend Vasari from the art critics who unanimously call his art superficial and garish...but doggone it, they're right.

With Vasari, who immortalized the Florentine Renaissance with his writing, that Renaissance ended.

BRANCACCI CHAPEL TOUR

(Cappella Brancacci)

In the Brancacci Chapel, Masaccio created a world in paint that looked like the world we inhabit. For the first time in a thousand years, Man and Nature were frozen for inspection. Masaccio's painting techniques were copied by many Renaissance artists, and his people—sturdy, intelligent, and dignified—helped shape Renaissance Men and Women's own self-images. They have an expression of understated astonishment, like people awakening to a new and wonderful world—the Renaissance.

ORIENTATION

Cost: €4, or €8 combo-ticket with Palazzo Vecchio.

Reservations: Call the chapel for free, mandatory reservations in English, often available for the same day (tel. 055-276-8224). Reservation times begin every 15 minutes, with a maximum of 30 visitors per time slot. You have 15 minutes in the actual chapel. Visits on the top of each hour include a free 40-minute video in English; ask about this when booking your visit.

Hours: Mon and Wed–Sat 10:00–17:00, Sun 13:00–17:00, closed Tue. Ticket office closes at 16:30. During visiting hours, enter through the paid entrance to the right of the church. Otherwise, enter the church (free admission, but the chapel is often blocked off or blacked out); the chapel is in the right transept.

Dress Code: Shorts and bare shoulders are OK if you enter through the paid entrance. If you enter through the church, modest dress is requested.

Photography: Allowed without a flash.

Brancacci Chapel

1 MASACCIO – Adam and Eve Banished

2 MASOLINO – Adam and Eve Tempted

3 MASACCIO – The Tribute Money

4 MASOLINO – Peter Preaches

5 MASACCIO – Peter Baptizing

6 MASOLINO – Peter Heals Cripple & Resurrects Tabitha

7 MASACCIO – Peter Resurrects Son of Theophilus

8 MASACCIO – Peter Heals the Sick

9 MASACCIO – Peter Shares the Wealth

10 ANONYMOUS – Madonna of the People

11 LIPPI (Filippino) – Peter Crucified

Getting There: The Brancacci Chapel (bran-KAH-chee) is in the Church of Santa Maria del Carmine, on Piazza del Carmine, in the Oltrarno neighborhood south of the Arno River.

Starring: Masaccio, Masolino, and Filippino Lippi.

THE TOUR BEGINS

Overview

The chapel has 12 frescoes, telling the story of Peter—half are by Masaccio and half by Masolino or Filippino Lippi. Although Masaccio is the star, the panels by his colleagues are interesting and a good contrast in styles. Masaccio's works are sprinkled among the others, mostly on the left and center walls.

We'll see them roughly in the order they were painted, from upper left to lower right—the upper six by Masaccio and Masolino (1424–1425), the lower ones by Masaccio (1426–1427) and Filippino Lippi (1481–1485).

• *Start with the left wall, the small panel in the upper left.*

Masaccio—*Adam and Eve Banished from Eden*

Renaissance Man and Woman—as nude as they can be—turn their backs on the skinny, unrealistic, medieval Gate of Paradise and take their first step as mortal humans in the real world. For the first time in a thousand years of painting, these figures cast a realistic shadow, seemingly lit by the same light we are—the natural light through the Brancacci Chapel's window.

Eve wails from deep within. (The first time I saw her, I thought Eve's gaping mouth was way over the top, until I saw the very same expression on someone dealing with a brother's death.) Adam buries his face in shame. These simple human gestures speak louder than the religious symbols of medieval art.

• Compare Masaccio's Adam and Eve *with the one on the opposite wall, by his colleague Masolino.*

Masolino—*Adam and Eve Tempted by the Serpent*

Masolino's elegant, innocent First Couple float in an ethereal Garden of Eden with no clear foreground or background (Eve hugs a tree or she'd float away). Their bodies are lit evenly by a pristine, all-encompassing, morning-in-springtime light that casts no shadows.

In 1424, Masolino da Panicale (1383–1435) was hired by the Brancacci family to decorate this chapel with the story of Peter (beginning with the Original Sin that Peter's "Good News" saves man from). Masolino, a 40-year-old contractor with too many other commitments, invited 23-year-old Masaccio (1401–1428) to help him. The two set up scaffolding and worked side by side—the older, workmanlike master and the young, intuitive genius—in a harmonious collaboration. They just divvied up the panels, never (or rarely) working together on the same scene.

• *Return to the left wall, upper level. From here, we'll work clockwise around the chapel. After Adam and Eve, the second panel is...*

Masaccio—*Jesus, Peter, and the Disciples Pay the Tribute Money*

The tax collector (in red miniskirt, with his back to us) tells Jesus he must pay a temple tax. Jesus gestures to say, "OK, but the money's over there." Peter, his right-hand man (gray hair and beard, brown robe), says, "Yeah, over there." Peter goes over there to the lake (left side of panel), takes off his robe, stoops down at an odd angle, and miraculously pulls a coin from the mouth of a fish. He puts his robe back on and (right side of panel) pays the man.

Some consider this the first modern painting, placing real humans in a real setting, seen from a single viewpoint—ours. Earlier painters had done far more detailed landscapes than Masaccio's sketchy mountains, lake, trees, clouds, and buildings, but they never fixed where the viewer was in relation to these things.

Masaccio tells us exactly where we stand—near the crowd, farther from the trees, with the sun to our right casting late-afternoon shadows. We're no longer detached spectators, but an extension of the scene. Masaccio lets us stand in the presence of the human Jesus. While a good attempt at three-dimensionality, Masaccio's work is far from perfect. Later artists would perfect mathematically what Masaccio eyeballed intuitively.

The disciples all have strong, broad-shouldered bodies, but each face is unique. Blonde, curly-haired, clean-shaven John is as handsome as the head on a Roman coin (Masaccio had just returned from Rome). Thomas (far right, with a five o'clock shadow) is intense. Their different reactions—with faces half in shadow, half in light—tell us they're divided over paying the tax.

Masaccio's people have one thing in common—a faraway look in the eye, as though hit with a spiritual two-by-four. They're deep in thought, reflective, and awestruck, aware they've just experienced something miraculous. But they're also dazzled, glazed over, and a bit disoriented, like tourists at the Brancacci Chapel.

• *Continuing clockwise, we move to the next panel, on the center wall.*

Masolino—*Peter Preaches to a Crowd*

Masolino and Masaccio, different in so many ways, were both fans of Giotto (c.1266–1337), who told stories with simple gestures and minimal acting, adding the human drama by showing the reaction of bystanders. Here, the miraculous power of the sermon is not evident in Peter (who just raises his hand) but in the faces of the crowd. The lady in the front row is riveted, while others close their eyes to meditate.

The big nun (far right) finds it interesting enough to come a little closer, while the tonsured monk's mouth slips open in awe. The gentleman to the left is skeptical but wants to hear more.

Masolino never mastered 3-D space like Masaccio. Peter's extreme profile is a cardboard cutout, his left leg stands too high to plant him realistically on flat ground, the people in the back have their gazes fixed somewhere above Peter, and the "Masacciesque" mountains in the background remain just that, background.

• *Continuing clockwise to the other side of the window...*

Masaccio—*Peter Baptizing Converts*

A muscular man kneels in the stream to join the cult of Jesus. On the bank (far right), another young man waits his turn, shivering in

his jockstrap. Among the crowd, a just-baptized man wrestles with his robe, while the man in blue, his hair still dripping, buttons up.

The body language is eloquent: the strongman's humility, the shivering youth's uncertainty, and the bowed heads of the just-baptized, reflecting on the life-altering choice they've just made.

Masaccio builds these bodies with patches of color (an especially effective technique in fresco, where colors can bleed together). He knew that a kneeling man's body, when lit from the left (the direction of the chapel window), would look like a patchwork of bright hills (his pecs) and dark crevasses (his sternum). He assembles the pieces into a sculptural, 3-D figure, "modeled" by light and shade.

Again, Masaccio was the first artist to paint real humans—with 3-D bodies and individual faces, reflecting inner emotions—in a real-world setting.

• *Continue clockwise to the right wall.*

Masolino—*Peter Heals a Cripple* (left side) *and* *Resurrects Tabitha* (right side)

Masolino takes a crack at the 3-D style of his young partner, setting two separate stories in a single Florentine square, defined by an arcade on the left and a porch on the right. Crude elements of the future Renaissance style abound—the receding buildings establish the viewer's point of reference; the rocks scattered through the square define 3-D space; there are secular details in the background (mother and child, laundry on a balcony, a monkey on a ledge); and the cripple (left) is shown at an odd angle (foreshortening). Masaccio may have helped on this panel.

But there's no denying that the stars of the work are the two sharp-dressed gentlemen strolling across the square, who help divide (and unite) the two stories of Peter. The patterned coat is a textbook example of the International Gothic style that was the rage in Florence—elegant, refined, graceful, with curvy lines creating a complex, pleasing pattern. The man walking is shown at a three-quarters angle, but Masolino shows the coat from the front to catch the full display. The picture is evenly lit, with only a hint of shadow, accentuating the colorful clothes and cheerful atmosphere.

In mid-project (1426), Masolino took another job in Hungary, leaving Masaccio to finish the lower half of the chapel. Masolino never again explored the Renaissance style, building a successful career with the eternal springtime of International Gothic.

• *We move to the lower level. Start on the left wall with the second panel and work clockwise.*

Masaccio—*Peter Resurrects the Son of Theophilus*

Peter (in that same brown robe...like Masaccio, who was careless about his appearance) raises the boy from the world of bones, winning his freedom from stern Theophilus (seated in niche to the left).

The courtyard setting is fully 3-D, Masaccio having recently learned a bit of perspective mathematics from his (older) friends Brunelleschi and Donatello. At the far right of the painting, there are three of the Quattrocento (1400s) giants who invented painting perspective (from right to left): Brunelleschi, who broke reality down mathematically; Alberti, who popularized the math with his book, *On Painting*; and Masaccio himself (looking out at us), who opened everyone's eyes to the psychologically powerful possibilities.

Little is known of Masaccio's short life. "Masaccio" is a nickname (often translated as "Big, Clumsy Thomas") describing his personality—stumbling through life with careless abandon, not worrying about money, clothes, or fame...a lovable doofus.

Next to Masaccio's self-portrait is a painting within a painting of Peter on a throne. On a flat surface with a blank background, Masaccio has created a hovering hologram, a human more 3-D than even a statue made in medieval times.

"Wow," said Brother Philip, a 20-year-old Carmelite monk stationed here when Masaccio painted this. Fra Filippo ("Brother Philip") Lippi was inspired by these frescoes and went on to become a famous painter himself. At age 50, while painting in a convent, he fell in love with a young nun, and they eloped. Nine months later, "Little Philip" was born, and he too grew to be a famous painter—Filippino Lippi...who, in 1481, was chosen to complete the Brancacci Chapel.

Filippino Lippi painted substantial portions of this fresco, including the group in the far left (five heads but only eight legs).

• *Moving clockwise to the center wall...*

Masaccio—*Peter Heals the Sick with his Shadow*

Peter is a powerful Donatello statue come to life, walking towards us along a Florentine street. Next to him, in the red cap, is bearded Donatello, Masaccio's friend and mentor.

Masaccio inspired more than painters. He gave ordinary people a new self-image of what it is to be human. Masaccio's people are

individuals, not generic Greek gods, not always pretty (like the old bald guy) but still robust and handsome in their own way. They exude a seriousness that makes them very adult. Compare these street people with Masolino's two well-dressed dandies, and you see the difference between Florence's working-class, urban, "democratic" spirit (Guelphs) and the courtly grace of Europe's landed gentry (Ghibellines).

• *The next panel, on the other side of the altar, is...*

Masaccio—*Peter Shares the Wealth with the Poor*

Early Christians practiced a form of communal sharing. The wealthy Ananias lied about his contribution, and drops dead at Peter's feet. Peter takes the missing share and gives it to a poor lady who can't even afford baby pants. The shy baby, the grateful woman, and the admiring man on crutches show Masaccio's blue-collar sympathies.

The scene reflects an actual event in Florence—a tax-reform measure to make things equal for everyone. Florentines were championing a new form of government where, if we all contribute our fair share through taxes, we don't need kings and nobles.

• *The altar under the window holds a painting that is not by Masaccio, Masolino, or Lippi.*

Anonymous (possibly Coppo di Marcovaldo)— *The Madonna of the People*

This medieval altarpiece replaces the now-destroyed fresco by Masaccio that was the centerpiece of the whole design—Peter's crucifixion.

With several panels still unfinished, Masaccio traveled to Rome to meet up with Masolino. Masaccio died there (possibly of poison) in

1428, at age 27. After his death, the political and artistic climate changed, the chapel was left unfinished (the lower right wall), and some of his frescoes were scraped off whole (his *Crucifixion of Peter*) or in part—we saw in *Peter Resurrects the Son of Theophilus* that several exiled Brancaccis were erased from history, later to be replaced.

Finally, in 1481, new funding arrived and Filippino Lippi, the son of the monk-turned-painter, was hired to complete the blank panels and retouch some destroyed frescoes.

• *The right wall, lower section, contains two panels by Filippino Lippi. The first and biggest is...*

Filippino Lippi—*Peter Crucified*

Lippi completes the story of Peter with his upside-down crucifixion. Lippi tried to match the solemn style of Masaccio, but his figures are less statuesque, more colorful, and more detailed, and the compositions are busier. Still, compared with Lippi's other, more hyperactive works found elsewhere, he's reined himself in admirably to honor the great pioneer.

In fact, while Masaccio's perspective techniques were enormously

influential, learned by every Tuscan artist, his sober style was not terribly popular. Another strain of Tuscan painting diverged from Masaccio—from the adult Fra Filippo Lippi to Botticelli, Ghirlandaio, and Filippino Lippi—mixing in the bright colors, line patterns, and even lighting of International Gothic. But Masaccio's legacy remained strong, emerging in the grave, statuesque, harsh-shadow creations of two Florentine giants—Leonardo da Vinci and Michelangelo.

SCIENCE MUSEUM TOUR

(Istituto e Museo di Storia della Scienza)

Enough art, already! Forget the Madonnas and Venuses for a while to ponder weird contraptions from the birth of modern science. The same spirit of discovery that fueled the artistic Renaissance helped free the sciences from medieval mumbo jumbo. The Science Museum is a historical overview of technical innovations from, roughly, A.D. 1000 to 1900, featuring early telescopes, clocks, experiments, and Galileo's finger in a jar.

English majors will enjoy expanding their knowledge. Art lovers can admire the sheer beauty of functional devices. Engineers will be in hog heaven among endless arrays of gadgets. Everyone will be fully amused by my feeble attempts to explain technical concepts.

ORIENTATION

Cost: €6.50.
Hours: Mon and Wed–Fri 9:30–17:00, Tue and Sat 9:30–13:00, closed Sun.
Getting There: It's at Piazza dei Giudici 1, one block east of the Uffizi, on the north bank of the Arno River.
Information: Tel. 055-265-311.
Length of This Tour: 90 minutes.
Photography: Not allowed.
Starring: Galileo's telescopes, experiment models, and finger.

THE TOUR BEGINS

Overview

There are two floors of rooms. The collection is not really chronological, but if you follow the rooms in order, you get a good

overview. Find the displays by their room number (I, II, III, etc.) and exhibit number (I.1, I.2, I.3, etc.).
• *Buy your ticket on the ground floor, then climb stairs to the first floor. Before entering Room I, pick up a free loaner guidebook in English.*

FIRST FLOOR

The objects displayed in the first three rooms measured the world around us—the height of distant mountains, the length of a man's arm, the movement of the stars across the sky. This was the bold, first step in science, to actually observe nature and measure it. What they found is that nature—apparently so ever-changing and chaotic—actually behaves in an orderly way, mirroring rather simple mathematical formulas.

Room I: Mathematical Instruments
• *In the center of Room I, you'll find...*

Exhibit I.1—Arabic Celestial Globe
(*Globo Celeste Arabo*, 1080)
Looking down on this map of the heavens, you have a God's-eye view of the night sky. Find familiar constellations like the fish, hunter, snake, and bear (our "Big Dipper"). Arab traders mapped the dome of heaven that arches overhead to help them navigate by the stars.

    The universe only got bigger with each new bit of knowledge.
• *In the first glass case to the left, on the middle shelf, find...*

Exhibit I.10—Quadrant (*Quadranti e cursore*)
You'd grab this wedge-shaped quadrant by its curved edge, point it away from you, and sight along the top edge toward, say, a distant tower or star. Then you'd read the scale etched along the curved edge to find how many degrees above the horizon the object is.

    A quadrant measures the triangle formed by you, the horizon, and a distant object. Once you know some of the triangle's six variables (three angles and three sides), you can figure the others. (That's trigonometry.)

Armed with this knowledge, you could use the quadrant to measure all kinds of things. On land, you could calculate how high or how far away a building is. At sea, you could figure your position in relation to the sun and stars.

Most of the instruments in Rooms I, II, and III are variations on the earliest, simplest device—the quadrant. (A *quad*-rant is one-*fourth* of a 360-degree circle, or 90 degrees.)
• *Just above the quadrant, find...*

Exhibits I.2 through I.9—Arabic Astrolabes
(Astrolabi Arabi)
Astrolabes, invented by the ancient Greeks and pioneered by medieval Arab sailors, combined a quadrant with a map of the sky (a star chart), allowing you to calculate your position against the stars without doing all the math. You'd hang the metal disk from your thumb and sight along the central crossbeam, locate a star, then read its altitude above the horizon on the measuring scale etched around the rim.

Next, you entered this information in by turning the little handle on the astrolabe's face. This set the wheels-within-wheels into motion, and you'd watch the constellations spin across a backdrop of coordinates. You kept turning until the astrolabe mirrored the current heavens. With your known coordinates dialed in, the astrolabe calculated the unknowns, and you could read out your position along the rim.

In addition, knowing the position of the stars and sun told you the current time of day (see the 24-hour clock around the rim), which was especially useful for Muslims in their daily prayers.
• *In the glass case in the far right corner of the room, on the middle shelf, look for...*

Exhibit I.102—Michelangelo's Compass
(Compasso detto di Michelangelo)
Maybe Michelangelo once used this (it's said to be his), and I suppose it's even conceivable he used it to measure, say, *David*'s hand or to draw a circle on the Sistine ceiling. Regardless, dividers like this were a common way for Renaissance Men and Women to measure the world and marvel at its harmonious proportions.
• *Enter the next room...*

Room II: More Quadrants
and Various Combinations
In the 1500s, improvements were made on the relatively crude quadrants and astrolabes, spurred by the need to navigate the open oceans.
• *Straight ahead, just to the left of the exit doorway, see...*

Exhibit II.27—Quadrant (*Quadrante Universale,* 1608)
Like a Popeil's Pocket-Navigator, this all-purpose unit has 1,001 uses. The quadrant measures angles. A magnetic compass points to north. A sundial (in the compass's removable cap) tells the time of day, as the sun casts a shadow from the vertical piece onto a scale of hours.

On the backside of the quadrant, a big half-dial arcs across rows of numbers, allowing even non–trig majors to calculate the trajectory of cannon balls. The movable arm even passed through a table of zodiac signs to cast your horoscope—how the stars' alignment affects you personally.
* *On the bottom shelf of the glass case back by the entrance doorway, is...*

Exhibit II.88—Calculator (*Macchina Calcolatrice,* 1664)
This calculator (mechanical, of course, not electrical) could add and subtract. Enter the numbers you're adding on the dials, and the dials turn gears inside that spin a tube marked with numbers in concentric rings. The answer appears in the digital readout.

Rooms IV and V: Galileo
Galileo Galilei (1564–1642) is known as the father of modern sci-ence. His discoveries pioneered many sci-entific fields, and he was among the first to blend mathematics with hands-on observation of nature to find practical applications. Raised in Florence, he achieved fame teaching at the University of Pisa before retiring back to Florence. The museum displays several of his actual possessions (lens, 2 telescopes, compass, and thermometer), models illustrating his early experiments, and his finger.

* *Preserved in a jar in the glass case is...*

**Exhibit IV.10—Galileo's Finger
(*Dito Medio della Mano Destra di Galileo*)**
Galileo is, perhaps, best known as a martyr for science. He popular-ized the belief (conceived by the Polish astronomer, Nicolas Copernicus, in the early 1500s) that the Earth orbited around the sun. At the time, the Catholic Church preached an Earth-centered universe, and, at the age of 70, Galileo was hauled before the Inquisition in Rome and forced to kneel and publicly proclaim that the Earth did not move around the sun. As he walked away, legend has it, he whispered to his followers, "But it does move!"

His students preserved this finger bone, displayed on a marble pedestal, as a kind of sacred relic in this shrine to science. Galileo's beliefs eventually triumphed over the Inquisition, and, appropriately, we have his middle finger raised upward for all those blind to science.

• *Also in the glass case, displayed in an ivory frame, is...*

Exhibit IV.1—Galileo's Telescope Lens
(Lente obiettiva di Galileo)
Galileo was the first earthling to see the moons of Jupiter. With a homemade telescope (in Room V), he looked through this lens (it wasn't cracked then) and saw three moons lined up next to Jupiter. This discovery also irked the Church, which insisted that only Earth had a satellite. You could see Jupiter's moons with your own eyes if you simply looked through the telescope, but few church scholars bothered to do so, content to believe what they'd read in ancient books.

Exhibit IV.5—Pendulum Clock Model
(Modello dell'Applicazione del Pendolo all' Orologio)
It's said that during a church service in Pisa, Galileo looked up to see the cathedral's chandelier swaying slowly back and forth, like a pendulum. He noticed that a wide-but-fast arc took the same amount of time as a narrow-but-slow arc. "Hmmm. Maybe that regular pendulum motion could be used to time things...."

Exhibit IV.7—Thermometer (Termoscopio, 19th century)
Galileo also invented the thermometer (similar to this one), though his glass tube filled with air would later be replaced by thermometers of mercury.

• *The big wooden ramp in Room IV is...*

Exhibit IV.13—Inclined Plane
Legend has it that Galileo dropped cannonballs from the Leaning Tower of Pisa to see whether heavier objects fall faster than lighter ones, as the ancient writer Aristotle (and most people) believed. In fact, Galileo probably did not drop objects from the Leaning Tower, but he likely rolled them down a wooden ramp like this reconstructed one.

Rolling balls of different weights down the ramp, he timed them as they rang the bells posted along the way. (The bells are spaced increasingly farther apart, but a ball—accelerating as it drops—will ring them in a regular time.) What Galileo found is that—if you discount air resistance—all objects fall at the same speed, regardless of their weight. (It's the air resistance that makes a feather fall more slowly than a cannonball, not the weight.)

He also found that falling objects accelerate (speed up) at a regular rate (9.8 meters per second faster every second) summed up in a mathematical formula (distance is proportional to the time squared).

Exhibit IV.15—Model of Water-Lifting Device
(Macchina da Alzare Acqua)

The horses walk in a circle, rocking the two crossbars back and forth. The crossbars alternately lift and lower buckets in wells, allowing two horses to draw water from four wells. Galileo was among the first research scientists to suggest practical applications of his principles.

• *Enter Room V, filled with telescopes. Galileo's two telescopes are in a glass case on the right-hand wall.*

Room V: Galileo's Telescopes

Galileo built these **telescopes** (Exhibits V.1 and V.2), based on reports he'd read from Holland. He was the first person to seriously study the heavens with telescopes. Though these only magnified the image about 30 times ("30 power," which is less than today's binoculars), he saw Jupiter's moons, Saturn's rings, the craters of the moon (which he named "seas"), and blemishes (sunspots) on the supposedly perfect sun.

A telescope is essentially two "magnifying glasses" (convex lenses) in a tube, one at either end. The farther apart the lenses, the greater the magnification, prompting the 15-foot **telescope hanging on the wall** (V.51). (The longest ever built was 160 feet, but the slightest movement jiggled the image.)

Room VI: Lenses and Prisms

A curved glass lens can bend light, magnifying an image. A **lens-grinding machine** (Exhibit VI.55) could make higher-quality lenses than human hands could.

The study of optics in the 1600s initially had few practical applications beyond optical illusions for the amusement of nobles. Party guests could look at a reflection and see a **man and woman switching genders** (Exhibit VI.53) or walk from side to side to see **Christ become Mary become a saint** (VI.54).

Room VII: Mapping the Cosmos

• *The large contraption in the center of Room VII is an...*

Exhibit VII.30—Armillary Sphere
(Sfera Armillare Tolemaica, c. 1590)

This is a 10-foot-high, gilded-wood model of the universe as conceived by ancient Greeks and medieval Europeans. You'd turn a crank (which is now missing), and watch the stars and planets orbit around the Earth in the center. (The map of North America is pretty accurate, but you're on your own past Reno.) This Earth-centered view of the universe—which matches our common-sense observations of the night sky—was codified by Ptolemy, a Greek-speaking Egyptian of the second century A.D.

Ptolemy (silent *P*) summed up Aristotle's knowledge of the heavens and worked out the mathematics explaining its movements. His math was complex, especially when trying to explain the planets, which occasionally lag behind the stars in their paths across the night sky. (We now know it's because fast-orbiting Earth passes the outer planets in their longer, more time-consuming orbits around the sun.)

Ptolemy's system dominated Europe for 1,400 years. It worked most of the time and fit well with medieval Christianity's human-centered theology. But, finally, Nicolas Copernicus (and Galileo) made the mental leap to a sun-centered system. This simplified the math, explained the movement of planets, and—most importantly—changed earthlings' conception of themselves forever.

• *On the wall near the entrance, find the large, round...*

Exhibit VII.40—Map of the World
(Fra Mauro—*Mappamondo*, 15th century)

With Columbus' voyages, the Europeans' world suddenly got bigger and rounder. This map portrays the spherical world on a flat surface. South is up. At the bottom, find *Europa, Norvegia* (Norway), and Russia. Africa's tip is on top, with India and China to the left.

Room VIII: Microscopes

The inner world was expanding, too. One day, a Dutchman picked something from his teeth, looked at it under his crude microscope, and discovered a mini-universe, crawling with thousands of "very little animalcules, very prettily a-moving" (i.e., bacteria and protozoa). Antoni van Leeuwenhoek (1632–1723) popularized the microscope, finding that fleas have fleas, semen contains sperm, and one-celled creatures are our fellow animals.

This room displays **simple** *(semplice)* and **compound** *(composto)* **microscopes.** A simple one is just a single convex lens—what we'd call a magnifying glass. A compound is two (or more) lenses in a tube, working like a telescope, where one lens magnifies the object and the eyepiece lens magnifies the magnified image. Van Leeuwenhoek opted for a simple microscope, since early compound ones often blurred and colored things around the edges. His glass bead–size lens could make a flea look 275 times bigger.

Room IX: Thermometers

Even nature's most changeable force—the weather—was analyzed by human reason.

You'll see many interesting **thermometers** *(termometri)*—spiral ones, tall ones, and skinny ones on distinctive bases. All operate on the basic principle that heat expands things. So, a liquid in a closed glass tube will expand and rise upward as the temperature rises.

Galileo's early thermometer held air, which is too easily affected by changing air pressure. So they experimented with various liquids in a vacuum tube—first water, then alcohol. Finally, G. D. Fahrenheit (1656–1736) tried mercury, the densest liquid, which expands evenly. He set his scale to the freezing point (32 degrees) and boiling point (212 degrees) of water. Anders Celsius (1701–1744) also used water as the standard, but called the freezing point 0 and boiling point 100.
• *Left of the entrance is...*

Room X: Meteorology
Exhibit X.3-5—Column Barometers

To make a barometer, take a long, skinny glass tube like the one in the wood frame, fill it with liquid mercury, then turn it upside down

and put the open end into a bowlful of more mercury. The column of mercury keeps standing as the air in the room "pushes back," pressing down on the surface of the bowl of mercury.

Changing air pressure signals a change in the weather. Hot air expands, pressing down harder on the bowl of mercury, pushing the mercury column up above 30 inches, "pushing away" clouds, and pointing to good, dry weather (called *Gran Secco* on this device). Low pressure lets the mercury drop, warning of "big rains" *(Gran Pioggia)*. Your home barometer probably has a round dial with a needle, but it operates on a similar principle.
• *To the right of the entrance...*

Exhibit X.54—Hygrometer

When it's humid (lots of water vapor in the air), your hair gets limp. When it's dry, it frizzes. In various humidity gauges displayed here, when it's humid, the thread or paper absorbs moisture, getting heavier and tilting the scale that measures the humidity.

Room XI: Reflecting Telescopes

The telescopes we saw in Room V were "refracting telescopes," made with lenses that bend (refract) light. The big ones in this room—thick-barreled, often with the eyepiece on the side—are more modern **reflecting telescopes.** They use mirrors to bounce the light rays back and forth through several (refracting) lenses to increase the magnification, thus avoiding the long tubes and distortion of refractors.

Finally, the big double-lensed contraption, *Grande Lente Ustoria* (Exhibit XI.5) was owned by the Medici Grand Duke of Florence, who, I believe, used it to burn bugs.

• *Take a break before heading upstairs.*

SECOND FLOOR

Room XII: Clocks

In an ever-changing universe, what is constant enough to measure the passage of time? The sun and stars passing over every 24 hours work for calendar time, but not for hours, minutes, or seconds. Medieval man used sundials, or the steady flow of water or sand through an opening, but these were only approximate.

By the 1600s, with overseas trade booming, there was a crying need for an accurate and durable clock to help in navigation. Sighting by the stars told you your latitude but was less certain on whether you were near Florence, Italy (latitude 44), or Portland, Maine (also latitude 44). You needed a way to time Earth's 24-hour rotation, to know exactly where you were on that daily journey—i.e., your longitude. Reward money was offered for a good clock that could be taken to sea, and science sprang into action.

• *The big clock to the left of the entrance is a...*

Exhibit XII.37—Big Clock

Tick. Tock.

This clock is powered by the big, suspended weights that slowly "fall." The energy turns a series of cogwheels that slowly move the clock hands around the dial. The whole thing is regulated by a horizontal ring (at the top) rocking back and forth, once a second. Though big and crude, this "grandfather"-type clock has the three essentials:

1. Power (falling weights).
2. An "escapement" (the cogs that transform the "falling" power into turning power).

3. A regulator that keeps the gears turning evenly. (This one has a rocking ring, while others used a swinging pendulum.)

• *In the glass case ahead in the left corner, find...*

Exhibit XII.1—Spring Clock

A clock powered by dangling weights won't work on a rocking ship. This clock is powered by a metal spring that slowly uncoils. (The spring is also the power behind most **watches.**) The power is regulated by a pendulum—Galileo's contribution. Unfortunately, a rocking pendulum on a rocking ship won't work either.

The longitude problem was finally solved—and a £20,000 prize won—by John Harrison of England (1693–1776), whose "chronometer" (not in this museum) was a spring-driven clock in a suspension device to keep it horizontal. It was accurate within three seconds a day, far better than any in this room.

• *In the glass case along the right wall...*

Exhibit XII.33—The Writing Hand *(La Mano che Scrive)*

A clockwork mechanism powers this mechanical hand of time that writes profundities in Latin (*Huic Domui Deus...* This is the House of God...). The hand gets an A for ingenuity and a B-minus for penmanship.

During the so-called Age of Reason (1600s) and Age of Enlightenment (1700s), the clock was the perfect metaphor for the orderly workings of God's well-crafted universe.

• *To the left of the glass case, find the big, black...*

Exhibit XII.28—"Perpetual Motion" Machine

This big, black clock rolls a ball down a spiral ramp, powering the very device that will launch it back up again. And so on, and so on, ad infinitum...or so hoped those pursuing the elusive machine that could power itself. In fact, in every energy exchange (as stated in the second law of thermodynamics), a certain amount is transformed into nonrecyclable heat, meaning a perpetual motion machine is impossible. This principle of entropy (trend toward dissipation of energy) leads philosophers to ponder the eventual cold, lifeless fate of the universe itself.

• *Head to the large Room XIV.*

Room XIV: Electricity (or, more precisely, Electromagnetism)

Lightning, magnets, and static cling mystified humans for millennia. Little did they know that these quite different phenomena are all generated by the same invisible force—electromagnetism.

In the 1700s, electricity began to be studied, harnessed...and played with. The big **static electricity–generating machine** (in the center of the room) was a popular party amusement. You turned a (missing) crank to spin the glass disk, which rubbed against cloth, generating static electricity. The electricity could be stored in the glass Leyden Jar (a jar coated with metal and filled with water). The metal rod sticking out the top of the jar gave off a small charge when touched, enough to create a spark, shock a party guest, or tenderize a turkey (as Ben Franklin attempted one Thanksgiving). But a static generator like this could never produce enough electricity for practical use.

• *In the glass case to the left of the entrance are several early batteries.*

Alessandro Volta (1745–1827) built the first **battery** in Europe (XIV.117 and XIV.134 are similar), which generates electricity from a chemical reaction. He stacked metal disks of zinc and copper between disks of cardboard soaked with salt water. The zinc slowly dissolves, releasing electrons into the liquid.

Hook a wire to each end of the battery, and the current flows. When the zinc is gone, your battery is dead.

The **electric motor**, *Motore elettrico* (XIV.132) generates electricity by moving a magnet through a coil of copper wire, a principle perfected by England's Michael Faraday in 1831. This invention soon led to production of electricity on a large scale.

Room XV: Pneumatic (Air) and Hydraulic (Water) Pumps
Exhibit XV.21-22—Archimedes Screw Models
(Modelli di Vite d'Archimede)

Back in 3rd-century-B.C. Greece, Archimedes—the man who gave

us the phrase "Eureka!" ("I've found it!")—invented a way to pump water that's still occasionally used today. It's a screw in a cylinder. Simply turn the handle and the screw spins, channeling the water up in a spiral path. Dutch windmills powered big Archimedes screws to push water over dikes, to reclaim land from the sea.

Rooms XVI and XVII: Models for Demonstrating Newton's Mechanics

Isaac Newton (1642–1727) explained all of the universe's motion ("mechanics")—from spinning planets to rolling rocks—in a few simple mathematical formulas.

Exhibit XVI.6—Double Rising Cone *(Doppio Cono Saliente)*

The double cone rolls up the incline, seemingly defying gravity and Newton's laws. Ah, but Newton would remind us, the cone's center of gravity is always descending.

The **collision balls in Room XVII** (the big wooden frame with hanging balls), a popular desktop toy in the 1970s, demonstrate Newton's three famous laws.

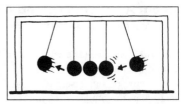

1. **Inertia.** The balls just sit there unless something moves them, and once they're set in motion, they'll keep moving the same way until something stops them.
2. **Force = Mass times Acceleration.** The harder you strike the balls, the farther they go. Use two balls to strike with, and you pack twice the punch.
3. **For every action, there's an equal and opposite reaction.** When one ball swings in and strikes the rest, one ball at the other end swings out, then returns and strikes back.

Room XVIII: Medicine

Back when the same guy who cut your hair removed your appendix, surgery was crude. In the 1700s, there were no anesthetics beyond a bottle of wine, and no knowledge of antiseptics.

The almost life-size wax **obstetrics models**—showing various breech-style complications—are a pregnant woman's nightmare.

Room XIX: Pharmacy
Exhibit XIX.1—Pharmaceutical Jars (late 1700s)

Read the labels on the jars to see what was considered therapeutic in the 1700s: cocaine *(Coca Boliviana)*, licorice *(Anice)*, poisonous plants *(Belladonna)*, tea *(The)*, ipecac *(Ipecacuana)*, and something I believe translates as "flies' nuts" *(Noci Mosca)*.

Room XX: Chemistry

• *On the wall, find the...*

Exhibit XX.34—Affinity Table
(*Tabula Affinitatum*, 18th century)

This is a precursor of modern periodic tables of the elements. Antoine Lavoisier (1743–94) was the Galileo of chemistry, introducing sound methodology and transforming the mumbo jumbo of medieval alchemy into hard science. He used the standardized terminology of suffixes that describe the different forms a single element can take (sulfur, sulf-ide, sulf-ate, sulf-uric, etc.).

Room XXI: Weights and Measures

• *In the glass case ahead, bottom shelf, find...*

Exhibit XXI.28—One Meter Rod *(Metro)*

Much of the purpose of science is to use constants to measure an ever-changing universe. Here's one constant, the meter, established in 1790 as the fundamental unit by which all distances are measured.

The rod is exactly one meter. Or 39.37 inches. Or 1/1,000th of the distance from the Science Museum to *David*. Or 1/10,000,000th of the distance from the equator to the North Pole. Or, according to the updated definition of 1960, a meter is the length of 1,650,763.73 wavelengths in a vacuum of the orange-red radiation of krypton 86.

Ain't science wonderful?

SLEEPING

For hassle-free efficiency, I favor hotels and restaurants handy to your sightseeing activities. Nearly all of my recommended accommodations are located in Florence's downtown core.

The accommodations scene varies wildly with the season. Spring and fall are very tight and expensive, while mid-July through August is wide open and discounted. November through February is also generally empty. I've listed prices for peak season: April, May, June, September, and October. If a price range is listed, the lower end reflects off-season (Aug, Nov–March), and the higher end reflects peak season.

With good information and an e-mail or phone call beforehand, you can find a stark, clean, and comfortable double with breakfast and a shower down the hall for about €80 (for the room, not per person). A typical room with a private bath costs around €100 (less at the smaller places, such as the *soggiorni*). You get elegance in peak season for €150. Virtually all of the accommodations are central, within minutes of the great sights. Some places listed are old and rickety, and described as such. Few hotels escape moped noise at night.

Book ahead. I repeat, book ahead (by e-mail, fax, or phone). Places will hold a room until early afternoon. If they say they're full, mention that you're using this book. If you're traveling off-season, you can show up without reservations and find huge discounts.

Book direct—not through a tourist agency. Tourist information room-finding services cannot give opinions on quality. A major advantage of this book is its extensive listing of good-value rooms. I like places that are clean, small, central, relatively quiet at night, traditional, inexpensive, and friendly—and not listed in other guidebooks. (In Florence, six out of eight means it's a keeper.)

Hotels

Most rooms cluster around €90–150 (with private bathrooms). Three or four people economize by sharing larger rooms. Solo travelers find that the cost of a *camera singola* is often only 25 percent less than a *camera doppia*. Most listed hotels have rooms for anywhere from one to five people. If there's room for an extra cot, they'll cram it in for you.

You normally get close to what you pay for. Prices are fairly standard. Shopping around earns you a better location and more character, but rarely a cheaper price.

However, prices at nearly any hotel can get soft if you do any of the following: arrive direct (without using a pricey middleman like the TI), offer to pay cash, stay at least three nights, mention this book, or visit off-season. Offer to skip breakfast for a better price. If you're on a budget, ask for a cheaper room or a discount. Always ask.

You'll save €30 if you request a room without a shower and just use the shower down the hall. Generally rooms with a bath or shower also have a toilet and a bidet (which Italians use for quick sponge baths). If a shower has no curtain, the entire bathroom showers with you. Even if there is a curtain, the toilet or sink may be inside the shower. The cord that dangles over the tub or shower is not a clothesline. You pull it when you've fallen and can't get up (though oddly, they're often bundled up out of reach to keep them out of the way).

Double beds are called *matrimoniale*, even though hotels aren't interested in your marital status. Twins are *due letti singoli.*

Air-conditioning sometimes costs an extra per-day charge, is worth seeking out in summer, and is rarely activated from fall through spring. Rooms in fancier hotels usually come with air-conditioning (included in the price), a little safe, and a small stocked fridge called a *frigo bar* (FREE-goh bar). Many hotel rooms have a TV and phone.

If you arrive on an overnight train, your room may not be ready. Drop your bag at the hotel and dive right into Florence.

When you check in, the receptionist will normally ask for your passport and keep it for a couple of hours. Hotels are legally required to register each guest with the local police. Relax. Americans are notorious for making this chore more difficult than it needs to be.

The hotel breakfast, while convenient, is often a bad value—€9 for a simple continental buffet with unlimited *caffè latte.* You can sometimes request cheese or salami (about €3 extra). I enjoy taking breakfast at the corner café. It's OK to supplement what you order with a few picnic goodies.

Rooms are safe. Still, zip cameras and keep money out of sight. More pillows and blankets are usually in the closet or available on request. In Italy, towels and linen aren't always replaced every day. Hang your towel up to dry.

Sleep Code

(€1 = $1.20)
To give maximum information in a minimum of space, I use the following code to describe the accommodations listed in this book. Prices listed are per room, not per person.

S = Single room (or price for one person in a double).

D = Double or Twin room. "Double beds" are often two twins sheeted together and are usually big enough for nonromantic couples.

T = Triple (generally a double bed with a single).

Q = Quad (usually two double beds).

b = Private bathroom with toilet and shower or tub.

s = Private shower or tub only (the toilet is down the hall).

no CC = Doesn't accept credit cards; pay in local cash.

SE = Speaks English. This code is used only when it seems predictable that you'll encounter English-speaking staff.

NSE = Does not speak English. Used only when it's unlikely you'll encounter English-speaking staff.

According to this code, a couple staying at a "Db-€140, SE" hotel would pay a total of €140 (about $170) for a double room with a private bathroom. The hotel accepts credit cards or Italian cash (euros); you can assume a hotel takes credit cards unless you see "no CC" in the listing. The staff speaks English.

To help you easily sort through these listings, I've divided the rooms into three categories based on the price for a standard double room with bath during high season:

$$$ **Higher Priced**—Most rooms €160 or more.
 $$ **Moderately Priced**—Most rooms between €110–160.
  $ **Lower Priced**—Most rooms €110 or less.

Your hotelier, a good source of advice, can direct you to the nearest launderette and Internet café.

To avoid the time-wasting line at the reception desk in the morning, settle up your bill the evening before you leave.

Country Code

To call Italy from the United States or Canada, dial 011-39 (the country code) and then the local number. If calling Italy from another European country, dial 00-39-local number.

Making Reservations

To reserve from home, e-mail, fax, or phone your request. You'll find a handy reservation form in the appendix (online at www .ricksteves.com/reservation). Europeans prefer e-mail to pricey faxing. If you don't get an answer to a faxed request, consider that a "no."

(Many little places get 20 faxes a day after they're full and can't afford to respond.) It's also easy to reserve by phone. (For details, see "Telephones" in this book's introduction.)

Most hotels listed are accustomed to English-speaking tourists. Simple English is usually fine. A two-night stay for the nights of August 16 and 17 would be "2 nights, 16/8/05 to 18/8/05" (Europeans write the date day/month/year and hotel jargon uses your day of departure). You'll often receive a response back requesting one night's deposit. If your credit-card number is accepted as the deposit (which is usually the case), you can pay with your card or cash when you arrive; if you don't show up, you'll be billed for one night. Always reconfirm your reservations a day or two in advance by phone.

Honor (or cancel by phone) your reservations. Long distance is cheap from public phone booths. Don't let these people down—I promised you'd call and cancel if for some reason you can't show up.

Between the Station and Duomo

$$$ **Palazzo Castiglioni** offers 16 grand rooms with all the conveniences and a peaceful, *palazzo* decor. Most rooms are spacious, several have frescoes, and all make a fine splurge (Db-€170, Db suite-€200, Tb-€210, 5 percent discount with cash, air-con, elevator, Via del Giglio 8, tel. 055-214-886, fax 055-274-0521, pal.cast @flashnet.it, Laura SE).

$$ **Hotel Accademia** is an elegant place with marble stairs, parquet floors, attractive public areas, 21 pleasant rooms, and a floor plan that defies logic (Db-€140, Tb-€170, prices promised through 2005 with this book, 5 percent additional discount with cash, air-con, tiny courtyard, Via Faenza 7, tel. 055-293-451, fax 055-219-771, www.accademiahotel.net, info@accademiahotel.net, Tea SE).

$$ **Hotel Bellettini** rents 30 bright, cool, well-cared-for rooms with inviting lounges (S-€78, Sb-€100, D-€105, Db-€140, Tb-€170, Qb-€210; 5 percent discount with this book through 2005 if claimed during checkout, air-con, Via de' Conti 7, tel. 055-213-561, fax 055-283-551, www.hotelbellettini.com, info@hotelbellettini.com, frisky Gina SE). Be warned, they rent much higher-priced rooms in a nearby annex.

$$ **Residenza dei Pucci,** a block north of the Duomo, has 12 tastefully decorated rooms—in soothing earth tones—with aristocratic furniture and tweed carpeting. It's fresh and bright (Sb-€130, Db-€145, Db in Aug and much of winter-€105, Tb-€165, suite with grand Duomo view-€207 for 2 people, €233 for 4, claim a 10 percent discount through 2005 with cash and this book, breakfast served in room, Via dei Pucci 9, tel. 055-281-886, fax 055-264-314, http://residenzapucci.interfree.it, residenzapucci@interfree.it, SE).

Florence Hotels

① Palazzo Castiglioni
   & Hotel Aldobrandini
② Hotel Accademia
③ Hotel Bellettini
④ Residenza dei Pucci
⑤ Hotel Basilea
⑥ Casa Rabatti
⑦ Affitacamere Freda Lucia
⑧ Soggiorno Magliani
⑨ Hotel Loggiato dei Serviti
⑩ Hotel Morandi alla Crocetta
⑪ Hotel Le Due Fontane
⑫ Oblate Sisters of the Assumption
⑬ Hotel Pendini

⑭ Residenza Giotto
⑮ Pensione Maxim
⑯ Soggiorno Battistero
⑰ Albergo Firenze
⑱ Hotel Torre Guelfa & Hotel
   Pensione Alessandra
⑲ In Piazza della Signoria B&B
⑳ Hotel Davanzati
㉑ Hotel Pensione Elite
㉒ Bellevue House
㉓ Hotel Sole
㉔ Hotel Bargellino
㉕ Florence Walking Tours

$ **Hotel Aldobrandini,** a budget choice in a drab old palazzo, has 15 basic, clean rooms, with the San Lorenzo market at its doorstep and the entrance to the Medici Chapels a few steps away (Ss-€40, Sb-€50, D-€65, Db-€80 with this book, lots of night noise but has double-paned windows, fans, hiding behind market stalls and mopeds at Piazza Madonna degli Aldobrandini 8, tel. 055-211-866, fax 055-267-6281, www.hotelaldobrandini.it, info@hotelaldobrandini.it; Ignazio SE, though his one-legged mother in wheelchair, who often greets people, speaks Italian).

Near the Central Market

$$ **Hotel Basilea** offers predictable three-star, air-conditioned comfort in its 38 modern rooms (Sb-€80–110, Db-€110–150, Tb-€150–210, 5 percent discount through 2005 with this book, lower prices Aug and Nov–March, elevator, terrace, Via Guelfa 41, at intersection with Nazionale—a busy street, ask for a room in the back, tel. 055-214-587, fax 055-268-350, www.hotelbasilea.net, basilea@florenceitaly.net, SE).

$ **Casa Rabatti** is the ultimate if you always wanted to be a part of a Florentine family. Its four simple, clean rooms are run with motherly warmth by Marcella, who speaks minimal English. Seeing 10 years of my family Christmas cards on their walls, I'm reminded of how long the Rabattis have been keeping budget travelers happy (D-€50, Db-€60, €25 per bed in shared quad or quint, prices good with this book, no breakfast, no CC, fans, no sign other than on doorbell, 5 blocks from station, Via San Zanobi 48 black, tel. 055-212-393, casarabatti@inwind.it). If booked up, Marcella will refer you to her daughter's place nearby on Via Nazionale.

$ **Affitacamere Lucia Freda** is basic, clean, and cheap. Its four ground floor-yet-quiet rooms share two bathrooms, a kitchenette, and a leafy garden terrace (S-€45, D-€55, T-€70, €5 less for 2 or more days, discounts in winter, cash only, no breakfast, Via San Zanobi 76, but ring at #31, tel. 055-487-533, luciafreda@libero.it, kind Lucia and son Claudio).

$ **Soggiorno Magliani,** central and humble with seven rooms, feels and smells like a great-grandmother's place (S-€38, D-€49, T-€65, cash only but secure reservation with CC, no breakfast, double-paned windows, near Via Guelfa at Via Reparata 1, tel. 055-287-378, hotel-magliani@libero.it, run by friendly family duo Vincenza and English-speaking daughter Cristina).

East of the Duomo

$$$ **Hotel Loggiato dei Serviti,** at the most prestigious address in Florence on the most Renaissance square in town, gives you Old World romance with hair dryers. Stone stairways lead you under open-beam ceilings through this 16th-century monastery's classy

public rooms. The 38 cells, with air-conditioning, TVs, mini-bars, and telephones, wouldn't be recognized by their original inhabitants. The hotel staff is both professional and friendly (Sb-€146, Db-€210, family suites from €263, 30 percent discount in Aug and late Nov–Feb, 5 elegant rooms in 17th-century annex, elevator, Piazza S.S. Annuziata 3, tel. 055-289-592, fax 055-289-595, www.loggiatodeiservitihotel.it, info@loggiatodeiservitihotel.it, Simonetta, Francesca, and Andrea SE). Ask for a backside room to avoid piazza night noise.

$$$ **Hotel Morandi alla Crocetta,** another former convent, envelops you in a 16th-century cocoon. Located on a quiet street, with period furnishings, parquet floors, and wood-beamed ceilings, it takes you back (10 rooms, Sb-€110, Db-€170, breakfast-€11, a block off Piazza S.S. Annunziata at Via Laura 50, tel. 055-234-4747, fax 055-248-0954, www.hotelmorandi.it, welcome@hotelmorandi.it, Claudio SE).

$$ **Hotel Le Due Fontane** faces the Renaissance Piazza S.S. Annunziata but fills its old building with a smoky, 1970s, business-class ambience. Its 57 air-conditioned rooms are big and comfortable (Sb-€110, Db-€160, Tb-€200, prices promised through 2005 only if you claim them upon reserving, elevator, Piazza S.S. Annunziata 14, tel. 055-210-185, fax 055-294-461, www.leduefontane.it, info@leduefontane.it, SE).

$ **Oblate Sisters of the Assumption** run an institutional 20-room hotel in a Renaissance building with a dreamy garden and a quiet, nice-place-to-relax-after-you-die feel. Not a hint of English spoken here (€37 per person, elevator, no CC, Borgo Pinti 15, tel. 055-248-0582, fax 055-234-6291).

Near Piazza Repubblica

These are the most central of my accommodations recommendations (and therefore a little overpriced). While worth the extra cost for many, given Florence's walkable core, nearly every hotel can be considered central.

$$ **Hotel Pendini,** a well-run and well-worn three-star hotel with Old World tiles, chandeliers, and 42 rooms, is popular and central, overlooking the grand Piazza Repubblica (Sb-€86–110, Db-€110–150 depending on season, elevator, fine lounge and breakfast room, air-con, Via Strozzi 2, tel. 055-211-170, fax 055-281-807, www.florenceitaly.net, Barbara SE).

$$ **Residenza Giotto** has six colorful, modern rooms, and a terrace so close to the Duomo you can almost touch it (Sb-€120, Db-€130, Tb-€145, 10 percent discount for cash with this book if claimed at time of reservation, breakfast in room, elevator, Via Roma 6, 4th floor, tel. 055-214-593, fax 055-264-8568, www.residenzagiotto.it, residenzagiotto@tin.it, SE).

$$ Pensione Maxim, right on Via dei Calzaiuoli, is a big, institutional-feeling place as close to the sights as possible. Its halls are narrow, but the 29 basic rooms are comfortable and well-maintained (Sb-€75, Db-€99, Tb-€125, Qb-€148, dorm bed-€30, takes CC but pay first night in cash, air-con, elevator, Via dei Calzaiuoli 11, tel. 055-217-474, fax 055-283-729, www.hotelmaximfirenze.it, hotmaxim@tin.it, Paolo Maioli SE).

$ Soggiorno Battistero, next door to the Baptistery, has seven simple, airy rooms, most with great views, overlooking the Baptistery and square. You're in the heart of Florence (Sb-€75, Db-€98, Tb-€135, Qb-€145, these prices good through 2005 with this book, 5 percent discount with cash, breakfast served in room, air-con, double-paned windows, Piazza San Giovanni 1, 3rd floor, no elevator, tel. 055-295-143, fax 055-268-189, www.soggiornobattistero.it, battistero@dada.it, lovingly run by Italian Luca and his American wife, Kelly).

$ Albergo Firenze, a big, efficient place, offers 58 good, basic rooms in a wonderfully central, reasonably quiet locale two blocks behind the Duomo (Sb-€80, Db-€100, Tb-€147, Qb-€170, cash only; prepay first night with traveler's check, bank draft, or international money order; elevator, air-con, off Via del Corso at Piazza Donati 4, tel. 055-214-203, fax 055-212-370, www.hotelfirenze-fi.it, firenze.albergo@tiscali.it, SE).

Near Piazza della Signoria and Ponte Vecchio

$$$ Hotel Torre Guelfa is topped by a fun medieval tower with a panoramic rooftop terrace and a huge living room. Its 29 rooms vary wildly in size (Sb-€110, small Db-€145, standard Db-€180, Db junior suite-€230, family deals, 5 percent discount with cash in 2005 with this book). Room #15, with a private terrace—€210—is worth reserving several months in advance (elevator, air-con, a couple blocks northwest of Ponte Vecchio, Borgo S.S. Apostoli 8, tel. 055-239-6338, fax 055-239-8577, www.hoteltorreguelfa.com, torre .guelfa@flashnet.it; Sabina, Giancarlo, Carlo, and Sandro all SE).

$$$ In Piazza della Signoria B&B is peaceful, classy, and homey at the same time and overlooks Piazza della Signoria. It comes with all the special touches—much like a top-end American B&B. Each of its eight rooms has a huge and lavish bathroom (Sb-€170–210, Db-€200–260, Tb-€280, lower prices without view, family apartments, tiny elevator, air-con, Via dei Magazzini 2, tel. 055-239-9546, fax 055-267-6616, mobile 348-321-0565, www .inpiazzadellasignoria.it, info@inpiazzadellasignoria.it, Sonia SE).

$$ Hotel Pensione Alessandra is a 16th-century, tranquil place with 27 big, modern rooms (S-€72, Sb-€113, D-€113, Db-€150, T-€150, Tb-€196, Q-€165, Qb-€217, 5 percent discount with cash, air-con, Borgo S.S. Apostoli 17, tel. 055-283-438, fax 055-210-619, www.hotelalessandra.com, info@hotelalessandra.com, SE).

$$ **Hotel Davanzati,** bright and shiny with artistic touches, has 21 cheery rooms with all the comforts. A family affair, friendly Tomasso and father Fabrizio also book dinners, museums, and excursions (Sb-€95, Db-€150, Tb-€195, prices soft in slow times and off-season, elevator, air-con, Via Porta Rossa 5, tel. 055-286-666, fax 055-265-8252, www.hoteldavanzati.it, info@hoteldavanzati.it, Laura and Stefano SE).

Near the Train Station

Note: As with any big Italian city, the area around the train station is a magnet for hardworking pickpockets on alert for lost, vulnerable tourists with bulging moneybelts hanging out of their khakis.

$ **Hotel Pensione Elite,** run warmly by sunny Nadia, is a fine value. It has 10 comfortable—if plainly furnished—rooms and a charm rare in this price range (Ss-€70, Sb-€80, Ds-€75, Db-€90, Tb-€110, Qb-€130, breakfast-€6, air-con, fans, Via della Scala 12, 2nd floor, tel. & fax 055-215-395, easy reservations by phone, SE).

$ **Bellevue House** is a fourth-floor oasis (no elevator) with six spacious rooms flanking a long, mellow yellow lobby. It's a peaceful time-warp run by Rosanna and Antonio di Grazia (Db-maximum €100 in April–June, Sept, and Oct, Db-maximum €80 off-season, prices promised through 2005 with this book, 5 percent cash discount, includes breakfast in a street level bar, oversized modern bathrooms, Via della Scala 21, tel. 055-260-8932, fax 055-265-5315, mobile 333-612-5973, www.bellevuehouse.it, info@bellevuehouse.it).

$ **Hotel Sole,** a clean, cozy, family-run place with eight bright, modern rooms, is just off Santa Maria Novella square toward the river. Friendly Anna makes you feel like a guest of the family (Sb-€50, Db-€80, Tb-€110, no breakfast, no CC, air-con, elevator, 1:00 curfew, Via del Sole 8, 3rd floor, tel. & fax 055-239-6094, NSE).

$ **Hotel Bargellino,** run by Bostonian Carmel and her Italian husband Pino, has a traditional faded-paint charm and funky antique furniture just a few blocks north of the train station. Some rooms face a large, peaceful common terrace complete with a tiny greenhouse (S-€43, D-€65, Db-€75, T-€100, CC OK but send deposit check to Carmel's sister in Boston to reserve, no breakfast, Via Guelfa 87, tel. 055-238-2658, fax 055-238-2698, www.ilbargellino .com, Carmel SE with a Boston accent).

Oltrarno, South of the River

Across the river in the Oltrarno area, between the Pitti Palace and Ponte Vecchio, you'll still find small traditional crafts shops, neighborly piazzas, and family eateries. The following places are an easy walk from the Ponte Vecchio.

$$$ Hotel Lungarno is *the* place to stay if money is no object. This deluxe, four-star hotel with 74 rooms strains anything stressful or rough out of Italy, and gives you (sometimes snooty) service, physical elegance everywhere you look, and fine views over the Arno and Ponte Vecchio (Sb-€250, Db-€400, Db facing river-€510, fancier suites, great riverside public spaces, air-con, elevator, 100 yards from Ponte Vecchio at Borgo San Jacopo 14, tel. 055-27261, fax 055-272-64-444, www.lungarnohotels.com, bookings @lungarnohotels.com, SE).

$$$ Hotel Silla, a classic three-star hotel with 36 cheery, spacious, pastel, and modern rooms, is a fine value. It faces the river and overlooks a park opposite the Santa Croce Church (Db-€170, Tb-€210, mention this book for a discount, elevator, air-con, Via dei Renai 5, tel. 055-234-2888, fax 055-234-1437, www.hotelsilla.it, hotelsilla@tin.it, Laura and Stefano SE).

$$ Hotel La Scaletta, ramshackle and reeking in character, is a dark, cool place with a labyrinthine floor plan, senseless stairs, loose tiles, lots of Old World lounges, and a romantic, panoramic roof terrace (16 rooms, S-€50, Sb-€95, D-€110, Db-€115–130, Tb-€130–160, Qb-€160–170, higher price is for quieter rooms in back, discount for cash, mostly air-con, elevator, bar with fine wine at good prices, Via Guicciardini 13 black, 150 yards south of Ponte Vecchio, tel. 055-283-028, fax 055-289-562, www.hotellascaletta.it, info@hotellascaletta.it). The new owners—Andrea, Fabrizio, and Paolo—and the manager, Giovanna, enjoy entertaining guests on their comfortable terrace. They serve a fine family-style dinner and a €15 "Taste of Tuscany for Two" deal (plate of quality Tuscan meats and cheeses with bread and 4 glasses of robust Chianti)—perfect for a light lunch or dinner.

$$ Pensione Sorelle Bandini is a rickety 500-year-old palace on a perfectly Florentine square, with 12 cavernous rooms, museum-warehouse interiors, a musty youthfulness, a balcony lounge-loggia with a view, and an ambience that, for romantic bohemians, can be a highlight of Florence. Mimmo or Sr. Romeo will hold a room until 16:00 with a phone call (D-€102, Db-€110, T-€137, Tb-€149, includes breakfast, no CC, elevator, Piazza Santo Spirito 9, tel. 055-215-308, fax 055-282-761, pensionebandini@tiscali.it, SE). This square can attract drug pushers; just don't invite them to your room.

$ Istituto Gould is a Protestant Church–run place with 41 clean but drab rooms with twin beds and modern facilities (S-€36, Sb-€41, D-€46, Db-€58, Tb-€72, €21 per person in quads, no breakfast, quieter rooms in back, Via dei Serragli 49, tel. 055-212-576, fax 055-280-274, www.istitutogould.it, gould.reception@dada.it). You must arrive when the office is open (Mon–Fri 9:00–13:00 & 15:00–19:00, Sat 9:00–13:00, no check-in Sun or holidays, SE).

Oltrarno Hotels

1 Hotel La Scaletta
2 To Hotel Silla
3 Pensione Sorelle Bandini
4 Hotel Lungarno
5 Istituto Gould
6 Ostello Santa Monaca

$ **Ostello Santa Monaca,** a cheap hostel, is a long block south of the Brancacci Chapel and attracts a young backpacking crowd (€17 beds with sheets, 4- to 20-bed rooms, 1:00 curfew, Via Santa Monaca 6, tel. 055-268-338, fax 055-280-185, www.ostello.it, info@ostello.it).

Away from the Center

$$ **Hotel Ungherese** is good for drivers. It's northeast of the city center (near *stadio,* en route to Fiesole), with easy, free street parking and quick bus access (#11 and #17) into central Florence (Sb-€72, Db-€123, extra bed-€31, prices good through 2005 only with this book, additional 7 percent discount for cash, rooms are 20 percent less off-season, includes breakfast, most rooms air-con, Via G. B. Amici 8, tel. & fax 055-573-474, www.hotelungherese.it, info @hotelungherese.it, Giovanni and Francesca SE). It has great singles and a backyard garden terrace (ask for a room on the garden). They can recommend good eateries nearby.

$ **Villa Camerata,** classy for an IYHF hostel, is in a pretty villa on the outskirts of Florence (€16.50 per bed with breakfast, 4- to 12-bed rooms, must have hostel membership card, no CC, ride bus #17 to Salviatino stop, Via Righi 2, tel. 055-601-451).

EATING

The Italians are masters of the art of fine living. That means eating…long and well. Lengthy, multicourse lunches and dinners and endless hours sitting in outdoor cafés are the norm. Americans eat on their way to an evening event and complain if the check is slow in coming. For Italians, the meal is an end in itself, and only rude waiters rush you. When you want the bill, mime-scribble on your raised palm or ask for it: *"Il conto?"*

Even those of us who liked dorm food will find that the local cafés, cuisine, and wines become a highlight of our Italian adventure. This is sightseeing for your palate, and even if the rest of you is sleeping in cheap hotels, your taste buds will relish an occasional first-class splurge. You can eat well without going broke. But be careful; you're just as likely to blow a small fortune on a disappointing meal as you are to dine wonderfully for €20.

To save money and time for sights, you can keep lunches fast and simple, eating in one of the countless pizzerias and self-service cafeterias (or picnicking, see below). For dessert, it's gelato (see page 190).

Restaurants

Good restaurants don't open before 19:00 for dinner. When restaurant-hunting, choose places filled with locals, not the place with the big neon signs boasting, "We speak English and accept credit cards." Restaurants parked on famous squares generally serve bad food at high prices to tourists. Locals eat better at lower-rent locales. Family-run places operate without hired help and can offer cheaper meals. The words *trattoria* and *osteria* (normally simple local-style restaurants) make me salivate. Any place called *ristorante* is generally more formal, with prices to match. While set menus can be cheap and easy, galloping gourmets order à la carte with the

Tipping

Tipping is an issue only at restaurants that have waiters and wait-resses. If you order your food at a counter, don't tip. (Many Italians don't ever tip.)

If the menu states that service is included *(servizio incluso)*, Italians generally don't tip any extra. But if you like to tip and you're pleased with the service, you could throw in €1 to €2 euros per person at your table.

If service is not included, tip 5 to 10 percent by rounding up or leaving the change from your bill. Leave the tip on the table or hand it to your server. It's best to tip in cash even if you pay with your credit card. Otherwise the money may never reach your waiter.

help of a menu translator. (The *Marling Italian Menu Master* is excellent. *Rick Steves' Italian Phrase Book* has enough phrases for intermediate eaters.)

A full meal consists of an appetizer (*antipasto*, €3–6), a first course (*primo piatto*, pasta or soup, €4–8), and a second course (*secondo piatto*, expensive meat and fish dishes, €6–14). Vegetables *(contorni, verdure)* may come with the *secondo* or cost extra (€3–4) as a side dish. Restaurants normally pad the bill with a cover charge (*pane e coperto*—"bread and cover charge," around €2–3) and a service charge (*servizio*, 15 percent); these charges are listed on the menu.

The euros can add up in a hurry. Light and budget eaters get by with a *primo piatto* each and sharing an *antipasto*. Italians admit that the *secondo* is the least interesting aspect of the local cuisine.

Delis, Cafeterias, Pizza Shops, and *Tavola Calda* (Hot Table) Bars

Florence offers many cheap alternatives to restaurants. Stop by a *rosticceria* for great cooked deli food; a self-service cafeteria for the basics without the add-ons; a *tavola calda* bar for an assortment of veggies; or a Pizza Rustica shop for stand-up or take-out pizza.

Pizza is cheap and everywhere. Key pizza vocabulary: *capricciosa* (generally ham, mushrooms, olives, and artichokes), *funghi* (mushrooms), *marinara* (tomato sauce, oregano, garlic, no cheese), *quattro formaggi* (four different cheeses), and *quattro stagioni* (different toppings on each of the four quarters for those who can't choose just one menu item). If you ask for *peperoni* on your pizza, you'll get green or red peppers, not sausage. Kids like spicy *diavola* (closest thing in Italy to American "pepperoni") or bland *margherita* (tomato and cheese) pizzas. At Pizza Rustica take-out shops, slices are sold by weight (100 grams, or *un etto*, is a hot, cheap snack; 200 grams, or *due etti*, makes a light meal).

For a fast, cheap, and healthy lunch, find a *tavola calda* bar with a buffet spread of meat and vegetables and ask for a mixed plate of vegetables with a hunk of mozzarella *(piatto misto di verdure con moz-zarella)*. Don't be limited by what you can see. If you'd like a salad with a slice of cantaloupe and a hunk of cheese, they'll whip that up for you in a snap. Step up to the bar and, with a pointing finger and key words from the chart in this chapter, you can get a fine mixed plate of vegetables. If something's a mystery, ask for *un assaggio* (oon ah-SAH-joh) to get a little taste.

Italian Bars/Cafés

Italian "bars" are not taverns but cafés. These local hangouts serve coffee, mini-pizzas, sandwiches, and drinks from the cooler. Many dish up plates of fried cheese and vegetables from under the glass counter, ready to reheat.

For quick meals, bars usually have trays of cheap ready-made sandwiches *(panini* or *tramezzini)*—some kinds are delightful grilled. To save time for sightseeing and room for dinner, my favorite lunch is a ham and cheese *panino* at a bar (called toast, have it grilled twice if you want it really hot). To get food "to go," say, *"Da portare via"* (for the road). All bars have a WC *(toilette, bagno)* in the back, and customers are entitled to use it.

Bars serve great drinks—hot, cold, sweet, or alcoholic. Chilled bottled water *(natural* or *frizzante)* is sold cheap to go.

Coffee: If you ask for *"un caffè,"* you'll get espresso. Cappuccino is served to locals before noon and tourists any time of day. (To an Italian, cappuccino is a breakfast drink and a travesty after anything with tomatoes.) Italians like it only warm. To get it hot, request *"Molto caldo"* (very hot) or *"Più caldo, per favore"* ("Hotter, please"; pew KAHL-doh, pehr fah-VOH-ray).

Experiment with a few of the options...
- *caffè freddo*: sweet and iced espresso
- *cappuccino freddo*: iced cappuccino
- *caffè hag*: instant decaf (any coffee drink is available decaffeinated; ask for it *decaffeinato:* day-kah-fay-een-AH-toh)
- *macchiato*: with only a little milk
- *caffè latte*: coffee with lots of hot milk, no foam. Note that ordering a latte gets you only milk.
- *caffè Americano*: espresso diluted with hot water
- *caffè corretto*: espresso with a shot of liqueur

Beer: Beer on tap is *"alla spina."* Get it *piccola* (33 cl), *media* (50 cl), or *grande* (a liter).

Wine: To order a glass *(bicchiere;* bee-kee-AY-ray) of red *(rosso)* or white *(bianco)* wine, say, *"Un bicchiere di vino rosso/bianco."* *Corposo* means full-bodied. House wine often comes in a quarter-liter carafe *(un quarto)*.

Ordering Food at *Tavola Caldas*

plate of	*piatto misto*	pee-AH-toh MEES-toh
mixed veggies	*di verdure*	dee vehr-DOO-ray
"Heated, please."	*"Scaldare,*	skahl-DAH-ray
	per favore."	pehr fah-VOH-ray
"A taste, please."	*"Un assaggio,*	oon ah-SAH-joh
	per favore."	pehr fah-VOH-ray
artichokes	*carciofi*	kar-CHOH-fee
asparagus	*asparagi*	ah-spah-RAH-jee
beans	*fagioli*	fah-JOH-lee
green beans	*fagiolini*	fah-joh-LEE-nee
broccoli	*broccoli*	BROK-oh-lee
cantaloupe	*melone*	may–LOH-nay
carrots	*carote*	kah-ROT-ay
ham	*prosciutto*	proh-SHOO-toh
mushrooms	*funghi*	FOONG-ghee
potatoes	*patate*	pah-TAH-tay
rice	*riso*	REE-zoh
spinach	*spinaci*	speen-AH-chee
tomatoes	*pomodori*	poh-moh-DOH-ree
zucchini	*zucchine*	zoo-KEE-nay
breadsticks	*grissini*	gree-SEE-nee

(Excerpted from *Rick Steves' Italian Phrase Book*)

Prices: You'll notice a two-tiered price system. Drinking a cup of coffee while standing at the bar is cheaper than drinking it at a table. If you're on a budget, don't sit without first checking out the financial consequences. Ask "Same price if I sit or stand?" by saying, *"Costa uguale al tavolo o al banco?"* (KOH-stah oo-GWAH-lay ahl TAH-voh-loh oh ahl BAHN-koh).

If the bar isn't busy, you'll often just order and pay when you leave. Otherwise, (1) decide what you want; (2) find out the price by checking the price list on the wall, the prices posted near the food, or by asking the barman; (3) pay the cashier; and (4) give the receipt to the barman (whose clean fingers handle no dirty euros) and tell him what you want.

Picnics

In Florence, picnicking saves lots of euros and is a great way to sample local specialties. For a colorful experience, gather your ingredients in the morning at Florence's Mercato Centrale (Central Market, near Church of San Lorenzo); you'll probably visit several market stalls to put together a complete meal. A local *alimentari* is your one-stop corner grocery store (most will slice and stuff your sandwich for you if you buy the ingredients there). The rare *super-mercato* gives you more efficiency with less color for less cost.

Juice-lovers can get a liter of O.J. for the price of a Coke or coffee. Look for "100% *succo*" (juice) on the label. Hang onto the half-liter mineral-water bottles (sold everywhere for about €1). Buy juice in cheap liter boxes, drink some, and store the extra in your water bottle. (I drink tap water—*acqua del rubinetto*.)

Picnics can be an adventure in high cuisine. Be daring. Try the fresh mozzarella, *presto* pesto, shriveled olives, and any UFOs the locals are excited about. In supermarkets, weigh your produce on the scale with the photo ID chart and print a price tag. In markets and small shops, you're expected to let the shopkeeper choose the produce for you. To get fruit that's ripe and ready to eat today, say *"per mangiare oggi"* (pehr mahn-JAH-ray OH-jee, meaning "to eat today"). Shopkeepers are happy to sell small quantities of produce.

A typical picnic for two might be fresh rolls, 100 grams of cheese, 100 grams of meat (100 grams = about a quarter pound, called *un etto* in Italy), two tomatoes, three carrots, two apples, yogurt, and a liter box of juice. Total cost—about €10.

FLORENTINE CUISINE

While many Florentine restaurants serve your basic Italian fare—pasta and pizza, veal cutlets, and mixed salad—there are a few local specialties you'll find without looking too hard. In general, Florentine cuisine is hearty, simple, farmers' food: grilled meats, high-quality seasonal vegetables, fresh herbs, prized olive oil, and rustic bread. Tuscans are frugal, not wasting a single breadcrumb. They are also known as *mangiafagioli* (bean-eaters)—and sorting through the many beans on Florentine menus you'll learn why.

Note that steak and seafood are often sold by weight (priced by the kilo—1,000 grams, or just over 2 pounds; or by the *etto*—100 grams). Sometimes, especially for steak, restaurants require a minimum order of four or five *etti*. Beware, or be shell-shocked by €50 entrées.

Here are some typical foods you'll encounter in Florence:

Appetizers (Antipasti)
- *Tuscan bread:* Rustic-style breads (not baguettes) with a thick crust and chewy interior. It's a type of sourdough bread, unsalted and nearly flavorless, used almost like a utensil to sop up the heartier-flavored cuisine. Slathered with olive oil and salt, it is a popular afternoon snack. Locals describe the action of dipping their crust repeatedly into the treasured olive oil as "making the *scarpetta* (little shoe)."

- *Bruschetta:* Toasted bread slices brushed with olive oil and rubbed with garlic, topped with chopped tomato, or a variety of spreads. *A la Toscana* (with liver paste) is traditional and common on menus.
- *Crostini:* Small toasted bread rounds topped with meat or vegetable pastes. *Lardo* (animal fat) is also a favorite traditional spread.
- *Panzanella:* A simple Tuscan salad made of chunks of day-old bread and chopped tomatoes, onion, and basil, tossed in a light vinaigrette.
- *Pecorino cheese:* Fresh *(fresco)* or aged *(secco)*, from ewe's milk.
- *Porcini mushrooms:* Harvested in the fall and used in pasta and soups.
- *Finocchiona sbriciolona:* A soft salami flavored with fennel seed.

First Course *(Primo Piatto)*
- *Ribollita:* "Reboiled" soup traditionally made with leftovers, including white beans *(fagioli)*, seasonal vegetables, and olive oil, with layers of day-old Tuscan bread slices.
- *Pappardelle sulla lepre:* This broad noodle is served with a rich sauce made from wild hare.
- *Pici al ragù:* A fat, spaghetti-like pasta served most often with a meat-tomato sauce.

Main Course *(Secondo Piatto)*
- *Bistecca alla fiorentina:* A thick T-bone steak, grilled and lightly seasoned. (The best is from the white Chiana breed of cattle you'll see grazing throughout Tuscany.) This dish is often sold by weight (per *etto*, or 100 grams), not per portion; ask what the minimum amount costs.
- *Cinghiale:* Wild boar, served grilled or in soups, stews, and pasta. It is also made into many varieties of sausage.
- *Arrosto misto:* Mixed roast meats or meats on a skewer *(spiedino)*.
- *Various game birds:* Squab, pheasant, and guinea hen.
- *Trippa alla fiorentina:* Tripe (intestines) and vegetables sautéed in a tomato sauce, baked with parmesan cheese.
- *...alla fiorentina:* Anything cooked "in the Florentine style." Can mean almost anything, but often means it's cooked with vegetables, especially spinach.

Dessert *(Dolci)*
- *Panforte:* Dense, dark, clove-and-cinnamon-spiced cake from Siena. *Panforte* makes a good, enduring gift.
- *Gelato:* The Florentines claim they invented Italian-style ice cream. Many think they serve some of the world's best. Consider skipping dessert at the restaurant and stretching your legs before finding a good *gelateria*.

Eating with the Seasons

Italian cooks love to serve you fresh produce and seafood at its tastiest. If you must have porcini mushrooms outside of October and November, they'll be frozen. To get the freshest veggies at a fine restaurant, request *"Il piatto di verdure della stagione, per favore"* (A plate of seasonal vegetables, please).

Here are a few examples of what's fresh when:

April–May:	Calamari, squid, green beans, asparagus, artichokes, and zucchini flowers
April, May, Sept, Oct:	Black truffles
May–June:	Mussels, asparagus, zucchini, cantaloupe, and strawberries
May–Aug:	Eggplant
Oct–Nov:	Mushrooms and white truffles
Fresh year-round:	Clams, meats, and cheese

- *Cantucci and Vin Santo:* Florentines love this simple way to end a meal, by dipping the crunchy almond *biscotti* in *Vin Santo* (literally "holy wine"), a sweet, golden dessert wine.

Wines (Vini)

Brunello di Montalcino: One of Italy's greatest red wines, made from Sangiovese *grosso* grapes, comes from the slopes of Montalcino south of Siena. This full-bodied wine is aged at least four years in wooden casks, resulting in a bold, smooth character. Called "the brunette," it is a dark, brownish red and has a rich, robust, complex aroma that is suitable to pair with hearty, meaty food. Really savor this one; bottles typically start at €25.

Rosso di Montalcino: This lower-priced, younger version of Brunello—a.k.a. "baby Brunello"—is also made in Montalcino from Sangiovese grapes. It lacks the Brunello's depth of flavor and complexity, but it's still a great wine at a bargain price, usually €8–15.

Chianti: The hearty red from the Chianti region (20 miles south of Florence), made mostly from the Sangiovese grape, is world-famous. "Chianti Classico," with a black rooster symbol on the bottle neck, is usually the best. Cheap, €2 Chiantis are acidic, while better ones, starting at €8, can be flavorful, sometimes earthy or fruity.

Vino Nobile di Montepulciano: This high-quality, ruby red, dry wine—also made of Sangiovese grapes—goes well with meat dishes, especially chicken. Don't confuse this one with the inferior (but drinkable) Montepulciano wine available in most U.S. grocery stores.

Super Tuscans: Ultra-expensive and rivaling the Brunello in taste, this newer breed of Italian wine is made from non-Italian grapes (usually from French grapes like Cabernet and Merlot), so the Italian regulating body does not rate them. Ask for help in choosing one of these at an *enoteca*. There are many choices, and at these prices, you don't want to be disappointed. Reliable brands are Sassicia and Tignanello.

Vernaccia di San Gimignano: In Tuscany, this is the only choice for white wine-lovers, but even finicky red-wine fans will be able to down a glass of this medium-dry white, which pairs well with pasta and salad.

RESTAURANTS

North of the River
Near Santa Maria Novella and the Train Station

Osteria Belledonne feels like eating dinner in a crowded terrarium. I loved the meal but had to correct the bill—read it carefully. They take only a few reservations; arrive early or wait (Mon–Fri 12:00–14:30 & 19:00–23:30, closed Sat–Sun, Via delle Belledonne 16 red, tel. 055-238-2609).

Ristorante La Spada is another fine local favorite serving typical Tuscan cuisine with less atmosphere and more menu. Order the €20 "Spada's Fantasy" for an unending parade of food (€12 lunch special, daily 12:00–15:00 & 19:00–22:30, evening reservations smart, air-con, near Via della Spada at Via del Moro 66 red, tel. 055-218-757). Their take-out *rosticceria* (at their Via della Spada entrance) serves the same food for picnic prices.

Trattoria Marione serves good home-cooked-style meals to a local crowd in a happy, food-loving, and steamy ambience. Dinners run about €15 plus wine (open daily, Via della Spada 27 red, tel. 055-214-756).

Trattoria Sostanza-Troia is a characteristic and well-established place with shared tables and a loyal local following. Whirling ceiling fans and walls strewn with old photos create a time-warp ambience. They offer two seatings, requiring reservations: one at 19:30 and one at 21:00 (dinners for about €30 plus wine, great steaks, lunch 12:00–14:00, closed Sat, Via del Porcellana 25 red, tel. 055-212-691).

Ristorante il Latini is a hugely popular institution packed with Florentines and tourists munching Tuscan cuisine noisily under pendulous hamhocks. Reserve in advance or arrive no later than 12:30—or 19:30 or join the mob waiting for a table (€7 pastas, €15 *secondi*, each table has a bottle of Chianti—you pay €1 per glass, closed Mon, off Via d. Vigna Nuova at Via Palchetti 6, tel. 055-210-916). Although good, it's not worth waiting for in a huge line when you can get similar-quality food elsewhere without the wait.

Ristorante Giglio Rosso has a sleek, modern interior and beautifully-presented, reasonably-priced dishes. Hip Italians, local clergy, and the occasional tourist all enjoy the homemade pasta, flambéed roasts, and luscious dessert cart (open daily, pasta and *secondi* under €10 each, Via Panzani 35 red, tel. 055-211-795).

Florence Restaurants

① Osteria Belledonne
② Ristorante La Spada
③ Trattoria Marione
④ Trattoria Sostanza-Troia
⑤ Ristorante il Latini
⑥ Ristorante Giglio Rosso
⑦ Mercato Centrale (Market)
⑧ Trattoria la Burrasca & Osteria la Congrega
⑨ Gran Caffè San Marco
⑩ Self-Service Rist. Leonardo
⑪ Antico Ristorante il Sasso di Dante
⑫ Ristorante il Ritrovo

⑬ Ristorante il Cavallino
⑭ Osteria Vini e Vecchi Sapori
⑮ Cantinetta dei Verrazzano & Ristorante Paoli
⑯ I Fratellini Wine & Sandwich Shop
⑰ Trattoria Icche C'è C'è
⑱ Osteria del Porcellino
⑲ Trattoria Nella
⑳ Gelateria Carrozze
㉑ Gelateria dei Neri
㉒ Vivoli's Gelateria
㉓ Café Rivoire

Near the Central and San Lorenzo Markets

For piles of picnic produce, people-watching, or just a rustic sandwich, try the huge **Central Market,** called Mercato Centrale (Mon–Sat 7:00–14:00, a block north of San Lorenzo street market).

Trattoria la Burrasca is a Flintstone-chic, family-run place ideal for Tuscan home cooking. It's small—10 tables—and often filled with our readers. Anna and Antonio Genzano have cooked and served here with passion since 1982. If Andy Capp were Italian, he'd eat here for special nights out. Everything is homemade except the desserts. And if you want good wine cheap, order it here (Fri–Wed 12:00–15:00 & 19:00–22:00, closed Thu, Via Panicale 6b, at north corner of Central Market, tel. 055-215-827, NSE).

Osteria la Congrega brags it's "a Tuscan wine bar designed to help you lose track of time." In a fresh and romantic two-level setting, chef/owner Mahyar takes pride in his fun, easy menu featuring modern Tuscan cuisine, with top-notch meat and seasonal produce. He offers quality vegetarian dishes, creative salads, and an inexpensive but excellent house wine. With just 10 uncrowded tables, reservations are required for dinner (€5–6 pasta, €12 nightly specials, daily 12:00–15:00 & 19:00–23:00, Via Panicale 43 red, tel. 055-264-5027).

Near the Accademia and Museum of San Marco

Gran Caffè San Marco, conveniently located on Piazza San Marco across from the entrance of the San Marco Museum, churns out cheap but tired cafeteria fare to cheap but tired tourists (no cover charge, self-service and restaurant, Piazza San Marco 11 but enter around the corner on Via Cavour near #50, tel. 055-215-833).

Near the Duomo

Self-Service Ristorante Leonardo is fast, cheap, air-conditioned, and handy, just a block from the Duomo, southwest of the Baptistery (€3 pastas, €4 main courses, Sun–Fri 11:45–14:45 & 18:45–21:45, closed Sat, upstairs at Via Pecori 5, tel. 055-284-446). Luciano (like Pavarotti) runs the place with enthusiasm.

Antico Ristorante il Sasso di Dante serves standard Tuscan fare in a surprisingly pleasant indoor/outdoor setting in the shadow of the Duomo (€20 meals, always good vegetarian dishes and special menu of the day, daily 12:00–14:30 & 19:00–22:30, come early to snare front-row seats, Piazza delle Pallottole 6, tel. 055-282-113).

Cavernous **Ristorante il Ritrovo** offers a bright, dressy ambience and meaty Tuscan cuisine cooked with family pride (€25 meals, Tue–Sun 12:30–15:00 & 19:00–23:00, closed Mon, 12 tables, air-con, a long block north of the Duomo at Via dei Pucci 4, tel. 055-281-688, Marco SE).

Near Palazzo Vecchio

Piazza della Signoria, the square facing Palazzo Vecchio, is ringed by beautifully situated yet touristy eateries. Any will do for a reasonably priced pizza. Perhaps the least of these evils is **Ristorante il Cavallino** with its glum crowd of tourists, dumbed-down menu, and great outdoor seating in the shadow of the palace (€18 fixed-price dinner *menu*, open daily, tel. 055-215-818). For a fancy dessert and hot chocolate, consider **Café Rivoire** (closed Mon).

Osteria Vini e Vecchi Sapori, half a block north of Palazzo Vecchio, is a colorful hole-in-the-wall serving traditional food, including plates of mixed *crostini* (€1 each—step right up and choose at the bar) and €10 daily specials (Tue–Sun 11:00–22:00, closed Mon, Via dei Magazzini 3 red, facing the bronze equestrian statue in Piazza della Signoria, go behind its tail into the corner and to your left, gruff Giorgio SE).

Cantinetta dei Verrazzano is a long-established bakery/café/wine bar, serving delightful sandwich plates in an elegant old-time setting, and hot focaccia sandwiches to go. Their *Specialità Verrazzano* is a fine plate of four little *crostini* (like mini *bruschetta*) featuring different local breads, cheeses, and meats (€7). The *Tagliere di Focacce,* a sampler plate of mini–focaccia sandwiches, is also fun. Either of these dishes with a glass of Chianti makes a fine light meal. Paolo describes things to make eating educational. As office workers pop in for a quick bite, it's traditional to share tables at lunchtime (Mon–Sat 8:00–21:00, closed Sun, just off Via Calzaiuoli on a side street across from Orsanmichele Church at Via dei Tavolini 18, tel. 055-268-590).

I Fratellini is a rustic little place where the "little brothers" have served peasants 27 different kinds of sandwiches and cheap glasses of Chianti wine (see list on wall) since 1875. Join the local crowd, then sit on a nearby curb or windowsill to munch, placing your glass on the wall rack before you leave (€4 for sandwich and wine, daily 8:00–20:00, 20 yards in front of Orsanmichele church on Via dei Cimatori).

Ristorante Paoli serves great local cuisine to piles of happy eaters under a richly frescoed Gothic vault. Because of its fame and central location, it's filled mostly with tourists, but for a dressy, traditional splurge meal, this is my choice (Wed–Mon 12:00–14:00 & 19:00–22:00, closed Tue, reserve for dinner, €20 tourist menu, à la carte is pricier, midway between old square and Duomo at Via de Tavolini 12 red, tel. 055-216-215). Salads are flamboyantly cut and mixed from a trolley right at your table.

Trattoria Icche C'è C'è (ee-kay chay chay; dialect for "whatever is, is") is a small, family-style eatery where fun-loving Gino serves good traditional meals (3-course €11 meals, not too touristy,

Tue–Sun 11:00–15:00 & 19:00–24:00, closed Mon, midway between Bargello and river at Via Magalotti 11 red, tel. 055-216-589).

Osteria del Porcellino has a romantic ambience and a fresh, seasonal menu. A rare place that serves late, this dark, dense, candlelit place is packed with a mix of locals and tourists and run with style and enthusiasm by friendly chef Enzo (daily 12:00–14:30 & 19:00–1:00, reserve for dinner, outdoor seating in summer, Via Val di Lamona 7 red, half a block behind Mercato Nuovo, tel. 055-264-148).

Trattoria Nella serves good, typical Tuscan cuisine at affordable prices. Arrive early or be disappointed—it's understandably popular (€20 meals, Mon–Sat 12:00–14:30 & 19:00–22:00, closed Sun, 3 blocks northwest of Ponte Vecchio, Via delle Terme 19 red, tel. 055-218-925).

Oltrarno, South of the River
Near Ponte Vecchio
Ristorante Bibo serves *"cucina tipica Fiorentina"* with a pink-tablecloth-and-black-bowtie dressiness and leafy, candlelit outdoor seating (good €15 three-course meal, leave this book face up on the edge of the table for a 15 percent discount, Wed–Mon 12:00–14:30 & 19:00–22:30, reserve for outdoor seating, Piazza Santa Felicita 6 red, tel. 055-239-8554, enthusiastic Tonino SE).

Golden View Open Bar is a lively, trendy place good for a salad, pizza, or pasta with a view of Ponte Vecchio and the Arno River. Reservations for window tables are recommended (reasonable prices, daily 11:30–24:00, impressive wine bar, Internet access, 50 yards upstream from Ponte Vecchio at Via dei Bardi 58, tel. 055-214-502). They have live jazz Mondays and Wednesdays at 21:00.

Via Santo Spirito and Borgo San Jacopo
Several good and colorful restaurants line this multinamed street a block off the river in Oltrarno. I'd survey the scene (perhaps following the self-guided Oltrarno walk described on page 43) before making a choice.

Trattoria Cammillo was formerly run by Cammillo, who is now slurping spaghetti in heaven. But his granddaughter Chiara carries on the tradition, mixing traditional Tuscan and creative, modern cuisine. With a charcoal grill and a team of white-aproned waiters cranking out wonderful food in a fun, dressy-but-down-to-earth ambience, this place is a hit (full dinners about €36 plus wine, Thu–Tue 12:00–14:30 & 19:30–22:30, closed Wed, reservations smart, Borgo San Jacopo 57 red, tel. 055-212-427).

Trattoria Angiolino serves good, old-fashioned local cuisine. Sit in the main hall rather than the stuffy side rooms (€20 for dinner plus wine, Tue–Sun 12:00–14:30 & 19:30–22:30, closed Mon, Via di Santo Spirito 36 red, tel. 055-239-8976).

Eating in Oltrarno

- **1** Ristorante Bibo
- **2** Golden View Open Bar
- **3** Trattoria Cammillo
- **4** Trattoria Angiolino
- **5** To Trattoria Sabatino
- **6** Borgo Antico, Osteria Santo Spirito, Ricchi Caffè & Café Cabiria
- **7** Trattoria Casalinga

Trattoria Sabatino, farthest away and least touristy, is spacious and disturbingly cheap, with family character, red-checkered table-cloths, and a simple menu. A wonderful place to watch locals munch, it's just outside the Porta San Frediano (medieval gate), a 15-minute walk from Ponte Vecchio (Mon–Fri 12:00–14:30 & 19:20–22:00, closed Sat–Sun, Via Pisana 2 red, tel. 055-225-955, NSE). If you eat here, let it be your reward after following my self-guided Oltrarno walk (on page 43).

Piazza Santo Spirito

This classic Florentine square (lately a hangout for drug pushers, therefore a bit seedy-feeling and plagued by bag-snatchers on mopeds) has several popular little restaurants and bars that are open nightly. They offer good local cuisine, moderate prices, and impersonal service, with a choice of indoor or romantic on-the-square seating (reservations smart): lively **Borgo Antico** (Piazza Santo Spirito 6 red, tel. 055-210-437) and the quieter yet more bohemian **Osteria Santo Spirito** (Piazza Santo Spirito 16 red, tel. 055-238-2383).

Ricchi Caffè, next to Borgo Antico, has fine gelato and shaded outdoor tables. After noting the plain facade of the Brunelleschi church facing the square, step inside the café and pick your favorite of the many ways it might be finished. **Café Cabiria,** on the other side of Borgo Antico, is a trendy local hangout with good light meals and a cozy Florentine-funky room in back. If you're a scene-crasher, try it here.

Trattoria Casalinga, an inexpensive standby, comes with aproned women bustling around the kitchen. You'll find more tourists than locals, but all seem to leave full and happy, with euros to spare for gelato (Mon–Sat 12:00–14:30 & 19:00–21:45, after 20:00 reserve or wait, closed Sun and all of Aug, just off Piazza Santo Spirito, near the church at Via dei Michelozzi 9 red, tel. 055-218-624).

Gelato

Gelato is an edible art form. Italy's best ice cream is in Florence—one souvenir that can't break and won't clutter your luggage. But beware of scams at touristy joints on busy streets that turn a simple request for a cone into a €10 "tourist special." A key to gelato-appreciation is sampling liberally and choosing flavors that go well together. Ask, as the locals do, for *"Un assaggio, per favore?"* (A taste, please?) and *"Che si sposano bene?"* (What marries well; kay spoh-ZAH-noh BEN-ay).

Gelateria Carrozze is very good (daily 11:00–24:00, closes at 21:00 in winter; on riverfront 30 yards from Ponte Vecchio toward the Uffizi, Via del Pesce 3, also has decent sandwiches to go). **Gelateria dei Neri** is another local favorite worth tracking down (2 blocks east of Palazzo Vecchio at Via dei Neri 20/22 red, daily in summer 12:00–23:00, closed Wed in winter).

Vivoli's, which serves "only today's production" is the most famous (Tue–Sun 8:00–01:00; closed Mon, the last 3 weeks in Aug, and winter; opposite the Church of Santa Croce, go down Via Torta a block, turn right on Via Stinche). Before ordering, try a free sample of their *riso* flavor—rice.

If you want an excuse to check out the little village-like neighborhood across the river from Santa Croce, enjoy a gelato at the tiny **no-name** *gelateria* at Via San Miniato 5 red (just before Porta San Miniato).

FLORENCE WITH CHILDREN

Florence with kids: not ideal. But it's certainly good for them! Here are a few thoughts on family fun in the art capital of Europe.

- Be certain to call ahead to get admission appointments whenever possible. Long museum lines add insult to injury for the preteen dragged into another old building filled with old paintings.
- Avoid the midday heat by planning on a cool break such as an air-conditioned, kid-friendly place for lunch.
- Eat dinner early (around 19:00), and you'll miss the romantic crowd. Skip the famous places. Look instead for self-serve cafeterias, bars (kids are welcome), or even fast-food restaurants where kids can move around without bothering others. Picnic lunches and dinners work well. For ready-made picnics, drop by the *rosticcerie* (delis) and Pizza Rustica shops (cheap take-out pizza; *diavola* is the closest thing on the menu to kid-friendly pepperoni).
- Public WCs are hard to find: Try museums, bars, gelato shops, and fast-food restaurants.
- The smart tour guide/parent incorporates the child's interests into each day's plans. When a child is unhappy, no one has fun.

SIGHTS AND ACTIVITIES

The **Science Museum** has cool old telescopes and early chemical and science lab stuff. But the case with Galileo's finger will likely be the main highlight here (closed Sun; see Science Museum Tour, page 152).

Climbing the dome of the cathedral is almost like climbing an urban mountain—you'll spiral up in a strange dome-within-a-dome space, see some musty old tools used in the construction, get a bird's-eye peek into the nave from way up, and then pop out with the best city view in town. Arrive by 8:30 to beat the crowds; otherwise it may not be worth the long, slow-moving line (closed Sun; see page 34).

Every kid will want to see Michelangelo's *David* (closed Mon; see Renaissance Walk, page 48). But the most interesting collection of statues—with many bizarre poses—is in the **Bargello** (closed on alternating Sun and Mon; see Bargello Tour, page 84).

The **Museum of Precious Stones** shows 500 different semi-precious stones and then demonstrates the fascinating techniques of inlay and mosaic work (closed Sun, around corner from *David*; see page 30).

The **Uffizi courtyard** is ringed by statues of all the famous Florentines (Amerigo Vespucci, Machiavelli, Leonardo, and so on)—great for putting a face on a sweep through history (see page 62 of Renaissance Walk).

Florence's various **open-air markets** are fun for kids (see Shopping, next page). Remember to haggle.

The **Boboli Gardens** are a landscaped wonderland. While designed to give adults a break from the city, they are kid-friendly compared to streets and museums (closed first and last Mon of month; see page 42). For a real playground-type park, head west of the old center along the north side of the river to **Parco dello Cascine** (10-min walk, lots of grass, a pool, and rental bikes).

Older kids may enjoy taking a **bike tour** through the countryside around Florence (bike rental at Parco dello Cascine, above) or hiking up to **Piazzale Michelangelo** for the view (see page 43).

Of all the side trips, a jaunt to see the leaning tower in **Pisa** is probably the most interesting for kids (see Pisa chapter, page 247).

EATING

For fast and kid-friendly **meals** in the old center, there are plenty of hamburger and pizza joints. For a good cafeteria, try Self-Service Ristorante Leonardo (a block from the Duomo; see page 186 of Eating). *Gelaterias* such as Festival del Gelato (Via del Corso 75 red) and Perchè No! (Via dei Tavolini 19 red) are brash, neon, and provide some of the best high-calorie memories in town.

SHOPPING

Florence is a great shopping town—known for its sense of style since the Medici days. Many people spend entire days shopping. Stores are open 9:00–13:00 and 15:30–19:30, usually closed on Sunday, often closed on Monday, and sometimes closed for a couple of weeks around August 15. Many stores have promotional stalls in the market squares.

For shopping ideas, ads, and a list of markets, see the *Florence Concierge Information* magazine (free from TI and many hotels).

Markets

Busy street scenes and markets abound. Prices are soft in the markets—bargain. Perhaps the biggest market fills the streets around the Church of San Lorenzo with countless stalls selling lower-end leather, clothing, T-shirts, handbags, and souvenirs. Beware of fakes (9:00–19:00, closed winter Mon, between the Duomo and train station). The shops behind the street stalls (and along nearby Via Faenza) are great for a workaday peek into Florentine life. The neighboring Mercato Centrale is a giant covered food market (early–14:00, a block north of the Church of San Lorenzo).

Other popular shopping centers are the Santa Croce area (known for leather; check out the "leather school," which is actually inside the Church of Santa Croce—enter to the right of altar); Ponte Vecchio (traditional spot for gold and silver); and the old, covered Mercato Nuovo (3 blocks north of Ponte Vecchio, described on page 39).

For antiques, wander the Oltrarno (south side of river), specifically along Borgo San Jacopo and Via Maggio.

A **flea market** litters Piazza dei Ciompi with antiques, odds, and ends Tuesday through Saturday, but is really big only on the first Sunday of each month (near Piazza Santa Croce).

Getting a VAT Refund

Wrapped into the purchase price of your Florentine souvenirs is a Value Added Tax (VAT) that's generally about 20 percent. If you purchase more than €155 worth of goods at a store that participates in the VAT refund scheme, you're entitled to get most of that tax back. Personally, I've never felt that VAT refunds are worth the hassle, but if you do, here's the scoop.

If you're lucky, the merchant will subtract the tax when you make your purchase (this is more likely if the store ships the goods to your home). Otherwise, you'll need to:

Get the paperwork. Have the merchant completely fill out the necessary refund document, called a "cheque." You'll have to present your passport.

Get your stamp at the border. Process your cheque(s) at your last stop in the European Union with the customs agent who deals with VAT refunds. It's best to keep your purchases in your carry-on for viewing, but if they're too large or dangerous (such as knives) to carry on, then track down the proper customs agent to inspect them before you check your bag. You're not supposed to use your purchased goods before you leave. If you show up at customs wearing your new shoes, officials might look the other way—or deny you a refund.

Collect your refund. You'll need to return your stamped document to the retailer or its representative. Many merchants work with services such as Global Refund or Premier Tax Free, which have offices at major airports, ports, or border crossings. These services, which extract a 4 percent fee, can refund your money immediately in your currency of choice or credit your card (within two billing cycles). If you have to deal directly with the retailer, mail the store your stamped documents and then wait. It could take months.

Boutiques and High Fashion

The entire area between the river and the cathedral is busy with inviting boutiques showing off ritzy Italian fashions. The street Via de' Tornabuoni is best for boutique browsing. The main **Ferragamo** store fills a classy 800-year-old building with a fine selection of shoes and boots and an interesting shoe museum upstairs (Via de' Tornabuoni 16, Mon 15:30–19:30, Tue–Sun 10:00–19:30, tel. 055-292-123). For more boutiques, meander the streets Via della Vigna Nuova (runs west from Via de' Tornabuoni) and Via Strozzi (runs east from Via de' Tornabuoni to Piazza Repubblica).

Department Stores

Typical chain department stores are **Coin,** the local "Macy's" (Mon–Sat 9:30–20:00, Sun 11:00–20:00, on Via Calzaiuoli, near

Orsanmichele Church); **Oviesse,** the local "Penney's," a discount clothing chain (Mon–Sat 9:00–19:55, closed Sun; at intersection of Via Panzani and Via del Giglio, near train station); and the upscale **La Rinascente**, the local "Nordstrom" (Mon–Sat 9:00–21:00, Sun 10:30–20:00, on Piazza della Repubblica, expensive café and view terrace on 4th floor).

Souvenir Ideas

Shoppers in Florence can easily buy art reproductions (posters, calendars, books, prints, and so on—a breeze to find in and near the Uffizi and Accademia museums); reproductions of old documents,

maps, and manuscripts; traditional stationery (Il Papiro chain stores); silk ties and scarves; ceramics; edible goodies (olives, Parmigiano-Reggiano cheese, and dried *porcini* mushrooms); and goofy knickknacks featuring Renaissance masterpieces (such as Botticelli mouse pads, Raphael lipstick-holders, and plaster *David*s). While I don't fly with bottles of wine, many bring home a special bottle of Chianti Classico or Brunello di Montalcino. For soaps, skin creams, herbal remedies, and perfumes, sniff out the antique and palatial perfumery, **Farmacia di Santa Maria Novella** (Via della Scala 16, see page 42).

Customs

You can take home $800 in souvenirs per person duty-free. The next $1,000 is taxed at a flat 3 percent. After that, you pay the individual item's duty rate. You can also bring in duty-free a liter of alcohol (slightly more than a standard-sized bottle of wine), a carton of cigarettes, and up to 100 cigars. To check customs rules and duty rates, visit www.customs.gov.

NIGHTLIFE

With so many American and international college students in town, Florence by night can have a frat-party atmosphere. Nighttime is for eating a late meal, catching a concert, strolling through the old-town pedestrian zone and piazzas, or hitting one of the many pubs.

The latest on nightlife and concerts is listed in several publications available free at the TI (such as the monthly *Florence Concierge Information*) or for a small price at newsstands (consider the monthly *Firenze Spettacolo*, which has an English section). Also check www.firenzeturismo.it. On some summer evenings, a few museums stay open late (pick up a current flyer listing sights and their hours at the TI).

The **Box Office** sells tickets for local events (Mon–Sat 10:00–20:00, closed Sun, on road that runs along west side of train station, Via Alamanni 39, tel. 055-210-804).

The best (and only) way to see the interior of the **Orsanmichele** church is by going to a concert in the evening. Tickets are sold on the day of the concert from the door facing Via dei Calzaiuoli (for description of church, see Sights, page 28 and Renaissance Walk, page 48).

The historic center has a good floodlit ambience, ideal for **strolling.** The entire pedestrian zone from the Uffizi to the Duomo is lively with people. Street musicians perk up famous squares. The Piazza della Repubblica, lined with venerable 19th-century cafés, offers good people-watching on the square. The Ponte Vecchio is a popular place to enjoy river views (and kiss). Of the great squares, only two feel creepy at night—Piazza Santa Maria Novella and, to a lesser extent, Piazza Santo Spirito (south of the Arno)—because they're known as rendezvous spots for drug pushers and users.

Piazzale Michelangelo, perched on a hilltop across the river (bus #12 or #13 from the train station), is awesome for sunsets and is packed with local Romeos and Juliets on weekend evenings. If you're going after dark, it's easier to get there and back by bus or taxi (rather than take a 60-minute round-trip hike). Consider going to **Fiesole** for the sunset (see page 45).

Wine bars *(enotecas)* are fun for sampling local wines and enjoying regional munchies. Consider these *enotecas*: **Boccadama** (closed Mon, Piazza San Croce 25–26 red), **All' Antico Vinaio** (open daily, Via dei Neri 65 red, between Piazza della Signoria and Santa Croce, tel. 055-282-738), and **Casa del Vino** (closed Sat night and Sun, Via dell' Ariento 16 red, near Mercato Centrale). The trendy bar **Chiaroscuro** offers a hearty snack buffet with the purchase of an *aperitivo*, a pre-dinner drink (buffet starts at 18:30, Via del Corso 36, tel. 055-214-247). There's live jazz at the **Golden View Open Bar** near Ponte Vecchio (21:00 on Mon and Wed; see Eating, page 177).

TRANSPORTATION CONNECTIONS

Florence is the transportation hub for Tuscany, with good connections to virtually anywhere in Italy. The city has a central train station, bus station (next to the train station), and an airport (plus Pisa's airport nearby).

Train Station

The station soaks up time and generates dazed and sweaty crowds. If you arrive by train, there's no need to linger at the station. Extremely user-friendly, coin-operated gray-and-yellow machines can display schedules, issue tickets, and even make reservations for railpass holders. Otherwise, get tickets and train information for your next destination from travel agencies away from the congested station (e.g., American Express, see page 12). The fake "Tourist Information" office in the station (next to McDonald's) is actually a room-booking service funded by the hotels. The real TI is across the square from the station (see page 23).

With your back to the tracks, look left to see many of my recommended hotels, a 24-hour pharmacy (*Farmacia Comunale,* near McDonald's), city buses, and the entrance to the underground mall/passage that goes across the square to the Church of Santa Maria Novella. (Note: Pickpockets frequent this tunnel, especially the surface point near the church.) Baggage check is near track 16.

Types of Trains

You'll encounter several types of trains in Italy. Along with the various local milk-run trains, there are the slow IR (Interregional) and *diretto* trains, the medium *espresso*, the fast IC (Intercity), the bullet-train T.A.V. *(Treno Alta Velocita),* and the space-age Eurostar Italia.

If you take a fast train, you'll need to pay a supplement and get

Italy's Public Transportation

KEY: — RAIL   •••• SHIP
       — PRIVATE RAIL   ---BUS

a reservation (even if you have a railpass). But despite the supplements, fast trains are affordable (e.g., including the express supplement, a first-class Florence-to-Venice ticket costs about $40; second-class about $28). Buying supplements on the train comes with a nasty penalty. Purchasing them at the station usually involves a long wait in line; try the machines in the station (mentioned above). Or—usually more convenient—drop by a travel agency (American Express or CIT) in town. The cost is the same, the lines and language barrier are smaller, and you'll save time.

Schedules

Newsstands sell up-to-date regional and all-Italy timetables (€5, ask for the *orario ferroviario*). On the Web, check http://bahn.hafas.de /bin/query.exe/en or www.trenitalia.it.

When using the schedules posted at the station, note that your final destination may be listed in fine print as an intermediate destination. If you're going from Florence to Chiusi or Cortona, scan the schedule and you'll notice that trains that go to Rome usually stop in Chiusi or Terontola (near Cortona) en route. Travelers who read the fine print end up with a greater choice of trains.

Strikes are common. They generally last a day, and train employees will simply say "*Sciopero*" (strike). But sporadic trains lumber down the tracks during most strikes.

By train to: Pisa (2/hr, 1.25 hrs), **Lucca** (9/day, 1.5 hrs), **Siena** (9/day, 1.75 hrs, more with transfer in Empoli; bus is better), **La Spezia** (for the Cinque Terre, 2/day direct, 2 hrs, or change in Pisa), **Milan** (12/day, 3–5 hrs), **Venice** (7/day, 3 hrs), **Assisi** (3/day, 2 hrs, more frequent with transfers, direction: Foligno), **Orvieto** (6/day, 2 hrs), **Rome** (hrly, 2.5 hrs), **Naples** (10/day, 4 hrs), **Brindisi** (3/day, 11 hrs with change in Bologna), **Frankfurt** (3/day, 12 hrs), **Paris** (1/day, 12 hrs overnight), **Vienna** (4/day, 9–10 hrs).

Bus Station

The SITA bus station, a block west of the Florence train station, is user-friendly. Schedules are posted everywhere, and TV monitors show looming departures. Bus service drops dramatically on Sunday.

By bus to: San Gimignano (€6, hrly, 1.75 hrs, change in Poggibonsi), **Siena** (€6.50, hrly, 75-min *corse rapide* buses are faster than the train, avoid the 2-hr *diretta* slow buses), and the **airport** (€4, hrly, 15 min). Bus info: tel. 800-373-760 or 055-214-721 9:30–12:30; some schedules are in the *Florence Concierge Information* magazine.

Taxis

If you don't want to mess with buses or trains, consider hiring a taxi to take you to nearby towns. For a small group or people with more

Driving In Italy

money than time, this can be a good value. For example, for around €100 you can arrange a ride directly from your Florence hotel to your Siena hotel. Ask your hotel to call a taxi or go to a taxi stand (e.g., at the train station).

Airports

The **Amerigo Vespucci Airport** (www.safnet.it), several miles northwest of Florence, has a TI, cash machines, car-rental agencies, and easy connections by airport shuttle bus with Florence's bus station, a block west of the train station (€4, 2/hr, 30 min, from Florence runs 5:30–23:00, from airport 6:00–23:30). Airport info: 055-306-1300, flight info: 055-306-1700 (domestic), 055-306-1702 (international). Allow about €16–20 for a taxi.

International flights often land at Pisa's **Galileo Galilei Airport** (also has TI and car-rental agencies, www.pisa-airport.com), a little over an hour from Florence by train (2/hr; if you're leaving Florence for this airport, catch train at Florence's train station at platform #5). Flight info: 050-849-300.

Greater Florence

Tips for Drivers

If you're taking the autostrada (north or south) to Florence, get off at the Certosa exit and follow signs to *Centro*; at Porta Romana, go to the left of the arch and down Via Francesco Petrarca. After driving around and trying to park in Florence, you'll understand why Leonardo never invented the car. Cars flatten the charm of the city.

Don't drive into the historic core of Florence. A new system photographs every car entering the center. You must register your car with your hotel, whether you just drove in to drop off luggage or if you have parking reserved at your hotel. If you don't, a hefty fine will appear on your rental-car statement. If you go into the city beyond the ring road, even accidentally, you need to report your license-plate number to avoid the fine.

Non-residents are not allowed to park on the streets anywhere near or in the old center. Many hotels listed in this book have a few parking spots they can rent to guests in the center—most charge €15–20 per day. In addition, the city has plenty of **parking lots.** For a short stay, park underground at the train station (€2/hr). The best options for a longer stay are parking at Piazza della Libertà (€15/24 hrs, perhaps cheaper with hotel reservation, 4 long blocks east of Fortezza di Basso, on the inner ring road) and Porta Romana (exit A1 at Firenze-Certosa, follow signs to Porta Romana; €15 per day). For parking information, ask at your hotel, call 800-055-055 in Italy, or consult the useful Web site, www.firenzeparcheggi.it.

TUSCANY

Tuscany

SIENA

Siena was medieval Florence's archrival. And while Florence ultimately won the battle, Siena still competes for the tourists. Sure, Florence has the most heavyweight sights. But Siena seems to be every Italy connoisseur's pet town. In my office, whenever Siena is mentioned, someone moans, "Siena? I looove Siena!"

Seven hundred years ago (from about 1260–1348), Siena was a major banking and trade center, and a military power in a class with Florence, Venice, and Genoa. With a population of 60,000, it was even bigger than Paris. Situated on the north-south road to Rome (the Via Francigena), Siena traded with all Europe. Then, in 1348, the Black Plague that swept through Europe hit Siena and cut the population by a third. Siena never recovered. In the 1550s, her bitter rival, Florence (with help from the Spanish army), forever made Siena a nonthreatening backwater. Siena's loss became our sightseeing gain, as its political and economic irrelevance pickled it purely medieval. Today, Siena's population is still 60,000, compared to Florence's 420,000.

Siena's thriving historic center, with redbrick lanes cascading every which way, offers Italy's best medieval city experience. Most people do Siena, just 30 miles south of Florence, as a day trip, but it's best experienced at twilight. While Florence has the blockbuster museums, Siena has an easy-to-enjoy soul: Courtyards sport flower-decked wells, alleys dead-end at rooftop views, and the sky is a rich blue dome.

For those who dream of a Fiat-free Italy, pedestrians rule in the old center of Siena. Sit at a café on the redbrick main square. Wander narrow streets lined with colorful flags and iron rings to tether horses. Take time to savor the first European city to eliminate automobile traffic from its main square (1966) and then, just to be silly, wonder what would happen if they did it in your city.

Planning Your Time

On a quick trip, consider spending two nights in Siena (or three nights with a whole-day side trip into Florence). Whatever you do, enjoy a sleepy medieval evening in Siena. After an evening in Siena, you can see its major sights in half a day.

ORIENTATION

Siena lounges atop a hill, stretching its three legs out from Il Campo. This main square, the historic meeting point of Siena's neighborhoods, is pedestrian-only. And most of those pedestrians are students from the local university.

Everything I mention is within a 15-minute walk of the square. Navigate by three major landmarks (Campo, Duomo, and church of San Domenico), following the excellent system of street-corner signs. The typical visitor sticks to the San Domenico–Il Campo axis. Make a point to stray from the current of this main artery.

Siena itself is one big sight. Its individual sights come in two little clusters: the square (Civic Museum and City Tower) and the cathedral (Baptistery and Duomo Museum with its surprise viewpoint). Check these sights off, and you're free to wander.

Tourist Information: This is an exasperating place. TI employees claim that transit officials and museum officials don't want them to know anything about the town's sights or buses. They do offer a decent free map (#56 on Il Campo, daily 9:00–19:00, tel. 0577-280-551, www.terresiena.it in Italian only, info@terresiena.it). The helpful booklet *Terre di Siena* lists current hours and prices for sights in Siena and outlying towns. The little TI at San Domenico, while primarily for hotel promotion, sells a €.50 Siena map and organizes daily walking tours of the old town and San Gimignano (across street from church).

Arrival in Siena

By Train: The small train station, located on the edge of town, has a bar and bus office (no baggage check or lockers). To get from the station to the city center, hike about 20 minutes uphill or catch a city bus or taxi. The **taxi stand** is to your far right as you exit the station (about €8 to Il Campo, taxi tel. 0577-49222 or 0577-289-350).

By City Bus: Before leaving the train station, buy a €1 ticket from the Bus Ticket Office in the station lobby (daily 6:15–19:30, ask for a city map—it's free and just a bus-route map, but it helps get you started), the newsstand, or from the blue machine in the lobby (touch screen for English and select "urban" for type of ticket). Then cross the parking lot and the street to reach the sheltered bus stop. The station fronts a wide round-about. Buses only drop off passengers at the station—they pick up travelers on the far side (at a covered stop 100 yards across from the station). Buses run about every 15 minutes (fewer on Sun and after 21:00).

Every orange bus goes from here to the center. (Caution: blue ones go to other cities.) Confirm by asking "centro," punch ticket in machine on bus to validate it, and ride to the last stop. (Buses go to Piazza Gramsci/Lizza, Piazza Sale, or Via Stufa Secca—all within several blocks of each other.)

When leaving Siena, you can catch the city bus to the train station from Piazza Gramsci, Piazza del Sale, or Via Stufa Secca (bus stops are marked with a posted schedule and sometimes with yellow lines painted on the pavement, showing a bus-sized rectangle and the word "bus"). Confirm with the driver that the bus is going to the *stazione* (stat-zee-OH-nay). Remember to purchase your ticket in advance from a *tabacchi* shop.

By Intercity Bus: Some buses arrive in Siena at the train station (see "By Train," above), others at Piazza Gramsci (a few blocks from city center), and some stop at both. The main bus companies are Sena and the confusingly named Tra-in (TRAAH-in). You can store baggage underneath Piazza Gramsci in Sotopassaggio la Lizza (€3.50, daily 7:00–19:45, no overnight).

By Car: Drivers coming from the autostrada take the Siena Ovest exit and follow signs for *Centro,* then *Stadio* (stadium, soccer ball). The soccer-ball signs take you to the stadium lot (Parcheggio Stadio, €1.50/hr, €12.50/day) at the huge, bare-brick San Domenico Church. The Fortezza lot nearby charges the same amount. Another option is to park in the lot under the train station. Technically, hotel customers are allowed to drop bags at their hotel, but I wouldn't bother. You can park free in the lot below the Albergo Lea, in white-striped spots behind Hotel Villa Liberty, behind the Fortezza, and overnight in most city lots from 20:00–8:00. (The signs showing a street cleaner and a day of the week indicate which day the street is cleaned; there's a €100 tow-fee incentive to learn the days of the week in Italian.)

Siena at a Glance

▲▲▲**Il Campo** Best square in Italy. **Hours:** Always open.

▲▲▲**Duomo** Art-packed cathedral with mosaic floors and statues by Michelangelo and Bernini. **Hours:** Mid-March–Oct Mon–Sat 7:30–19:30, Sun 10:15–14:00 worship only, Nov–mid-March Mon–Sat 7:30–17:00, Sun 14:30–17:30.

▲▲**Duomo Museum** Displays cathedral art (Duccio's Maestà) and offers sweeping Tuscan view. **Hours:** Daily mid-March–Sept 9:00–19:30, Oct 9:00–18:00, Nov–mid-March 9:00–13:30.

▲**Baptistery** Cave-like building has baptismal font decorated by Ghiberti and Donatello. **Hours:** Daily mid-March–Sept 9:00–19:30, Oct 9:00–18:00, Nov–mid-March 10:00–13:00 & 14:00–17:00.

▲**Civic Museum** City museum in City Hall with Sienese frescoes of Good and Bad Government. **Hours:** Daily 10:00–19:00, Nov–Feb 10:00–16:00. May be open summer evenings.

▲**City Tower** 330-foot tower climb. **Hours:** Same as Civic Museum.

▲**Pinacoteca** Fine Sienese paintings. **Hours:** Sun–Mon 8:30–13:15, Tue–Sat 8:15–19:15.

▲**Santa Maria della Scala** Museum with art, medieval hospital displays, and exhibitions. **Hours:** Daily 10:30–18:30, off-season 10:30–16:30.

Church of San Domenico Huge brick church with St. Catherine's head and finger. **Hours:** Daily March–Oct 7:00–13:00 & 14:30–18:30, Nov–Feb 9:00–13:00 & 15:00–18:00.

Sanctuary of Saint Catherine Home of St. Catherine. **Hours:** Daily 9:00–12:30 & 15:00–18:30.

Helpful Hints

Local Guide: Roberto Bechi, a hardworking Sienese guide, specializes in off-the-beaten-path tours of the surrounding countryside (mini-bus, up to six passengers, convenient pick-up at hotel). Married to an American (Patti) and having run restaurants in Siena and the United States, Roberto communicates well with Americans. His passions are Sienese culture, Tuscan history, and local cuisine. Book well in advance (full-day tours from €65–95 per person, half-day tours from €30–60 per person, mobile 328-727-3186 or 328-425-5648, www.toursbyroberto.com, tourrob@tin.it). Robert has a line on other good city guides.

Internet Access: In this university town, there are lots of places to get plugged in. **Internet Point** is just off Piazza Matteotti, on Via Paradiso (across street from McDonald's) and **Internet Train** is near Il Campo, at Via di Città 121 (tel. 0577-226-366).

Launderettes: Two modern, self-service places are Lavarapido Wash and Dry (daily 8:00–22:00; Via di Pantaneto 38, near Logge del Papa) and Onda Blu (daily 8:00–21:00; Via del Casato di Sotto 17, 50 yards from Il Campo).

Travel Agency: Palio Viaggi on Piazza Gramsci sells train and plane tickets but no bus tickets (Mon–Fri 9:00–13:00 & 15:00–18:00, closed Sat–Sun, La Lizza 12, tel. 0577-280-828, info@palioviaggi.it).

Wednesday Morning Market: The weekly market, consisting mainly of clothes, knickknacks, and food, sprawls between the Fortress and Piazza Gramsci along Viale Cesare Maccabi and the adjacent Viale XXV Aprile.

Combo-Tickets: A deranged person cobbled together a pile of illogically paired combo-tickets to give some travelers a small savings. Nothing covers everything and most are conflicting. You can buy a combo-ticket at the City Tower that also covers the Civic Museum (€10, saves €3). A different combo-ticket gets you into the Duomo Museum and Baptistery (€7.50, saves €2), but doesn't cover the actual Duomo (cathedral). Yet another is for the Civic Museum and Santa Maria della Scala Museum (€10, saves €2.50). There's also a big €16 combo-ticket that doesn't quite cover everything.

SIGHTS

Siena's Main Square

Il Campo, a ▲▲▲ sight, is the heart—geographically and metaphorically—of Siena. Seen from the top of the City Tower, this "heart" appears to pump people through the busy city's veins. The square fans out from the City Hall (Palazzo Pubblico) to create an amphitheater, where the citizens are the stars.

Originally, this area was just a "field" (campo) located outside the former city walls. You can still see some of the old tufa-stone blocks incorporated into today's redbrick Caffe Fonte Gaia, along the right side of the square ("right" as you face City Hall).

As the city expanded, Il Campo eventually became the historic junction of Siena's various competing districts, or *contrade,* on the old marketplace. The brick surface is divided into nine sections, representing the council of nine merchants and city bigwigs who ruled medieval Siena. The square and its buildings are the color of the soil upon which they stand...a color known to artists and Crayola-users as "Burnt Sienna."

The square is dominated by **City Hall** and its 330-foot tower. In medieval Siena, this secular building was the center of the city, and the whole focus of the Campo flows down to it.

The City Hall features the various symbols of the city. The sun on the facade remembers Saint Bernardino of Siena. Born the day Saint Catherine of Siena died, he grew up here, and went on to travel throughout Italy giving spirited and humorous sermons preaching peace between warring political factions. His sermons often ended with reconciling parties exchanging a *bacio di pace* (kiss of peace). In Siena, he would stand in front of the Palazzo and preach to crowds discreetly segregated by gender with a curtain down the middle. Bernardino personally designed the sun logo to attract crowds, and later became the patron saint of advertising (and of Siena).

To either side of the sun logo, she-wolf gargoyles lean out and snarl, "Don't mess with Siena, Mister Pope!" Siena, a Ghibelline city, prided itself on its political independence from the papacy, and embraced the pagan she-wolf (who suckled Romulus and Remus, Siena's legendary founder) as a city symbol. The black-and-white shields over the windows are another city symbol. Near ground level, the metal rings are for tying up your horse, while the fixtures above those held flags.

The City Hall's 330-foot-tall **Torre del Mangia,** Italy's tallest secular tower, was named after a hedonistic watchman who consumed his earnings like a glutton consumes food—his chewed-up statue is in the courtyard, to the left as you enter. (Tower admission details below.)

The chapel located at the base of the tower was built in 1348 as thanks to God for ending the Black Plague (after it killed more than a third of the population). It should also be used to thank God that the tower—just plunked onto the building with no extra foundation—still

Siena Sights

FORTEZZA

VIALE FRANCHI

VIALE MACCARI

25 APR.-MACCARI

ENOTECA ITALIA

STADIO

P - PARKING

TO TRAIN STATION

V. GARI.

PIAZZA SALE

PIAZZA GRAMSCI

BUSES TO FLORENCE

PIAZZA MATTEOTTI

100 YDS.

100 m

PIAZZA SALIMBENI

PIAZZA TOLOMEI

POST

POST

V. DEI MILLE

WC

VIA CURTATONE

PARADISIO

McD

VIA DI SAPIENZA

CAMPOREGIO

PITTOR.

SAN DOMENICO

SANCT. S. CAT.

S. CAT.

BANCHI

ROSSI

TERMINI

P. SOPRA

CECCO

CIVIC MUSEUM,
CITY HALL
& TOWER

ESTERINA FONT.

COSTONE

BAPT.

DUOMO

FRANC.

SANTA MARIA DELLA SCALA

PIAZZA DUOMO

DUOMO MUSEUM

VIA PELL.

IL CAMPO

BANCHI

P. IND.

WC

VIA DI CITTA

CASTORO

CAPITANO

STALLOREGGI

S. PIETRO

CAS. DI SOTTO

GIO. DUPRÈ

SALICOTTO

PANT.

TORRIONE

PINACOTECA
-PICTURE GALLERY-

❶ Sottopassaggio La Lizza   ❷ Palio Movie

stands. These days, the chapel is only used to bless the Palio contestants and the tower's bell only rings for the race.

The *Fountain of Joy* (Fonte Gaia) by Jacopo della Quercia marks the square's high point. Find the snake-handler woman, the two naked guys about to be tossed in, and the pigeons politely waiting their turn to gingerly tightrope down slippery spouts to slurp a drink from wolves' snouts. The relief panel on the left (as you face the fountain) shows God creating Adam by helping him to his feet. It's said that this reclining Adam influenced Michelangelo when he

Siena's Palio

In the Palio, the feisty spirit of Siena's 17 *contrade* (neighborhoods) lives on. These neighborhoods celebrate, worship, and compete together. Each even has its own historical museum. *Contrada* pride is evident any time of year in the colorful neighborhood banners and parades. (If you hear distant drumming, run to it for some medieval action, often featuring flag-throwers.) But *contrada* passion is most visible twice a year—on July 2 and August 16—when they have their world-famous horse race, the Palio di Siena.

Ten of the 17 neighborhoods compete (chosen by rotation and lot), hurling themselves with medieval abandon into several days of trial races and traditional revelry. Jockeys are considered hired guns...paid mercenaries. But on the big day, the horses are taken into their *contrada's* church to be blessed. ("Go and win," says the priest.) It's considered a sign of luck if a horse leaves droppings in the church.

On the evening of the big day, Il Campo is stuffed to the brim with locals and tourists, as the horses charge wildly around the square in this literally no-holds-barred race. A horse can win even if its rider has fallen off. Of course, the winning neighborhood is the scene of grand celebrations afterward. Winners receive a *palio* (banner), typically painted by a local artist and always featuring the Virgin Mary. But the true prize is simply proving your *contrada* is *numero uno*. All over town, sketches and posters depict the Palio. This is not some folkloristic event. It's a real medieval moment. If you're packed onto the square with 15,000 people, each of whom really wants to win, you won't see much, but you'll feel it. While the actual Palio packs the city, you could side-trip in from Florence to see horse-race trials each of the three days before the big day (usually at 9:00 and around 19:30). For more information, visit www.ilpalio.org.

▲**Palio al Cinema**—This 20-minute film, *Siena, the Palio, and its History,* helps recreate the craziness. See it at the Cinema Moderno in Piazza Tolomei, two blocks from Il Campo (€5.25, with this book pay €4.25/person or €8/2; runs May–Oct only, Mon–Sat 9:30–17:30, closed Sun, English showings generally hrly at half past the hour—schedule posted on door, air-con, tel. 0577-289-201). Call or drop by to confirm when the next English showing is scheduled—there are usually nine a day.

painted his Sistine Ceiling. This fountain is a copy. You can see parts of the original fountain in an interesting exhibit at Siena's Santa Maria della Scala Museum, listed on page 218.

To say Siena and Florence have always been competitive is an understatement. In medieval times, a statue of Venus stood on Il Campo. After the plague hit Siena, the monks blamed the pagan statue. The people cut it to pieces and buried it along the walls of Florence.

The "heart" of Siena beats fastest at Palio time. Picture the Campo when the famous horse races are held (July 2 and Aug 16). Ten snorting horses and their nervous riders (selected from 17 *contrade,* or neighborhoods) line up near the "Antica Siena" shop (right side of square) to await the starting signal. Then they race like crazy three times around the perimeter (the gray pavement), which is covered with dirt. Mattresses pad the sharpest turns. Spectators waving the banners of their

neighborhoods cram (for free) into the center of the square or watch from temporary bleachers or, if they have the money, from the balconies. The winner crosses the line, and 1/17th of Siena goes berserk for the next 365 days.

▲**Civic Museum (Museo Civico)**—At the base of the tower is Siena's City Hall, the spot where secular government got its start in early Renaissance Europe. There, you'll find city government still at work, along with a sampling of local art, including Siena's first fresco (with a groundbreaking down-to-earth Madonna). Stroll through the dramatic halls for more frescoes and portraits extolling Siena's greats, saints, and the city-as-utopia.

Take a moment to savor one of those to-sigh-for rural panoramas out the window of the *Sala della Pace.* The view out the window is essentially the same as that from the top of the big stairs (€7, €10 combo-ticket includes tower—sold only at tower, March–Oct daily 10:00–19:00, Nov–Feb daily 10:00–16:00, last entry 45 min before closing, audioguide-€3.75/person and €5.25/2, tel. 0577-292-111). See **☉** Civic Museum Tour, page 234.

▲**City Tower (Torre del Mangia)**—Siena gathers around its City Hall, not its church. It was a proud republic and this tall tower is the exclamation point of its "declaration of independence." Its 300 steps get pretty skinny at the top, but the reward is one of Italy's best views (€6, €10 combo-ticket with Civic Museum only sold here, March–Oct daily 10:00–19:00, Nov–Feb daily 10:00–16:00, closed in rain, sometimes long lines, avoid midday crowd, limit of 30 tourists at a time, often sold out).

Near Il Campo

Via Banchi di Sopra and Via Banchi di Sotto—These main drags in town are named "upper row of banks" and "lower row of banks." In medieval times, they were part of the Via Francigena, the main thoroughfare between London and Santiago di Compostela in Spain. The medieval Sienese traded wool with passing travelers, requiring money-changers, which led to banks. As Siena was a secular town, local Christians were allowed to loan money and be bankers. Today, strollers out each evening for their *passegiata* fill via Banchi di Sopra.

▲**Pinacoteca**—It rarely rains in Siena, but when it does, I prefer the Pinacoteca to getting drenched. But others may find this quiet, uncrowded, colorful museum delightful. The museum takes you on a walk through Siena's art chronologically from the 12th through the 16th centuries, when a revolution in realism was percolating in Tuscany. Here are a few highlights from this large collection:

Room 1 (up several floors) features the art world pre-Duccio. Altarpieces emphasize the heavenly and otherworldly, rather than the human realism the Sienese artist helped pioneer. **Rooms 2–4** contain a number of works by Duccio (and assistants), whose groundbreaking innovations are subtle to the layman's eyes: less gold-leaf background, fewer gold creases in robes, transparent garments, inlaid-marble thrones, and a more human Mary and Jesus. (Duccio is the artist who did the *Maestà* in the Duomo Museum, the Duomo's big stained-glass window, and a fresco in the Civic Museum).

In **Room 5** are works by Duccio's assistant, Simone Martini, including his *St. Augustine of Siena.* The saint's life is set in pretty realistic Sienese streets, buildings, and landscapes. The saint occasionally pops out at the oddest of angles (difficult to draw) to save the day. (Simone Martini also did the *Maestà* and Guidoriccio frescoes in the Civic Museum.)

In **Room 7** are religious works by the Lorenzetti brothers, best known for the secular masterpiece, *Effects of Good and Bad Government,* in the Civic Museum. The rest of the rooms on this floor are a menagerie of gold-backed saints and Madonnas.

Descend one floor down to **Room 20,** and suddenly the gold is gone—Madonna is set on earth. See works by the painter/biographer Vasari **(Room 22),** a stunning view out the window **(Room 26),** and several colorful rooms **(Rooms 27–30)** dedicated to Domenico Beccafumi (1486–1551). Beccafumi designed many of the Duomo's inlaid pavement panels (including *Slaughter of the*

Innocents), and his original cartoons are displayed in **Room 30.** With strong bodies, twisting poses, and dramatic gestures, Beccafumi's works epitomize the Mannerist style.

Room 31 has "Il Sodoma's" sympathetic *Christ Being Whipped,* and the long **Room 32** displays large-scale works by Il Sodoma, Beccafumi, and others. And finally, Bernardino Mei **(Rooms 33–35)** gives a Sienese take on the wrinkled saints and dark shadows of Caravaggio.

To reach the museum from Il Campo, walk out Via di Città and go left on Via San Pietro (€4, Sun–Mon 8:30–13:15, Tue–Sat 8:15–19:15, audioguide-€4, tel. 0577-281-161).

Siena's Cathedral Area

▲▲▲**Duomo**—This 13th-century Gothic cathedral with its six-story striped bell tower, Siena's ultimate tribute to the Virgin Mary, is heaped with statues, plastered with frescoes, and paved with art. Soak up the richly ornamented facade before venturing inside, where a passel of popes keep watch from on high. The interior is a Renaissance riot of striped columns, intricate marble inlays, Michelangelo statues, and Bernini sculptures. The Piccolomini Library features a series of 15th-century frescoes chronicling the adventures of Siena's philanderer-turned-pope, Aeneas Piccolomini.

Cost and Hours: €3 includes Cathedral and Piccolomini Library. Both are open mid-March–Oct Mon–Sat 7:30–19:30, worship only Sun 10:15–14:00; Nov–mid-March Mon–Sat 7:30–17:00, Sun 14:30–17:30. Modest dress is required to enter.

○ See Duomo Tour on page 221.

▲▲**Duomo Museum (Museo dell' Opera e Panorama)**—On the Campo side of the church (look for the yellow signs), Siena's most enjoyable museum was built to house the cathedral's art. Upstairs to the left is Duccio's *Maestà* (*Enthroned Virgin,* 1311), one of the great pieces of medieval art. The flip side of the *Maestà* (displayed on the opposite wall), with 26 panels—the medieval equivalent of pages—shows scenes from the Passion of Christ.

Climb onto the "Panorama dal Facciatone." From the first landing, take the skinnier second spiral for Siena's surprise view (€5.50, €7.50 combo-ticket with Baptistery, worthwhile 40-min audioguide-€3, daily mid-March–Sept 9:00–19:30, Oct 9:00–18:00, Nov–mid-March 9:00–13:30, tel. 0577-283-048). ○ See Duomo Museum Tour on page 230.

▲**Baptistery**—Siena is so hilly that there wasn't enough flat ground on which to build a big church. What to do? Build a big church and prop up the overhanging edge with the Baptistery. This dark and quietly tucked-away cave of art is worth a look (and €2.50) for its cool tranquility and the bronze panels and angels—by

Ghiberti, Donatello, and others—adorning the pedestal of the baptismal font (daily mid-March–Sept 9:00–19:30, Oct 9:00–18:00, Nov–mid-March 10:00–13:00 & 14:00–17:00). Note: The "crypt" of the cathedral (entrance above the baptistery) is important archeologically, but of little interest to the average tourist. I'd skip it.

▲Santa Maria della Scala Museum—This museum (opposite the Duomo entrance) was used as a hospital until the 1980s. Its labyrinthine 12th-century cellars—carved out of tufa and finished with brick—go down several floors. They once stored supplies for the medieval hospital upstairs. Today the hospital and its cellars are filled with museum exhibits, including these main attractions: the fancy frescoed hall (Pellegrinaio Hall, ground floor), the *Fountain of Joy* and St. Catherine's Oratory chapel (first basement), and the Etruscan collection in the Archeological Museum (second basement).

Cost and Hours: €6, €10 combo-ticket with Civic Museum, daily 10:30–18:30, off-season 10:30–16:30. The chapel just inside the door to your left is free (English description inside chapel entrance).

Pellegrinaio Hall: Sumptuously frescoed, this hall shows medieval Siena's innovative health care and social welfare system in action (c. 1442, wonderfully described in English). From the 11th century, the hospital nursed the sick and cared for abandoned children, as is vividly portrayed in these frescoes. The good works paid off, as bequests and donations poured in, creating the wealth that's evident throughout this building.

Fountain of Joy **Exhibit:** Downstairs you'll find an engaging exhibit on Jacopo della Quercia's early 15th-century Fountain of Joy (Fonte Gaia)—and the disassembled pieces of the original fountain itself. In the 19th century, after serious deterioration, the ornate fountain was dismantled and plaster casts were made. (From these casts, they made the replica that graces Il Campo today.) Here you'll see the eroded original panels paired with their restored casts, along with the original statues that originally stood on the edges of the fountain.

On the same floor, pop into the small chapel or oratory where St. Catherine prayed and received visions. A holy nail thought to be from Jesus' cross is on the altar.

Archaeological Museum: Descend into the second basement under fat groin vaults to be alone with piles of ancient Etruscan stuff excavated from tombs centuries before Christ. Remember, the Etruscans dominated this part of Italy before the Roman Empire swept through—Rome originated as an Etruscan town.

St. Catherine of Siena
(1347–1380)

The youngest of 25 children born to a Sienese cloth dyer, Catherine began experiencing heavenly visions even in childhood. At 16, she became a Dominican nun, locking herself away for three years in a room in her family's house. She lived the life of an ascetic, which culminated in a vision wherein she married Christ. Catherine emerged from solitude to join her Dominican sisters, sharing her experiences, caring for the sick, and gathering both disciples and enemies. At age 23, she lapsed into a spiritual coma, waking with the heavenly command to spread her message to the world. She wrote essays and letters to kings, dukes, bishops, and popes, imploring them to find peace for a war-ravaged Italy. While visiting Pisa during Lent of 1375, she had a vision in which she received the stigmata, the wounds of Christ.

Still in her twenties, Catherine was invited to Avignon, France, where the pope had taken up residence. With her charm, sincerity, and reputation for holiness, she helped convince Pope Gregory XI to return the papacy to the city of Rome. Catherine also went to Rome, where she died young. She was canonized in the next generation (by a Sienese pope) and her relics were distributed to churches around Italy.

Siena's San Domenico Area

Church of San Domenico—This huge brick church is worth a quick look. The bland interior (except for the colorful flags of the city's 17 *contrada* or neighborhoods) fits the austere philosophy of the Dominicans. Walk up the steps in the rear for paintings from the life of Saint Catherine, patron saint of Siena. Halfway up the church on the right, find a metal bust of Saint Catherine and a small case containing her finger (sometimes loaned out to other churches). In the chapel (five yards to the left) surrounded with candles, you'll see Catherine's actual head atop the altar (free, daily March–Oct 7:00–13:00 & 14:30–18:30, Nov–Feb 9:00–13:00 & 15:00–18:00; WC for €0.50 at far end of parking lot—facing church entrance, it's to your right).

Sanctuary of Saint Catherine—Step into Catherine's cool and peaceful home. Siena remembers its favorite hometown gal, a simple, unschooled, but mystically devout soul who, in the mid-1300s, helped convince the pope to return from France to Rome. This schism split the Continent in the 14th century, but because of her intervention, Catherine is honored today as Europe's patron saint. Pilgrims have come to her home since 1464. Since then, architects and artists have greatly embellished what was probably a humble home (her family worked as wool-dyers). Enter through the courtyard and walk to the far end. The chapel on your right contains the wooden crucifix upon which Catherine was meditating when she received the stigmata. The chapel on your left used to be the kitchen. Go down the stairs to the left of the chapel/kitchen to reach the saint's room. Catherine's bare cell is behind see-through doors. Much of the art throughout the sanctuary depicts scenes from her life (free, daily 9:00–12:30 & 15:00–18:30, Via Tiratoio). It's a few downhill blocks toward the center from San Domenico (follow signs to Santuario di Santa Caterina).

SHOPPING AND NIGHTLIFE

Shopping

Siena has long been an important trade crossroads. Its two main streets, Via Banci di Sopra and Via Banci di Sotto, are literally translated as the "upper street of banks" and the "lower street of banks." Via Banchi di Sopra, Siena's top *passeggiata* route, is a can-can of fancy shops today. The big local department store is Upim (Mon–Sat 9:30–19:50, closed Sun, Piazza Matteotti). The Feltrinelli bookstore closest to the Campo sells books and magazines in English (daily 9:00–19:30, Banchi di Sopra 52). The large, colorful scarves/flags, each depicting the symbol of one of Siena's 17 different neighborhoods (such as the wolf, the turtle, and the snail), are easy-to-pack souvenirs, fun for decorating your home (€7 apiece for large size, sold at souvenir stands).

Local Sweets: All over town, **Prodotti Tipici** shops sell Sienese specialties. Siena's claim to caloric fame is its *panforte,* a rich, chewy concoction of nuts, honey, and candied fruits that impresses even fruitcake-haters. There are a few varieties to try: *margherita,* dusted in powdered sugar, is more fruity; *panpepato* has a spicy, peppery crust. Locals prefer a chewy white macaroon-and-almond cookie called *ricciarelli.*

Nightlife

Join the evening *passeggiata* (peak strolling time is 19:00) along Via Banchi di Sopra with gelato in hand.

The **Enoteca Italiana** is a good wine bar in a cellar in the Fortezza/Fortress (sample glasses in 3 different price ranges: €2, €3, €5.50; Mon 12:00–20:00, Tue–Sat 12:00–24:00, closed Sun; bottles and snacks available; cross bridge and enter fortress, go left down ramp, not to be confused with Enoteca Toscana—same location but not as nice, tel. 0577-288-497).

Sightseeing geeks take note: Museums are often open late on summer Fridays and Saturdays (check with the TI for current hours).

SIENA DUOMO TOUR

This ornate but surprisingly secular shrine to the Virgin Mary is stacked with colorful art inside and out, from the inlaid-marble floors to the stained-glass windows. Along with sculptures by Bernini and Michelangelo, the church features the Piccolomini Library with a series of captivating Pinturicchio frescoes telling the story of Siena's consummate Renaissance Man who became Pope Pius II.

ORIENTATION

Cost: €3.

Hours: Mid-March–Oct Mon–Sat 7:30–19:30, Sun 10:15–14:00 worship only; Nov–mid-March Mon–Sat 7:30–17:00, Sun 14:30–17:30.

Getting There: Just look up and head for the green- and white-striped tower.

Information: Audioguide for church-€3.50, add the library-€4, add the Duomo Museum-€5.50. Church and museum only-€4.50. Two headphones are available at a price break. Modest dress is required. Tel. 0577-283-048.

Length of This Tour: 1 hour.

THE TOUR BEGINS

Exterior
If the Campo is the heart of Siena, the Duomo is its soul. The white and dark-green church, sitting on an artificial platform atop Siena's highest point, is visible for miles around.

Grab a spot on a stone bench opposite the entry to admire the colorful entrance facade of green, white, pink, and gold. Like a medieval altarpiece, the facade is divided into sections, each frame

Siena's Duomo

1 Exterior View
2 Interior View
3 Ticket Office for Library, Audioguides
4 She-Wolf of Siena (in floor)
5 Slaughter of the Innocents (in floor)
6 Pulpit
7 Stained Glass Window
8 BERNINI - Mary Magdalene & St. Jerome
9 Piccolomini Altar
10 Piccolomini Library
11 DONATELLO - St. John the Baptist

filled with patriarchs and prophets, studded with roaring gargoyles, and topped with prickly golden pinnacles.

The current structure dates from 1215, with the major decoration done during Siena's heyday from 1250–1350. This huge cathedral (described later in this chapter) was supposed to be even bigger, but the plague got in the way.

The lower story, by Giovanni Pisano (worked 1284–1297), features remnants of the fading Romanesque style (round arches over the doors) topped with the pointed arches of the new Gothic style seeping in from France. The upper half, in full-blown Gothic, was done a century later by a different architect.

The six-story bell tower (c. 1315) looks even taller, thanks to an optical illusion: the white marble stripes get narrower toward the top, making the upper part seem farther away.

On a column to the right of the entrance is a statue of the Roman she-wolf suckling Romulus and Remus, the legendary founders of Rome. Legend has it that Remus' son Senio ("Siena") rode north on a black horse to found the city of Siena. Step inside (with a maximum of 700 allowed in, you may have to wait—current number is indicated on computer screen at turnstile).

Interior—Nave

The heads of 172 popes peer down from above, looking over the fine inlaid art on the floor. With a forest of striped columns, a coffered dome, a large stained-glass window at the far end, and a museum's worth of early Renaissance art, this is one busy interior. Looking closer at the popes, you see the same four faces repeated over and over.

For almost two centuries (1373–1547), 40 artists paved the marble floor with scenes from the Old Testament, allegories, and intricate patterns. The earliest are simple black-and-white, with engraved details, but the later ones use inlay technique with many colored marbles. The series starts with historical allegories near the entrance. The larger, more elaborate scenes surrounding the altar are mostly stories from the Old Testament. Many of the floor panels may be protected with sheet flooring.

• On the floor, find the second pavement panel from the entrance.

She-Wolf Inlaid Pavement Panel

Depicted as a she-wolf, the proud city of Siena is the center of the Italian universe, orbited by such lesser lights as Roma, Florentia, and Pisa. This is pretty secular stuff for such prime church real estate. Five yards to the left and right are panels with still more non-Christian imagery—the ancient pagan prophetesses known as sibyls.

• The fourth pavement panel from the entrance is the...

Fortune Panel

Lady Luck (lower right) parachutes down to earth, where she teeters back and forth (on a ball and a tipsy boat). The lesson? Fortune provides an unstable foundation for life. Truth-seekers wind their way up the precarious path to the top, where Socrates accompanies Lady Wisdom. Having attained wisdom, the world's richest man ("Cratis," upper right) realizes that money doesn't buy happiness, and he dumps his jewels out. They fall to earth, and the cycle of Fortune begins again.

• *On the right wall hangs a dim painting (fourth from entrance).*

St. Catherine Painting

Siena's homegrown saint (see page 219) had a vision where she mystically married Christ. Here's the wedding ceremony in heaven. Jesus places the ring on Catherine's finger as her future mother-in-law Mary looks on.

• *On the left wall is a marble altarpiece decorated with statues.*

Piccolomini Altar—in part by Michelangelo

The Piccolomini altar, designed for the tomb of the Sienese-born Pope Pius III, is most interesting for its statues—one by Michelangelo, three by his students. Michelangelo was originally contracted to do 15 statues, but the marble blocks had been started by another sculptor, and his heart was never in the project. He personally finished only one—Paul (lower right, who is clearly more interesting than the bland, bored popes above him).

Paul has the look of Michelangelo's *Moses*, the broken-nosed self-portrait of the sculptor himself, and the dangling hand of his *David*. It was the chance to sculpt *David* in Florence that convinced Michelangelo to abandon the Siena project.

Dome

Grab a seat under the dome. It sits on a 12-sided base but its "coffered" ceiling is actually a painted illusion.

Get oriented to the array of sights by thinking of the church floor as a big clock. You're the middle, and the altar is high noon: You'll find the *Slaughter of the Innocents* roped off on the floor at 10:00, Pisano's pulpit between two pillars at 11:00, Duccio's round stained-glass window at high noon, Bernini's chapel at 3:00, the Michelangelo statue (next to doorway leading to a shop, snacks, and WC) at 7:00, the Piccolomini Library at 8:00, and a Donatello statue at 9:00.

Attached to columns (at 7:00 and 5:00) are two 65-foot tall wooden poles—dear to any Sienese heart. These were the **flagpoles** bearing the Florentine flag, captured during the pivotal Battle of Montaperti (1260, fought near Siena), when 20,000 Sienese squared off against 35,000 from their arch-rival Florence. The two armies battled back and forth all day, until one of the Florentine soldiers—actually, a Sienese spy under cover—attacked the Florentine standard-bearer from behind. Florence's flag fell to the ground, the army lost its bearings and confidence, and Siena seized the moment to counter-attack and win. It was the city's finest hour, ushering in an 80-year golden age.

Look into the right transept and mentally blow a hole in the wall. You'd be looking down the nave of a massive church, if the original grandiose plan had been completed.

Pulpit

The octagonal Carrara marble pulpit (1268) rests on the backs of lions, symbols of Christianity triumphant. Like the lions, the Church eats its catch (devouring paganism) and nurses its cubs. The seven relief panels tell the life of Christ in rich detail. (Buy light from a coin-op machine.) The pulpit is the work of Nicola Pisano (c. 1220–1284), the "Giotto of sculpture," whose revival of classical forms (columns, sarcophagus-like relief panels) signaled the coming Renaissance. His son Giovanni (c. 1250–1314) carved many of the panels, mixing his dad's classicism and realism with the decorative detail and curvy lines of French Gothic—a style that would influence Donatello and the other Florentines.

The Crucifixion panel, facing the center, is proto-Renaissance. Christ's anatomy is realistic. Mary (bottom left) swoons into the arms of the other women, a very human outburst of emotion. And a Roman soldier (to the right, by Giovanni) turns to look back with an easy motion that breaks the stiff, frontal Gothic mold.

If you're visiting Pisa, you'll see two more quite similar Pisano pulpits there. (See pages 258 and 163 for more on the Pisanos and their pulpits).

• *It can be difficult to get a good view of Duccio's stained-glass window. Try viewing it from left of the pulpit.*

Duccio's Stained-Glass Window

Above and behind the altar, the round 20-foot window (1288) is dedicated—like the church and the city itself—to the Virgin Mary. In the window's bottom panel, Mary (in blue) lies stretched across a red coffin (not always visible, sometimes covered by canopy) while a crowd of mourners looks on. Miraculously, Mary was spared the pain of death (the Assumption, central panel), and winged angels carry her up in a holy bubble to heaven (top panel), where Christ sets her on a throne beside him and crowns her.

The work was designed by Siena's most famous artist, Duccio di Buoninsegna (c. 1225–1319). Duccio combined elements from rigid Byzantine icons (Mary's almond-shaped bubble or *mandorla,* and the full-frontal saints that flank her) with a budding sense of 3-D realism (the throne turned at three-quarter angle to simulate depth, with angels behind). Also notice how the angels in the central panel spread their wings out over the border of the window frame.

The Sienese army defeated Florence in the bloody battle of Montaperti, thanks to the miraculous help of the Virgin. For the next 80 years of prosperity, Sienese artists cranked out countless Madonnas as a way of saying *grazie*. Bear in mind that the main altar was originally dominated by Duccio's *Maestà,* a huge golden altarpiece of the Virgin in Majesty (now kept in the Duomo Museum—today's altar is less noteworthy), which was bathed in the golden-blue light from this window.

Slaughter of the Innocents Inlaid Pavement Panel

Herod (left), standing amid Renaissance arches, orders the massacre of all babies, to prevent the coming of the promised Messiah. It's a chaotic scene of angry soldiers, grieving mothers, and dead babies reminding locals that a republic ruled by a tyrant will experience misery.

The work was designed by the Sienese Il Beccafumi (1486–1551) and inlaid with a colorful array of marble, including yellow, a Sienese specialty quarried nearby.

Donatello—*St. John the Baptist*

The rugged saint in his famous rags stands in a chapel to the right of the library. Donatello, the aging Florentine sculptor, whose style was now considered passé in Florence, came here to build bronze doors for the church (similar to Ghiberti's in Florence). He didn't complete the door project, but he finished this bronze statue (1457).

Bernini—*Cappella della Madonna del Voto*

To understand why Bernini is considered the greatest Baroque sculptor, step into his sumptuous chapel. This last work in the cathedral, from 1659, is enough to make even a Lutheran light a candle. Move up to the altar and look back at the two Bernini statues: Mary Magdalene in a state of spiritual ecstasy, and St. Jerome playing the crucifix like a violinist lost in beautiful music.

The chapel is classic Baroque, combining colored marble, statues, stained glass, a dome, and golden angels holding an oil painting, creating a multimedia extravaganza that offers a glimpse of heaven.

Over the altar is the *Madonna del Voto,* a Madonna and Child painted by Duccio and adorned with a real crown of gold and jewels. In typical medieval fashion, the scene is set in the golden light of heaven. Mary has the almond eyes, long fingers, and golden folds in her robe that are found in orthodox icons of the time. Still, this Mary tilts her head and looks out sympathetically, ready to listen to the prayers of the faithful. This is the Mary that the Palio is dedicated to, special in the hearts of the Sienese.

• *The faithful's prayers to Mary are accompanied by offerings, found outside the chapel, hanging on the wall to the left as you exit.*

Offerings to the *Madonna del Voto*

For untold generations, the Sienese have prayed to the *Madonna del Voto* for her help. In thanks, they give offerings, many of which hang now on the church wall. Silver hearts and medallions express thanks.

Piccolomini Library

The Piccolomini Library, brilliantly frescoed, captures the exuberant, optimistic spirit of the 1400s, when humanism and the Renaissance were born. The frescoes, never restored, look nearly as vivid today as the day they were finished 550 years ago. (With the bright window light, candles—which soot up the art—were never necessary in this room.) The painter Pinturicchio (c. 1454–1513) was hired to celebrate the life of one of Siena's hometown boys. Each episode is framed with an arch, as if Pinturicchio were opening a window onto the spacious 3-D world we inhabit. Start from the window and work clockwise, following 10 scenes in the life of the man many call "the first humanist," Aeneas Piccolomini (1405–1464).

1. Leaving for Basel: Twenty-seven-year-old Aeneas, riding a white horse and decked out in an outrageous hat, pauses to take one last look back as he leaves Siena to charge off on the first of many adventures in his sometimes sunny, sometimes stormy life. Born poor but noble, he got all A's in his classics classes in Siena. Now, having soaked up all the secular knowledge available, he leaves home to crash a church council in Switzerland, where he would take sides against the pope.

2. Meeting James II of Scotland: Aeneas (with long brown hair) charmed King James and the well-dressed, educated, worldly crowd of Europe's courts. Among his many travels, he visited London (writing home about Westminster Abbey and St. Paul's), barely survived a storm at sea, negotiated peace between England and France, and fathered (at least) two illegitimate children.

3. Crowned poet by Frederick III: Next we find Aeneas in Vienna, working as secretary to the German king. Aeneas kneels to ceremonially receive the laurel crown of a poet. Aeneas wrote love poetry, bawdy stories, and a play, and is best known for his candid autobiography. Everyone was talking about Aeneas—a writer, speaker, diplomat, and lover of the arts and pretty women, who was the very essence of the *uomo universale*, or Renaissance Man.

4. Submitting to Pope Eugene IV: At age 40, after a serious illness, Aeneas changed his life. He journeys to Rome and kisses the pope's foot, apologizing for his heretical opposition. He repents of his wild youth and becomes a priest. (In his autobiography, he says it was time to change anyway, as women no longer aroused him...and he no longer attracted them.)

5. Introducing Frederick III and Eleanora: Quickly named Bishop of Siena, Aeneas (in white, pointed bishop's hat) makes his hometown a romantic getaway for his friend Frederick and his fiancée. Notice the Duomo's bell tower in the distance and the city walls (upper left). Aeneas always seemed to be present at Europe's most important political, religious, and social events.

6. Made Cardinal: Kneeling before the pope, with shaved head and praying hands, Aeneas receives the flat red hat of a Cardinal. In many of these panels, the artist Pinturicchio uses all the latest 3-D effects—floor tiles and carpets, distant landscapes, receding lines—to suck you into the scene. He tears down palace walls and lets us peek inside into the day's centers of power.

7. Made Pope: In 1458, at age 53, Aeneas is elected to be Pope Pius II. Carried in triumph, he blesses the crowd. One of his first acts as pope was to declare as heresy the anti-pope doctrines he had championed in his youth. (Pius II fans can visit his birthplace in Pienza—see page 289.)

8. Proclaims a Crusade: He calls on all Europe to liberate the Christian city of Constantinople, which had recently fallen to the Ottoman Turks. Europe was reluctant to follow his call, but Aeneas pushes the measure through.

9. Canonizes St. Catherine: From his papal throne, Aeneas looks down on the mortal remains of Catherine (clutching her symbol, the lily) and proclaims his fellow Sienese a saint. The well-dressed candle-holders in the foreground pose proudly.

10. Arrival in Ancona: Old and sick, the pope has to be carried everywhere on a litter because of rheumatic feet. He travels to Ancona, ready to board a ship to go fight the Turks. But only a handful of Venetian galleys arrive at the appointed time, the crusade peters out, and Aeneas, disheartened, dies. He wrote: "I do not deny my past. I have been a great wanderer, wandering away from the right path. But at least I know it, and hope the knowledge has not come too late."

The library also contains intricately decorated, illuminated music scores, and a statue (a Roman copy of a Greek original) of the Three Graces.

• *Exit the Duomo and make a U-turn to the left, walking alongside the church to Piazza Jacopo della Quercia.*

The Unfinished Church

The nave of the Duomo was supposed to be where the piazza is today. Worshipers would have entered the church from the far end of the piazza through the unfinished wall. Some of the nave's green- and white-striped columns were built, now filled in with a brick wall. Round white stones in the pavement mark where a row of pillars would have been. Look through the unfinished entrance facade, seeing blue sky where the stained-glass windows would have been, and ponder the struggles, triumphs, and failures of the human spirit...or of humanism.

DUOMO MUSEUM TOUR

(Museo dell' Opera e Panorama)

Siena's most enjoyable museum was built to house the cathedral's art. Stand eye-to-eye with the saints and angels who once languished unknown on the church's upper reaches (where copies stand today). The museum's centerpiece—an altarpiece by Duccio—once stood in the center of the church. And the museum's high point is one of the highest points in the city, offering expansive views of the church and the city.

ORIENTATION

Cost: €6 (includes crypt—basically just a basement with faded frescoes).
Hours: Daily mid-March–Sept 9:00–19:30, Oct 9:00–18:00, Nov–mid-March 9:00–13:30.
Getting There: It's next to the Duomo, on the Campo side; look for the yellow signs.
Information: There's a good 40-minute audioguide for €3. Tel. 0577-283-048.
Length of This Tour: 1 hour.
Starring: Duccio, the Virgin Mary, and the Tuscan view.

THE TOUR BEGINS

Ground Floor
The ground floor houses the church's original statues, mainly from the facade and exterior. You immediately run face-to-face with **Donatello's *Madonna and Child,*** a round, carved relief. A slender, tender Mary gazes down at her chubby-cheeked baby. The thick folds of her headdress stream down around her smooth face. Her sad eyes say she knows the eventual fate of her son. Donatello creates the illusion of Mary's three-dimensional "lap" using only a few

inches of depth cut into the creamy-rose stone.

Lining the main room are **Giovanni Pisano's statues.** Giovanni spent a decade (c.1285–1296) carving and orchestrating the decoration of the cathedral—saints, prophets, sibyls, animals, and the original she-wolf with Romulus and Remus. These life-size, robed saints stand in a relaxed *contrapposto,* with open mouths and expressive gestures. Their heads jut out—Giovanni's way of making them more visible from below. Some turn and seem to converse with their neighbors, especially evident with Moses *(Mose)* and the sister who raised him like a mother, Miriam *(Maria di Mose,* on the left side of the room). The copies of these two stand on the right side of the church, where they appear to interact.

Down a few steps in Rooms 11 and 12 are the two lions who once looked down from the church's main entrance, and Giovanni's 12 apostles who once lined the nave. Tastes changed over the centuries, and the apostles were later moved up to the roof, where they eroded. Giovanni's relaxed realism and expressive gestures were a major influence on later Florentine sculptors like Donatello.

• *Upstairs to the left awaits a private audience with Duccio's* Madonna.

Duccio di Buoninsegna—Altarpiece panels (*Maestà* and 26 Passion panels, 1311)

The panels in this room were once part of the Duomo's main altarpiece. Grab a seat and study one of the great pieces of medieval art. The former altarpiece was disassembled (and the frame lost) and now most of the pieces are displayed here—the front side (*Maestà,* with Mary and saints) at one end of the room, back side (Passion panels) at the other.

Imagine these separate panels pieced together, set into their original gold, prickly, 15-by-15-foot wood frame and placed on the main altar in the Duomo. For two centuries it gave the congregation something to look at while the priests turned their backs at Communion time. The Christ child stared back.

At the center of the front side sits the Virgin and Child, surrounded by angels and saints (*Maestà,* or *Enthroned Virgin*). Mary's a melancholy queen on an inlaid marble throne. Young angels lean their elbows on the back of the throne and sigh. We see the throne head-on, unnaturally splayed open (a Byzantine style popular at the time in Siena). Mary is massive, twice the size of the saints around her, and she clearly stands out from the golden background. Unlike traditional full-frontal Byzantine icons, she turns slightly sideways to touch her baby, who does not bless us.

The city of Siena is dedicated to this Lady, who backed the Sienese in a bloody battle against Florence (Montaperti, 1260). Here, she's triumphant, visited by Siena's four patron saints (kneeling in front), John the Baptist and other saints (the first choir row), more angels in a row (soprano section), and, chiming in from up in the balcony, James the Great and the 12 apostles.

The painting was revolutionary for the time in its sheer size and opulence, and in Duccio's budding realism that broke standard conventions. Duccio (c. 1225–1319), at the height of his powers, used every innovative arrow in his quiver. He replaced the standard gold-leaf background (symbolizing heaven) with a gold, intricately patterned curtain draped over the throne. Mary's blue robe opens to reveal her body, and the curve of her knee suggests real anatomy beneath the robe. Baby Jesus wears a delicately transparent garment. Their faces are modeled with light—a patchwork of bright flesh and shadowy valleys, as if lit from the left (a technique he likely learned from his contemporary Giotto during a visit to Florence).

Along the base of Mary's throne is an inscription (*"Mater sancta dei..."* or "Holy Mother of God...") asking Mary to bring peace to Siena *(Senis)* and long life to Duccio *(Ducio)*—quite a tribute in a time when painters were usually treated as anonymous craftsmen.

• *Look on the opposite wall.*

The flip side of the altarpiece featured 26 smaller panels—the medieval equivalent of pages—showing colorful **scenes from the Passion of Christ.**

The panels showcase the budding Tuscan style—realism and storytelling. It doesn't take a Bible scholar to "read" these panels, left to right. Christ on a donkey (lower left) makes his triumphal entry into the city gate of Jerusalem (or is it Siena?). Next, he washes his disciples' feet in a realistic, three-dimensional room. But Duccio hasn't fully mastered perspective—in the Last Supper, we see Christ eye-to-eye, but view the table from above. Christ is arrested in Gethsemane, and so on, until the climactic Crucifixion. The Crucifixion is given the standard gold background, but the cross is set on a terraced hillside, amid the crowd. Jesus' followers express human emotion rarely seen in earlier art.

The Passion panels' crowd scenes aren't arranged in neat choir rows, but in more natural-looking groups. Duccio sets figures in motion, with individual faces expressing sorrow, anger, and agitation. Duccio's human realism would be taken to the next level by his Florentine counterpart Giotto, often called the first proto-Renaissance painter.

Duccio and assistants (possibly including Simone Martini) spent three years on this massive altarpiece. It was a triumph, and at its dedication the satisfied Sienese marched it around the Campo and into the church in a public procession.

But by 1506, at the height of the Renaissance, Duccio's medieval altarpiece looked musty and old-fashioned, and was moved to a side altar. In 1771 it was disassembled and stored in the church offices (today's Duomo Museum). Today scholars debate how to reassemble it accurately, and hail it as a quantum leap in the evolution of art.

• *Continue up the stairs. At the landing on the top floor, walk to the end of the room on the right—the entrance is through the small doorway. Climb down the steps and then up the claustrophobic spiral staircase to the viewpoint...*

Panorama del Facciatone

Standing on the wall from this high point in the city, you're rewarded with a stunning view of Siena...and an interesting perspective on its place in history.

Look toward the Duomo, and consider this: After rival republic Florence began its grand cathedral (1296), proud Siena made plans to build one even bigger, the biggest church in all Christendom. Construction began in the 1330s on an extension off the right side of the existing Duomo. Today's cathedral would have been used as a transept.

You're standing on what would have been the entrance facade (see map on page 222). Had the church been completed, you'd be looking straight down the nave toward the altar—white stones mark where columns would have stood.

Unfortunately, this wall was as far as Siena got. The vision was grand but it underestimated the complexity of constructing such a building without enough land for it to sit upon. That, coupled with the devastating effects of a plague, killed the city's ability to finish the project. Many Sienese saw the plague as a sign from God punishing them for their pride. They canceled their plans and humbly faded into the background of Tuscan history.

CIVIC
MUSEUM
TOUR
(Museo Civico)

The City Hall (Palazzo Pubblico), at the base of the tower, stands as a symbol of a republic independent of the pope and the Holy Roman Emperor and of the rising secular society that appeared first in Tuscany before spreading around Europe in the Renaissance. Still the seat of city government, the City Hall also has a fine and manageable museum housing a good sample of Sienese art. Stroll through this civic center, featuring day-in-the-life frescoes and a fine real-life view of the surrounding countryside.

ORIENTATION

Cost: €7, €10 combo-ticket with City Tower (sold only at the tower) or €10 combo-ticket with Santa Maria della Scala Museum.

Hours: Daily March–Oct 10:00–19:00, Nov–Feb 10:00–16:00, last entry 45 min before closing. May be open summer evenings.

Getting There: The focus of the main square, it's hard to miss.

Information: The audioguide costs €3.75 for 1 person, €5.25 for 2. Tel. 0577-292-111.

Length of This Tour: 1 hour.

THE TOUR BEGINS

Hall of Italian Unification (Sala del Risorgimento)

This hall has dramatic scenes of the 19th-century unification of Italy (surrounded by statues that don't seem to care). See Victor Emmanuel II (left wall, with beard and pointy moustache), king of a small northern Italian province, on horseback at the Battle of San Martino (1859), leading a united Italian nation against their Austrian oppressors. Beneath the painting, you'll see the coat he's wearing in

Civic Museum

PIAZZA
DEL
MERCATO

GIFT SHOP

VIA SALICOTTO

COURT-YARD

SALA DEL MAPPAMONDO

SALA PACE

VIA GIOVANNI DUPRE

CHAPEL

WC

SALA DEL RISORG.

SALA DI BALIA

PIAZZA
DEL CAMPO

TORRE DEL MANGIA (TOWER)

DCH

20 YARDS

20 METERS

❶ Victor Emmanuel II at Battle of San Martino

❷ Victor Emmanuel II Receives Politicians

❸ Inlaid Chairs in Chapel

❹ MARTINI - Maesta

❺ MARTINI - Guidoriccio da Fogliano

❻ St. Catherine fresco

❼ Good Government

❽ Bad Government

the painting. Next (long wall), the king's red-shirted troops cheer as he shakes hands with the dashing general Garibaldi. Victorious, Victor receives politicians (next painting) who bow and present the election results that made Italy united and democratic, with Victor as a symbolic head. When Victor Emmanuel died in 1878 (see his funeral on the far wall), Italy was on the road to modern nationhood.
• *Pass through the next two rooms and turn left to find the chapel where the city's governors and bureaucrats prayed. Continue into the large...*

Sala del Mappamondo

On opposite ends of the room where the Grand Council met, you'll find two large frescoes by Siena's great Simone Martini (c. 1280–1344). His *Maestà* (*Enthroned Virgin*, 1315) was the secular counterpart to Duccio's *Maestà* in the Duomo (now in the Duomo

Museum). Mary sits on a throne under a red silk canopy, a model to Siena's city council of what a just ruler should be. Siena's black-and-white coat of arms is woven into the canopy and also the picture frame. She's surrounded by saints and angels, clearly echoing the *Maestà* of Simone's teacher, Duccio.

But this is a groundbreaking work. It's Siena's first fresco showing a Madonna not in a faraway, gold-leaf heaven, but under the blue sky of the real world that we inhabit. The canopy creates a three-dimensional stage, with saints in front of, behind, and under the canopy. Some saints' faces are actually blocked by the support poles. These saints are not a generic conga-line of Byzantine icons, but a milling crowd of 30 individuals with expressive faces. Some look straight out, some are in profile, and some turn at that difficult-to-draw three-quarter angle, grabbing onto the canopy poles. And the Virgin's brooch is painted so well that it almost looks... uh, real.

Facing the *Maestà* is Simone Martini's *Guidoriccio da Fogliano*. It's the year "MCCCXXVIII" (1328), and Siena's renowned mercenary general—one of Simone's compatriots—rides across a barren landscape surveying the two castles his armies have just conquered. Guido and his horse have the same tailor. This is one of Europe's first secular portraits.

The Surrender of the Castle of Giuncarico, by Duccio (1314), shows a man in green about to hand over his sword to the Sienese general (not pictured; the fresco was damaged). In the background is the man's castle and village on a rocky outcropping. Duccio's Surrender apparently inspired the 3-D landscape of *Guidoriccio da Folignano,* by Duccio's pupil.

Also in the room (painted between the arches) are frescoes of two saints with local connections, St. Catherine (see page 219) and St. Bernardine (1380–1444). Bernardine's charismatic sermons in Siena brought together sworn enemies to share a *bacio di pace*—kiss of peace.

Room of Peace
(Sala della Pace, a.k.a. Sala dei Nove)

This is the council room where the Council of Nine met. Looking down on the oligarchy during their meetings were two interesting frescoes showing the *Effects of Good and Bad Government,* by Ambrogio Lorenzetti (1337–40).

Good Government (on the short wall) is represented by a stately, bearded man on a throne, surrounded by virtuous females, especially the central virtue Peace (PAX), who lounges back on a pile of discarded armor. Justice holds a scale with angels on either side to execute her judgments. Wrongdoers (lower right) are rounded up by the authorities. At the foot of the stage, prominent Sienese file by.

On the long wall (with the better-preserved fresco), notice the whistle-while-you-work happiness of the utopian community ruled by the utopian government. Amid Siena's skyline (Duomo at upper left), young people dance to the beat of a tambourine, workers repair roofs, and the conversation flows. The blessings of a good government extend even to the countryside, which feels safe and prosperous. The fields are tilled, the Via Francigena is busy, and angels fly overhead.

But under Bad Government (other long wall, damaged fresco), a horned, fanged, wine-drinking devil sets the vices loose ("Avarice," "Vainglorious"). Arsonists torch homes and fields, soldiers rape and pillage, the fields are barren, and frescoes get damaged. Justice slumps at the devil's feet, bound, and too depressed to look up. The message: Without justice, there can be no prosperity.

The rural view out the window is essentially the same view as from the top of the big stairs—enjoy it from here.

SLEEPING, EATING, AND TRANSPORTATION CONNECTIONS

SLEEPING

Finding a room is tough during Easter or the Palio in early July and mid-August. Call ahead any time of year, as all the guidebooks list Siena's few budget places. While day-tripping tour groups turn the town into a Gothic amusement park in midsummer, Siena is basically yours in the evenings and off-season.

Most of the listed hotels lie between Il Campo and the Church of San Domenico. Part of Siena's charm is its lively, festive character—this means that all hotels can be plagued with noise, even (and sometimes especially) the hotels in the pedestrian-only zone. If tranquility is important for your sanity, ask for a room that's off the street or consider staying at the recommended places outside the center.

Near Il Campo
Each of these listings is forgettable but inexpensive, and just a horse wreck away from one of Italy's most wonderful civic spaces.

$ Albergo Tre Donzelle is a fine budget value with 28 plain, institutional rooms. Don't hang out here...think of Il Campo, a block away, as your terrace (S-€33, D-€46, Db-€60, T-€65, Tb-€82, no breakfast; with your back to the tower, leave Il Campo to the right at 2:00, Via Donzelle 5; tel. 0577-280-358, fax 0577-223-933, Signora Valentina SE).

$ Piccolo Hotel Etruria, with 19 decent rooms but not much soul, is a bit overpriced but well-located and sleepable (S-€43, Sb-€48, Db-€78, Tb-€105, Qb-€127, breakfast-€5, curfew at 00:30, next to Albergo Tre Donzelle at Via Donzelle 1—3, tel. 0577-288-088, fax 0577-288-461, info@hoteletruria.com, Fattorini family SE).

$ Locanda Garibaldi is a modest, very Sienese restaurant/ *albergo*. Gentle Marcello wears two hats, running a busy restaurant

Sleeping and Eating in Siena

1 Piccolo Hotel Etruria

2 Albergo Tre Donzelle

3 Locanda Garibaldi & Rist. Guidoriccio

4 Hotel Cannon d'Oro

5 To Hotel Duomo, Pen. Pal. Ravizza, & Ost. Nonna Gina

6 To Hotel Villa Liberty & Albergo Lea

7 Hotel Chiusarelli

8 Alma Domus

9 Albergo Bernini & Ost. la Chiacchera

10 To Hotel Sta. Caterina & Res. d'Epoca Borgognini

11 To Hostel

12 Antica Osteria Da Divo

13 To Taverna San Giuseppe

14 Osteria il Tamburino

15 Le Campane Rest.

16 Pizzeria Spadaforte

17 Gelateria Artigiana

18 Ciao Cafeteria, Spizzico Pizza & Key Largo Bar

19 Consorzio Agrario Siena Grocery

20 Lavarapido Launderette

21 Onda Blu Launderette

Sleep Code

(€1 = about $1.20, country code: 39)
S = Single, D = Double/Twin, T = Triple, Q = Quad,
b = bathroom, s = shower only, no CC = Credit Cards not
accepted, SE = Speaks English, NSE = No English. Breakfast is
generally not included. Have breakfast on Il Campo or in a
nearby bar. Credit cards are generally accepted. If not, there are
ATMs all over town.

To help you sort easily through these listings, I've divided
the rooms into three categories based on the price for a standard
double room with bath:

$$$ **Higher Priced**—Most rooms €120 or more.
 $$ **Moderately Priced**—Most rooms between €90–120.
  $ **Lower Priced**—Most rooms €90 or less.

downstairs and renting seven pleasant rooms up a funky, artsy staircase (Db-€75, Tb-€95, 10 percent discount through 2005 with this
book, family deals, no CC, takes reservations only a week in advance,
half a block downhill off the square at Via Giovanni Dupre 18, tel.
0577-284-204, NSE).

$ **Hotel Cannon d'Oro,** a few blocks up Via Banchi di Sopra,
is spacious and comfortable, if a bit noisy and group-friendly (30
rooms, Sb-€69, Db-€86, Tb-€109, Qb-€128, these discounted
prices promised through 2005 with this book, family deals, break-
fast-€6, Via Montanini 28, tel. 0577-44321, fax 0577-280-868,
cannondoro@libero.it, Maurizio and Debora SE). This is just a
couple blocks from the bus station.

Sleeping Fancy, Southwest of Il Campo

These two classy and well-run places are a 10-minute walk from Il
Campo.

$$$ **Hotel Duomo,** with 23 spacious rooms and a bizarre floor
plan, is a great value (Sb-€110, Db-€130, Tb-€175, Qb-€200,
includes breakfast, air-con, elevator, picnic-friendly roof terrace,
free parking; follow Via di Città, which becomes Via Stalloreggi,
to Via Stalloreggi 38; tel. 0577-289-088, fax 0577-43043, www
.hotelduomo.it, booking@hotelduomo.it, Alessandra SE). If you
arrive by train, take a taxi (€8); if you drive, go to Porta San Marco
and follow the signs to the hotel, drop off your bags, and then park
in nearby "Il Campo" lot.

$$$ **Pensione Palazzo Ravizza,** elegant and friendly, with an
aristocratic feel and a peaceful garden, is a worthwhile splurge (Sb-
€130, small loft Db-€120, standard Db-€160, superior Db-€180—
see Web for differences, Tb-€220–310, suites available, includes

breakfast, cheaper mid-Nov–Feb, air-con, elevator, free Internet, back rooms face open country, good restaurant, free parking, Via Pian dei Mantellini 34, tel. 0577-280-462, fax 0577-221-597, www.palazzoravizza.it, bureau@palazzoravizza.it, SE).

Near San Domenico Church

These hotels are within a 10-minute walk northeast of Il Campo. Albergo Bernini and Alma Domus, which enjoy views of the old town and cathedral, are about the best values in town.

$ **Alma Domus** is ideal—unless nuns make you nervous, you need a double bed, or you plan on staying out past the 23:30 curfew (no mercy given). This quasi-hotel (not a convent) is run with firm but angelic smiles by sisters who offer clean and quiet rooms for a steal and save the best views for foreigners. Bright lamps, quaint balconies, fine views, grand public rooms, top security, and a friendly atmosphere make this a great value. The checkout time is strictly 10:00, but they will store your luggage in their secure courtyard (Db-€60, Tb-€70, Qb-€90, no CC, ask for view room—*con vista*, elevator; from San Domenico walk downhill with the church on your right toward the view, turn left down Via Camporegio, make a U-turn at the little chapel down the brick steps to Via Camporegio 37; tel. 0577-44177, fax 0577-47601, NSE).

$ **Albergo Bernini** makes you part of a Sienese family in a modest, clean home with nine fine rooms. Friendly Nadia and Mauro welcome you to their spectacular view terrace for breakfast and picnic lunches and dinners. Outside of breakfast and checkout time, Mauro, an accomplished accordionist, might play a song for you if you ask (Sb-€77, D-€62, Db-€82, breakfast-€7, less in winter, no CC, midnight curfew, on the main San Domenico–Il Campo drag at Via Sapienza 15, tel. & fax 0577-289-047, www.albergobernini.com, hbernin@tin.it, son Alessandro SE). When full, they recommend their bigger but more expensive, less central, and less charming apartments.

$$$ **Hotel Chiusarelli,** a proper hotel with 49 rooms in a beautiful building with a handy location, comes with traffic noise at night—ask for a quieter room in the back (S-€64, Sb-€82, Db-€121, Tb-€164, includes buffet breakfast, suites available, air-con, pleasant garden terrace, €4 rental bikes, reasonable dinner menu, across from San Domenico at Viale Curtatone 15, tel. 0577-280-562, fax 0577-271-177, www.chiusarelli.com, info@chiusarelli.com, Barbara SE).

$$$ **Hotel Villa Liberty,** a bit farther out, has 18 big, bright, comfortable rooms and lots of street noise (S-€75, Db-€130, includes breakfast, only one room with twin beds, elevator, bar, air-con, TVs, courtyard, free and easy street parking, facing fortress at Viale V. Veneto 11, tel. 0577-44966, fax 0577-44770, www.villaliberty.it, info@villaliberty.it, SE).

$$ Albergo Lea is a creaky, old-fashioned place in a residential neighborhood a few blocks past San Domenico with 11 rooms and easy parking (S-€50, Db-€90, Tb-€110, cheaper in winter, includes breakfast, yard, and rooftop terrace, Viale XXIV Maggio 10, tel. & fax 0577-283-207, hotellea@libero.it, SE).

Southeast of Il Campo and farther from the Center

The first two places are near each other, in the direction of Porta Romana city gate. The last two are well-served by city buses, but are less convenient.

$$ Residenza d'Epoca Borgognini is a grand old building with seven cool, solid, and tastefully decorated rooms. You'll find high ceilings, lots of stairs, and a warm welcome from Maria Antonietta (D-€70, €110 in July and Aug, Db-€80, €120 in July and Aug, Tb-€110–140, 10 percent discount with this book, includes breakfast at nearby bar, Via Pantaneto 160, tel. & fax 0577-44055, mobile 338-7640933, www.hotelborgognini.it, hotelborgognini@yahoo.it).

$$$ Hotel Santa Caterina is a three-star, 18th-century place, great for drivers who need air-conditioning. Professionally run with real attention to quality, it has 22 comfortable rooms with a delightful garden (Sb-€105, small Db-€105, Db-€140, Tb-€190, prices promised through 2005 with this book, includes buffet breakfast, elevator; garden side is quieter, but street side—with multipaned windows—isn't bad; fridge in room, parking-€15/day—request when you reserve, 100 yards outside Porta Romana at Via E.S. Piccolomini 7, tel. 0577-221-105, fax 0577-271-087, www.hscsiena .it, info@hscsiena.it, Lorenza SE). A city shuttle bus runs frequently (4/hr) to the town center.

$$$ Frances' Lodge is a small farmhouse B&B a mile out of Siena. English-speaking Franca and Franco rent four modern rooms in a rustic yet elegant old place with a swimming pool, peaceful garden, eight acres of olive trees and vineyards, and great Siena views (Db-€150–180 depending upon the room, Tb-€210, easy parking, great breakfast, near shuttle bus "B" into town, Strada di Valdipugna 2, tel. 0577-281-061, fax 0577-222-224, www.franceslodge.it, info@franceslodge.it).

$ Siena's Guidoriccio Youth Hostel has 100 cheap beds, but, given the hassle of the bus ride and the charm of downtown Siena at night, I'd skip it (€13 beds in doubles, triples, and dorms with sheets, no CC, cheap breakfast, lock-out 9:30–15:00, bus #10 from train station or bus #10 or #15 from Piazza Gramsci—about 20 min, Via Fiorentina 89 in Stellino neighborhood, tel. 0577-52212, SE).

Outside of Siena

The following accommodations are in the lush, peaceful countryside surrounding Siena.

$ Poste Regie B&B has three beautifully-furnished rooms run by spunky Beatrice. Owned by her family for generations, this farm-house has a genuinely welcoming feel (D-€65, includes breakfast, on a country road in Ancaiano west of Siena, Via della Montagnola 68; mobile 349-475-4995, fax 0577-45387, www.posteregie.com, reservations@posteregie.com, SE).

$ Agriturismo le Trappoline, on I Sodi Farm in Chianti east of Siena, is a renovated farmhouse with panoramic vistas and ample grounds for country walks. Danilo and Gabriella Casini rent by the week (Sat to Sat, mid-June–mid-Sept) and for a minimum of three nights otherwise (4-person apartments-€100, discounts off-season, pool, Località Monti Gaiole, tel. 0577-747-012, www.letrappoline .it, info@agrisodi.com).

$ Parri Nada Farmhouse, a good choice for families, is tucked away in the vineyards in the hills of Chianti northeast of Siena. Luca and Elena Masti rent two rooms in their comfortable home (D-€70, T-€85, Q-whole apartment-€105, 1-night rentals OK, kitchen, pool, private yard, Località Santa Chiara 4, tel. & fax 0577-359-072, mobile 333-840-8448, www.farm-house.it, info@farm-house.it).

EATING

Sienese restaurants are reasonable by Florentine and Venetian stan-dards. Enjoy ordering high on the menu here without going broke.

Antica Osteria Da Divo is *the* place for a fine €40 meal. The kitchen is creative, the ambience is candlelit, and the food is fresh and top-notch. The lamb goes *baaa* in your mouth. They offer a basket of exotic fresh breads and excellent seasonal dishes. And the chef is understandably proud of his desserts (daily 12:00–14:30 & 19:00–22:00, reserve for summer eves; Via Franciosa 29, facing bap-tistery door, take the far right and walk one long curving block, tel. 0577-286-054). Readers of this book finish their meal with a com-plimentary biscotti and vin santo or coffee.

Ristorante Guidoriccio—just a few steps below Il Campo—feels warm, dressy, and inviting, with friendly service by Ercole and Elis and prices good for the locale (pastas-€7, *secondi*-€13, closed Sun, air-con, Via G. Dupre 2, tel. 0577-44350).

Taverna San Giuseppe, a local favorite, offers modern Tuscan cuisine in a dressy grotto atmosphere. Check the posters tacked around the entry for daily specials. Reserve or arrive early to get a table (Mon–Sat 12:15–14:30 & 19:15–22:00, closed Sun, 7-min walk up street to the right of the City Hall, Via Giovanni Dupre 132, tel. 0577-42286).

Osteria il Tamburino is friendly, popular, and serves up tasty, inexpensive meals in a narrow dining room (Mon–Sat 12:00–14:30 & 19:00–21:30, closed Sun; follow Via di Città off Il Campo, becomes Stalloreggi, Via Stalloreggi 11; tel. 0577-280-306).

Le Campane, two blocks off Il Campo, is more formal. It features modern Tuscan fare with a dressy interior and outdoor tables on a quiet square (pastas-€8, *secondi*-€13, daily 12:15–14:30 & 19:15–22:00, closed Mon in winter, indoor/outdoor seating, a few steps off Via di Città at Via delle Campane 6, tel. 0577-284-035, reservations smart).

Osteria Nonna Gina wins praise from locals for its good quality and prices (Tue–Sun 12:30–14:30 & 19:30–22:30, closed Mon, 10-min walk from Il Campo, 2 blocks beyond Hotel Duomo, Piano dei Mantellini 2, tel. 0577-287-247).

Osteria la Chiacchera is a youthful hole-in-the-brick-wall playing hip music and serving "peasant food" at peasant prices on rustic tables and paper place mats (pastas-€3, *secondi*-€5, daily 12:00–15:30 & 19:00–23:00, reservations wise, understandably proud of their cakes, skip the *trippa*—tripe, 2 rooms, below Pension Bernini at Costa di San Antonio 4, tel. 0577-280-631). Their outside tables cling to a steep lane.

Locanda Garibaldi offers authentic Sienese dining at a fair price (pastas-€6, secondi-€9, €20 menu, Sun–Fri 12:00–14:00 & 19:00–21:00, closed Sat, arrive early to get a table, within a block of Il Campo down Via Giovanni Dupre at #18). Marcello does a little *piatto misto dolce* for €4, featuring several local desserts with sweet wine.

Even with higher prices, lousy service, and lower-quality food, consider eating on Il Campo—a classic European experience. Considering the real estate, the prices (if you order carefully and are treated fairly) are actually pretty good. Wander across the square and sit wherever your stomach and heart tell you to. **Pizzeria Spadaforte,** at the edge of Il Campo, has a fine perch, decent food, and slanted tables (€7 pizza and pasta, daily 12:00–16:00 & 19:30–22:30, to far right of city tower as you face it, tel. 0577-281-123).

Drinks or Snacks Overlooking Il Campo

Three places have skinny balconies with benches overlooking the main square for their customers. Sipping a coffee or nibbling a pastry here while marveling at the Il Campo scene is one of my favorite European experiences. And it's very cheap. Survey these three places from Il Campo (from the base of the tower, they are at 10:00, high noon, and 3:00, respectively).

Gelateria Artigiana has good ice cream, drinks, and light snacks (off Via di Città). **Bar Paninoteca,** with a youthful pub ambience, has a row of stools overlooking the square and serves 50 kinds of sandwiches (hot and cold, €3 each, €0.50 extra if you sit out-side, on Vicolo di S. Paolo on the stairs leading down to Il Campo). **Key Largo Bar** has two benches in the corner offering a great secret perch (Mon–Sat 7:00–22:00 or 23:00, closed Sun, corner left of the tower). Buy your drink or snack at the bar (no extra charge to sit), climb upstairs, and slide the ancient bar to open the door and suddenly...you're imagining Palio ponies zip-ping wildly around your corner.

Eating Cheaply in the Center
At the bottom of Il Campo, a **Ciao** cafeteria offers easy self-service meals, no ambience, and no views. The crowded **Spizzico,** a pizza counter in the front half of Ciao, serves huge, inexpensive quarter pizzas; on sunny days, people take the pizza, trays and all, out on Il Campo for a picnic (daily 11:00–22:00, non-smoking section—*non fumatori*—in back, to left of city tower as you face it).

Budget eaters look for *pizza al taglio* shops, scattered through-out Siena, selling pizza by the slice. Of all the grocery shops, the biggest is **Consorzio Agrario Siena** (Mon–Sat 8:00–19:30, a block off Piazza Matteotti, toward Il Campo at Via Pianigiani 5).

TRANSPORTATION CONNECTIONS

Siena has sparse train connections, but is a great hub for buses to the hill towns.

By train to: Florence (9/day, 1.75 hrs, more with transfer in Empoli), Rome (every 2 hrs, 2.75–4 hrs, transfer in Florence or Chiusi).

By bus to: Florence (2/hr, 1.25–2 hrs, by Tra-in bus, last bus at 20:45), **San Gimignano** (6/day, 1.25 hrs, by Tra-in bus, more fre-quent with transfer in Poggibonsi), **Assisi** (2/day, 2 hrs, €9, by Sena bus; the morning bus goes direct to Assisi, the afternoon bus might terminate at Santa Maria degli Angeli, from here catch a local bus to Assisi, 2/hr, 20 min), **Rome** (7/day, 3 hrs, by Sena bus, arrives at Rome's Tiburtina station), **Milan** (4/day, 5 hrs). Schedules get sparse on Sundays and holidays.

Buses depart Siena from Piazza Gramsci, the train station, or both; confirm when you purchase your ticket. You can get tickets for Tra-in buses or Sena buses at the train station (there's a ticket window for both companies at the station, Mon–Sat 5:50–20:00) or, more centrally, under Piazza Gramsci at Sottopassaggio La Lizza (Tra-in bus office: daily 5:50–20:00, tel. 0577-204-246, toll-free tel. 800-570-530, www.trainspa.it; Sena bus office: Mon–Sat 7:45–19:45, closed Sun, tel. 800-930-960, www.senabus.it).

Sottopassaggio La Lizza, under Piazza Gramsci, has a cash machine (neither bus office accepts credit cards), luggage storage

(€3.50/day, daily 7:00–19:45, no overnight storage), posted bus schedules, TV monitors (listing imminent departures for all three companies), an elevator, and expensive WCs (€0.55). Those departing Siena after the bus offices close can buy the ticket directly from the driver (and pay a supplement). On schedules, the fastest buses are marked *corse rapide*. I'd stick with these. Note that if a schedule lists your departure point as Via Tozzi or La Lizza, you catch the bus at Piazza Gramsci (Via Tozzi is the street that runs alongside Piazza Gramsci and La Lizza is the name of the bus station).

Travel agency: Palio Viaggi on Piazza Gramsci sells train and plane tickets but no bus tickets (Mon–Fri 9:00–13:00 & 15:00–18:00, closed Sat–Sun, La Lizza 12, tel. 0577-280-828, info@palioviaggi.it).

PISA

In A.D. 1200, Pisa's power peaked. For nearly three centuries (1000–1300), Pisa rivaled Venice and Genoa as a sea-trading power, exchanging European goods for luxury items in Muslim lands. As a port near the mouth of the Arno River (six miles from the coast), the city enjoyed easy access to the Mediterranean plus the protection of sitting a bit upstream. ("Pisa" is an ancient word meaning delta.) The Romans had made it a navy base, and by medieval times, it was a major player.

Pisa's 150-foot galleys cruised the Mediterranean, gaining control of the islands of Corsica, Sardinia, and Sicily, and trading with Europeans, Muslims, and Byzantine Christians as far south as North Africa and as far east as Syria. European Crusaders hired Pisan boats to carry them and their supplies to conquer the Muslim-held Holy Land. The Pisan "Republic" prided itself on its independence from both popes and emperors. The city used its sea-trading wealth to build the grand monuments of the Field of Miracles, including the now-famous Tower.

But the Pisa fleet was routed in battle by Genoa (1284, at Meloria, off Livorno), their overseas outposts were taken away, the port silted up, and Pisa was left high and dry, with only its Field of Miracles and its university keeping it on the map.

Pisa's three important sights—the Duomo, Baptistery, and bell tower—float regally on the best lawn in Italy. The style throughout is Pisa's very own "Pisan Romanesque." Even as the church was being built, the Piazza del Duomo was nicknamed the "Campo dei Miracoli," or Field of Miracles, for the grandness of the undertaking. The Leaning Tower recently reopened after a decade of restoration and topple prevention. To ascend, you'll have to make a reservation when you buy your €15 ticket (for details, see "Sights," page 251).

Planning Your Time

Seeing the Tower and the square and wandering through the church are 90 percent of the Pisan thrill. Pisa is a touristy quickie. By car, it's a headache. By train, it's a joy. Train travelers may need to change trains in Pisa anyway. Hop on the bus and see the Tower. If you want to climb it, go straight to the ticket booth to snare an appointment—usually for a couple of hours later (or for an extra €2, you can book a time online at www.opapisa.it). Sophisticated sightseers stop more for the Pisano carvings in the Duomo and Baptistery than for a look at the tipsy Tower. There's nothing wrong with Pisa, but I'd stop only to see the Field of Miracles and get out of town. By car, it's a 45-minute detour from the freeway.

If you explore the rest of the city, it stretches southeast of the Field of Miracles, framed by the Arno on the south and bordered on the east and west by two streets, Borgo Stretto and Via Santa Maria.

ORIENTATION

Tourist Information: One TI is about 200 yards from the train station—exit and walk straight up the street to the big, circular Piazza Vittorio Emanuele II. The TI is on the left, around the corner from #16 (Mon–Fri 9:00–19:00, Sat 9:00–13:30, closed Sun, tel. 050-42-291, www.pisa.turismo.toscana.it). The other, less enthusiastic TI is behind the Leaning Tower, next to the ticket office (summer daily 8:00–20:00, winter Mon–Fri 9:00–18:00, Sat–Sun 10:30–16:30, tel. 050-560-464). There's also one at the airport (daily 10:30–16:30 & 18:00–22:00, tel. 050-503-700).

Markets: An open-air produce market attracts picnickers to Piazza della Vettovaglie, one block north of the Arno River near Ponte di Mezzo (Mon–Sat 7:00–18:00, closed Sun). A street market is held Wednesday and Saturday mornings between Via del Brennero and Via Paparrelle (just outside of wall, about 6 blocks east of the Tower).

Festivals: The month of June has many events, centered around Pisa's patron saint's feast day on June 16.

Arrival in Pisa

By Train: Baggage deposit *(deposito bagagli)* is to the right at the far end of platform #1, past the police office (€3/bag per 12 hrs, daily 6:00–22:00, ignore nonfunctional lockers). In the likely event that this is closed, bags can also be left at Pisa Incoming tourist service company (€3/bag per day, daily 9:30–19:30, in front of station under arcade on the right, Viale Gramsci 23).

To get to the Field of Miracles from the station, you can **walk** (45 min, get free map from TI and they'll mark the best route; or, follow the walk below), take a **taxi** (€8, at taxi stand at station or tel. 050-541-600), or catch a **bus** (10-min ride, plus traffic jams, to the

Pisa

FIELD OF MIRACLES

❶ TI & Ticket Office
❷ Cathedral (Duomo)
❸ Baptistery
❹ Duomo Museum
❺ Camposanto Cemetery
❻ Museum of the Sinopias

TO AUTOSTRADA

VIALE CASCINE

TO LUCCA

VIA CONTESSA MATILDE

OLD CITY WALLS

PIAZZA MANIN

TACKY SOUVENIR STANDS

VIA GABBA

PISANO

BONANNO

VIA ROMA

SANTA MARIA

VIA MILLE

PIAZZA CAVALIERI

S. STEFANO

VIA ULPINI

PIAZZA CAVALOTTI

PIAZZA DANTE

MARKET

BORGO STRETTO

PONTE DI MEZZO

PONTE SOLFERINO

RIVER ARNO

SANTA MARIA DELLA SPINA

VIA FRAN. CRISPI

VIA ITALIA

CORSO ITALIA

VIA MANZ.

VIA BATTISTI

PIAZZA VITTORIO EMANUELE

VIA BONAINI

BUS STOP

Ⓣ - TAXI STAND

¼ MILE

400 METERS

TRAIN STATION

DCH

❼ Hotel Minerva
❽ Hotel Villa Kinzica
❾ Hotel Milano
❿ Hotel Alessandro della Spina
⓫ Pizzeria/Trattoria La Buca
⓬ Ristorante Galileo
⓭ Paninoteca il Canguro
⓮ La Lupa Ghiotta Cafeteria

Tower). Take bus #3 (3/hr) or Navette A (4/hr)—both leave from the street that runs directly away from the station, in front of the Jolly Hotel. Buy an €0.80 ticket from the *tabacchi*/magazine kiosk in the station's main hall or at any *tabacchi* shop (good for 1 hr, round-trip OK). These buses let you off at Piazza Manin, in front of the gate to the Field of Miracles. Confirm the latest information on the bus route (posted in the train information office in Pisa's station lobby, or ask at the TI) or risk taking a long tour of Pisa's suburbs. To return to the train station from the Tower, catch the bus across the street from where you got off (again, confirm the stop with a local or at the TI).

By Car: To get to the Leaning Tower, follow signs to the Duomo or Campo dei Miracoli, located on the north edge of town. If you're coming from the Pisa Nord autostrada exit, you won't have to mess with the city center, but you will have to endure some terrible traffic. There's no option better than the €1/hour pay lot just outside the town wall a block from the Tower.

By Plane: From Pisa's airport, take bus #3 (€0.80, 3/hr, 7 min) or a taxi (€6) into town.

Introductory Pisa Walk:
From the Train Station to the Tower

A leisurely 45-minute stroll from the station to the Tower is a good way to get acquainted with the more subtle virtues of this Renaissance city. It's also a more pleasant alternative to the tourist-mobbed buses. You'll find Pisa to be a student-filled, classy, Old World town with an Arno-scape much like its rival upstream.

Exit straight out of the station, walking north up Viale Gramsci to the circular Piazza Vittorio Emanuele II (where the TI is). Continue straight north, up the pedestrian-only shopping street Corso Italia, and cross the Arno River over Ponte di Mezzo. This modern bridge, constructed on the same site where the Romans built their bridge, is the center of Pisa and the heart of local festivals. Cross and continue north up the elegantly arcaded Borgo Stretto, Pisa's main shopping street.

The first left, Via delle Colonne, is a worthwhile one-block detour, leading to Piazza Vettovaglie, some atmospheric restaurants, and the small but lively open-air market just beyond (Mon–Sat 7:00–18:00, closed Sun).

Continue north on Borgo Stretto another 100 yards or so. Take the second left on nondescript Via Ulisse Dini (it's not obvious). From here, angle northwest to the Tower. Along the way, you pass through Pisa's historic core, including Piazza dei Cavalieri with its colorfully-decorated palace and statue of Cosimo I de' Medici (the Florentine who ruled Pisa in the 16th century). The frescoes on the exterior of the square's buildings, though damaged by salty sea air and years of neglect, reflect the fading glory of Pisa under the Medicis.

The palace and the compound behind the gates to the left *(Scuola Normale)* house Pisa's famous university. The university is one of Europe's oldest, with roots in a law school dating as far back as the 11th century. In the mid-16th century, it was a hotbed of controversy, as professors like Galileo Galilei were exploring the natural sciences, often in conflict with church doctrine.

From here, continue straight on to Via Corsica. Take a quick peek into the humble church of San Sisto, ahead on the left. With simple bricks, assorted reused columns, heavy walls, and few windows, this is the typical "Romanesque" style before the more lavish "Pisan Romanesque" of the Campo dei Miracoli structures.

Follow Via Corsica to Via Santa Maria, where a right turn leads you north, through increasingly touristy clap-trap, directly to the Tower.

SIGHTS

▲▲**Field of Miracles (Campo dei Miracoli)**—Scattered across a golf-course-green lawn are four large white buildings that make up Pisa's religious center—the cathedral (or Duomo), its bell tower (the

Leaning Tower), Baptistery, and Camposanto Cemetery. The four buildings share similar building materials, similar decoration, and a tendency toward circular designs—giving the Campo a pleasant unity. (They also share centuries-long construction schedules.)

The style is dubbed Pisan Romanesque. Where traditional Romanesque has a heavy fortress feel—thick walls, barrel arches, few windows—Pisan Romanesque is light and elegant. At ground level, most of the structures have a solid Romanesque base of simple pilasters and blind arches (columns and arches in relief). On the upper levels, you'll see a little of everything—tight rows of thin columns borrowed from the Lombards (barbarians); pointed Gothic gables and prickly spires; Byzantine mosaics and horseshoe arches; and geometric designs (such as diamonds) and striped colored marbles inspired by mosques in Muslim lands.

All the Campo's buildings have bright white marble, a simple ground floor, and rows of delicate columns and arches forming open-air arcades. Architecturally, the Campo is unique and exotic, like the fantasy city of Minas Tirith from *The Lord of the Rings*. Theologically, the Campo's buildings mark the main events of every Pisan's life: christened in the Baptistery, married in the Duomo, honored in ceremonies at the Tower, and buried in the Camposanto.

Campo dei Miracoli Tickets

Pisa has a scheme to get you into its neglected secondary sights: the Baptistery, the Duomo Museum, Camposanto Cemetery, and the Museum of the Sinopias (fresco museum). Since you may be visiting these lesser sights anyway, I give more sightseeing information on these than they may deserve.

For any one monument, you'll pay €5; for two monuments the cost is €6; for four monuments minus the Duomo it's €8.50; and for the works (including the Duomo) you'll pay €10.50. By comparison, the Duomo alone is a bargain (€2). You can buy any of these tickets at the usually crowded ticket office (behind Tower and Duomo entrance), or more easily at the Camposanto Cemetery, the Duomo Museum, or the Museum of the Sinopias (near the Baptistery, almost suffocated by souvenir stands); note that you can buy a ticket just for, say, the Duomo at any of these points.

No matter what ticket you get, you'll have to pay another €15 to climb the Leaning Tower. Tickets for the ascent are sold only at the crowded ticket office behind the Tower and Duomo or online at www.opapisa.it.

Lining this field of artistic pearls is a gauntlet of Europe's tackiest souvenir stands, as well as dozens of amateur mimes "propping up" the Leaning Tower while tourists take photos.

✪ For more information, see the Pisa Duomo Tour (page 256) and Field of Miracles Tour (page 262).

▲▲**Leaning Tower**—The Tower is nearly 200 feet tall, 55 feet wide, weighs 14,000 tons, and leans at an 85-degree angle (15 feet off the vertical axis). It started to lean almost immediately after construction began. There are eight stories—a simple base, plus six stories of columns (forming arcades), and a belfry on top. The inner, structural core is a hollow cylinder built of limestone bricks, faced with white marble barged here from San Giuluano, northeast of the city. The thin columns of the open-air arcades make the heavy Tower seem light and graceful.

The Tower was built over two centuries by at least three different architects. You can see how each successive architect tried to "correct" the problem of leaning—once half-way up (after the fourth story), once at the belfry on the top.

The first stones were laid in 1173, probably under the architect

Bonanno Pisano (who also designed the Duomo's bronze back door). Five years later, just as they'd finished the base and the first arcade, someone said, "Is it just me, or does that look crooked?" The heavy Tower—resting on a very shallow 13-foot foundation—was obviously sinking on the south side into the marshy, multilayered, unstable soil. (Actually, all the Campo's buildings tilt somewhat.) They carried on anyway, until they'd finished four stories (the base plus three arcade floors). Then, construction was suddenly halted— no one knows why—and for a century the Tower sat half-finished and visibly leaning.

Around 1272, the next architect continued, trying to correct the problem by angling the next three stories backward, in the opposite direction of the lean. The project then sat (mysteriously) idle for nearly another century. Finally, Tommaso Pisano put the belfry on the top (c. 1350–1372), also kinking it backward.

Man versus Gravity: After the Tower's completion, several attempts were made to stop its slow-motion fall. The architect/ artist/writer Giorgio Vasari reinforced the base (1550), and it actually worked. But in 1838, well-intentioned engineers pumped out ground water, destabilizing the Tower, causing it to fall at a rate of a millimeter a year.

It got so bad that, in 1990, it was closed for repairs. Thirty million dollars were spent to stabilize the Tower. Engineers dried the soil with steam pipes, anchored the Tower to the ground with steel cables, and buried 600 tons of lead on the north side as a counterweight (not visible)—all with little success. The breakthrough came when they drilled 15-foot holes in the ground on the north side and sucked out sixty tons of faulty soil, allowing the Tower to sink on the north side. The Tower has actually been straightened by about six inches, turning the clock back 200 years on the still-leaning (and probably still falling) Tower.

As well as gravity, erosion attacks or threatens the Tower. Since its construction, 135 of the Tower's 180 marble columns have had to be replaced. Stone decay, deposits of lime and calcium phosphate, accumulations of dirt and moss, cracking from the stress of the lean—all of these are factors in its decline.

Thanks to the Tower's lean, there are special trouble spots. The lower south side (which is protected from cleansing rain and wind) is black from dirty airborne particles, while the upper areas, though clean, have more stone decay (from eroding rain and wind).

The Tower, now stabilized, is getting cleaned. Cracks are filled, and accumulations removed, using atomized water sprays and poultices of various solvents.

Climbing the Tower: Thirty people every half-hour can clamber up the 294 tilting stairs to the top for €15 (daily 8:30–20:30, off-season 9:00–17:00, ticket office opens 30 min early).

If you want to make the necessary reservation in person (rather than online), go straight to the ticket office behind the Tower. You choose a (30-min) time slot for your visit at the time of purchase; it will likely be a couple of hours before you're able to go up (you could see the rest of the monuments and grab lunch while waiting), but the wait will probably be much shorter if you arrive at the beginning or end of the day. For an extra €2, you can book a time online at www.opapisa.it. Online bookings are accepted no more that 45 days in advance, but at least 14 days prior.

You must show up 10 minutes early for your appointment and you can't take any bags up the Tower, but teensy lockers are available in a room behind the TI desk to store daypacks (a guard opens the room every half-hour). Even though the ticket-office sign says the visit is guided, that only means you'll be accompanied by a museum guard to make sure you don't stay up past your scheduled 30-minute appointment time. Not including the climb, you'll have about 15 minutes for vertigo on top.

Caution: There are no railings, the steps are slanted, and rain makes the marble slippery. Anyone with balance issues of any sort should think twice before ascending.

▲▲Duomo (Cathedral)—The gargantuan Pisan Romanesque church has a Pisano pulpit, modest dress code, and no baggage check (€2, summer Mon–Sat 10:00–19:40, Sun 13:00–19:40; spring and fall Mon–Sat 10:00–17:40, Sun 13:00–17:40; winter Mon–Sat 10:00–12:45 & 15:00–16:45, Sun 15:00–16:45). ✪ See Pisa Duomo Tour on page 256.

Baptistery—The round Baptistery next to the cathedral has superb acoustics and another fine Pisano pulpit (summer daily 8:00–20:00, spring and fall 9:00–17:40, winter 9:00–16:40, located in front of the Duomo). ✪ See Field of Miracles Tour on page 262.

Camposanto Cemetery—Lined with faint frescoes, the ancient cemetery is famous for its "Holy Land" dirt, said to reduce a body into a skeleton within a day. Artillery fire during World War II set the lead roof ablaze, greatly damaging the building, and especially its frescoes (same hours as Baptistery, on north side of Field of Miracles). ✪ See page 265.

Museum of the Sinopias (Museo delle Sinopie)—Housed in a 13th-century hospital, the museum displays some of the original sketches (made on walls) used to make the frescoes in the Camposanto Cemetery (same hours as Baptistery, entrance smothered by souvenir stands, across from Baptistery). ✪ See page 266.

Duomo Museum (Museo dell' Opera del Duomo)—The museum is big on Pisan art, displaying treasures of the cathedral, sculptures (12th–14th centuries, particularly by the Pisano dynasty), paintings, and silverware, as well as ancient Egyptian, Etruscan, and Roman artifacts (same hours as Baptistery, behind Leaning Tower, Piazza Arcivescovado 18). ✪ See page 267.

Panoramic Walk on the Wall—This much-advertised walk, which includes just a small section of the 12th-century wall, isn't worth your time or €2 (March–Dec daily 10:00–18:00, entrance near Baptistery, at Porta Leone).

Museo Nazionale di San Matteo—On the river and in a former convent, this art museum displays 12th- to 15th-century sculptures, illuminated manuscripts, and paintings by Martini, Ghirlandaio, Masaccio, and others (€4, Tue–Sat 8:30–19:30, Sun 9:30–13:30, closed Mon, near Piazza Mazzini at Lungarno Mediceo, tel. 050-541-865).

PISA DUOMO TOUR

The huge Pisan Romanesque cathedral, with its carved pulpit by Giovanni Pisano, is artistically more important than its more famous bell tower.

ORIENTATION

Cost: €2 (see page 252 for combo-ticket).

Hours: Summer—Mon–Sat 10:00–19:40, Sun 13:00–19:40. Spring and fall—Mon–Sat 10:00–17:40, Sun 13:00–17:40. Winter—Mon–Sat 10:00–12:45 & 15:00–16:45, Sun 15:00–16:45.

Dress Code: Shorts are OK as long as they're not short shorts, but shoulders should be covered (although it's not really enforced).

Baggage: Big backpacks are not allowed, nor is storage provided, but if you're climbing the Tower you can leave your daypack in its locker room (see page 254; technically, these small lockers are for Tower climbers, but they could work for clever cathedral visitors).

THE TOUR BEGINS

Exterior

The Duomo is the centerpiece of the Field of Miracles' complex of religious buildings. Begun in 1063, it was financed by a galley-load of booty ransacked that year from the Muslim-held capital of Palermo, Sicily. The architect Buschetto created the style of Pisan Romanesque that set the tone for the Baptistery and Tower. Five decades later (1118), the architect Rainaldo added the impressive main-entrance facade (which also leans out about a foot).

The lower half of the church is simple Romanesque, with blind arches. The upper half has four rows of columns forming arcades.

Black and white marble in stripes, mosaics, stone inlay, and even recycled Roman tombstones complete the decoration.

• *Tourists enter the church from the back end, near the Leaning Tower.*

Bronze Back Door (Porta San Ranieri)

Designed by Bonnano Pisano (c. 1186), thought by some historians to be the first architect of the tower, the doors have 24 different

panels that show Christ's story using the same simple, skinny figures found in Byzantine icons.

It starts in the lower right panel ("Magis"), as the three Wise Men ride up a hill, heading toward...the panel to the left, where tiny baby Jesus lies in a manger while angels and shepherds look down from above. Above the manger scene, King Herod ("Erodi") sits under a

canopy (in Pisan Romanesque style) and orders a soldier to raise his sword to kill all potential Messiahs. The terrified mother pulls her hair out. In the panel to the right, John the Baptist stands under a swaying palm and baptizes the adult Jesus. Jesus wears the rippling River Jordan like a blanket.

Cast using the lost-wax technique, this door was an inspiration for Lorenzo Ghiberti's bronze doors in Florence.

Nave

The 320-foot nave was the longest in Christendom when it was built.

The model was traditional Roman basilicas—68 Corinthian columns of granite that divide the nave into five aisles. But the striped marble and arches-on-columns give it an exotic, almost mosque-like feel. Dim light filters in from the small upper windows of the galleries, where the women worshiped. The gilded coffered ceiling has shields of Florence's Medici family (featuring the six "pills" of these medics-turned-cloth merchants-turned-bankers), who took over Pisa after its glory days.

• *In the apse (behind the altar) is the...*

Apse Mosaic

The mosaic (c. 1300, partly done by Cimabue) shows Christ as the Ruler of All (Pantocrator) between Mary and John the Evangelist.

The Pantocrator image of Christ is a bit foreign to Protestants, Catholics, and secularists, but is standard fare among Orthodox Eastern Christians—that is, the "Byzantine" people that were Pisa's partners in trade.

As King of the Universe, Christ sits on a throne, facing directly out, with penetrating eyes. He wears a halo divided with a cross, worn only by the Trinity. In his left hand is a Bible open to the verse, "Ego Lux Sum Mundi"—"I am the light of the world." Christ blesses with his right hand, with the fingers forming the Greek letters Chi and Rho, the first two letters of "Christos." The thumb (almost) touches the fingers, symbolizing how Christ unites both his divinity and his humanity.

Dome

Looking up into the dome, the heavens open and rings of saints and angels spiral up to a hazy God. Beneath the dome is an inlaid-marble Cosmati-style floor.

• *Near the center of the church you'll find...*

Giovanni's Pulpit (1301–1311)

The 15-foot-tall, octagonal pulpit by Giovanni Pisano (c. 1250–1319) is the last, biggest, and most complex of the four pulpits by the Pisano father-and-son team. Giovanni's father, Nicola, started the family tradition four decades earlier, carving the pulpit in the Baptistery. Giovanni grew up working side-by-side with dad on numerous projects. Now on his own, he crams every-thing he's learned into his crowning achievement.

Giovanni left no stone uncarved in his pursuit of beauty. Four hundred intricately sculpted figures smother the pulpit, blurring the architectural outlines. In addition, the relief panels are actually curved, making it look less like an octagon than a circle. The creamy white Carrara marble has the look and feel of carved French ivories, which the Pisanos loved. Originally, this and the other pulpits were frosted with paint, gilding, and colored pastes.

At the base, lions roar and crouch over their prey, symbolizing how Christ (the lion) triumphs over Satan (the horse, as in Four Horsemen of the Apocalypse).

Four of the pulpit's support "columns" are statues. The central "column" features three graceful ladies representing Faith, Hope, and Charity, the three pillars of Christianity. They in turn stand on the sturdy base of knowledge, represented by the liberal arts taught at the U. of Pisa. Another "column" is Hercules, standing *contrapposto,* nude, holding his club and lion skin. Nearby, Lady Church suckles the babies of the Old and New Testaments, while at her feet are the Four Virtues, including Justice (with her scales), Moderation (modestly covering her nakedness), Courage (holding a lion), and Wisdom (with a horn of plenty).

Around the top of the pulpit, Christ's life unfolds in a series of panels saturated with carvings. The panels tilt out from the top, so the viewer below has a better look, and they're bordered on top with a heavy cornice as a backdrop. Since the panels are curved and unframed, you "read" Christ's life less like a nine-frame comic strip and more like a continuous scroll.

The story unfolds from left to right, beginning at the column.

1. Story of Elizabeth and Zechariah: John the Baptist's parents.

2. Nativity: Mary lounges across a bed, unfazed by labor and delivery. Her pose is clearly inspired by carved Roman sarcophagi (which you can see in the Camposanto), showing the dearly departed relaxing for eternity atop their coffins. Mary and the babe are surrounded by angels (above) and shepherds (right).

3. Adoration of the Magi: The wise men ride in with horses and camels.

4. Presentation in the Temple (left side): Joseph and Mary hold baby Jesus between them. On the right side of the panel, Giovanni adds the next scene in the story, when the nuclear family gets on a donkey and escapes into Egypt.

5. Massacre of the Innocents: Herod (at the top) turns and gestures dramatically, ordering the slaughter of all babies. A mother (bottom left corner) grabs her head in despair. Giovanni uses thick lips and big noses to let the faces speak the full range of human emotions. The soldiers in the tangled chaos are almost freestanding.

6. Kiss of Judas: Jesus is betrayed by a kiss (left side).

7. Crucifixion: An emaciated Christ is mourned by his followers who turn every which way. A Roman horseman (bottom right corner) rides directly away from us—an example of Renaissance "foreshortening" a century before its time.

8 and **9. Last Judgment:** Christ sits in the center, the dead rise from their graves, and he sends the good to heaven (left) and hell (right).

Giovanni was a better pure sculptor than his father. Armed with more sophisticated chisels, he could cut even deeper into the marble, freeing heads from the marble backdrop, creating almost-freestanding, 3-D figures. Where Nicola shows figures either facing forward or in profile, Giovanni mastered the difficult three-quarters angle.

If the pulpit seems a bit cluttered and asymmetrical, blame Mussolini. Originally, Giovanni built the pulpit standing on the right side of the altar (the traditional location). But after a massive fire in 1595 (when the roof burned), the pulpit was disassembled and stored away for three centuries. In 1926 they pulled it out of storage, reassembled it on this spot...and ended up with pieces left over (now in other museums), leading scholars to debate the current look.

• *Hanging from the ceiling of the north transept (to the left of the altar) is...*

Galileo's Lamp

The bronze incense burner is said to be the one (actually, this is a replacement for the original) that caught teenage Galileo's attention one day in church. Someone left a church door open, and a gust of wind set the lamp swinging. Galileo timed the swings, and realized that the burner swung back and forth in the same amount of time regardless of how wide the arc. (This pendulum motion was a constant that allowed Galileo to measure this ever-changing universe.)

Galileo Galilei (1564–1642) was born in Pisa, grew up here on Via Giuseppe Giusti (where the family home still stands, adorned with a humble plaque), and taught math at the University (1584–91). He supposedly threw things off the Tower to time their fall, fascinated by gravity.

• *Find the following two sights in the right (south) transept, near the tourists' entrance.*

Emperor Henry VII's Tomb

In the corner of the south transept, pause at the tomb of Holy Roman Emperor Henry VII, whose untimely death plunged Pisa into its centuries-long decline. Henry lies sleeping, arms folded, his head turned to the side, resting on a soft pillow.

This German king (c. 1275–1313) invaded Italy and was welcomed by Pisans as a nonpartisan leader who could bring peace to Italy's warring Guelphs and Ghibellines. In 1312 he was crowned Emperor by the pope in Rome. He returned to his base in Pisa, and was preparing to polish off the last opposition when he caught a fever (or was poisoned by a priest) and died. Ghibelline Pisa was suddenly at the mercy of Guelph rivals like rising Florence, and Pisa never recovered.

St. Ranieri's Body

In a glass-lined casket on the altar, Pisa's patron saint lies mummified, encased in silver at his head and feet, with his hairshirt covering his body.

Ranieri Scuggeri (1117–1161) was born into the city of Pisa at its peak, when the Campo dei Miracoli was a construction zone. (Ranieri was a year old when this Duomo was consecrated in thanks for Pisa's lucrative victory over the Muslims.) The son of a rich sea-trader, Ranieri chose the life of a hard-partying, popular touring musician. Backstage one night, he met a mysterious stranger who changed his life. Ranieri was inspired to take his musical instrument and set it on fire, while opening his arms to the heavens (à la Jimi Hendrix). He returned to his father's shipping business and amassed a fortune. Then one day, he smelled something funky— his own money. He gave it all away, joined a monastery, and put on a hair shirt.

The former wandering troubadour, traveling salesman, and pilgrimaging monk finally settled down in his hometown of Pisa. He devoured the Bible, then used his showmanship to wow audiences here in the Duomo when he took stage atop the pulpit (Giovanni's predecessor) to deliver spirited sermons.

Ranieri's feast day (June 16) is Pisa's biggest local event, the "Luminara," celebrated along the Arno with tens of thousands of candles lining the buildings and floating on the river. The next day, rowing teams play a game of capture-the-flag, racing to a boat in the Arno and shinnying up a long rope to claim the prize.

FIELD OF MIRACLES TOUR

The Leaning Tower nearly steals the show from the massive cathedral, which muscles out the other sights. But if you have extra time to wander and ponder in Pisa, consider exploring the rest of the Field of Miracles: the Baptistery, Camposanto Cemetery, Museum of the Sinopias (sketches), and the Duomo Museum.

ORIENTATION

Cost: €8.50 for the four sights, €10.50 includes the Duomo (see page 252 for more on prices).

Hours: All the sights are open daily in summer (daily 8:00–20:00), spring and fall (9:00–17:40), and winter (9:00–16:40).

Location: The Bapistery is located in front of the Duomo. The Camposanto Cemetery is on the north side of the Field of Miracles. The Museum of Sinopias is hidden behind souvenir stands, across the street from the Baptistery entrance. The Duomo Museum is housed behind the Tower (Piazza Arcivescovado 18).

THE TOUR BEGINS

Baptistery
Pisa's Baptistery is Italy's biggest. It's interesting for its pulpit and interior ambience, and especially great for its acoustics.

Exterior
The building is 180 feet tall—John the Baptist on top looks eye-to-eye with the tourists atop the nearly 200-foot Leaning Tower. Notice that the Baptistery leans nearly six feet to the north (the Tower leans 15 to the south). The building (begun 1153) is modeled

on the circular, domed church of the Holy Sepulchre in Jerusalem, seen by Pisan Crusaders who occupied Jerusalem in 1099.

From the outside, you see three distinct sections reflecting changing tastes spanning the 150-year construction—simple Romanesque blind arches at the base (1153), ornate Gothic spires and pointed arches in the middle (1250), and a Renaissance dome (15th-century). The roofing looks unfinished, but was intentionally designed with red tiles on the seaward side and the more-prestigious lead tiles (which would corrode) on the sheltered side. The statues of the mid-section are by Nicola Pisano, who sculpted the pulpit inside.

Interior

Inside, it's simple, spacious, and baptized with light. Tall arches atop thin columns once again echo the Campo's architectural theme of arches above blank spaces. The columns encircle just a few pieces of religious furniture.

In the center sits the **octagonal font** (1246). A statue of the first baptist, John the Baptist, stretches his hands and says, "Welcome to my Baptistery." The font contains plenty of space for baptizing adults by immersion (the medieval custom), plus four wells for dunking babies.

Baptismal fonts—where sinners symbolically die and are reborn again—are traditionally octagons. The shape suggests a cross (symbolizing Christ's death), and the eight sides symbolize the eighth day of Christ's ordeal, when he was resurrected. The font's sides, carved with inlaid multicolored marble, feature circle-in-a-square patterns, symbolizing the interlocking of heaven and earth. The circles are studded with interesting faces, both human and animal. Behind the font, the altar features similar inlaid-marble work.

Nicola Pisano's Pulpit

Is this the world's first Renaissance sculpture? It's the first authenticated (signed) work by the "Giotto of sculpture," working in what came to be called the "Renaissance" style. It's a freestanding sculpture with classical columns, realistic people and animals, and 3-D effects in the carved panels.

The 15-foot-tall, hexagonal pulpit is by Nicola Pisano (c. 1220–1278, Giovanni's father), the earliest (1260) and simplest of the four pulpits by the Pisano father-and-son team. Nicola, born in southern Italy, settled in Pisa where he found steady work.

Ten-year-old Giovanni learned the art of pulpit-making here at the feet of his father.

The speaker's platform stands on columns that rest on the backs of animals, representing Christianity's triumph over paganism. The white Carrara marble panels are framed by dark, rose-colored marble, making a pleasant contrast. Originally, this and the other pulpits were touched up with paint, gilding, and colored pastes.

The relief panels, with scenes from the life of Christ, are more readable than the Duomo pulpit, which shows bigger, simpler figures in dark-marble "frames." Read left to right, starting from the back.

1. Nativity: Mary reclines across a bed like a Roman matron, a pose inspired by Roman sarcophagi, which had been found around Pisa in Nicola's day (also on display in the Camposanto).

2. Adoration of the Magi: The three kings kneel before baby Jesus in simple profile; but notice the strong 3-D of the horses' heads coming straight out of the panel.

3. Presentation in the Temple: It lacks the star of the scene, baby Jesus, who got broken off, but on the panel's right side, a powerful, bearded man in a voluminous robe epitomizes Nicola's solemn classical style.

4. Crucifixion: Everyone faces either straight out or in profile; the Roman in front has to actually look back over his shoulder to razz Christ.

5. Last Judgment: Christ reigns over crowded, barely-controlled chaos. The pulpit's lectern is an eagle clutching its prey, echoing the theme of the base.

Acoustics

Make a sound in here and it echoes for a good 10 seconds (a 10-second "decay"). A priest standing atop the pulpit (or a security guard today) can sing three tones within the 10 seconds—"Ave Maria"—and make a chord, singing haunting harmonies with himself. This medieval form of digital delay is due to the 250-foot-wide dome. Recent computer analysis suggests that the 15th-century architects who built the dome intended this building to be not just a Baptistery but also a musical instrument.

To hear the acoustics, you can:
1. Wait for a tour group to come through, and the guard will sing.
2. Ask nicely *(Mi scusi...Canta, per favore?)* and leave a tip of a couple euros—the guard may give you a command performance. The bigger the audience, the more likely they are to do it.

3. Stand near the center, cough, and count to 10. (Singing by yourself is tacky, unless there are no crowds and you have a good voice.)

Climb to the Galleries
Climb 75 steps to the interior gallery (midway up) with an impressive view back down on the baptismal font. Ascend 75 more steps to the upper gallery with views outside—through grills or dirty windows—looking over the town and across to the Leaning Tower.

Camposanto Cemetery
The long white building (1278–1465) with a nondescript entrance borders the Campo dei Miracoli on the north. This site has been a cemetery since ancient times. Highlights are the building's cloistered interior courtyard, some ancient sarcophagi, and the large 14th-century fresco, *The Triumph of Death* (same hours as Baptistery).

Inside is a delightful open-air **courtyard,** surrounded by an arcade with intricate carved tracery in the arches. The courtyard's grass grows on special dirt (said to turn a body into a skeleton in a day) originally shipped by returning Crusaders from Mount Calvary, where Christ was crucified.

The arcade floor is paved with the **coats-of-arms** of some 600 dearly-departed Pisans. Displayed in the arcade are dozens of ancient Roman sarcophagi. These coffins once held dead Romans (not currently buried here). Just to the right of the entrance door, you'll find the 3rd-century A.D. rectangular **Roman sarcophagus** with the myth of Melagus. It's carved along the side with a couple—the deceased—shown relaxing atop their coffin. Carved reliefs like this inspired Nicola and Giovanni Pisano.

Circle the courtyard clockwise, noticing **traces of fresco** on the bare-brick walls. (We'll see some reconstructed frescoes later.) Huge **chains** on the west wall once stretched across the mouth of Pisa's harbor as a defense. Then Genoa attacked, broke the chains, carried them off as a war trophy, and gave them to Pisa's arch-rival Florence. Finally, they were returned here as a token of friendship.

Straight ahead is the cemetery's oldest object, an ochre-colored Greek tombstone—the 4th-century B.C. **stele,** dating from the time of Alexander the Great. It shows a woman (seated) who's just given birth. A maid (standing) shows the baby while the mother gazes adoringly. In the floor nearby is one of the newest memorials, a **pavement slab** dedicated to an American artist, Deane Keller. After serving in Italy in World War II, he helped rebuild the Camposanto and restore its frescoes.

At the back of the courtyard, step through the door to see **photos** of the Camposanto bombed during World War II (yikes!). By the summer of 1944, Allied troops had pushed Nazi forces to the north bank of the Arno, and German Field Marshal Kesselring dug in at Pisa, surrounded by the United States' 91st Infantry. Germans and Americans lobbed artillery shells at each other. (The Americans even considered blowing up the Leaning Tower—the "Tiltin' Hilton"—suspected to be the German lookout point.) Most of the Campo dei Miracoli was miraculously unscathed, but the Camposanto took a direct hit with a Yankee incendiary grenade. It melted the lead-covered arcade roof and peeled historic frescoes from the walls. The Americans liberated the city on September 2 and rebuilt the Camposanto. Some restored frescoes are now displayed in the adjoining room.

The 1,000-square-foot *Triumph of Death* (on the left wall, c. 1350, artist unknown, perhaps by Francesco Traini or Bonamico Buffalmacco) captures Pisa's mood in the wake of the bubonic plague (1348), which killed one in three Pisans. Well-dressed ladies and gents (left half of the painting) are riding gaily through the countryside when they come across three coffins with corpses (bottom left). Confronted with death, they each react differently—a woman puts her hand thoughtfully to her chin, a man holds his nose against the stench, while a horse leans in for a better whiff. Above them, a monk scours the Bible for the meaning of death. Mr. Death, a winged demon with a scythe, stands to the right of center and eyes his future victims.

In the right half of the painting, young people gather in a garden (bottom right) to play music (symbolizing earthly pleasure), oblivious to the death around them. Winged demons swoop down from above to pluck souls from a pile of corpses, while winged angels fight them for the souls. The action continues in the next fresco (the room's far wall), where Christ and Mary judge the dead at the Last Judgment. The wicked are led away to Hell (the right wall of the room) to be tortured by a horned Satan. Grim stuff, but appropriate for the Camposanto's permanent residents.

Museum of the Sinopias

Housed in a 13th-century hospital, this museum (Museo delle Sinopie) features the preparatory sketches (sinopias) for the Camposanto's frescoes. If you loved *The Triumph of Death* and others in the Camposanto, or if you're interested in fresco technique, this museum is worthwhile.

Climb the stairs to the first floor to find (along the right wall) the red-tinted sinopias for *The Triumph of Death*, the *Last Judgment*, and (at the far end) the multi-ringed, earth-centric, Ptolomaic universe of the *Theological Cosmography*.

Sinopias are sketches in red paint painted directly on the wall just before the final colored version. The master always did the sinopia himself. It was a way for him (and for those who paid for the work) to see exactly how the scene would look in its designated spot. If it wasn't quite right, the master changed a detail here and there. Assistants then copied or traced the sinopia onto paper to make a cartoon. Then the wall was covered with plaster (completely covering up the sinopia), and the assistants redrew the outlines—either by tracing a cut-out of the cartoon or by perforating the drawing on the cartoon and coloring it with charcoal to make dotted lines to follow on the plaster. While the plaster was still wet, the master quickly filled in the color and details, producing the final frescoes (now on display at the Camposanto). The sinopias—never meant to be seen—were uncovered by the bombing and restoration of the Camposanto and brought here.

Duomo Museum

Near the Tower is the entrance to the Duomo Museum (Museo dell' Opera del Duomo), which houses many of the original statues that once adorned the Campo's buildings (where copies stand today), notably the statues by Nicola and Giovanni Pisano. You can stand face-to-face with the Pisanos' very human busts that ring the outside of the Baptistery. Giovanni Pisano's stone *Madonna del Colloquio* solemnly exchanges gazes with baby Jesus in her arms. The most charming piece is Giovanni's carved ivory *Madonna and Child*. Mary leans back gracefully to admire baby Jesus, her pose matching what she's carved from—an elephant's tusk.

You'll see a mythical sculpted hippogriff (a medieval jackalope) and other oddities brought back from the Holy Land by Pisan Crusaders. The museum also has several large-scale wooden models of the Duomo and Baptistery. The church treasury is here, with vestments, chalices, and bishops' staves. There are some Etruscan funerary urns upstairs with reclining people—the inspiration for the Roman sarcophagi that inspired the Pisanos.

Beyond the Etruscan collection are beautiful small-scale copies of the Camposanto frescoes, painted in the 1830s. There's also a scene showing what the building looked like inside before it was bombed.

The museum's interior courtyard has a two-story, tourist-free view of the Tower, Duomo, and Baptistery.

SLEEPING, EATING, AND TRANSPORTATION CONNECTIONS

SLEEPING

To locate the hotels, see the map on page 249.

$$ **Hotel Minerva,** a classy, peaceful place with all the comforts, is a seven-minute walk from the train station (Sb-€85, Db-€110, Tb-€128, air-con, garden terrace, Piazza Toniolo 20, tel. 050-501-081, fax 050-501-559, hotelminerva@pisaonline.it, SE).

$$$ **Hotel Alessandro della Spina,** located in a nondescript neighborhood near the train station, has 16 elegant and colorful rooms each named after a flower (Sb-€105, Db-€125, air-con, free parking, Via Alessandro della Spina 7, tel. 050-502-777, fax 050-20583, www.hoteldellaspina.it, info@hoteldellaspina.it).

$$ **Hotel Villa Kinzica,** with 33 decent rooms, is just steps away from the Field of Miracles—ask for a room with a view of the

---

Sleep Code

(€1 = about $1.20, country code: 39)
S = Single, **D** = Double/Twin, **T** = Triple, **Q** = Quad, **b** = bathroom, **s** = shower only, **no CC** = Credit Cards not accepted, **SE** = Speaks English, **NSE** = No English. Unless otherwise noted, credit cards are accepted and breakfast is included (but usually optional). English is generally spoken.

To help you sort easily through these listings, I've divided the rooms into three categories based on the price for a standard double room with bath:

    $$$ **Higher Priced**—Most rooms €120 or more.
    $$ **Moderately Priced**—Most rooms between €80–120.
    $ **Lower Priced**—Most rooms €80 or less.

Tower (Sb-€78, Db-€108, Tb-€124, Qb-€135, elevator, air-con, attached restaurant, Piazza Arcivescovado 2, tel. 050-560-419, fax 050-551-204).

$ Hotel Milano, near the station, offers 10 spacious, tidy rooms (D-€53, Db-€73, breakfast-€3, air-con, Via Mascagni 14, tel. 050-23162, fax 050-44237, hotelmilano@pisaonline.it).

EATING

For a quick lunch or dinner, the pizzeria/trattoria **La Buca,** just a block from the Tower, is adequate and convenient (Sat–Thu 12:00–15:30 & 19:00–23:00, closed Fri, at Via Santa Maria 171 and Via G. Tassi, tel. 050-560-660).

Ristorante Galileo, south of the Arno, has excellent pizza and pasta (Wed–Mon 12:00–15:00 & 19:30–22:00, closed Tue, Via Silvestri 12, tel. 050-28-287).

Paninoteca il Canguro makes warm, hearty sandwiches to order. Try their popular *primavera* sandwich (Mon–Fri 12:00–22:00, closed Sat night and Sun, Via Santa Maria 151, tel. 050-561-942).

For a cheap, fast, and tasty meal a few steps from the train station, drop by cheery **La Lupa Ghiotta Tavola Calda.** It's got everything you'd want from a *ristorante* at half the price with faster service (build your own salad—5 ingredients for €4.50, Mon and Wed–Sat 12:15–15:30 & 19:15–24:00, Sun 19:00–24:00, closed Tue, Viale Bonaini 113, tel. 050-21018).

The street that houses the daily market, Via delle Colonne (a block north of the Arno), has several atmospheric, mid-priced restaurants and several fun, greasy take-out options.

TRANSPORTATION CONNECTIONS

By train to: Florence (hrly, 1.5 hrs), **Rome** (14/day, 3.25 hrs), **La Spezia,** gateway to Cinque Terre (hrly, 1 hr), **Siena** (change at Empoli: Pisa–Empoli, hrly, 30 min; Empoli–Siena, hrly, 1 hr), **Lucca** (hrly, 30 min). Even the fastest trains stop in Pisa, and you might be changing trains here whether you plan to stop or not.

By car: The drive between Pisa and Florence is that rare case where the non-autostrada highway (free, more direct, and at least as fast) is a better deal than the autostrada.

LUCCA

Surrounded by well-preserved ramparts, layered with history, alternately quaint and urbane, Lucca charms its visitors. Romanesque churches seem to be around every corner, as do fun-loving and shady piazzas filled with soccer-playing children. Despite Lucca's appeal, few tourists seem to put it on their maps, and it remains a city for the Lucchese (loo-KAY-zee).

The city was a Roman settlement. In fact, the grid layout of the streets (and the shadow of an amphitheater) survives from Roman times. Trace the rectangular Roman wall—indicated by today's streets—on the map. As in typical Roman towns, two main roads quartered the fortified town, crossing at what was the forum (main market and religious/political center)—today's Piazza San Michele.

Christianity came early here; it's said that the first bishop of Lucca was a disciple of St. Peter. While churches were built here as early as the fourth century, the majority of Lucca's elegant Romanesque churches date to around the 12th century.

Feisty Lucca, though never a real power, enjoyed a long period of independence (maintained by clever diplomacy). While Pisa ruled the town for 30 years in the 14th century, Lucca was basically an independent city-state (until Napoleon came to town).

In the Middle Ages, wealthy Lucca's economy was built on the silk industry, dominated by the Guinigi (gwee-NEE-gee) family. Without silk, Lucca would have been just another sleepy Italian town. In 1500 the town had 3,000 silk looms employing 25,000 workers. Banking was also big. Many pilgrims stopped here on their way to the Holy Land, deposited their money for safety...and never returned to pick it up.

In its heyday, Lucca packed 160 towers—one on nearly every corner—and 70 churches within its walls. Each tower was the home of a wealthy merchant family. Towers were many stories tall, with single rooms stacked atop each other: ground-floor shop, upstairs living room, and top-floor fire-safe kitchen, all connected by exterior wooden staircases. The rooftop was generally a vegetable garden with trees providing shade. Later, the wealthy city folk moved into the countryside—trading away life in their city palazzos to establish farm estates complete with fancy villas (popular to visit today).

In 1799 Napoleon stormed into Italy and took a liking to Lucca. He liked it so much, he gave it to his sister as a gift. It was later passed on to Napoleon's widow, Marie Louise. With a feminine sensitivity, Marie Louise was partially responsible for turning the city's imposing (but no longer particularly useful) fortified wall into a fine city park much enjoyed today.

ORIENTATION

Tourist Information: The TI is just inside the Porta Santa Maria gate, on Piazza Santa Maria (daily 9:00–20:00, Nov–March 9:00–13:00 & 15:00–18:00, Internet access, Piazza Santa Maria 35, tel. 0583-919-931, fax 0583-469-964, www.luccatourist.it, info@luccaturismo.it, SE).

There is also a glossy, privately-owned information office, marked with an "i," on Piazzale Verdi that offers information and a room- and tour-booking service (daily 9:00–19:00, off-season 9:00–17:30, rents bikes, 80-min city-walk audioguide-€9, futuristic WC, tel. 0583-583-150, SE).

Arrival in Lucca: To reach the city center from the train station, walk toward the walls and head left, to the entry at Porta San Pietro. Taxis are sparse at midday, but try calling 0583-333-434. There is no baggage check at the train station, but you can leave bags at the TI on Piazzale Verdi—for a price (one piece: €2/hr, €11/day).

Helpful Hints

Combo-Tickets: A €5.50 combo-ticket includes visits to Ilaria Guinigi memorial tomb in San Martino Cathedral (€2), Cathedral Museum (€3.50), and Santi Giovanni Church (€2.50). A different €6.50 combo-ticket covers just Palazzo Mansi and Villa Guinigi. Yet another ticket combines Guinigi Tower (€3.50) and Torre delle Ore (€3.50) for €5.

Bike Rental: Several places with identical prices cluster around Piazza Santa Maria (€2.10/hr, €11/day, tandem bikes available, open daily, last rental around 19:00). **Antonio Poli** (Piazza Santa Maria 42, tel. & fax 0583-493-787, enthusiastic Christina SE) and **Cicli Bizzarri** (Piazza Santa Maria 32, tel. 0583-496-031)

Lucca

N

TO →

PORTA ELISA

DCH

TO AGOSTINO →

MARTI

MARCONI

GUGLIELMO

BATONI

M. ROSI

P.S. MARIA

ROMAN AMPHITHEATER

VILLA GUINIGI

ELISA

GIUSTI

PORTA SANTA MARIA

S. FRED.

FILLUNGO

TORRE GUINIGI

CATH. MUSEUM

CATHEDRAL

RAMPARTS

S. CROCE

VIA

ANDREA

S. GION.

PUCCINI'S HOUSE

S. GIUSTINA

POGGIO

BECC.

S. PAOLINO

SAN MICHELE

EMAN.

P. NAP.

VITT.

GARIBA.

GIUSEPPE

MARG.

REG.

PAL. MANSI

VIA

BUS

VITT.

CORSO

VEN.

VITT.

PORTA SAN PIETRO

CALVOUR

TO TRAIN STN.

PORTA SAN DONATO

P

PRETI

CARLO

PORTA VITT. EMAN.

V. NIERI

CAT.

TO AUTO STRADA

CARDUCCI

P

Legend:
1. To Hotel San Marco
2. Albergo La Luna
3. La Boheme B&B
4. Da Elisa B&B
5. Hostel San Frediano
6. Puccini Ristorante
7. Ristorante Canuleia
8. Vecchia Trattoria Buralli
9. Trattoria da Leo
10. Osteria Baralla
11. Bike Rental

200 YARDS
200 METERS

⋯ PATHWAY ATOP RAMPARTS

are each easygoing and rent good bikes. A one-hour rental gives you two leisurely loops around the ramparts.

Launderette: Lavanderia Self-Service Niagara is just off Piazza Santa Maria at Via Rosi 26 (daily 8:00–22:00).

Markets: Lucca's atmospheric markets are worth visiting. Every third Saturday and Sunday of the month, one of the largest **antiques market** in Italy unfurls in the blocks around Piazza Antelminelli (8:00–15:00). The last weekend of the month, local artisans sell **arts and crafts** throughout the town (also 8:00–15:00). At the **general market,** held Wednesdays and Saturdays, you'll find produce and household goods (8:00–13:00, outside of the walls, a few blocks north of Porta Elisa).

Shops and Museums Alert: Shops close most of Sunday and Monday mornings. Many museums are closed on Monday as well.

Festival: On September 13 and 14 the city celebrates Volto Santo ("Holy Face"), with a procession of the treasured local crucifix and a fair in Piazza Antelminelli.

SIGHTS

▲▲**Bike the Ramparts**—Lucca's most remarkable feature, its Renaissance wall, is also its most enjoyable attraction—especially when circled on a rental bike. Stretching for 2.5 miles, this is *the* place to come for a stroll, a bike ride, or an overview of the city.

Lucca has had a protective wall for 2,000 years. You can read three walls into today's map: the first rectangular Roman wall, the later medieval wall (nearly the size of today's), and the 16th-century Renaissance wall.

With the advent of cannons, thin medieval walls were suddenly vulnerable. A new design—the same one that stands today—was

state-of-the-art when it was built (1550–1650). Much of the old medieval wall (look for the old stones) was incorporated into the Renaissance wall (with uniform bricks). The new wall was squat: a 100-foot-wide mound of dirt faced with bricks, engineered to absorb a cannonball pummeling. The townspeople cleared a wide no-man's-land around the town, exposing any attackers from a distance. Ten heart-shaped bastions (inviting picnic areas today) were designed to minimize exposure to cannonballs and maximize defense capabilities. The ramparts were armed with 130 cannons.

The town invested a third of its income for over a century to construct the wall, and—since it kept away the Florentines and nasty Pisans—it was considered a fine investment. In fact, nobody ever bothered to try to attack the wall. Locals say the only time it actually defended the city was during an 1812 flood, when the gates were sandbagged and its ramparts kept the high water out.

Today the ramparts seem made-to-order for a leisurely bike ride (20-min pedal, wonderfully smooth). You can rent bikes cheap and easy from one of several bike-rental places in town (see "Helpful Hints," above).

Roman Amphitheater—Just off the main shopping street, the architectural ghost of a Roman amphitheater can be felt in the delightful Piazza Amfiteatro. With the fall of Rome, the theater (which seated 10,000) was gradually cannibalized for its stones and inhabited by a mish-mash of huts. These were cleared away in the last century to better appreciate the town's illustrious past, and today the square is a circle of touristy shops and mediocre restaurants that becomes a lively bar scene after dark. Today's street level is nine feet above the original arena floor. The only bits of surviving Roman stonework are a few arches on the northwest exterior (#42).

Via Fillungo—This main pedestrian drag, *the* street to stroll, takes you from the amphitheater almost all the way to the cathedral. Along the way you'll get a taste of this town's rich past, including many elegant century-old storefronts. Many of the original storefront paintings, reliefs, or mosaics survive—even if today's occupant of that shop sells something entirely different.

At #97 is a classic old **jewelry store** with a rare storefront that has kept its T-shaped arrangement (when closed, you see a wooden T, and during open hours it unfolds with a fine old-time display). This arrangement dates from a time when the merchant sold his goods in front, did his work in the back, and lived upstairs.

Di Simo Caffè at #58 has long been the hangout of Lucca's artistic and intellectual elite. Composer and hometown boy Giacomo Puccini tapped his foot while sipping coffee here. Pop in to check out the 1880s ambience.

A surviving five-story **tower house** is at #67. Remember, there was a time when each corner sported its own tower. The stubby stones that still stick out once supported wooden staircases (there were no interior connections up or down). So many towers cast shadows over this part of town that the next street is called Via Buia (literally "dark street").

Opposite Via Buia a few yards off Via Fillungo is **Piazza Guidiccioni**. Filled with chairs, it serves as an outdoor theater each summer (pick up a program at the little office desk, nightly, €5).

At #45 and #43 you'll see two more good examples of **tower houses.** Across the street, the clock tower has a "hand"-wound Swiss clock that has clanged four times an hour since 1754 (€4 to climb up and see the mechanism flip into action on the quarter hour).

The intersection of Via Fillungo and Via Roma/Via Santa Croce marks the center of town (where the two original Roman roads crossed). Just down Via Santa Croce (past the Leonardo exhibit—€5 to see a room full of "don't touch" modern models of his sketches...not worth the money) is **Piazza San Michele** (once the Roman Forum). Towering above the church's fancy Pisan Romanesque facade, the archangel Michael stands ready to flap his wings—which he actually did on special occasions. (See the stairs behind the facade, which church officials would climb to pull some strings and wow their gullible flock.) Piazza San Michele is as fun a people center today as it has been since Roman times.

▲**San Martino Cathedral**—This church, begun in the 11th century, is an entertaining mix of architectural and artistic styles. Its elaborate Pisan-Romanesque **facade**—featuring Bible scenes, animals, and candy-cane-striped columns—dominates the piazza. The central figure of the facade is St. Martin, a Roman military officer from Hungary who, by offering his cloak to a beggar, more fully understood the beauty of Christian compassion. (The impressive original, a fine example of Romanesque sculpture, is just inside, hiding from the pollution.) Each of the columns on the facade is unique. On the lower right, the architect Guideo from Como holds a document declaring he finished the facade in 1204. On the right (at eye level), a labyrinth set into the wall relates the struggle and challenge our souls face in finding salvation. The Latin plaque just left of the main door is where moneychangers and spice traders met to seal deals (on the doorstep of the church—to underscore the reliability of their promises). Notice the date: An Dni MCXI (A.D. 1111).

The **interior** features Gothic arches, Renaissance paintings, and stained glass from the 19th century. On the left side of the nave, a small temple displays the wooden crucifix called Volto Santo. It's said to have been sculpted by Nicodemus in Jerusalem and set afloat in an unmanned boat that landed on the coast of Tuscany, from where wild oxen carried it to Lucca in 782. The sculpture (which is actually 12th-century Byzantine-style) has quite a jewelry collection, which you can see in the Cathedral Museum (see below). On the right side of the nave, the sacristy houses the enchantingly beautiful memorial tomb of Ilaria del Carretto by Jacopo della Quercia (1407). The young bride of silk baron Paolo Guinigi is decked out in the latest, most expensive fashions. She's so realistic that the statue was nicknamed "sleeping beauty." Her nose is partially rubbed off because of a long-standing tradition of lonely young ladies rubbing it for luck in finding a boyfriend (cathedral is free, Ilaria tomb-€2, included in €5.50 combo-ticket, Mon–Sat 9:30–19:00, Sun 13:00–16:45, Piazza San Martino).

Cathedral Museum (Museo della Cattedrale)—This beautifully-presented museum houses original paintings, sculptures, and vestments from the cathedral and other Lucca churches. The first room displays jewelry made to dress up the Volto Santo crucifix, including gigantic gold shoes. Nearby, notice the fine red silk—a reminder that this precious fabric is what brought riches and power to the city. The exhibits in this museum take on meaning only with the €1 audioguide—if you're not in the mood to listen to this, I'd skip the place altogether (€3.50; included in €5.50 combo-ticket, daily 10:00–18:00, off-season 10:00–14:00; Piazza Antelminelli, next to cathedral).

Santi Giovanni Church—This first cathedral of Lucca is interesting only for its excavations. The entire floor of the 12th-century church was excavated (1969–1992), revealing layers of Roman houses, early churches, and ancient hot tubs dating back to the time of Christ. Eager students can request an English translation of the floor plans to know what's what. As you climb under the church's present-day floor and wander the lanes of Roman Lucca, remember that the entire city sits on similar ruins (€2.50, included in €5.50 combo-ticket, daily 10:00–18:00, off-season Sat–Sun only 10:00–17:00, Piazza S. Giovanni, diagonal from cathedral).

Puccini's House—Opera enthusiasts (but nobody else) will want to visit the home where Giacomo Puccini (1858–1924) grew up. The museum has the great composer's piano and a small collection of his personal belongings (€3, daily 10:00–18:00, off-season Tue–Sun 10:00–13:00 & 15:00–18:00, closed Mon and Jan–mid-March, Corte San Lorenzo 9, tel. 0583-584-028).

Guinigi Tower (Torre Guinigi)—Many Tuscan towns have towers, but none quite like the Guinigi family's. Up 227 steps is a small garden with fragrant trees (and a bar) surrounded by fantastic views (€3.50, daily mid-May–mid-Sept 9:00–24:00, March–mid-May and late Sept 9:00–19:00, Oct–Feb 10:00–18:00, Via S. Andrea, tel. 0583-316-846). Tower-climbers can also purchase a combo-ticket (€5) that covers both the Guinigi Tower and the medieval **Torre delle Ore,** the city clock tower (daily 10:00–18:30, corner of Via Fillungo and Via del'Arancio).

Palazzo Mansi—Minor paintings by Tintoretto, Pontormo, Veronese, and others vie for attention, but the palazzo itself, a furnished and decorated 17th-century confection, steals the show. This is your chance to appreciate the wealth of Lucca's silk merchants (€4, €6.50 combo-ticket includes Villa Guinigi, Tue–Sat 8:30–19:30, Sun 8:30–13:30, closed Mon, Via Galli Tassi 43, tel. 0583-55-570).

Villa Guinigi—Built by Paolo Guinigi in 1418, the family villa is now a museum displaying artifacts, sculptures, and paintings. Monumental paintings by multitalented Giorgio Vasari are the best reason to visit (€4, €6.50 combo-ticket includes Palazzo Mansi, Mon–Sat 8:30–19:30, Sun 8:30–13:30, Via della Quarquonia, tel. 0583-496-033).

SLEEPING

$$$ Hotel San Marco is a postmodern palace a seven-minute walk outside the Porta Santa Maria. Its 42 rooms are sleek, with all the comforts (Sb-€87, Db-€126, nice breakfast spread, air-con, elevator, pool, free parking, taxi from station-€6, Via San Marco 368, tel. 0583-495-010, fax 0583-490-513).

$$ Albergo la Luna has 29 professional, spotless rooms in the heart of the city. Updated rooms are split between two adjacent buildings right off of the main shopping street. Frescoed top-floor suites are a palatial, romantic splurge (Sb-€80, Db-€90–110, suite-€175, breakfast-€10.50, air-con, elevator, parking-€10.50/day, Via Fillungo Corte Compagni 12, tel. 0583-493-634, fax 0583-490-021, www.hotellaluna.com, info@hotellaluna.com, Barbieri family).

$$ La Boheme B&B has a cozy yet elegant ambience, offering five spacious, chandeliered rooms, each painted a different, rich color (Db-€110, less off-season, 5 percent discount with cash and this book, includes breakfast, air-con, Via del Moro 2, tel. & fax 0583-462-404, www.boheme.it, info@boheme.it, gracious Ranieri SE).

$ Da Elisa B&B is cheap and cheery, with six simple, old-fashioned rooms sharing three worn-but-clean bathrooms and a common kitchen (S-€47, D-€54, T-€69, Q-€84, breakfast-€5, some

---

Sleep Code

(€1 = about $1.20, country code: 39)
S = Single, **D** = Double/Twin, **T** = Triple, **Q** = Quad, **b** = bathroom, **s** = shower only, **no CC** = Credit Cards not accepted, **SE** = Speaks English, **NSE** = No English. Unless otherwise noted, credit cards are accepted and breakfast is included (but usually optional). English is generally spoken.

To help you sort easily through these listings, I've divided the rooms into three categories based on the price for a standard double room with bath:

    $$$ Higher Priced—Most rooms €120 or more.
      $$ Moderately Priced—Most rooms between €80–120.
        $ Lower Priced—Most rooms €80 or less.

street noise, Via Elisa 25, tel. 0583-494-539, fax 0583-471-609, www.daelisa.com, info@daelisa.com)

$ Ostello San Frediano is a cut above the average hostel. In a central palazzo with a peaceful garden, the rooms are bright and modern, some with fun lofts (Db-€41, Qb-€82, €17 beds in 6- to 8-person dorms, €3 extra for non-members, no CC, lock-out 10:00–15:30, free parking, cheap restaurant, Via della Cavallerizza 12, tel. 0583-469-957, fax 0583-461-007, www.ostellolucca.it, info @ostellolucca.it).

EATING

Puccini Ristorante is the place for a fancy €50 dinner. Fish and meat are featured here, with gourmet preparations and elegant presentation. Skip the basic sidewalk seats for the classy, modern art–strewn dining room (€38 tasting *menu*, daily 12:30–14:30 & 19:30–22:30, closed Tue in winter, reserve on weekends, across the street from Puccini's House, Corte San Lorenzo 1, tel. 0583-316-116).

Ristorante Canuleia makes everything fresh in their small kitchen. While the portions aren't huge, the food is great. You can eat in their tiny dining room or garden courtyard (€18 tourist *menu*, daily 11:30–23:00, Via Canuleia 14, tel. 0583-467-470).

Vecchia Trattoria Buralli, on quiet Piazza S. Agostino, is a good bet for traditional cooking, with fine indoor and piazza seating. Service can be uneven (€20–40 dinner, Thu–Tue 12:00–14:45 & 19:15–22:45, closed Wed, Piazza S. Agostino 10, tel. 0583-950-611).

Trattoria da Leo, a cousin of Trattoria Buralli above, packs in chatty locals for typical, low-priced home-cooking. Arrive early or reserve a spot (daily 12:00–15:00 & 19:00–22:00, Via Tegrimi 1, tel. 0583-492-236).

Osteria Baralla, steps from the Roman Amphitheater, is popular with locals for its quality meals. They have a breezy and spacious dining room under medieval vaults or a few quiet tables on the pedestrian street (Mon–Sat 12:30–15:00 & 19:30–22:00, closed Sun, Via Anfiteatro 7, tel. 0583-440-240).

TRANSPORTATION CONNECTIONS

By train to: Florence (9/day, 90 min), **Pisa** (hrly, 30 min), **Milan** (nearly hrly, 4-5 hrs, transfer in Florence or Prato), **Rome** (5/day, 3 hrs).

Drivers: Lucca has a serious lack of public parking places. Try parking lots at Porta Santa Maria and Porta Sant' Anna, or consider parking outside of the gates near the train station or on the boulevard surrounding the city.

TUSCAN HILL TOWNS

Tuscany is rich in history, and proud locals will remind you that their ancestors, the Etruscans, were thriving long before anyone had heard of Julius Caesar.

The Middle Ages were formative times for many cities, with warring factions dividing towns between those loyal to the Pope (Guelphs) and the Holy Roman Emperor (Ghibellines). Cities developed monumental defensive walls and built towers, many of which are still being attacked—by tourists. The bubonic plague in 1348, combined with increasing dominance from Florence, turned many bustling cities into docile backwaters.

Tuscan towns retain their medieval charm, and are best enjoyed by adapting to the pace of the countryside. So...slow...down...and enjoy the delights that Tuscany offers. Spend the night if you can, as many hill towns are mobbed by day-trippers from Florence and Siena.

But how in Dante's name does a traveler choose from the literally hundreds of Tuscan hill towns? I've listed some of my favorites in this chapter. The one(s) you visit will depend on your interests, time, and mode of transportation. Multi-towered San Gimignano is a classic, but peak-season crowds can overwhelm the town's charms. Wine aficionados won't want to miss Montalcino or Montepulciano. Art-lovers and those eager to trace Frances Mayes' footsteps will make the pilgrimage to Cortona. Fans of architecture and urban design will appreciate Pienza's well-planned streets and squares. Chiusi and Volterra rate highly on the Etruscan trail. And San Galgano's ruined church offers solitude in the midst of a peaceful landscape.

One of the greatest Tuscan treats—the food—varies wildly depending on where you are. The areas around Florence and Siena are famed for serving hearty "farmer food," but as you move west, dishes become lighter, based more on seafood and grains. Siena is

Tuscan Hill Towns

the only town that excels at sweets, but if you look, you might find good local desserts anywhere (watch for the phrase *"fatta in casa,"* or homemade). Wine is good throughout Tuscany, with pleasing selections for both amateurs and connoisseurs (see page 284 for a description of Tuscan wines).

Getting Around

You'll find manageable public transportation in most places, but to really explore the countryside at your own pace, a car is ideal.

By Bus or Train: Traveling by public transportation is an economical way to see the countryside and rub elbows with the locals. While trains connect some of the smaller towns like Cortona and Chiusi, the train stations are likely to be in the valley a couple miles from the town center, usually connected by a local bus.

Buses are most often the better, if not the only, choice to connect destinations. Siena is a great hub of local bus lines. You can find schedules at local TIs and buy tickets at newsstands or tobacco shops (look for the black sign with a big white T on it). Confirm the departure point *(Dov'è la fermata?)*—some piazzas have more than one bus stop, so double-check that the posted schedule lists your destination and departure time. In general, orange buses are local city buses and blue buses are for long distances.

Once the bus arrives, confirm the destination with the driver. You are expected to stow big packs underneath the bus (open the luggage compartment if it's closed). Sundays and holidays are problematic. Buses, even from large cities like Siena, have sparse schedules. The few departing ones are usually jam-packed. Bus-ticket offices are often closed on Sundays, so make plans and buy your ticket ahead of time. If you must travel on a day when there are few choices (like Easter), drop into a travel agency and ask for help. Most agencies book bus and train tickets with little or no commission.

By Car: A car is the best way to maximize your time in small-town Tuscany. Since a car is a headache in big cities (such as Florence and Siena), pick up your car in the last big city you visit, then head to the countryside. Get a big, detailed Tuscany road map at a newsstand. Although roads are numbered on the map, you will not find any numbers referenced on the actual road signs. Roads are indicated by blue signs with a city name on them (e.g., if you want to take route 146 out of Montepulciano to the west, look for signs leading to Pienza, the next town along this route to the west). For two particularly scenic drives, from Siena to Montalcino, and from Montalcino to Montepulciano, see the Crete Senese Drives suggested on page 297.

If you are staying overnight, ask your hotelier for parking suggestions. Keep all valuables out of sight and locked in the trunk of the car.

SLEEPING

Hotels, Rooms, and Apartments

In small towns, there are often few hotels to choose from. Prices are lower than in Florence, but a nice double will still run around €80 including breakfast. Many small towns have an abundance of *affita-camere*, or rental rooms. This can be anything from a cozy B&B with your own Tuscan grandmother, to a set of keys and a basic bed. The TI can give you a list of possibilities. These rooms are generally a good budget option, but since they vary in quality, shop around to find the best value. Apartment rentals are also listed at the TI and are very common in small towns. Apartments generally offer a couple of bedrooms, a sitting area, and a teensy *cucinetta*, usually stocked with dishes and flatware—a great value for families or couples traveling together. Once you have the keys, you will probably be on your own.

Tips for Enjoying an *Agriturismo* or Farmhouse Stay

- Avoid peak season to sleep cheap. Rental prices follow the old rule of supply and demand. For instance, a Tuscan farmhouse that rents for as much as $1,900 a week at peak times can go for as little as $600 in late September or October.
- Make sure your trip fits their requirements. Many properties rent on a traditional Saturday to Saturday time period. You might be unable to rent for a different or shorter time, especially during peak season.
- If you want amenities, be willing to pay more. A private pool can add substantially to the cost, but at the height of summer, could be worth every extra euro.
- Consider renting a rural apartment rather than an entire villa or farmhouse. Often the owners have renovated an original rambling farmhouse or medieval estate into a series of well-constructed apartments with private kitchens, bathrooms, living areas, and outdoor terraces. They usually share a common pool.
- You will need private transportation, such as a rental car, to fully enjoy—or even reach—your accommodations.
- To make the most of your time, ask an expert—the owner—for suggestions on local restaurants, sights, and activities. Make sure you know how to operate the appliances.
- Slow down. One of the joys of staying for at least a week in one location is you can develop a true *dolce far niente* (sweetness of doing nothing) attitude. If it rains, grab a book from the in-house library and curl up on the sofa.
- While your time in the countryside may not be action-packed, staying put in one spot leaves you open to the unexpected pleasures that come when you just let the days unwind without a plan.

Agriturismo

Agriturismo (agricultural tourism), or rural B&Bs, began in the 1980s as a way to encourage farmers to remain on their land, to produce food, and to offer accommodations to tourists. A peaceful home base for exploring the region, these rural Italian B&Bs are ideal for couples or families traveling by car.

It's wise to book several months in advance for high season (May–Sept). Weeklong stays are preferred in July and August, but shorter stays are possible off-season. In the winter you might be charged extra for heat, so confirm the price ahead of time. Payment policies vary, but generally a 25 percent deposit is required (lost if you cancel), and the balance is due one month before arrival.

As the name implies, *agriturismi* are in the countryside,

Sleep Code

(€1 = about $1.20, country code: 39)
S = Single, **D** = Double/Twin, **T** = Triple, **Q** = Quad,
b = bathroom, **s** = shower only, **no CC** = Credit Cards not
accepted, **SE** = Speaks English, **NSE** = No English. Unless otherwise noted, credit cards are accepted and breakfast is included
(but usually optional). English is generally spoken.

To help you sort easily through these listings, I've divided
the rooms into three categories based on the price for a standard
double room with bath:

$$$ **Higher Priced**—Most rooms €100 or more.
$$ **Moderately Priced**—Most rooms between €70–100.
$ **Lower Priced**—Most rooms €70 or less.

although some are located within a mile of town. Most are family-
run and vary wildly in quality. Some properties are simple and rustic,
while others are downright luxurious, offering amenities such as
swimming pools and riding stables. The rooms are usually clean and
comfortable. Breakfast is often included, and *mezza pensione* (half-
pension, which in this case, means a home-cooked dinner) may be
built into the price whether you want it or not. Most places serve
tasty homegrown food; some are vegetarian or organic, others are
gourmet. Kitchenettes are often available to cook up your own feast.

To qualify officially as an *agriturismo*, the farm must generate
more money from its farm activities than from tourism, thereby
insuring that the land is worked and preserved.

Some farmhouse B&Bs are simply that, and are not really
working farms, though are still fine places to stay. But if you want
the real thing, make sure the owners call their place an *agriturismo*.

In this chapter, I've listed some *agriturismi* and farmhouses under
the towns they're nearest, but there are many more than this. Local
TIs can give you a list of farms in their area, and many *agriturismi* now
have their own Web sites. For a sampling, visit www.agriturismoitaly.it.
For a booking agency, consider Farm Holidays in Tuscany (closed
weekends, tel. 0564-417-418, www.byfarmholidays.com).

South Tuscany

Montalcino

On a hill overlooking vineyards and valleys below, Montalcino—
famous for its delicious and pricey Brunello di Montalcino red
wines—is a must-sip for wine lovers.

Wines in Tuscany

The region of Tuscany produces some of the most famous and tastiest wines in Italy. Wines are particular to their village. The characteristics of the soil, temperature, and exposure make each wine unique to its area. Strictly regulated by the government, wines must meet certain recipe requirements to be considered, say, a Chianti or a Vino Nobile (with the exception of the "Super Tuscans").

Even if you don't often drink wine, try some in Tuscany. Choosing a wine can be intimidating, but the Italian government has made it easy to choose something decent, even if you don't know much about it. In general, three categories are designated to wines: *Vino da Tavola* (table wine) is the lowest grade—drink this one with hot dogs. *Denominazione di Origine Controllata* (DOC), a cut above table wine, is usually cheap, but can be surprisingly good. *Denominazione di Origine Controllata e Guarantita* (DOCG) is the highest grade, and can be identified by the pink or green label on the neck and the scary price tag on the shelf. DOCGs are generally a good bet if you want a quality wine but don't know anything else about the winemaker.

The *Vino della Casa* at local restaurants is absurdly cheap and ranges from mouthwash (rarely) to impressive (often). "House Wine" doesn't mean that it comes out of a box. Many restaurants, even modest ones, have agreements with local wineries or occasionally bottle their own. For the most part, it is good enough and the best value on the menu.

Words to Live By, or...
How to Describe Wine in Italian

dry	**secco**	SAY-koh
sweet	**dolce**	DOHL-chay
earthy	**terre**	TAY-ray
fruity	**fruttoso**	froo-TOH-zoh
full-bodied	**corposo**	kor-POH-zoh

In the Middle Ages, Montalcino (mohn-tahl-CHEE-noh) was considered Siena's biggest ally. Originally allied with Florence, the town switched sides after the Sienese beat up Florence in the battle of Monteaperti in 1260. The Sienese persuaded the Montalcini to join their side by forcing them to sleep one night in the bloody, Florentine-strewn battlefield.

Montalcino prospered under Siena, but like its ally, it waned after the Medici family took control of the region. The village regained fame when, in the late 19th century, the Biondi Santi family created a fine, dark red wine, calling it "the brunette."

Non–wine-lovers may find Montalcino a bit too focused on *vino*, but one sip of Brunello makes even wine skeptics believe that Bacchus was on to something. Note that Rosso di Montalcino (a younger version of Brunello) is also good at half the price. Those with sweet tooths will enjoy munching Ossi di Morta ("bones of the dead"), a crunchy cookie with almonds.

Day-trippers be warned: Montalcino has no baggage-check service.

Tourist Information: The TI is just off Piazza Garibaldi, in the city hall (daily 10:00–13:00 & 14:00–17:50, closed Mon in winter, tel. & fax 0577-849-331, www.prolocomontalcino.it in mostly Italian).

SIGHTS

Fortezza—The 14th-century fort, built under the rule of Siena, now houses an *enoteca*, or wine bar (see below). Climb the ramparts to enjoy a panoramic view of the Asso and Orcia valleys, or enjoy a picnic in the park surrounding the fort (€3.50 for rampart walk, €6 combo-ticket includes Civic Museum, daily 9:00–20:00, closed Monday off-season).

Civic Museum (Museo Civico)—Gothic art is the star of this museum, with works from Montalcino's heyday, the 13th- to 16th-centuries. Wooden sculptures and religious objects round out the collection (€4.50, €6 combo-ticket includes Fortezza, Tue–Sun 10:00–13:00 & 14:00–17:50, closed Mon, Via Ricasoli, tel. 0577-846-014).

Wineries—While there are plenty of *enoteche*, there are no real wineries inside the city. The countryside, however, is littered with them, and most wineries will give tastings, but require an appointment. Banfi, the most touristy, produces well-respected wines (daily 10:00–17:00, tours Mon–Fri at 16:00, reserve in advance, 10 min south of Montalcino in Sant'Angelo Scalo, tel. 0577-840-111, www.castellobanfi.com, reservations@banfi.it).

The Montalcino TI can give you the list of more than 150 regional wineries. Or check with the vintners' consortium (www.consorziobrunellodimontalcino.it, consbrun@tin.it, tel. 0577-848-246).

SLEEPING

(€1 = about $1.20, country code: 39)

$ **Albergo il Giglio,** although lacking in warmth, has 12 comfortable rooms, some with vaulted ceilings. Ask for a room with a view (Sb-€58, Db-€50, Tb-€95, breakfast-€6.50, Via Saloni 5, tel. & fax 0577-848-167, hotelgiglio@tin.it).

$ **Ristorante il Moro** rents four pleasant, modern rooms around the corner from their restaurant. The two upper rooms have views, the lower have terraces, and they all share a cozy common room with a kitchen (Db-€50, no breakfast, Via Mazzini 4, tel. 0577-849-384, Alessandro and Julia SE).

$ **Affittacamere Mariuccia** is basic and drab, but central and cheap (Sb-€35, Db-€46, no breakfast, air-con, check-in at Enoteca Pierangioli, Piazza del Popolo 16, tel. & fax 0577-849-113, www.enotecapierangioli.com, enotecapierangioli@hotmail.com, Stefania NSE).

Near Montalcino: $$ *Agriturismo*: **La Crociona,** a farm and working vineyard, rents seven fully-equipped apartments. Fiorella Vannoni and Roberto and Barbara Nannetti offer cooking classes and tastes of the Brunello wine grown and bottled on the premises (Db-€95, Qb-€130, lower weekly rates, pool, La Croce 15, 7-min drive from Montalcino, tel. 0577-847-133, tel. & fax 0577-848-007, www.lacrociona.com, crociona@tin.it, SE).

EATING

Taverna Il Grappolo Blu is dressy yet friendly, serving local specialties and vegetarian options (Sat–Thu 12:00–15:30 & 19:00–22:00, closed Fri, Scale di Via Moglio 1, tel. 0577-847-150).

Trattoria Sciame, a family-run hole-in-the-wall, has nine small tables and homemade desserts (pasta-€7, meat-€8, Wed–Mon 12:00–14:30 & 19:00–21:30, closed Tue, Via Ricasoli 9, tel. 0577-848-017).

Gather ingredients for a picnic at the **Co-op supermarket** on Via Ricasoli, then enjoy your feast in front of the Fortezza. **Market day** is Friday, in Viale della Liberta (7:00–13:00).

Wine Tasting

The medieval setting inside Montalcino's fort at **Enoteca La Fortezza** makes this a fun place for a glass or three of local wine. Spoil yourself with Brunello in the cozy *enoteca* or at outdoor tables (3 tastes for €13, snacks for 2-€8, daily 9:00–20:00, closes at 18:00 and on Mon off-season, inside the Fortezza, tel. 0577-849-211, www.enotecalafortezza.it).

Ferruccio Biondi-Santi, the founder of the café **Fiaschetteria**

Italiana, was also the creator of the famous Brunello wine. The wine library in the back boasts many choices of local wine, including a prized bottle from 1955, a vintage year. A meeting place since 1888, this grand café also serves light lunches and espresso to tourists and locals alike (€8–10 for glass of Brunello and plate of snacks, daily 7:30–24:00, Piazza del Popolo 6, tel. 0577-849-043).

TRANSPORTATION CONNECTIONS

To: Siena (8 buses/day, 90 min), **Montepulciano/Pienza** (10/day, change to line #114 in Torrenieri, 60 min plus changing time). Bus tickets are sold at tobacco shops or on board.

Montepulciano

Curving its way along a ridge, Montepulciano (mohn-tay-pull-chee-AH-noh) delights visitors with *vino* and views. Alternately under Sienese and Florentine rule, the city still retains its medieval *contrade* districts, each with a mascot and flag. The neighborhoods compete the last Sunday of August in the *Bravio delle Botti,* where teams of men push large wine casks uphill from Piazza Marzocco to Piazza Grande, all hoping to win a banner and bragging rights.

The city is a collage of architectural styles, but the elegant San Biagio Church, at the base of the hill, is the most impressive Renaissance building. Most ignore the architecture and focus more on the city's other creative accomplishment, the tasty Vino Nobile di Montepulciano red wine.

The action in Montepulciano centers on two streets, the steep Via di Gracciano nel Corso, and Via Ricci, but the quiet back streets are well worth a visit.

Tourist Information: The TI is on Via Gracciano nel Corso 26, not to be confused with the more central and less helpful "Strada del Vino" office on Piazza Grande (daily March–Oct 9:30–13:00 & 15:00–18:30, closed Tue, tel. 0578-757-341, www.comune .montepulciano.si.it—Italian only, prolocomp@bccmp.com).

Helpful Hints: Market day is Thursday, and a larger market takes place at the bus station on Saturday (8:00–14:00). Public WCs are located next to Palazzo del Comune and the church of St. Augustine.

SIGHTS

Piazza Grande—This pleasant, lively piazza is surrounded by an architectural grab bag. The medieval Palazzo Comunale has a Florentine-style **clock tower** that you can climb for a windy, panoramic view (€1.55, daily 10:00–18:00). The Palazzo de' Nobili-Tarugi is a Renaissance arcaded confection, while the unfinished Duomo glumly looks on, wishing the city hadn't run out of money for the facade. Dream up a way to finish it while you enjoy a cappuccino at the café on the square.

Civic Museum (Museo Civico)—Small and eclectic, this well-presented museum is worthwhile if only for its colorful della Robbia ceramic altarpieces (€4.13, Tue–Sat 10:00–13:00 & 15:00–18:00, Sun 10:00–18:00, closed Mon, Via Ricci 10, tel. 0578-717-300).

San Biagio Church—Down a picturesque driveway lined with cypress, this church—designed by Antonio da Sangallo—is Renaissance perfection. The proportions of the Greek cross plan give the building a pleasing rhythmic quality. The lone tower was supposed to have a twin, but it was never built. The soaring interior is impressive, with a high dome and lantern (daily 9:00–13:00 & 15:00–19:00). The street Via di San Biagio, leading from the church up into town, makes for an enjoyable, if challenging walk.

Cantinas—Montepulciano's most popular attraction is its Vino Nobile. This robust red wine can be tasted in any of the cantinas lining Via Ricci and Via nel Corso, but **Contucci** is the most famous. Lively Adamo has been making wine since 1953 and welcomes tourists into his cellar with warmth and wisecracks (€5.50 for guided visit and 4 tastes, no reservation necessary, Piazza Grande 7, tel. 0578-757-006).

The information office for the "Strada del Vino" on Piazza Grande may not give out much city information, but it does organize **wine tours** in the city and minibus winery tours farther afield (call for current days and times, tel. 0578-717-484, www.stradavinonobile.it, info@stradavinonobile.it).

SLEEPING

(€1 = about $1.20, country code: 39)
$$ Mueble il Riccio (hedgehog in Italian) is medieval-elegant, with modern rooms, a view terrace, and friendly owners. When Giorgio isn't manning the desk, he's out giving country tours in one of his classic Italian cars (Sb-€77, Db-€88, Tb-€110, breakfast-€8, Via Talosa 21, tel. & fax 0578-757-713, www.ilriccio.net, info@ilriccio .net, *poco* English).

$ **Camere Bellavista** has simple rooms with views, and nicer rooms without. Room 6 has a view terrace worth reserving (standard Db-€55, nicer Db-€65, no CC, no breakfast, no elevator, Via Ricci 25, mobile 347-823-2314, bellavista@bccmp.com, NSE).

EATING

Ai Quattro Venti is fresh, flavorful, fun, and right on Piazza Grande. Mushroom fans should try anything with the word *bosco* in it (pasta-€7, Fri–Wed 12:00–14:00 & 19:00–22:00, closed Thu, next to city hall on Piazza Grande, tel. 0578-717-231).

Osteria dell'Aquacheta serves pasta and salads at reasonable prices, with a mix of locals and tourists (€5 pasta and salads, Wed–Mon 12:30–15:00 & 19:30–22:30, closed Tue, Via del Teatro 22, tel. 0578-717-086).

TRANSPORTATION CONNECTIONS

To: Siena (8 buses/day, 1.25 hrs, few in afternoon, none on Sun), **Pienza** (8 buses/day, 30 min). The town has no baggage-check service.

Drivers: Route 146 to Montalcino is particularly scenic (see Crete Senese Drives, page 297). It isn't wise to drive the tiny roads inside the city, so park outside the walls, either at the bus station or at the numerous lots on the edges of town.

Pienza

Set on a crest, surrounded by green, rolling hills, the small town of Pienza packs a lot of Renaissance punch. In the 1400s, locally born

Pope Pius II of the Piccolomini family (see page 227) decided to remodel his birthplace in the current Renaissance style. Propelled by papal clout, the town of Corsignano was transformed—in only five years' time—into a jewel of Renaissance architecture. It was renamed Pienza, after Pope Pius. The plan was to remodel the whole town, but work ended in 1564 when both the pope and his architect, Bernardo Rossellino, died. The architectural focal point is the square Piazza Pio II, surrounded by the Duomo and the pope's family residence, Palazzo Piccolomini. The culinary focal point is Pecorino cheese, a pungent sheep's cheese, which can be found at almost any shop and can be eaten fresh *(fresco)* or aged *(secco)*.

Tourist Information: The TI is on Piazza Pio II, across from the Duomo (Mon–Sat 9:30–13:00 & 15:00–18:30, closed Sun, tel. & fax 0578-749-071). Audioguides are available for self-guided walking tours (€5, 50 min). The town has no baggage-check service. **Market day** is Friday.

SIGHTS

Piazza Pio II—One of the classic piazzas in Italy, this square is famous for its elegance and artistic unity. The square and the surrounding buildings were all designed by Rossellino to form an "outdoor room."

Duomo—Its classic, symmetrical Renaissance facade dominates Piazza Pio, but it cannot disguise the fact that the altar is slowly sliding down the mountain. It began sagging only 10 years after construction and, despite attempts to shore it up, remains downwardly mobile. The interior is charming, with several Gothic altarpieces and painted arches. Windows feature the crest of Pius II, with five half-moons advertising the number of crusades that his family funded. The left side of the church suffers the most from the faulty foundation. To measure the movement, bow-tie-shaped pieces of glass were recently set into the floor, bridging the cracks. Although it was thought that the foundation had been fixed, the glass pieces cracked. To the left of the altar, two slanty chapels might make you feel dizzy.

Palazzo Piccolomini—The home of Pius II and the Piccolomini family until 1962, the interior can be visited with a guided tour. Check out the well-preserved painted courtyard for free. In Renaissance times, most buildings were covered with elaborate paintings like these (€3, Tue–Sun 10:00–12:30 & 15:00–18:00, closed Mon, tel. 0578-749-071).

Museo Diocesano—This museum contains religious paintings from local churches (€4.10, Wed–Mon 10:00–13:00 & 15:00–18:30, closed Tue, in winter open Sat–Sun only, Corso il Rossellino 30).

View Terrace—Romantics walk up Via dell' Amore (Street of Love) or Via del Bacio (Street of the Kiss) to the panoramic promenade next to the Duomo. Views from the terrace include the Tuscan countryside and Monte Amiata, the largest mountain in southern Tuscany, in the distance.

SLEEPING

(€1 = about $1.20, country code: 39)

$ **Oliviera Camere** has six simple rooms in the center of town and is run by soft-spoken Nello (Db-€50, no CC, breakfast in room, Via Condotti 4, tel. 0578-748-205, NSE).

   $$ *Agriturismo*: **Agriturismo Terrapille** sits just below Pienza,

surrounded by dreamy scenery. Four country rooms and two apartments with modern comforts—all within a mile of town—make this a possibility for those without wheels (Db-€88, Qb-€190, breakfast-€6.50, dinner available, pool, take road #18 in direction of Monte Amiata, tel. & fax 0578-749-146, www.terrapille.it, terrapille@bccmp.com, SE).

EATING

Latte di Luna is a good, quality choice in a town of mediocre food (Wed–Mon 12:30–14:30 & 19:30–21:30, closed Tue, Via San Carlo 2, reservations suggested, tel. 0578-748-606).

La Taverna di Re Artu serves bruschetta and a variety of wines (daily 10:30–20:30, Via della Rosa 4).

Assemble a picnic at any of the numerous cheese and wine shops, and dine with a fantastic view along the walls of the view terrace.

TRANSPORTATION CONNECTIONS

Bus tickets are sold at the bar just inside Pienza's town gate.

To: Siena (6 buses/day, 90 min), **Montepulciano** (8 buses/day, 30 min).

Cortona

Cortona clings by its fingernails to the top of a mountain (1,700 feet), dangling above views of the Tuscan and Umbrian landscape below. Frances Mayes' books, such as *Under the Tuscan Sun*, have placed this

town in the touristic limelight, just as Peter Mayle's books popularized (and populated) the Luberon region in France. But even before Mayes ever published a book, Cortona was considered one of the classic Tuscan hill towns.

The city began as one of the largest Etruscan settlements, the remains of which can be seen at the base of the city walls, as well as in the nearby tombs. It grew to its present size in the 13th to 15th centuries, when it was a colorful and crowded city, eventually allied with Florence. The farmland that fills almost every view from the city was marshy and uninhabitable until about 300 years ago, when it was drained and turned into some of the most fertile land in Tuscany.

Bring good walking shoes; the streets here can be steep and unforgiving. Mercifully, most of Cortona's sights and shops cluster around the level streets on the Piazza Garibaldi–Piazza del Duomo axis.

Art-lovers will know Cortona as the home of Renaissance painter Luca Signorelli, Baroque master Pietro della Cortona (Berretini), and the 20th-century Futurist artist Gino Severini. Cortona's museums and churches reveal many of the works of these native sons.

Tourist Information: The helpful TI is on the main drag, Via Nazionale 42 (daily March–Oct 9:00–13:00 & 15:00–19:00, cash machine, also sells train tickets, tel. 0575-630-352, www.cortonaweb .net, www.cortona-musei.it for museums, infocortona@apt.arezzo.it, SE). **Market day** is Saturday (early–14:00, Piazza Signorelli).

Arrival in Cortona: You'll probably arrive at Piazza Garibaldi, where the bus stop is located outside the massive town walls. From here, it's a level five-minute walk down bustling shop-lined Via Nazionale (stop by the TI) to Piazza della Repubblica, the heart of the town, dominated by City Hall (Palazzo della Comune). From this square it's an easy five-minute walk past the interesting Etruscan Museum and theater to Piazza Duomo, where you'll find the recommended Diocesan Museum. Steep streets, many of them stepped, lead from Piazza della Repubblica up to the San Niccolo and Santa Margherita churches and the Medici Fortress (30 min).

SIGHTS

Etruscan Museum (Museo dell' Accademia Etrusca)— Established in 1787, this was one of the first galleries dedicated to artifacts from the Etruscan civilization. The impressive display includes an intricate fifth-century B.C. chandelier and some fantastic gold and turquoise jewelry. This eclectic museum also has an Egyptian section and a room dedicated to modern works by Severini (€4.20, Tue–Sun 10:00–19:00, closed Mon off-season, Palazzo Casali on Piazza Signorelli, tel. 0575-637-235).

Diocesan Museum (Museo Diocesano)—This collection, housed in the Gesu Church, has pieces by Fra Angelico and Duccio, but the highlights are the paintings by hometown hero and Renaissance master, Luca Signorelli (€5, daily 10:00–19:00, Nov–March closed Mon, Piazza del Duomo 1, tel. 0575-62830). For more on Signorelli, see page 298.

San Niccolo Church—Signorelli fans will want to make the pilgrimage up to this tiny church. Ring the bell and the caretaker will give you a short tour (in Italian). The highlight of this humble church is an altarpiece by Signorelli painted on both sides. The caretaker will

Cortona

★ = PIAZZA DELLA REPUBBLICA

100 YARDS
100 METERS

❶ Albergo San Luca
❷ San Marco Hostel
❸ Trattoria la Grotta
❹ Rest. la Locanda nel Loggiato
❺ Enoteca Molesini

TO MEDICI FORTRESS

SANTA MARGHERITA

PORTA MONTANINA

PORTA COLONIA

PORTA BERARDA

CITY WALLS

PUBLIC GARDENS

SAN NICOLÒ

SAN DOMENICO

TO TERONTOLA

VIA SEVERINI

VIA BERRETTINI

THEATER

S. FRAN.

VIA MAFFEI

POST

VIA NAZIONALE

VIA BATTISTI

BUS STOP

PIAZZA GARIBALDI

DUOMO

CASALI

VIA ROMA

VIA GUELFA

CITY HALL

DIOCESAN MUSEUM

ETRUSCAN MUSEUM

PORTA SANTA MARIA

VIA MERCATO

PORTA SAN AGOSTINO

DCH

activate a tricky arm mechanism that moves the picture away from the wall to reveal the painting behind it. There's no admission fee, but you should tip the caretaker a euro or two.

From San Niccolo, a steep path leads uphill 10 minutes to the...

Santa Margherita Church—This church houses the remains of the town's patron saint. Saint Margaret, an unwed mother from Montepulciano, found her calling with the Franciscans in Cortona, tending to the sick and poor. Her son eventually became a Franciscan monk.

Still need more altitude? Head uphill five minutes more to the Medici Fortress. It's usually closed, but the views are stunning, stretching all the way to distant Lake Trasimeno, where Hannibal defeated the Romans (217 B.C.) in the Punic Wars.

Near Cortona: Etruscan Tombs—Visits to nearby *melone* (tombs, named for their melon-like shape) can easily be arranged with the Etruscan Museum. Just a couple miles out of town, the road is dotted with tombs dating as back as far as seventh-century B.C. (accessible only through guided visit-€10.50, arrange through museum or Aioncultura, tel. 0575-637-235, meet at tomb site, www.aioncultura.org, aioncultura@aioncultura.org).

SLEEPING

(€1 = about $1.20, country code: 39)

$$ **Albergo San Luca,** perched on a cliffside, has 54 modern, business-class, impersonal rooms, half with stunning views of Lago Trasimeno. Right at the bus stop, it's perfect if you want to avoid dragging your bags up the hill (Sb-€73, Db-€105, popular with Americans and groups, reserve view rooms ASAP, Piazza Garibaldi 1, tel. 0575-630-460, fax 0575-630-105, www.sanlucacortona.com, info@sanlucacortona.com, SE).

$ **San Marco Hostel,** at the top of town, housed in a remodeled 13th-century palace, is one of Italy's best (€12, in rooms with 2, 4, or 8 beds, lockout 11:00–17:00, Via Maffei 57, tel. 0575-601-392, SE).

Near Cortona

$$$ **Casa San Martino,** 12 miles east of Cortona near the isolated village of Lisciano Niccone, is a 250-year-old countryside farmhouse run as a B&B by American Italophile Lois Martin. While Lois reserves the summer (June–Aug) for one-week stays, she'll take guests staying a minimum of three nights for the rest of the year (Db-€160, 10 percent discount for my readers—mention this book when you reserve, includes breakfast, pool, washer/dryer, house rental available, Casa San Martino 19, Lisciano Niccone, tel. 075-844-288, fax 075-844-422, casam@tuscanyvacation.com). Lois' neighbors, Ernestine and Gisbert Schwanke, run the tidy **La Villetta**

di San Martino B&B (Db-€110 includes breakfast, 2-night min, common kitchen and sitting room, San Martino 36, tel. & fax 075-844-309, erni@netemedia.net, SE).

$$ Castello di Montegualandro is a well-preserved castle on a hill opposite Cortona, overlooking the lake and countryside. The Marti family rent four charming medieval apartments, formerly peasant's quarters, inside the peaceful castle walls. Each one is unique and named for its former use—the Fornacci's sunken living room used to be a kiln. The castle's chapel is a popular spot for weddings (3- or 4-person apartment starts at €120, 3-night min, mention this book for a 7 percent discount, discounts for longer stays, no CC, 10 min southeast of Cortona, Tuoro sul Trasimeno, tel. & fax 075-8230-267, www.montegualandro.com, info@montegualandro.com, SE).

EATING

Trattoria la Grotta, just off Piazza Repubblica, is a traditional, cave-like place with daily specials and a fun outdoor seating area (pasta-€7, meat-€8, Wed–Mon 12:00–15:00 & 19:00–22:00, closed Tue, Piazza Baldelli 3, tel. 0575-630-271).

La Locanda nel Loggiato, run by Lara and Marco, serves up big portions of Tuscan cuisine (pasta-€7, meat-€7–15, Thu–Tue 12:00–15:00 & 19:00–23:00, closed Wed, Piazza Pescheria 3, tel. 0575-630-575).

Put together a **picnic** at the ultra-touristy **Enoteca Molesini** (Piazza della Repubblica 23) and munch with a million-euro view from Piazza Garibaldi or the public gardens behind San Domenico Church.

TRANSPORTATION CONNECTIONS

To: Rome (10 trains/day, 2.25 hrs), **Florence** (hrly, 1.5 hrs), **Montepulciano** (8/day, 1.25 hrs, change in Chiusi). Most trains stop at Cortona's Camucia train station (tel. 0575-603-018), but fast trains from Rome and Florence also stop at Terontola, 10 miles away (tel. 0575-670-034). From Terontola and the Camucia train station, orange buses depart for Piazza Garibaldi twice hourly (€1.60, buy tickets at newsstand).

Drivers: Some free parking is available inside the town walls—if you can find it. The best bets are Piazzale del Mercato and Piazzale di Santa Margherita.

San Galgano Monastery

Of southern Tuscany's several evocative monasteries, San Galgano is the best. Set in a forested area called the *Montagnolo* (medium-sized mountains), the isolated abbey and chapel are postcard-perfect.

San Galgano was a 12th-century saint who renounced his past as a knight to become a hermit. Lacking a cross to display, he created his own by miraculously burying his sword up to its hilt into a stone, à la King Arthur, but in reverse. After his death, a large Cistercian monastery complex grew. Today all you'll see is the roofless, ruined abbey and, on a nearby hill, the Chapel of San Galgano with its fascinating dome and sword in the stone.

Getting There: Although a bus reportedly comes here from Siena, this sight is realistically accessible only for drivers. It's just outside of Monticiano (not Montalcino), about an hour south of Siena. A warning to the queasy: These roads are curvy.

The Abbey—This picturesque, Cistercian abbey was once a powerful institution in Tuscany. Known for their skill as builders, the Cistercians oversaw the construction of Siena's cathedral. But the abbey, after losing most of its population in the plague of 1348, never really recovered and was eventually deconsecrated.

The Cistercian order was centered in France, and the architecture of the abbey shows a heavy French influence. Notice the large, high windows and the pointy, delicate arches. This is pure French Gothic, a style that never fully caught on in Italy (compare it with the chunky cathedral in Siena, built about the same time).

As you enter the church, notice the small section of the cloister wall to the left. This used to surround the garden, and was the only place that the monks were allowed to talk, for one hour each day. From inside the church, the empty windows frame the view of the chapel up on the hill.

The Chapel—A path from the abbey leads up the hill to the Chapel of San Galgano. The unique beehive-like interior houses San Galgano's sword and stone, recently confirmed to date back to the 12th century. Don't try and pull the sword from the stone. The small chapel to the left displays the severed arms of the last guy who tried. The chapel also contains some deteriorated frescoes and more interesting *sinopie*, or fresco sketches. The adjacent gift shop sells a little bit of everything, from wine to postcards to herbs, some of it made by religious orders (free, daily 8:00–sunset). For a quick snack, a small, touristy bar at the end of the driveway is your only option.

Other more accessible Tuscan monasteries worth visiting include Sant' Antimo (six miles south of Montalcino) and Monte Oliveto Maggiore (15 miles south of Siena).

MORE SOUTH TUSCAN SIGHTS

▲**Chiusi**—This small hill town (rated ▲▲ for Etruscan fans), once one of the most important Etruscan cities, is now a key train junction on the Florence–Rome line. The region's trains (to Siena, Orvieto, and Assisi) go through or change at this hub.

Highlights include the Archaeological Museum and the Etruscan tombs located just outside of town near Lago di Chiusi (€4, daily 9:00–20:00, Via Porsenna 93, tel. 0578-20177). One of the tombs is multichambered, with several sarcophagi. Another, the Tomba della Scimmia (Tomb of the Monkey), has some well-preserved frescoes. Visiting the tombs requires a guide, arranged through the TI or the Archaeological Museum (five people allowed to view at a time).

Troglodyte alert! The Cathedral Museum on the main square has a dark, underground labyrinth of Etruscan tunnels (bring a flashlight). The mandatory guided tour of the tunnels ends in a large Roman cistern from which you can climb the church bell tower for an expansive view of the countryside (museum-€2, labyrinth-€3, combo-ticket-€4, daily 9:30–12:45 & 16:00–19:00, tunnel tours at 11:00 and 16:00, Piazza Duomo 1, tel. 0578-226-490).

The TI is on the main square (Mon–Fri 10:00–13:00, maybe afternoons in summer, closed Sun, tel. 0578-227-667, prolocochiusi @bcc.tin.it). Trains connect Chiusi with Rome, Florence, Siena, and more. Buses link the train station with the town center two miles away.

▲**U.S. Cemetery**—Whatever one's feelings about war, the sight of endless rows of white marble crosses and Stars of David never fails to be moving. This particular cemetery is the final resting place of more than 4,000 Americans who died in the liberation of Italy during World War II. Their memory lives on in two Italian cemeteries, one in Nettuno near Rome and this one just south of Tavernuzze, seven miles south of Florence. Climb the hill past the perfectly manicured lawn, lined with grave markers, to the memorial, where maps and a history of the Italian campaign detail the Allied advance (daily mid-April–Sept 9:00–18:00, Oct–mid-April 9:00–17:00, WC, just off Via Cassia road that parallels the *superstrada* between Florence and Siena, 2 miles south of Florence Certosa exit on A-1 autostrada). Buses from Florence stop just outside the cemetery.

▲▲**Crete Senese Drives**—South of Siena, the hilly area known as the "Sienese Crests" is full of colorful fields and curvy, scenic roads.

You'll see an endless parade of classic Tuscan scenes, rolling hills topped with medieval towns, olive groves, rustic stone farmhouses, and a skyline punctuated with cypress trees. You won't find many wineries here, since the clay soil is better for wheat and sunflowers, but you will find the pristine, panoramic Tuscan countryside that you find on calendars and postcards.

During the spring, the fields are painted in yellow and green with fava beans and broom, dotted by red poppies on the fringes. Sunflowers decorate the area during July and August, and expanses of wind-blown grass fill the landscape almost all year.

Most roads to the southeast of Siena will give you a taste, but one of the most scenic stretches is the Laurentina road (Siena-Asciano-San Giovanni D'Asso, #438 on road maps, can easily continue to Montalcino). There are plenty of turnouts on this road for panoramic photo opportunities, and a few roadside picnic areas.

For a break from the winding road, about 15 miles from Siena, you'll find the quaint and non-touristy village of **Asciano.** With a medieval town center and several interesting churches and museums, this is a great place for lunch (TI at Corso Matteotti 18, tel. 0577-719-510). If you're in town on Saturday, gather a picnic at the outdoor market (Via Amendola, 8:00–14:00).

Five miles south of Asciano, the **Abbey of Monte Oliveto Maggiore** houses a famous fresco cycle of the life of St. Benedict, painted by Renaissance masters Sodoma and Luca Signorelli (free, daily April–Oct 9:15–12:00 & 15:15–18:00, Nov–March closes at 17:00, Gregorian chanting Sun at 11:00 and Mon–Fri at 18:15, call to confirm, tel. 0577-707-611, www.ftbcc.it/monteoliveto). Once you reach the town of **San Giovanni d'Asso,** it's only another 12 miles southwest to Montalcino.

Another scenic drive is the lovely stretch between Montalcino and Montepulciano (#146 on road maps). This route alternates between the grassy hills of the Crete Senese and sun-bathed vineyards of the Orcia River valley. Stop by Pienza en route.

Sleeping in the Crete Senese: **Agriturismo il Molinello** rents four apartments, two built over a medieval mill. Hardworking Alessandro and Elisa share their organic produce and sometimes offer wine-tastings. With children, friendly dogs, toys, and a swimming pool, this is ideal for families (Qb-€70–100, apartment for up to 8-€130, 1-week stay required in summer, discounts and 2-night min off-season, mountain-bike rentals, near Asciano, 30 min southeast of Siena, tel. 0577-704-791, mobile 335-692-5720, fax 0577-705-605, www.molinello.com, info@molinello.com, SE).

North Tuscany

San Gimignano

The epitome of a Tuscan hill town, with 14 medieval towers still standing (out of an original 72!), San Gimignano is a perfectly preserved tourist trap, so easy to visit and visually pleasing that it's a good stop.

In the 13th century, back in the days of Romeo and Juliet, feuding noble families ran the towns. They'd periodically battle things out from the protection of their respective family towers. Pointy skylines were the norm in medieval Tuscany. But in San Gimignano, fabric was big business, and many of its towers were built simply to hang dyed fabric out to dry.

While the basic three-star sight here is the town of San Gimignano itself, there are a few worthwhile stops. From the town gate, shop straight up the traffic-free town's cobbled main drag to Piazza della Cisterna (with its 13th-century well). The town sights cluster around the adjoining Piazza del Duomo. Thursday is market day (on Piazza Duomo), but for local merchants, every day is a sales frenzy.

Tourist Information: The helpful TI is in the old center on Piazza Duomo (daily March–Oct 9:00–13:00 & 15:00–19:00, Nov–Feb 9:00–13:00 & 14:00–18:00, free maps, sells bus tickets, books rooms, tel. 0577-940-008, www.sangimignano.com, prolocsg@tin.it, SE). A public WC is just off Piazza della Cisterna (€.50).

SIGHTS

Collegiata—The Romanesque church, with round windows and wide steps, is filled with fine Renaissance frescoes, some painted by Domenico Ghirlandaio (€3.50, €5.50 combo-ticket includes mediocre Religious Art Museum, Mon–Fri 9:30–19:30, Sat 9:30–17:00, Sun 12:30–17:00).

Civic Museum (Museo Civico)—This small, fun museum is inside City Hall (Palazzo Comunale). Enter the room called Sala di Consiglio. It's *molto* medieval and covered in festive frescoes, including the *Maestà* by Lippo Memmi. This virtual copy of Simone Martini's *Maestà* in Siena proves that Memmi doesn't have quite the same talent as his famous brother-in-law. Upstairs the Pinacoteca displays a classy little painting collection, with a 1422 altarpiece by Taddeo di Bartolo honoring Saint Gimignano. You can see the saint

San Gimignano

TO CERTALDO & S-429

SANT' AGOSTINO

PORTA SAN JACOPO

PORTA SAN MATTEO

VIA FOLGORE DI SAN GIM.

PORTA DELLE FONTI

PIAZZA DEL DUOMO

COLLEGIATA

ROCCA

PRUN.

QUERCECCHIO

WC

PORTA QUERCECCHIO

PIAZZA DELLA CISTERNA

POST

CIVIC MUSEUM, TORRE GROSSA

N

DCH

BUS STOP -DEPART-

TO VOLTERRA, POGGIBONSI, SIENA

VIA ROMA

PORTA SAN GIOVANNI

BUS STOP -ARRIVAL-

TO ①

300 YARDS

300 METERS

STEPPED STREETS

① To Podere Ponte a Nappo Rooms
② Hotel la Cisterna
③ Arco di Goro Rooms
④ Santa Fina Rooms
⑤ Tortoli Rooms
⑥ Osteria del Carcere
⑦ Trattoria Chiribiri
⑧ La Grotta Ghiotta Rest.
⑨ Co-Op Supermarket
⑩ Assoc. Strutture Extralberghiere

with the town in his hands surrounded by events from his life. As you exit, be sure to stop by the Camera del Podesta to check out the medieval dating scene (€5, includes Torre Grossa, daily 9:30–19:00, Nov–Feb 10:00–17:00, audioguide-€2).

Torre Grossa—The city's tallest tower, at 200 feet, can be scaled (€5, includes Civic Museum, same hours as museum).

Sant' Agostino Church—This peaceful church, at the opposite end of town, has fewer crowds and more soul. Behind the altar, a lovely fresco cycle by Benozzo Gozzoli (who painted a chapel in the Medici-Riccardi Palace in Florence) tells of the life of Saint Augustine, a North African monk who preached simplicity. The kind, English-speaking friars are happy to tell you about their church and way of life, and also have Mass in English on Sundays. Pace the tranquil cloister before heading back into the tourist mobs (free, but €.50 lights the frescoes, daily 7:00–12:00 & 15:00–19:00).

Rocca—Formerly Florentine fortifications, these walls now enclose a park that's perfect for picnicking. Climb the steep stairs on the corner tower for a great (and free) view of the towers.

SLEEPING

(€1 = about $1.20, country code: 39)
Although a zoo during the daytime, when evening comes, locals outnumber tourists and San Gimignano becomes peaceful and enjoyable.

$$ **Hotel la Cisterna,** right on Piazza della Cisterna, offers 49 clean, predictable rooms, some with panoramic view terraces (Sb-€70, Db-€90, Db with view-€105, Db with terrace-€115, buffet breakfast, elevator, good restaurant with great view, discounts off-season, closed Jan–Feb, Piazza della Cisterna 24, tel. 0577-940-328, fax 0577-942-080, www.hotelcisterna.it, info@hotelcisterna.it, Alessio SE).

$$ Enterprising **Carla Rossi** rents rooms and apartments—most with views—throughout the town. **Podere Ponte a Nappo,** just outside the city gates, is a comfortable farmhouse with taste-fully-decorated apartments and town views (Db-€100, Tb-€115, Qb-€130, 15-min walk or 5-min drive from Porta San Giovanni, air-con, parking). Rossi also rents rooms in the charming little houses of **Arco di Goro** and **Santa Fina** right in town. **Tortoli** has elegant rooms in a medieval tower overlooking Piazza della Cisterna (Db-from €60, most around €100, Tb and Qb around €110–150, no breakfast, office at Via di Cellole 81, tel. & fax 0577-955-041, mobile 349-882-1565, www.appartamentirossicarla.com, businirossicarla@tiscalinet.it, son Francesco SE).

$ **Associazione Strutture Extralberghiere** is a clearinghouse for reasonably-priced private rooms around the city (Db-€60, €70 with breakfast, Piazza della Cisterna 6, maurizio@temainf.it, tel. & fax 0577-943-190).

EATING

Osteria del Carcere serves high-quality, classic Tuscan dishes in a cozy atmosphere (12:30–15:00 & 19:30– 22:00, closed Wed and lunch Thu, Via del Castello 13, just off Piazza della Cisterna, tel. 0577-941-905).

The tiny **Trattoria Chiribiri,** just inside Porta San Giovanni, serves homemade pasta and desserts at a remarkably fair price (daily 11:00–23:00, Piazza della Madonna 1, tel. 0577-941-948).

La Grotta Ghiotta makes good soup and sandwiches that can be packed up *portare via*—to go (daily 12:00–21:00, Via Santo Stefano 10, tel. 0577-942-074).

Picnics: Co-Op sells all you need for a nice spread (Mon–Sat 8:30–20:00, closed Sun, at parking lot below Porta San Giovanni). Or browse the shops guarded by wild boar statues to buy boar by the gram. Pick up some boar (*cinghiale;* cheeng-gee-AH-lay), cheese, bread, and wine and enjoy a picnic in the garden at the Rocca or the park outside Porta San Giovanni.

TRANSPORTATION CONNECTIONS

By bus to: Florence (hrly, 75 min, change in Poggibonsi), **Siena** (5/day, 1.25 hrs, more with change in Poggibonsi), **Volterra** (4/day, 2 hrs, change in Colle di Val d'Elsa). Sunday buses are few, far between, and crowded. In San Gimignano, bus tickets are sold at the bar just inside the town gate or at the TI. The town has no baggage-check service.

Drivers: You can't drive within the walled town of San Gimignano, but a parking lot waits just a few steps outside the town.

Volterra

Encircled by impressive walls and topped with a grand fortress, Volterra sits high above the rich farmland below. More than 2,000 years ago, Volterra was one of the most important Etruscan cities, a city much larger than the one we see today. Greek-trained Etruscan artists worked in the city and outlying areas, leaving a significant stash of art, particularly funerary urns. Eventually absorbed into the Roman Empire, the city bitterly fought against the Florentines in the Middle Ages, but like many Tuscan towns, it lost in the end and was given a fortress atop the city to "protect" its citizens.

Compact and walkable, the city stretches out from the pleasant

Who Were the Etruscans?

Centuries before the Romans conquered the world as they knew it, another civilization inhabited parts of the Italian peninsula. Tuscany is named for these ancient people, the Etruscans. Their settlements and tombs, many of them discovered between Volterra and Chiusi, date back to the 6th century B.C. Contemporary with the Greeks, it appears the Etruscans—with many farmers and merchants in their society—were a peaceful people.

While the Etruscan language has not yet been completely deciphered, we do know they were excellent artists. Bronze devotional figures and delicately carved funerary urns show the high level of skill that the Etruscans achieved, suggesting that they may have sent artists to Greece for training. But while Greek art focused on the idealized human form, the Etruscans represented people realistically, with wrinkles, crooked noses, silly smiles, and funny haircuts. Women played an important role in their society, enjoying equal rights and importance with their male counterparts, a concept that many would say still hasn't resurfaced in Italy.

Etruscan tombs and artifacts are still being discovered, often by farmers in the countryside. Museums in Volterra and Cortona house fine collections of urns, pottery, and devotional figures. You can visit several domed tombs outside of Cortona.

While we don't know precisely why the Etruscans disappeared, it is likely that they were either steamrolled by the Roman war machine or simply absorbed into the Roman culture.

Piazza dei Priori to the old city gates. Time here is best spent in the Etruscan Museum or Roman Theater, but a couple of the city's other sights are worth a peek. With multiple connections and limited bus schedules, public transportation here is doable but tricky. Check bus schedules carefully for return trips.

Tourist Information: The information-packed TI is in Piazza dei Priori, next to City Hall (daily 9:00–13:00 & 14:00–19:00, Nov–March closes at 18:00, books rooms, guided tours available, tel. 058-887-257, www.volterratur.it, info@volterratur.it). Rent audioguides here for use around the city and in the museums (€5, 40–90 min).

SIGHTS

Etruscan Museum (Museo Etrusco Guarnacci)—Filled top to bottom with rare Etruscan artifacts, this museum—even with few English explanations—makes it easy to appreciate how advanced this pre-Roman culture was. Don't miss the oddly modern figurine

Ombre della Sera or the wrinkled, realistic faces on the funerary urn, *Urna degli Sposi* (€7, includes—like it or not—Pinacoteca and Sacred Art Museum, daily 9:00–19:00, Nov–March closes at 13:00, mildly interesting English pamphlet available, audioguide at TI, Via Don Minzoni 15, tel. 058-886-347).

Pinacoteca—See this eerily-lit museum for the last room, two huge Luca Signorelli paintings and another by Rosso Fiorentino. You might as well; it's included in the Etruscan Museum admission (€7 combo-ticket, daily 9:00–19:00, Nov–March closes at 13:00, Via dei Sarti 1, tel. 058-887-580).

Roman Theater—This well-preserved ancient theater is one of the few to have part of the stage remaining (€2, includes less-interesting Etruscan Acropolis in Parco Archeologico, or view it free from Via Lungo le Mure, daily 10:30–17:30, Nov–March weekends only 11:00–16:00).

Palazzo dei Priori—When not in use for meetings, the city council chambers—lavishly painted and lit with fun dragon lamps—are open to visitors (€1, may be possible to scale tower, daily 10:00–13:00 & 14:00–18:00).

Duomo—This 13th-century church is not as elaborate as its cousin in Pisa, but the simple facade and golden-coffered ceiling are beautiful examples of the Pisan Romanesque style. The chapel to the left of the entry has unusual, large dioramas with painted terra-cotta figures (Mon–Sat 8:00–12:00 & 15:00–18:00, Sun 15:00–18:00).

SLEEPING

(€1 = about $1.20, country code: 39)
$$ **Hotel la Locanda,** near the Roman Theater, is fancy, with nicely furnished rooms and huge bathrooms (Sb-€92, Db-from €115, air-con, elevator, Via Guarnacci 24, tel. 058-881-547, fax 058-881-541, www.hotel-lalocanda.com, staff@hotel-lalocanda.com, SE).

$ **Albergo Nazionale,** with 40 rooms, is clean, simple, and steps from the bus stop (Sb-€50, Db-€69, Tb-€80, less off-season, breakfast-€6, Via dei Marchesi 11, tel. 058-886-284, fax 058-884-097, nazionalevolterra@tiscalinet.it).

$ **Ostello della Gioventu** has budget beds a short walk from the Etruscan Museum (bed-€13, no CC, Via del Poggetto 3, tel. & fax 058-885-577).

EATING

Ristorante Etruria makes tasty ravioli, served in a frescoed dining room or on the piazza (€15 *menu turistico*, daily 12:00–15:00 & 19:00–22:00, closed Wed in winter, Piazza dei Priori 6, tel. 058-886-064).

For fresh sandwiches and wine, try friendly **Enoteca Scali** (daily 9:00–21:00, Via Guarnacci 13, tel. 058-881-170).

You can assemble a picnic at the few *alimentari* around town (try Spar Market, Via Gramsci 12) and eat in the breezy Parco Archeologico.

TRANSPORTATION CONNECTIONS

To: Florence (4 buses/day, 2 hrs, change in Colle Val d'Elsa), **Siena** (4 buses/day, 2 hrs, change in Colle Val d'Elsa), **San Gimignano** (4 buses/day, 2 hrs, change in Colle Val d'Elsa), **Pisa** (9 buses/day, 2 hrs, change in Pontedera). Buses arrive in and depart from Volterra's Piazzi Martiri della Liberta (buy tickets at any tabacchi shop). For Siena, Florence, and San Gimignano, Tra-in bus tickets only get you as far as Colle Val d'Elsa; you must buy another ticket (for the other bus company) at the newsstand near the bus stop. There is virtually no bus service in or out of Volterra on Sundays or holidays.

Drivers: There are easy parking lots are near the Roman Theater and underground, near Porta all'Arco (€1.40/hr or €10/24 hrs) and a cheaper lot at the train station (€3/24 hrs).

FIORENZA

FLORENTINE HISTORY

EIGHT CENTURIES IN SEVEN PAGES

59 B.C.–A.D. 1200:
Roman, Early Christian, Medieval

It's the usual Rome story—military outpost, thriving provincial capital, conversion to Christianity, over-
run by barbarians—except Florence
really didn't fall. Proud medieval
Florentines traced their roots back
to civilized Rome, and the city
remained a Tuscan commercial
center during the Dark Ages.

Sights
- Piazza Repubblica (the old Forum)
- Find the ancient Roman military camp on today's street map.
  You can still see the rectangular grid plan—lined up with com-
  pass points, rather than the river.
- Baptistery (built c. 1050), likely on site of Roman temple
- Roman and Etruscan fragments (Duomo Museum)

1200s: Urban Growth

Woolen cloth manufacture, trade,
and banking made urban merchants—organized into guilds—
more powerful than rural, feudal
nobles. Florence, now a largely
independent city-state, allied
with nearby cities.

Sights
- Bargello (it was built as the city hall)
- Santa Croce, Santa Maria Novella, and Badia Fiorentina churches
- Baptistery interior mosaics

1300s: Prosperity, Plague, Recovery

As part of a budding democracy with civic pride, Florence's guilds and merchants financed major construction projects (some begun in late 1200s). But the population of 90,000 was suddenly cut in half by the Black Death (bubonic plague) of 1348.

Recovery was slowed by more plagues, bank failures, and political rivalries.

Sights
- Duomo and Campanile (original decorations in Duomo Museum)
- Palazzo Vecchio
- Orsanmichele Church
- Santa Croce, Santa Maria Novella, and Giotto's bell-tower design and his paintings in Uffizi

1400s: Renaissance and Medici

While 1500 marks Europe's Renaissance, in Florence—where the whole revival of classical culture got its start—the Renaissance began

and ended in the 1400s (the Quattrocento). The Medici (MED-ee-chee), a rich textile-and-banking family whose wealth gave them political leverage around Europe, ruled the most prosperous city in Italy, appeasing the masses with philanthropy and public art.

Sights
- Brunelleschi's Duomo dome and Pazzi Chapel
- Donatello's statues in Bargello and Duomo Museum and on Orsanmichele exterior
- Ghiberti's two bronze doors on Baptistery (originals in Duomo Museum)
- Botticelli's paintings in Uffizi
- The Uffizi, tracing painting from medieval to Michelangelo
- The Bargello, tracing sculpture
- Masaccio's frescoes in Santa Maria Novella and Brancacci Chapel
- Fra Angelico paintings (and Savonarola history) in San Marco Museum

1500–1800:
Decline, Medici Dukes, Renaissance Goes South

Bankrupt, the anti-democratic Medicis were exiled to Rome, where they married into royalty and returned—backed by foreign powers—as even less democratic nobles. The "Renaissance spirit" moved elsewhere, taking Michelangelo, Leonardo, and Raphael with it. In succeeding centuries, the Medici dukes ruled an economically and politically declining city, but still financed art.

Sights
- Michelangelo's Florentine works—*David*, Medici Chapels, and Laurentian Library
- Pitti Palace and Boboli Gardens (the later Medici palace)
- Later paintings (Uffizi) and statues (Bargello)
- Destruction of the original Duomo facade (Duomo Museum)
- Medici Chapels—pompous tombs of (mostly) later Medici
- Ponte Vecchio cleaned up for jewelry shops
- Baroque interiors of many older churches
- Galileo's finger, telescopes, and experiments in Science Museum

1800s: Italian Unification

After years of rule by Austrian nobles, Florence peacefully booted the *ausländers* and joined the Italian unification movement. It even briefly served as modern Italy's capital (1865–1870). Artistic revival of both medieval (neo-Gothic) and Renaissance (neoclassical) styles.

Sights
- Duomo's current neo-Gothic facade
- Piazza Repubblica, commemorating unification, fine 19th-century cafés

1900s: Uncontrolled Urbanization, Urban Renewal

Population growth, rapid industrialization, WWII destruction, and the

20-foot-high flood of 1966 made Florence a chaotic, noisy, dirty, traffic-choked city. In the last 30 years, however, the tourist zone has been cleaned and cleared, museums revamped, hours extended, and the people have adapted to welcoming foreign visitors. Now if they could just do something about those Vespas....

FLORENCE TIMELINE

500 B.C.–A.D. 1000:
Etruscans, Romans, and "Barbarians"

c. 550 B.C.   Etruscans settle in Fiesole, near Florence.

59 B.C.   Julius Caesar establishes the Roman town of Florentia (meaning flowering or flourishing) at a convenient crossing point of the Arno River.

c. A.D. 200   Thriving Roman city, pop. 10,000.

c. 350   In the wake of Constantine's legalization of Christianity, Bishop (and Saint) Zenobius builds a church where the Duomo stands today.

450   Rome falls. Ostrogoths from the east, Byzantines from modern-day Turkey, and Germanic barbarians sweep through in waves. But Florence survives as a small trading town.

800   Charlemagne's Franks sweep through; he becomes the first Holy Roman Emperor. Florence is part of the Empire for the next 300 years, and is the regional capital (rather than Fiesole).

1000–1400:
Medieval Rise and Political Squabbles

c. 1050   Baptistery built, likely on site of ancient Roman temple.

1100   Matilda, Countess of Tuscany, allies with the pope and rises against the German-based Holy Roman Empire, gaining independence for Florence.

1200   Florence is the leading city in Tuscany, thriving on wool manufacture, trade, banking, and moneylending.

1215   Political assassination of Buondelmonte epitomizes power struggles between nobles (Ghibellines), rich merchants and craftsmen (Guelphs), and laborers. The different factions seek support from outsiders—Guelphs ally with pope, Ghibellines with emperor. In general, Ghibellines dominate in first half of 1200s.

1222–1235   Florentine armies defeat Pisa, Siena, and Pistoia. Florence is the dominant city-state in Tuscany, heading a rich, commercial marketplace.

1252   Gold florin minted, one of Europe's strongest currencies.

1266   Merchants and craftsmen (Guelphs), organized into guilds, oust nobles and establish the *primo popolo*, the first "rule by the people."

1293   Guelphs solidify rule by the rich middle class, establishing a constitution that forbids nobles and laborers from holding office. The Ghibellines are gone, but

Guelphs vs. Ghibellines

Pope	Emperor
Middle-class merchants and craftsmen	Aristocrats of feudal order
Urban (new economy)	Rural (traditional economy)
Independence of city-states under local Italian leaders	Unification of small states under traditional dukes and kings

But really, the fight was about power, not ideology. (It wasn't what you believed, but with whom you were allied.) The names always mean something different depending on the particular place and time.

bitter political infighting continues, with Florence divided between Black and White Guelphs.

1296 Construction begins on the Duomo. Santa Croce and Santa Maria Novella are also being built.

1302 The poet Dante, a prominent White Guelph, is exiled. Traveling around Europe and Italy, he writes his epic poem *The Divine Comedy*.

1347 Florence's population is 90,000, making it one of Europe's biggest cities.

1348 Population halved after the horrific bubonic plague. In addition, recent bank failures and ongoing political squabbles make recovery more difficult.

1378 The Ciompi revolt, led by wool-factory workers, is suppressed by rich merchant families. The guilds (workers' unions) lose power as a few wealthy families rise—the Strozzi, Ricci, Alberti, and...Medici.

1400s, The "Quattrocento": A Prosperous Renaissance City under Medici Princes

1401 Baptistery door competition energizes an already civic-minded city.

1406 Florence, by conquering Pisa, gains a port and becomes a sea-trading power.

1421 Giovanni de' Medici, a shrewd businessman, expands the Medici family business from wool manufacture into banking.

1434 Cosimo the Elder (Giovanni's son) returns triumphant from exile to rule Florence. Outwardly, he honors the

Florentine constitution, but, in fact, he uses his great wealth to rule as a tyrant, buying popularity with lavish patronage of public art.

1436 Dedication of the Duomo, topped by Brunelleschi's dome.

1440 Battle of Anghiari—Florence defeats Milan.

c. 1440 Donatello's *David*.

1458 Cosimo the Elder creates a rubber-stamp Council of the Hundred.

1464 Cosimo's son, Piero the Gouty, rules stiffly but ably.

1469 Lorenzo the Magnificent, Cosimo's grandson, rules over the most powerful city in Italy. He is a popular politician but a so-so businessman.

1492 Lorenzo dies. Many Medici banks go bankrupt. Lorenzo's son, Piero the Unfortunate, facing an invasion force from France, appears to side with the foreigners.

1494 The Medici family, reviled as bankrupt morally, financially, and politically, is exiled. In the political vacuum, the monk Girolamo Savonarola appears as a voice of moral authority. He re-establishes the Florentine constitution.

1498 Savonarola is hanged and burned on Piazza della Signoria by political enemies and a citizenry tired of his morally strict rule. The constitution-driven republic continues.

1500–1800:
The "Later" Medicis Oversee Florence's Decline

1501 Michelangelo begins sculpting *David*.

1512 The Medici family, having established a power base in Rome, returns to take political power as tyrants, backed by the pope and the Spanish army of Holy Roman Emperor Charles V.

1513 Lorenzo the Magnificent's son, Giovanni, becomes Pope Leo X.

1523 Lorenzo's nephew becomes Pope Clement VII.

1527 Renegade, unpaid mercenary troops loot Rome. In the political chaos that follows, Florentines drive the Medicis from Florence, reestablishing a republic.

1530 After a year-long siege, Pope Clement VII and Charles V retake Florence, abolishing the republic and reinstalling Medici rulers.

1533 The Medicis marry off Catherine de' Medici to the future King Henry II of France.

1537   Cosimo the Younger, a Medici descended from Cosimo the Elder's brother, is made Duke of Florence. He and his wife, Eleanor of Toledo, rule as tyrannical nobles but beautify the city with the Uffizi, a renovated Palazzo Vecchio, and a rebuilt Pitti Palace.

1574   Francesco I becomes duke, soon to be followed by various Ferdinandos and Cosimos. Florence is now a minor player in world affairs, a small dukedom with a stagnant economy.

1587   The medieval facade of the Duomo is torn down. It remains bare brick for the next 200 years while different proposals are debated.

1600   Maria de' Medici marries Henry IV to become Queen of France.

1610–1633   Galileo, backed by the Medici family, works in Florence.

1737   Gian Gastone, the last of the Medici line, dies. Florence is ruled by Austrian Hapsburg nobles.

1800–Present:
Florence Enters the Modern World

1799   Napoleon "liberates" the city, briefly establishing a pseudo-democracy with his sister as duchess.

1814   Napoleon falls and the city returns to Austrian rule, under a distant descendant of the Medici family.

1848   Florentine citizens join an uprising all over Italy against foreign rule. The Risorgimento is on.

1860   Florence joins the kingdom of Victor Emmanuel, forming the nucleus of united, democratic, modern Italy.

1865   Florence is made Italy's capital (until the liberation of Rome in 1870).

1944   Under Nazi occupation as the Allies close in, all of the Arno bridges except the Ponte Vecchio are blown up.

1966   A disastrous flood, up to nearly 20 feet high, covers the city's buildings and art treasures in mud. The city is a cultural, economic, and touristic mess. An international effort of volunteer "mud angels" slowly brings these treasures back into view.

1993   The Mafia tries to strike terror with a bomb that destroys a section of the Uffizi, but the museum and the city recover. With a thriving university, scads of Internet cafés, and sparkling clean museums, Florence is a model cultural destination.

2005   You visit Florence, the art capital of Europe.

RENAISSANCE FLORENCE: CRADLE OF THE MODERN WORLD

There was something dynamic about the Florentines. Pope Boniface VIII said there were five elements: earth, air, fire, water...and Florentines. For 200 years, starting in the early 1300s, their city was a cultural hub.

Florence's contributions to Western culture are immense: the whole revival of the arts, humanism, and science; the seeds of democracy; the modern Italian language (which grew out of the popular Florentine dialect); the art of Botticelli, Leonardo, and Michelangelo; the writings of Machiavelli, Boccaccio, and Dante; and the explorations of Amerigo Vespucci, who gave his name to a newly discovered continent. Florentines considered themselves descendants of the highly cultured people of the Roman Empire. But Florence, even in its Golden Age, was always a mixture of lustiness and refinement. The streets were filled with tough-talking, hardened, illiterate merchants who strode about singing verses from Dante's *Divine Comedy*.

Florentine culture came from money, and that money came from the wool trade, silk factories, and banking. The city had a large middle class and strong guilds (labor unions for skilled craftsmen). Success was a matter of civic pride, and Florentines showed that pride in the mountains of money they spent to rebuild and beautify the city.

Technically, Florence was a republic, ruled by elected citizens rather than a nobility. While there was some opportunity for upward mobility among the middle class, most power was in the hands of a few wealthy banking families. The most powerful was the Medici family. The Medici bank had branches in 10 cities in Europe, including London, Geneva, Bruges (Belgium), and Lyon (France). The pope kept his checking account in the Rome branch. The Florentine florin was the monetary standard of the Continent.

Florence dominated Italy economically and culturally, but not militarily. The independent Italian city-states squabbled and remained scattered until the nationalist movement four centuries later. (When someone suggested to the Renaissance Florentine Niccolò Machiavelli that the Italian city-states might unite against their common enemy, France, he wrote back, "Don't make me laugh.")

Lorenzo de' Medici (1449–1492), inheritor of the family's wealth and power and his grandfather Cosimo's love of art, was a central figure of the Golden Age. He was young (20 when he took power), athletic, and intelligent, in addition to being a poet, horseman, musician, and leader. He wrote love songs and humorous dirty songs to be sung loudly and badly at carnival time. His marathon drinking bouts and illicit love affairs were legendary. He learned Greek and Latin and read the classics, yet his great passion was hunting. He was the Renaissance Man—a man of knowledge and action, a patron of the arts, and a scholar and man of the world. He was Lorenzo the Magnificent.

Lorenzo epitomized the Florentine spirit of optimism. Born on New Year's Day and raised in the lap of luxury (Donatello's *David* stood in the family courtyard) by loving parents, he grew up feeling that there was nothing he couldn't do. Florentines saw themselves as part of a "new age," a great undertaking of discovery and progress in man's history. They boasted that within the city walls, there were more "nobly gifted souls than the world has seen in the entire thousand years before." These people invented the term "Dark Ages" for the era that preceded theirs.

Lorenzo surrounded himself with Florence's best and brightest. They formed an informal "Platonic Academy," based on that of ancient Greece, to meet over a glass of wine under the stars at the Medici villa and discuss literature, art, music, and politics—witty conversation was considered an art in itself.

Their "neo-Platonic" philosophy stressed the goodness of man and the created world; they believed in a common truth behind all religion. The Academy was more than just an excuse to go out with the guys: The members were convinced that their discussions were changing the world and improving their souls.

Botticelli was a member of the Platonic Academy. He painted scenes from the classical myths that the group read, weaving contemporary figures and events into the ancient subjects. He gloried in the nude body, which he considered God's greatest creation.

Artists such as Botticelli thrived on the patronage of wealthy individuals, government, the Church, and guilds. Botticelli commanded as much as 100 florins for one work, enough to live for a year in high style, which he did for many years. In Botticelli's art we see the lightness, gaiety, and optimism of Lorenzo's court.

Another of Lorenzo's protégés was the young **Michelangelo.** Impressed with his work, Lorenzo took the poor, unlearned 13-year-old boy into the Medici household and treated him like a son.

Michelangelo's playmates were the Medici children, later to become Popes Leo X and Clement VII, who would give him important commissions. For all the encouragement, education, and contacts Michelangelo received, his most important gift from Lorenzo was simply a place at the dinner table, where Michelangelo could absorb the words of the great men of the time and their love of art for art's sake.

Even with all the art and philosophy of the Renaissance, violence, disease, and warfare were present in medieval proportions. For the lower classes, life was as harsh as it had always been. Many artists and scholars wore swords and daggers as part of everyday dress. This was the time of the ruthless tactics of the Borgias (known for murdering their political enemies) and of other families battling for power. Lorenzo himself barely escaped assassination in the cathedral during Easter Mass; his brother died in the attack.

The center of the Renaissance gradually shifted to Rome, but its artists were mostly Florentine. In the 15th century, the Holy City of Rome was a dirty, decaying, crime-infested place. Then a series of popes, including Lorenzo's son and nephew, launched a building and beautification campaign. They used fat commissions (and outright orders) to lure Michelangelo, Raphael, and others to Rome. The Florentine Renaissance headed south.

APPENDIX

Let's Talk Telephones

Here's a primer on making phone calls. For information specific to Italy, see "Telephones" in the Introduction.

Making Calls within a European Country: About half of all European countries use area codes; the other half use a direct-dial system without area codes.

To make calls within a country that uses a direct-dial telephone system (Italy, Belgium, the Czech Republic, Denmark, France, Portugal, Norway, Spain, and Switzerland), you dial the same number whether you're calling across the country or across the street.

In countries that use area codes (such as Austria, Britain, Finland, Germany, Ireland, the Netherlands, and Sweden), you dial only the local number when calling within a city, and you add the area code if calling long distance within the country.

Making International Calls: You always start with the international access code (011 if you're calling from the United States or Canada, or 00 from Europe), then dial the country code of the country you're calling (see chart below).

What you dial next depends on the phone system of the country you're calling. If the country uses area codes, drop the initial zero of the area code, then dial the rest of the number.

Countries that use direct-dial systems (no area codes) vary in how they're accessed internationally by phone. For instance, if you're making an international call to Italy, the Czech Republic, Denmark, Norway, Portugal, or Spain, simply dial the international access code, country code, and phone number. But if you're calling Belgium, France, or Switzerland, drop the initial zero of the phone number.

European Calling Chart

Just smile and dial, using this key:
AC = Area Code, LN = Local Number.

European Country	Calling long distance within...	Calling from the U.S.A./ Canada to...	Calling from a European country to...
Austria	AC + LN	011 + 43 + AC (without the initial zero) + LN	00 + 43 + AC (without the initial zero) + LN
Belgium	LN	011 + 32 + LN (without initial zero)	00 + 32 + LN (without initial zero)
Britain	AC + LN	011 + 44 + AC (without initial zero) + LN	00 + 44 + AC (without initial zero) + LN
Czech Republic	LN	011 + 420 + LN	00 + 420 + LN
Denmark	LN	011 + 45 + LN	00 + 45 + LN
Estonia	LN	011 + 372 + LN	00 + 372 + LN
Finland	AC + LN	011 + 358 + AC (without initial zero) + LN	00 + 358 + AC (without initial zero) + LN
France	LN	011 + 33 + LN (without initial zero)	00 + 33 + LN (without initial zero)
Germany	AC + LN	011 + 49 + AC (without initial zero) + LN	00 + 49 + AC (without initial zero) + LN
Gibraltar	LN	011 + 350 + LN	00 + 350 + LN From Spain: 9567 + LN
Greece	LN	011 + 30 + LN	00 + 30 + LN

European Country	Calling long distance within ...	Calling from the U.S.A./ Canada to ...	Calling from a European country to ...
Ireland	AC + LN	011 + 353 + AC (without initial zero) + LN	00 + 353 + AC (without initial zero) + LN
Italy	LN	011 + 39 + LN	00 + 39 + LN
Morocco	LN	011 + 212 + LN (without initial zero)	00 + 212 + LN (without initial zero)
Netherlands	AC + LN	011 + 31 + AC (without initial zero) + LN	00 + 31 + AC (without initial zero) + LN
Norway	LN	011 + 47 + LN	00 + 47 + LN
Portugal	LN	011 + 351 + LN	00 + 351 + LN
Spain	LN	011 + 34 + LN	00 + 34 + LN
Sweden	AC + LN	011 + 46 + AC (without initial zero) + LN	00 + 46 + AC (without initial zero) + LN
Switzerland	LN	011 + 41 + LN (without initial zero)	00 + 41 + LN (without initial zero)
Turkey	AC (if no initial zero is included, add one) + LN	011 + 90 + AC (without initial zero) + LN	00 + 90 + AC (without initial zero) + LN

- The instructions above apply whether you're calling a fixed phone or cell phone.

- The international access codes (the first numbers you dial when making an international call) are 011 if you're calling from the U.S.A./Canada, or 00 if you're calling from anywhere in Europe.

- To call the U.S.A. or Canada from Europe, dial 00, then 1 (the country code for the U.S.A. and Canada), then the area code and number. In short, 00 + 1 + AC + LN = Hi, Mom!

Country Codes

After you've dialed the international access code (00 if you're calling from Europe, 011 if you're calling from the United States or Canada), dial the code of the country you're calling.

Austria—43	Ireland—353
Belgium—32	Italy—39
Britain—44	Morocco—212
Canada—1	Netherlands—31
Croatia—385	Norway—47
Czech Rep—420	Poland—48
Denmark—45	Portugal—351
Estonia—372	Slovenia—386
Finland—358	Spain—34
France—33	Sweden—46
Germany—49	Switzerland—41
Gibraltar—350	Turkey—90
Greece—30	United States—1

Useful Italian Phone Numbers

Emergency (English-speaking police help): 113
Emergency (military police): 112
Ambulance: 118
Road Service: 116
Directory Assistance (for €0.50, an Italian-speaking robot gives the number twice, very clearly): 12
Telephone help (in English; free directory assistance): 170

Festivals in Florence and National Holidays in 2005

This list includes Florence's major festivals, plus national holidays observed throughout Italy. Many sights close down on national holidays. Note that this isn't a complete list; holidays strike without warning.

For specifics and a more comprehensive listing of festivals, contact the Italian tourist information office in the U.S. (see page 4) and visit www.discoveritalia.com, www.whatsonwhen.com, and www.hostetler.net.

Jan 1:	New Year's Day
Jan 6:	Epiphany
Mid-Feb:	Carnival Celebrations/Mardi Gras in Florence (costumed parades, street water fights, jousting competitions).
March 27:	Easter Sunday (2005). Explosion of the Cart *(Scoppio del Carro)* in Florence (fireworks, bonfire in wooden cart).
March 28:	Easter Monday (2005)
April 25:	Liberation Day

2005

JANUARY
S	M	T	W	T	F	S
						1
2	3	4	5	6	7	8
9	10	11	12	13	14	15
16	17	18	19	20	21	22
23/30	24/31	25	26	27	28	29

FEBRUARY
S	M	T	W	T	F	S
		1	2	3	4	5
6	7	8	9	10	11	12
13	14	15	16	17	18	19
20	21	22	23	24	25	26
27	28					

MARCH
S	M	T	W	T	F	S
		1	2	3	4	5
6	7	8	9	10	11	12
13	14	15	16	17	18	19
20	21	22	23	24	25	26
27	28	29	30	31		

APRIL
S	M	T	W	T	F	S
					1	2
3	4	5	6	7	8	9
10	11	12	13	14	15	16
17	18	19	20	21	22	23
24	25	26	27	28	29	30

MAY
S	M	T	W	T	F	S
1	2	3	4	5	6	7
8	9	10	11	12	13	14
15	16	17	18	19	20	21
22	23	24	25	26	27	28
29	30	31				

JUNE
S	M	T	W	T	F	S
			1	2	3	4
5	6	7	8	9	10	11
12	13	14	15	16	17	18
19	20	21	22	23	24	25
26	27	28	29	30		

JULY
S	M	T	W	T	F	S
					1	2
3	4	5	6	7	8	9
10	11	12	13	14	15	16
17	18	19	20	21	22	23
24/31	25	26	27	28	29	30

AUGUST
S	M	T	W	T	F	S
	1	2	3	4	5	6
7	8	9	10	11	12	13
14	15	16	17	18	19	20
21	22	23	24	25	26	27
28	29	30	31			

SEPTEMBER
S	M	T	W	T	F	S
				1	2	3
4	5	6	7	8	9	10
11	12	13	14	15	16	17
18	19	20	21	22	23	24
25	26	27	28	29	30	

OCTOBER
S	M	T	W	T	F	S
						1
2	3	4	5	6	7	8
9	10	11	12	13	14	15
16	17	18	19	20	21	22
23/30	24/31	25	26	27	28	29

NOVEMBER
S	M	T	W	T	F	S
		1	2	3	4	5
6	7	8	9	10	11	12
13	14	15	16	17	18	19
20	21	22	23	24	25	26
27	28	29	30			

DECEMBER
S	M	T	W	T	F	S
				1	2	3
4	5	6	7	8	9	10
11	12	13	14	15	16	17
18	19	20	21	22	23	24
25	26	27	28	29	30	31

May 1: Labor Day

May 5: Ascension Day. Annual Cricket Festival in Florence (music, entertainment, food, crickets sold in cages).

June 1–30: Annual Flower Display in Florence (carpet of flowers on the main square, Piazza della Signoria).

June 2: Anniversary of the Republic

June 11–24: Festival of St. John in Florence (parades, dances, boat races).

June 24: Calcio Fiorentino (costumed soccer game on Florence's Piazza Santa Croce).

July–August: Annual Florence Dance Festival

Late June–Early Sept: Florence's annual outdoor cinema season (contemporary films).

July 2: Palio horse race in Siena

Aug 15: Assumption of Mary

Aug 16:	Palio horse race in Siena
Sept, first week:	Festa della Rificolona in Florence (children's procession with lanterns, street performances, parade).
Oct:	Musica dei Popoli Festival in Florence (ethnic and folk music and dances).
Nov 1:	All Saints' Day
Dec 8:	Feast of the Immaculate Conception
Dec 25:	Christmas
Dec 26:	St. Stephen's Day

Numbers and Stumblers

- Europeans write a few of their numbers differently than we do: 1 = $\mathcal{1}$, 4 = $\mathcal{4}$, 7 = $\mathcal{7}$. Learn the difference or miss your train.
- In Europe, dates appear as day/month/year, so Christmas is 25/12/05.
- Commas are decimal points and decimals commas. A dollar and a half is $1,50, and there are 5.280 feet in a mile.
- When pointing, use your whole hand, palm down.
- When counting with fingers, start with your thumb. If you hold up your first finger to request one item, you'll probably get two.
- What Americans call the second floor of a building is the first floor in Europe.
- Europeans keep the left "lane" open for passing on escalators and moving sidewalks. Keep to the right.

Metric Conversion (approximate)

1 inch = 25 millimeters	32 degrees F = 0 degrees C
1 foot = 0.3 meter	82 degrees F = about 28 degrees C
1 yard = 0.9 meter	1 ounce = 28 grams
1 mile = 1.6 kilometers	1 kilogram = 2.2 pounds
1 centimeter = 0.4 inch	1 quart = 0.95 liter
1 meter = 39.4 inches	1 square yard = 0.8 square meter
1 kilometer = .62 mile	1 acre = 0.4 hectare

Florence's Climate Chart

First line, average daily low; second line, average daily high; third line, days of no rain.

J	F	M	A	M	J	J	A	S	O	N	D
32°	35°	43°	49°	57°	63°	67°	66°	61°	52°	43°	35°
40°	46°	56°	65°	74°	80°	84°	82°	75°	63°	51°	43°
25	21	24	22	23	21	25	24	25	23	20	24

Converting Temperatures: Fahrenheit and Celsius

Making Your Hotel Reservation

Most hotel managers know basic "hotel English." Faxing or e-mailing are the preferred methods for reserving a room. They're more accurate than telephoning and much faster than writing a letter. Use this handy form for your fax or find it online at www.ricksteves.com/reservation. Photocopy and fax away.

One-Page Fax

To: _____ @ _____
           hotel   **fax**

From: _____@ _____
              name   **fax**

Today's date: _____/_____ /_____
                 day   month   year

Dear Hotel _____ ,
Please make this reservation for me:

Name: _____

Total # of people:_____ # of rooms: _____ # of nights: _____

Arriving: _____/____/____   My time of arrival (24-hr clock): _____
           day month year   (I will telephone if I will be late)

Departing: ____/____/____
             day month year

Room(s): Single _____ Double ____ Twin _____Triple ____ Quad_____

With: Toilet _____ Shower _____Bath _____ Sink only _____

Special needs: View____ Quiet ____ Cheapest ____ Ground Floor ____

Please fax, mail, or e-mail confirmation of my reservation, along with the type of room reserved and the price. Please also inform me of your cancellation policy. After I hear from you, I will quickly send my credit-card information as a deposit to hold the room. Thank you.

_____
Signature

_____
Name

_____
Address

_____
City   **State**   **Zip Code   Country**

_____
E-mail Address

Italian Survival Phrases

English	Italian	Pronunciation
Good day.	Buon giorno.	bwohn JOR-noh
Do you speak English?	Parla inglese?	PAR-lah een-GLAY-zay
Yes. / No.	Si. / No.	see / noh
I (don't) understand.	(Non) capisco.	(nohn) kah-PEES-koh
Please.	Per favore.	pehr fah-VOH-ray
Thank you.	Grazie.	GRAHT-seeay
I'm sorry.	Mi dispiace.	mee dee-speeAH-chay
Excuse me.	Mi scusi.	mee SKOO-zee
(No) problem.	(Non) c'è un problema.	(nohn) cheh oon proh-BLAY-mah
Good.	Va bene.	vah BEHN-ay
Goodbye.	Arrivederci.	ah-ree-vay-DEHR-chee
one / two	uno / due	OO-noh / DOO-ay
three / four	tre / quattro	tray / KWAH-troh
five / six	cinque / sei	CHEENG-kway / SEHee
seven / eight	sette / otto	SEHT-tay / OT-toh
nine / ten	nove / dieci	NOV-ay / deeAY-chee
How much is it?	Quanto costa?	KWAHN-toh KOS-tah
Write it?	Me lo scrive?	may loh SKREE-vay
Is it free?	È gratis?	eh GRAH-tees
Is it included?	È incluso?	eh een-KLOO-zoh
Where can I buy / find...?	Dove posso comprare / trovare...?	DOH-vay POS-soh kohm-PRAH-ray / troh-VAH-ray
I'd like / We'd like...	Vorrei / Vorremmo...	vor-REHee / vor-RAY-moh
...a room.	...una camera.	OO-nah KAH-meh-rah
...a ticket to ___.	...un biglietto per ___.	oon beel-YEHT-toh pehr
Is it possible?	È possibile?	eh poh-SEE-bee-lay
Where is...?	Dov'è...?	DOH-veh
...the train station	...la stazione	lah staht-seeOH-nay
...the bus station	...la stazione degli autobus	lah staht-seeOH-nay DAYL-yee OW-toh-boos
...tourist information	...informazioni per turisti	een-for-maht-seeOH-nee pehr too-REE-stee
...the toilet	...la toilette	lah twah-LEHT-tay
men	uomini, signori	WOH-mee-nee, seen-YOH-ree
women	donne, signore	DON-nay, seen-YOH-ray
left / right	sinistra / destra	see-NEE-strah / DEHS-trah
straight	sempre diritto	SEHM-pray dee-REE-toh
When do you open / close?	A che ora aprite / chiudete?	ah kay OH-rah ah-PREE-tay / keeoo-DAY-tay
At what time?	A che ora?	ah kay OH-rah
Just a moment.	Un momento.	oon moh-MAYN-toh
now / soon / later	adesso / presto / tardi	ah-DEHS-soh / PREHS-toh / TAR-dee
today / tomorrow	oggi / domani	OH-jee / doh-MAH-nee

In the Restaurant

I'd like...	Vorrei...	vor-REHee
We'd like...	Vorremmo...	vor-RAY-moh
...to reserve...	...prenotare...	pray-noh-TAH-ray
...a table for one / two.	...un tavolo per uno / due.	oon TAH-voh-loh pehr OO-noh / DOO-ay
Non-smoking.	Non fumare.	nohn foo-MAH-ray
Is this seat free?	È libero questo posto?	eh LEE-bay-roh KWEHS-toh POH-stoh
The menu (in English), please.	Il menù (in inglese), per favore.	eel may-NOO (een een-GLAY-zay) pehr fah-VOH-ray
service (not) included	servizio (non) incluso	sehr-VEET-seeoh (nohn) een-KLOO-zoh
cover charge	pane e coperto	PAH-nay ay koh-PEHR-toh
to go	da portar via	dah POR-tar VEE-ah
with / without	con / senza	kohn / SEHN-sah
and / or	e / o	ay / oh
menu (of the day)	menù (del giorno)	may-NOO (dayl JOR-noh)
specialty of the house	specialità della casa	spay-chah-lee-TAH DEHL-lah KAH-zah
first course (pasta, soup)	primo piatto	PREE-moh peeAH-toh
main course (meat, fish)	secondo piatto	say-KOHN-doh peeAH-toh
side dishes	contorni	kohn-TOR-nee
bread	pane	PAH-nay
cheese	formaggio	for-MAH-joh
sandwich	panino	pah-NEE-noh
soup	minestra, zuppa	mee-NEHS-trah, TSOO-pah
salad	insalata	een-sah-LAH-tah
meat	carne	KAR-nay
chicken	pollo	POH-loh
fish	pesce	PEH-shay
seafood	frutti di mare	FROO-tee dee MAH-ray
fruit / vegetables	frutta / legumi	FROO-tah / lay-GOO-mee
dessert	dolci	DOHL-chee
tap water	acqua del rubinetto	AH-kwah dayl roo-bee-NAY-toh
mineral water	acqua minerale	AH-kwah mee-nay-RAH-lay
milk	latte	LAH-tay
(orange) juice	succo (d'arancia)	SOO-koh (dah-RAHN-chah)
coffee / tea	caffè / tè	kah-FEH / teh
wine	vino	VEE-noh
red / white	rosso / bianco	ROH-soh / beeAHN-koh
glass / bottle	bicchiere / bottiglia	bee-keeAY-ray / boh-TEEL-yah
beer	birra	BEE-rah
Cheers!	Cin cin!	cheen cheen
More. / Another.	Ancora un po.' / Un altro.	ahn-KOH-rah oon poh / oon AHL-troh
The same.	Lo stesso.	loh STEHS-soh
The bill, please.	Il conto, per favore.	eel KOHN-toh pehr fah-VOH-ray
tip	mancia	MAHN-chah
Delicious!	Delizioso!	day-leet-seeOH-zoh

For hundreds more pages of survival phrases for your trip to Italy, check out *Rick Steves' Italian Phrase Book & Dictionary* or *Rick Steves' French, Italian, and German Phrase Book*.

INDEX

RESEARCHERS

To annually update his four books on Italy, Rick relies on the help of these *fantastica* researchers:

SARAH MURDOCH

Sarah Murdoch is passionate about Italy (and gelato). Trained as an architect, she abandoned her drafting board to research guidebooks and lead tours for Rick Steves. She lives in Seattle with her husband, Patrick, and their new baby.

HEIDI SEWELL

Heidi Sewell lived in Italy for two years, learning to speak Italian and roll her own pasta. When she's not leading tours and scouring the Italian Peninsula for Back Doors worthy of Rick Steves' guidebooks, she resides in Seattle with her husband Ragen.

Start your trip at
www.ricksteves.com

Rick Steves' website is packed with over 3,000 pages of timely travel information. It's also your gateway to getting FREE monthly travel news from Rick — and more!

Free Monthly European Travel News

Fresh articles on Europe's most interesting destinations and happenings. Rick will even send you an e-mail every month (often direct from Europe) with his latest discoveries!

Timely Travel Tips

Rick Steves' best money-and-stress-saving tips on trip planning, packing, transportation, hotels, health, safety, finances, hurdling the language barrier...and more.

Travelers' Graffiti Wall

Candid advice and opinions from thousands of travelers on everything listed above, plus whatever topics are hot at the moment (discount flights, packing tips, scams...you name it).

Rick's Annual Guide to European Railpasses

The clearest, most comprehensive guide to the confusing array of railpass options out there, and how to choo-choose the railpass that best fits your itinerary and budget. Then you can order your railpass (and get a bunch of great freebies) online from us!

Great Gear at the Rick Steves Travel Store

Enjoy bargains on Rick's guidebooks, planning maps and TV series DVDs—and on his custom-designed carry-on bags, wheeled bags, day bags and light-packing accessories.

Rick Steves Tours

Every year more than 5,000 lucky travelers explore Europe on a Rick Steves tour. Learn more about our 26 different one-to-three-week itineraries, read uncensored feedback from our tour alums, and sign up for your dream trip online!

Rick on TV

Read the scripts and see video clips from the popular Rick Steves' Europe TV series, and get an inside look at Rick's 13 newest shows.

Respect for Your Privacy

Ordering online from us is secure. When you buy something from us, join a tour, or subscribe to Rick's free monthly travel news e-mails, we promise to never share your name, information, or e-mail address with anyone else. You won't be spammed!

Have fun raising your Travel I.Q. at
www.ricksteves.com

Travel smart...carry on!

The latest generation of Rick Steves' carry-on travel bags is easily the best—benefiting from two decades of on-the-road attention to what really matters: maximum quality and strength; practical, flexible features; and no unnecessary frills. You won't find a better value anywhere!

Convertible, expandable, and carry-on-size:

Rick Steves' Back Door Bag $99

This is the same bag that Rick Steves lives out of for three months every summer. It's made of rugged water-resistant 1000 denier Cordura nylon, and best of all, it converts easily from a smart-looking suitcase to a handy backpack with comfortably-curved shoulder straps and a padded waistbelt.

This roomy, versatile 9" x 21" x 14" bag has a large 2600 cubic-inch main compartment, plus three outside pockets (small, medium and huge) that are perfect for often-used items. And the cinch-tight compression straps will keep your load compact and close to your back—not sagging like a sack of potatoes.

Wishing you had even more room to bring home souvenirs? Pull open the full-perimeter expando-zipper and its capacity jumps from 2600 to 3000 cubic inches. When you want to use it as a suitcase or check it as luggage (required when "expanded"), the straps and belt hide away in a zippered compartment in the back.

Attention travelers under 5'4" tall: This bag also comes in an inch-shorter version, for a compact-friendlier fit between the waistbelt and shoulder straps.

Convenient, durable, and carry-on-size:

Rick Steves' Wheeled Bag $119

At 9" x 21" x 14" our sturdy Rick Steves' Wheeled Bag is rucksack-soft in front, but the rest is lined with a hard ABS-lexan shell to give maximum protection to your belongings. We've spared no expense on moving parts, splurging on an extra-long button-release handle and big, tough inline skate wheels for easy rolling on rough surfaces.

This bag is not convertible! Our research tells us that travelers who've bought convertible wheeled bags never put them on their backs anyway, so we've eliminated the extra weight and expense.

Rick Steves' Wheeled Bag has exactly the same three-outside-pocket configuration as our Back Door Bag, plus a handy "add-a-bag" strap and full lining.

Our Back Door Bags and Wheeled Bags come in black, navy, blue spruce, evergreen and merlot.

For great deals on a wide selection of travel goodies, begin your next trip at the Rick Steves Travel Store!

Visit the Rick Steves Travel Store at
www.ricksteves.com

Rick Steves

COUNTRY GUIDES 2005

France
Germany & Austria
Great Britain
Greece
Ireland
Italy
Portugal
Scandinavia
Spain
Switzerland

CITY GUIDES 2005

Amsterdam, Bruges & Brussels
Florence & Tuscany
London
Paris
Prague & The Czech Republic
Provence & The French Riviera
Rome
Venice

BEST OF GUIDES

Best European City Walks & Museums
Best of Eastern Europe
Best of Europe

More *Savvy*. More *Surprising*. More *Fun.*

PHRASE BOOKS & DICTIONARIES

French
French, Italian & German
German
Italian
Portuguese
Spanish

MORE EUROPE FROM RICK STEVES

Easy Access Europe
Europe 101
Europe Through the Back Door
Best European City Walks & Museums
Postcards from Europe

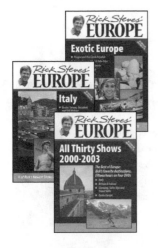

DVD
RICK STEVES' EUROPE

Rick Steves' Europe All Thirty
    Shows 2000–2003
Britain & Ireland
Exotic Europe
Germany, The Swiss Alps
    & Travel Skills
Italy